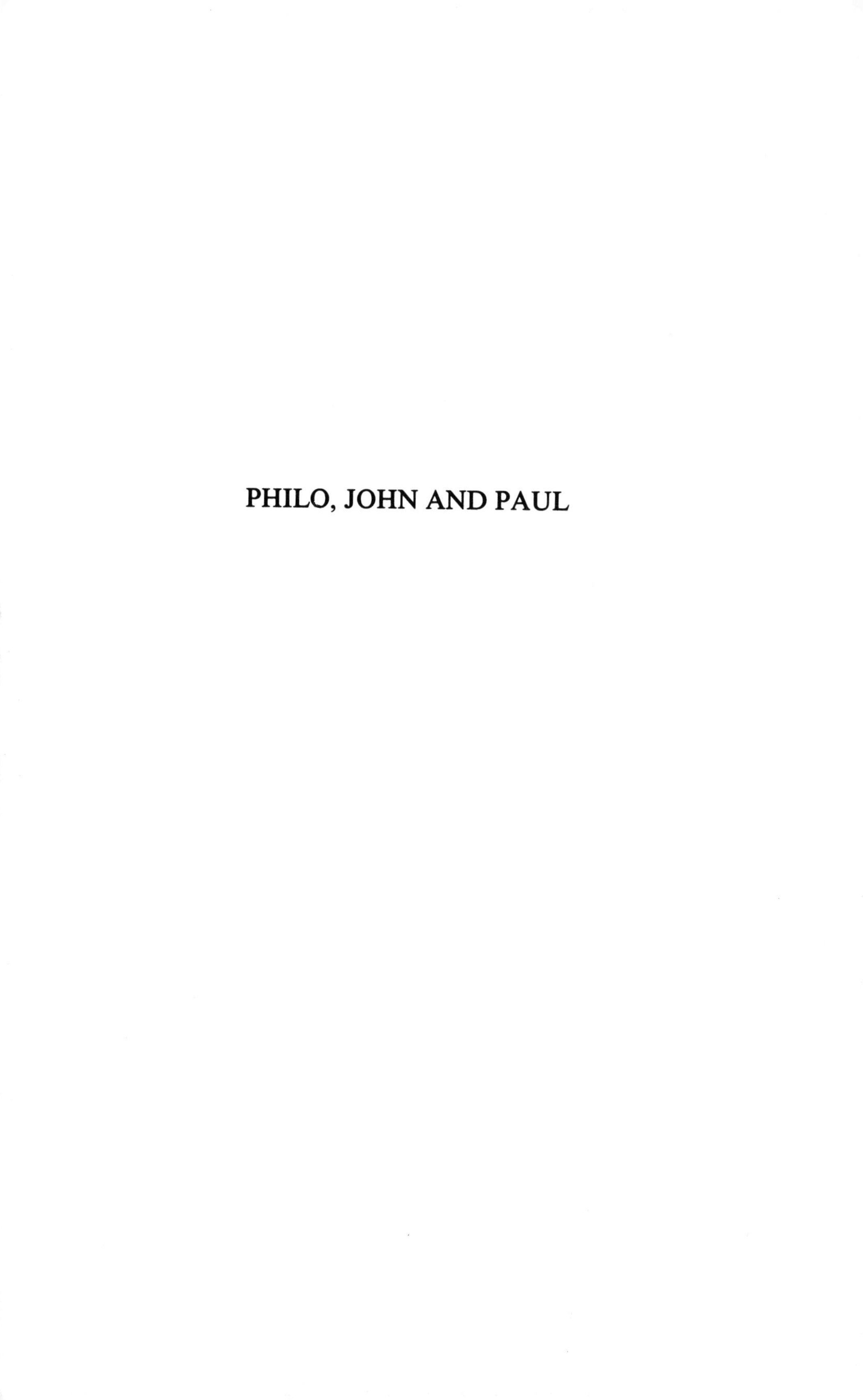

PHILO, JOHN AND PAUL

Program in Judaic Studies
Brown University
BROWN JUDAIC STUDIES

Number 131

PHILO, JOHN AND PAUL

New Perspectives on Judaism and Early Christianity

by
Peder Borgen

PHILO, JOHN AND PAUL

New Perspectives on Judaism and Early Christianity

by
Peder Borgen

Scholars Press
Atlanta, Georgia

PHILO, JOHN AND PAUL
New Perspectives on Judaism and Early Christianity

Library of Congress Cataloging-in-Publication Data

Borgen, Peder.
Philo, John, and Paul.

(Brown Judaic studies : no. 131)
Includes indexes.
1. Bible. N.T. John--Relation to the Old Testament.
2. Philo, of Alexandria. 3. Paul, the Apostle, Saint.
4. Judaism--Relations--Christianity. 5. Christianity
and other religions--Judaism. I. Title. II. Series.
BS2615.B638 1987 296'.09'015 87-23368
ISBN 1-55540-183-0 (alk. paper)

Printed in the United States of America
on acid-free paper

CONTENTS

PREFACE

PART I: PHILO

PART II: JOHN

PART III: PAUL

Dedicated to Jacob Neusner,
Outstanding Scholar and
Treasured Colleague

PREFACE

In recent years many scholars have emphasized that no sharp distinction can be drawn between Palestinian Judaism and Hellenistic Judaism. Instead, attempts are made to analyse the variety of attitudes, views and practices in the Jewish communities, whether in Palestine or in Diaspora. There had been a considerable degree of influence from Greco-Roman culture in Palestinian Judaism both before, during and after New Testament times, and the Judaism of the Diaspora was by no means free from the kind of features often labelled "Palestinian".

Philo

If no sharp distinction can be drawn between Palestinian Judaism and Hellenistic Judaism, then research in the writings of Philo and other Jewish writings from Alexandria gains a greater significance. The Jewish community of Alexandria is in this book represented through three essays. All three are focused on the exegetical activity of Alexandrian Jews. The first essay compares the exegesis of Aristobulus with that of Philo. In the second essay a survey is given of Philo's writings from the understanding that he primarily was an exegete. Finally, debates and conflicts among Alexandrian Jews are illustrated by the various views wich existed on circumcision.

John

Also the essays on the Gospel of John are centered on the expository use of the Old Testament. Expository methods and forms in the targum were of special interest for my study of the Prologue of John, although a wide range of background material is utilized at specific points. In an additional note answers are given on some comments of criticism raised in connection with my analysis.

On the other hand material found in the midrashim was more central for the analysis of John 6, and halakhic parallels in the Mishna and the Talmud provide background material for the discussion of agency in John's Gospel. The Son of Man - Saying in John 3:13-14 is primarily understood on the basis of Jewish traditions on the theophany at Mt. Sinai.

My clarification of the midrashic character of John 6:31-58 in the monograph _Bread from Heaven : An Exegetical Study of the Concept of Manna in the Gospel of John and the Writings of Philo_ (Leiden, 1965; second edition with revisions, 1981) has received broad acceptance, but it has also brought forth some debate. Some comments on disputed points are made in the chapter on "Bread from Heaven : Aspects of Debates on Expository Method and Form."

In two essays John's expository use of the Old Testament is related to the broader questions of sources and of theology.

Paul

As in the study of Philo, so also in the section on Paul, the interplay between exegesis of the Old Testament and the contemporary historical contexts is examined. From this perspective the relationship between the Church and the Hellenistic Synagogue is discussed, with emphasis on the understanding and practice of circumcision.

In the two last essays, light is thrown on the similarities and differences in the views of Paul and other Jews with regard to Jewish nationalism and Jewish geographical perspectives. They illustrate the functional aspect of exegesis and have as their point of departure the fact that the Laws of Moses and the other sacred writings were woven into the very fabric of the Jewish nation and community life.

The sections on John and Paul, just as the one on Philo, demonstrate that no sharp distinction can be drawn between Palestinian Judaism and Hellenistic Judaism. Correspondingly, no sharp distinction existed between the Palestinian Church and the Hellenistic Church. A variety of views existed both in Palestine and in and around the Jewish settlements of the Diaspora.

PART I: PHILO

CHAPTER ONE
ARISTOBULUS AND PHILO

Introduction

There was a rich variety of groups and trends within Judaism before the fall of Jerusalem in the year 70 A.D. (1) Of these only two survived, namely the Pharisaic-rabbinic branch and Christianity. The Pharisaic-rabbinic form of Judaism produced a comprehensive body of sources, largely written down between the second and the tenth centuries A.D. These rabbinic writings have preserved many traditions from the Second Temple period, but it has proved difficult to find criteria by which these early tradition can be identified with certainty. (2)

Moreover, if we were dependent on the rabbinic sources alone, we would, for example, know very little about the Jewish war against the Romans in 66-70 A.D. Much information is available to us, however, because the writing of the Jewish historian, Flavius Josephus, survived in Christian hands. Likewise, the Christian church preserved the writings of the Jewish philosopher and exegete Philo of Alexandria (20 B.C. - 50 A.D.), the writings called the Apocrypha - as part of the Septuagint -, as well as many other Jewish writings from the Second Temple period. Much scholarly effort has been put into examining these writings in order to gain an as clear picture as possible of the diversity of Jewish religious expression in New Testament times. Archaeology has also added much to this picture, especially through the discovery of the Dead Sea Scrolls.

In recent years many scholars have emphasized that no sharp distinction can be drawn between Palestinian Judaism and Hellenistic Judaism. Instead, attempts are made to analyse the variety of attitudes, views and practices in the Jewish communities, whether in Palestine or in the Diaspora. Such research will increase our knowledge and understanding of Judaism itself during the Second Temple period, and will illuminate the historical setting of the New Testament and Christian origins.

Against this background research in the writings of Philo and other Jewish writings from Alexandria gain greater significance. Thus, some Alexandrian fragments preserved by Eusebius also should be brought more into the foreground, among others those of Aristobulus' writings. The kinship between

Aristobulus and Philo supports the view that Philo was not an isolated individualist in his authorship. As for the New Testament Aristobulus shows that the exegetical debate on God's resting on the Seventh Day (Gen 2:1ff) was known in Judaism already in the Second Century B.C. This exegetical tradition, also evidenced in Philo and in rabbinic writings, is presupposed in John 5:17.

It is also to be noted that Aristobulus adduces the Stoic Aratus as witness to the existence of one invisible God, of the one creation and of God's rule over the universe. The verses from Aratus are taken from Phaenomena 1-9, part of which is found in Acts 17:28 where Phaenomena 5 is cited: "For we are indeed his offspring." Thus, Aristobulus shows that Aratus was part of Jewish apologetics even before New Testament times.

The Sources

The chief fragments of Aristobulus' writings are found in Eusebius, Historia Ecclesiastica (HE) 7, 32:17-18 (Fragment 1, taken from the writing of Anatolius), Praeparatio Evangelica (PE) 8, 10:1-17/(Fragment 2); PE 13,12:1-2 (Fragment 3); PE 13, 12:3-8 (Fragment 4); PE 13, 12:9-16 (Fragment 5, partly found also in PE 7, 14:1). Clement of Alexandria has parallels to parts of Fragments 2-5. References to Aristobulus are also found several places elsewhere in the writings of Clement and Eusebius, as well as in Origenes Contra Celsum 4:51 and 2 Macc 1:10. (3)

According to 2 Macc 1:10 Aristobulus came from a high-priestly family, and (as also stated by Clement and Eusebius) he is to be dated to the time of Ptolemy VI Philometor (ca 181-145 B.C.). (4) See further Clement, Strom 1, 150:1 - 3; Eusebius, PE 9, 6:6; 8,9:38. According to Eusebius, HE 7,32:16, however, Aristobulus lived at the time of Ptolemy II Philadelphus (285 B.C.). The latter dating is not reliable, but the dating to the time of Ptolemy VI Philometer is probable. (5)

There has been much debate as to the authenticity of these fragments and their date. (6) Scholars as H. Grätz, A. Elter, P. Wendland and E. Bréhier attacked their authenticity and dated the fragments to the time after Philo of Alexandria. Several scholars have defended the authenticity of the fragments, and in 1964 N. Walter, Der Thoraausleger Aristobulus, convincingly showed that the doubts were unwarranted, and that Aristobulus' work is to be dated to the second century B.C.

As to the form of Aristobulus' expositions no certain conclusion can be reached. They had the form of a dialogue in which Aristobulus answered questions raised by the Ptolemaic King.

Thus, the expositions contained problem-solving exegesis, akin to the form of exegesis found in Philo's quaestiones et solutiones. (7)

By Clement and Eusebius Aristobulus is described as a Peripatetic. However, the fragments of the work itself have few affinities with Peripatetic philosophy, and rather show influence from Platonic and Pythagorean thinking. More properly Aristobulus is to be characterized as a Jew who drew on Greek ideas and traditions in an eclectic manner.

On the basis of the fragments two concerns of Aristobulus become evident: 1) He develops the idea that the Jewish philosophy found in the Law of Moses has many points of agreement with Greek philosophy. The main reason for such agreements is that the Greek philosophers have learned from Moses. 2) He wants to solve the problem created by anthropomorphisms ascribed to the divinity. In his interpretation of anthropomorphism he largely uses the allegorical method.

<u>The Greek Philosophers and Moses</u>

In Fragment three, PE 13,12:1-2, Aristobulus states that Plato and Pythagoras derived ideas from the Jewish Law, allegedly known to them from pre-Alexandrian translations. Philo entertained similar theories. Thus in referring to Heraclitus' theory of the opposites, he described Heraclitus as conceiving these opinions from Moses or as snatching them from Moses like a thief (Quaes Gen III:5; IV:152; cf. Heres 214). Similarly, referring to certain Greek laws, he said that the Grecian legislators copied from the Laws of Moses (Spec IV:61). More cautiously, he stated that the Greek philosopher Zeno seemed to have learned from the Laws of Moses (Omn 53-54). Philo here draws on the same traditional view which already is documented in Aristobulus. Aristobulus was even more specific than Philo, however, since he presents a particular theory of pre-Alexandrian translations. (8)

Fragment four, PE 13,12:3-8, develops two related topics. The first topic is the understanding of the phrase "the divine voice". Contemplating the construction of the world Pythagoras, Socrates and Plato were led to the recognition of the truth of the creation story in the Laws of Moses. At the same time Aristobulus tells what in his opinion is the proper understanding of the "divine voice". It was not a real spoken word, but the preparation to the works of creation. He finds the scriptural basis of this interpretation in Gen. 1, where it is stated in relation to each thing: "and God said, - and it was done."

It cannot be said that Aristobulus here develops an allegorical interpretation in the strict sense of the term. He does not bring out the inner, spiritual meaning of the "divine voice", but only modifies the phrase to mean God's creative activity in general. (9)

Philo renders interpretation of God's word, Logos, when he says: God spoke and at the same time acted, setting no interval between the two; or it might suggest a truer view to say that His word was deed, Sacr 65.

The second topic found in Fragment 4 treats another aspect of the doctrine of God : the existence of one invisible God, of the one creation and of God's rule over the universe. Aristobulus adduces the 'Sacred Book' - an imaginary book - of Orpheus and verses of the Stoic Aratus as witnesses.

Orpheus and Aratus were inferior to Moses, however. This is seen by the fact they had no 'holy concepts of God'. They were therefore to be corrected. The passages quoted contained originally the polytheistic names 'Dis' and 'Zeus'. These names are in Aristobulus replaced by 'Theos' God: "We have interpreted the passage as necessary by removing the names 'Dis' and 'Zeus' which occur in the poems, since their meaning relates to God... For all philosophers agree that one must have holy concepts of God, and this is something with which our school is most concerned." (PE 13,12:7-8). For Aristobulus, the Jews are basically a nation of philosophers. Although other philosophers to some degree have views of value, the true philosophy is found among the Jews. (10)

The quotations from Orpheus and Aratus call for a comment. (11) The Orphic poem exists in various forms in Clement of Alexandria and in writings attributed to Justin Martyr. However, it is a Jewish fabrication, attributed to Orpheus. The verses from the Stoic Aratus is taken from Aratus Phaenomena 1-9, part of which is found in Acts 17:28 where Phaenomena 5 is cited.

In Fragments five (PE 13,12:9-16) and one (HE 7,32:17-18) Aristobulus discusses the feasts of the Sabbath and Passover. The Sabbath is interpreted on the basis of the creation story in Gen 1:1-2:4a and the words on Wisdom and creation in Prov 8:22f. (PE 13,12:9-16). Among the many observations which might be made on this fragment, F 5, the following deserve special attention:

Aristobulus modifies the concept of time found in the creation story. The enumeration six days was for the purpose of establishing the course of time and of gradation within the created world. In this way Aristobulus attempted to bring the biblical conception of creation in time in agreement with the Greek idea of timeless activity of God. Only God's creation is subject to the category of time, not God himself (PE 13,12:12).

In an even more developed way Philo stresses that the time was formed as part of creation and did not exist prior to it, Leg all I:2; Opif 26; Sacr 68. Moreover, the enumeration of six days indicate to him that in creation there was need of order (Opif 13; 27-28; 67; cf Leg all I:3f.). (12)

Aristobulus refers to Prov 8:22f., that Wisdom was created before heaven and earth. In this "midrashic" elaboration he goes beyond Proverbs when he says that all light comes from Wisdom. This conjunction of Wisdom and primal light has received further development in Wisdom 7:22-26.

Correspondingly, Philo associates light and _Logos_: the invisible light perceptible only by the mind has come into being as an image of the divine _Logos_ (Opif 31). Aristobulus, Philo and Wisdom offer here varied philosophical formulations of the concept of primal light which was current in Judaism.

In his exposition of Wisdom and light in F 5 Aristobulus furthermore refers to the view of wisdom among the Peripatetic philosophers. In a way similar to Jewish understanding these philosophers say that "wisdom has the role of a lamplighter, because those who perservere in following her find that their life continues long in a state of rest". (13)

In his interpretation of the Sabbath, the seventh day, Aristobulus makes the number seven to serve as the ordering principle of cosmos. Those who see, find here the proof of the divine ordering of the world, the order which the Jewish feast of the Sabbath makes manifest.

The Sabbath and the structure of seven is also the basis of human capacity of knowledge. The seventh day is to be kept holy "as a symbol of our 'sevenfold logos' to which we owe our knowledge of human and divine things" (PE 13,12:12-13). Here the Stoic definition of philosophy has been applied to the Jewish religion and the celebration of the Sabbath. Thereby Aristobulus claims that this definition belongs to the Jewish philosophy. Thus, the Law of Moses is basic for gaining knowledge of human and divine things.

In a similar way, 4 Macc (1.cent AD) 1:16f. describes 'wisdom' in Stoic fashion as 'the knowledge of divine and human things', and he then qualifies the Stoic phrase by defining it as the training of the Law. Philo also uses the Stoic definition to characterize the Jewish philosophy and way of life (Congr 79). (14)

Verses attributed to Hesiod, Homer and the legendary poet Linus are quoted by Aristobulus in order to show how non-Jewish writers glorify the Sabbath, by confirming the cosmic and spiritual significance of the number seven (PE 13,12:13-16). (15)

Two quotations are listed for Hesiod, three for Homer, and four for Linus. Walter finds Hesiod 1 (from Works and Days, 770) authentic, and Homer 2, taken from the Odyssey 5:262. But Homer's 'The fourth day came, and he had finished all', reads in Aristobulus: 'The seventh day came, and he had finished all'. Homer 3 is apocryphal: 'On the morning of the seventh day, we left the flood of Acheron'. Aristobulus adds allegorical comment to the verse. It means liberation from the forgetfulness which afflicts the soul, and from evil, through the sevenfold Logos from which we receive knowledge of the truth. Since seven is the key term in the quotation, the comment most probably refers to the Sabbath as central in the Jewish religion. Only the cosmic force of seven can repress the evil forces of the soul. This liberation comes through the contemplation done on the seventh day, the Sabbath. The other verses cited can only be mentioned in a summary fashion. Hesiod 2, probably Homer 1 , and Linus 2-5, come from a non-Jewish Pythagorean source. A Jewish editor seems to have produced Linus 1 (which Clement, Strom. 5:107, assigns to Callimachus) and to have modified Homer 1 and 2, and Linus, 4-5.

Aristobulus' emphasis on the theological significance of the Sabbath has its background in the fact that already the Old Testament offers cosmic interpretation of the Seventh day, Gen 2:1-4a. These cosmic speculations on the Sabbath are rendered in even more developed forms in Philo (Mos II:21ff.; Opif 89; Dec 96-101, etc.) and in Josephus (C Ap II:282). Moreover, the discussion of God's resting on the seventh day (Gen 2:1-4a) is broadly documented, here in Aristobulus, in Philo in rabbinic writings, and is alluded to in John 5:17. (16)

In Fragment 1 Aristobulus discussed another feast, the Passover. Here he gives answer to calendaric questions. He bases his calculation as to the date of Passover on the solar calendar. Passover is to be celebrated after the vernal equinox, at the middle of the first month. At the same time Aristobulus also pays attention to the lunar calendar, and states that not only the sun should be passing through an equinoctial sign, but the moon also.

Aristobulus is here to be seen within the context of the broad debates on calendaric questions in Judaism. He betrays knowledge of a Hellenistic Egyptian solar calendar. The calendar developed by the Essenes is a special expression of a solar calendar and it may depend upon such a Hellenistic-Egyptian calendar tradition.

Eusebius' report on Aristobulus' view in the dating of Passover is brief. The theological implications are not made explicit. It is probable, however, that Aristobulus by his calendaric discussion wanted to express the cosmic significance of the feast of Passover. (17)

Anthropomorphisms

The problem of anthropomorphisms is treated in Fragment two, PE 8, 10:1-17. We are told that king Ptolemy himself raised the objection against the Mosaic Law that it ascribed bodily organs and human passion to God. Aristobulus begins his answer by stating his hermeneutical principle. If men are to understand the real meaning of the Law of Moses, they should not fall victim to mythological and human conceptions. For those who merely cling to the letter, Moses does not appear as anyone who proclaims great things. Anthropomorphic statements are to be interpreted in such a way as to preserve the appropriate conception of God (8,10:1-6). Aristobulus' formulations indicate that he does not only attack the Greek critics of the Law of Moses, but also its conservative Jewish defendants.

Aristobulus' understanding of the anthropomorphic terms may be summarized as follows: When the Pentateuch talks about the 'hands of God', it means his powers, as seen by use of the term in Exod 3:20; 9:3; 13:19.16. When the phrase 'the standing of God' is used, it means the existence and immutability of the world that he has created. For instance, heaven never becomes earth, nor the sun the moon, nor the moon the sun, etc. Things are not exchangable. Furthermore, the descent of God on the mount Sinai, Exod 19:17-20, was not local, for God is everywhere. The appearance of fire and the sound of the trumpet were brought by God in a miraculous way without human intervention, as a display of the energy of God, Deut 4:11; 5:23; 9:15.

Aristobulus exemplifies the broader trend in Judaism to modify and remove anthropomorphisms ascribed to God. This anti-anthropomorphic tendency has it parallel in Greek interpretations of Homer's poems. Such anti-anthropomorphic re-phrasing is found in the Septuagint, in the targumim and in the midrashim. Thus, Tg Onq may interpret the phrase "God's hand" in the same way as Aristobulus: the term means God's power in Exod 3:20. Moreover, in Mek Exod 19:20 it is stated that God did not descend on Mount

Sinai, but Moses heard the call from God as if it came from the top of the mountain (cf. b Sukk 5a).

Anti-anthropomorphic interpretations are further developed in Philo. As for the term "the hands of God" Philo states a general hermeneutical principle: "... to say that he uses hands or feet or any created part at all is not the true account" (Conf 98). As for the "standing of God", Philo has a corresponding interpretation of Exod 24:10 to that of Aristobulus: "they saw the place where the God of Israel stood, for by standing or establishment he indicates his immutability" (Somn II; 222). Finally, in Conf 134-140 the phrase "the Lord came down" (Gen 11:5) makes Philo to state the following principle: "For to suppose that the Deity approaches or departs, goes down or goes up ... is an impiety." (18)

Conclusion

Some scholars, as P. Wendland, has put forth the view that the fragments attributed to Aristobulus presuppose Philo and are dependent upon his writings. E. Stein, and especially N. Walter, have convincingly shown that this cannot be the case. (19) Philo represents a developed allegorical exposition and often draws a distinction of principal nature between the literal and the allegorical/spiritual meanings. Aristobulus, on the other hand, applies a modest form of allegorical interpretation to the problematic anthropomorphic designations of God. His expositions, therefore, remain within the context of midrashic and allegorical exegesis as are also found in the Septuagint, the targumim and the midrashim. Nevertheless, his employment of Greek philosophical terminology and ideas, and his use of Greek quotations make him to be a reprsentive of an Alexandrian Jewish emphasis which points toward Philo's expositions. Moreover, both Aristobulus and Philo are part of the trend in contemporary Judaism to stress the cosmic basis of Jewish community life and of Jewish existence in general. Likewise, the kinship between Aristobulus and Philo supports the view that Philo was not an isolated individualist in his authorship.

Within his own historical context Aristobulus builds a bridge between traditional Judaism and the Greek surroundings. His exegesis of the Law of Moses therefore must be understood as a positive effort to adapt the traditional conceptions of the Jewish tradition to the spiritual demands of a new situation, that of a Jewish community who wanted to assert herself vis a vis the Hellenistic civilization at large.

This Jewish-Alexandrian concern was shared by the early Church. Clement of Alexandria and Eusebius of Caesarea then use fragments from Aristobulus in order to document their thesis that Greek wisdom depends on Jewish wisdom as revealed in the Law of Moses.

NOTES

1) See M. Stone, Scriptures, Sects and Visions, (London, 1980) esp. 46-56.

2) See J. Neusner, Formative Judaism: Religious, Historical, and Literary Studies. Fourth Series, (BJS 76; Chico, California, 1984); id., Formative Judaism: Religious, Historical, and Literary Studies. Fifth Series, (BJS 91; Chico, California, 1985).

3) N. Walter, Der Thoraausleger Aristobulus, (Berlin, 1964) 7-9.

4) 2 Macc 1:10 is probably an editorial addition from about 50 B.C. It testifies to the general knowledge of Aristobulus' writings in Alexandria at that time. See N. Walter, Der Thoraausleger, 16-19.

5) ibid., 13-26; 35-40.

6) ibid., 1-4; E. Stein, Die allegorische Exegese des Philo aus Alexandrien, (Giessen, 1929) 7-8.

7) N. Walter, Der Thoraausleger, 29-31, emphasizes too much the difference between the dialogue form of Aristobulus and the form of quaestiones et solutiones. Walter suggests that Aristobulus' work probably was a thematic treatise which presented the right hermeneutical principle for the interpretation of the Law of Moses, and some of the valuable philosophical insights gained from such an approach. Concerning the form of quaestiones et solutiones in various parts of Philo's works, see P. Borgen and R. Skarsten, "Quaestiones et Solutiones: Some Observations on the Form of Philo's Exegesis", Studia Philonica 4, (1976-77) 1-15.

8) Cf. E. Stein, Die allegorische Exegese, 10-11; M. Hengel Judaism and Hellenism, (2nd ed.; London, 1974) 1,165-166; H.A. Wolfson, Philo, (4th repr.; Cambridge, Mass., 1982) 1, 141-142.

9) Cf. E. Stein, Die allegorische Exegese, 10; N. Walter, Der Thoraausleger, 141-149.

10) Cf. M. Hengel, Judaism, 1, 164.

11) N. Walter, Der Thoraausleger, 103-123.

12) See M. Hengel, Judaism, 1, 166; H.A. Wolfson, Philo, 1, 311-312. N. Walter, Der Thoraausleger, 65-66.

13) See M. Hengel, Judaism, 1, 166-169; S. Aalen, Die Begriffe "Licht" und "Finsternis" im Alten Testament, im Spätjudentum und im Rabbinismus, (Oslo, 1951) 175ff.; Str.-B. 4, 960ff.

14) M. Hengel, Judaism, 1, 166-167; N. Walter, Der Thoraausleger, 68-75.

15) N. Walter, Der Thoraausleger, 150-171.

16) ibid., 170-171. C.K. Barrett, The Gospel According to St. John, (2nd ed.; London, 1978) 255-256.

17) M. Hengel, Judaism, 1, 235; 2, 157-158, n.813; See especially A. Strobel, "Der Termin des Todes Jesu," ZNW, 51, (1960), 92; id., "Zur Funktionsfähigkeit des essenischen Kalenders," Rev Q, 3 (1961/62) 410; cf. M. Limbek, Die Ordnung des Heils, (Düsseldorf, 1971) 134-175, concerning the Essene Calendar; M.D. Herr, "The Calendar," CRINT, (Assen, 1984) I:2, 834-864.

18) See S. Maybaum, Die Anthropomorphien und Anthropathien bei Onkelos und den späteren Targumim mit besonderer Berücksichtigung der Ausdrücke Memra, Jekara und Schechintha, (Breslau, 1870); J.Z. Lauterbach, "The Ancient Jewish Allegorists in the Talmud and Midrash," JQR, (NS) 1, (1910) 129-136. I. Heinemann, Altjüdische Allegoristik, (Leiden, 1936); R.J. Zwi Werblowsky, "Anthropomorphism," Enc Jud, 3, (3rd ed.; Jerusalem, 1974) cols. 50-56; C. Fritsch, The Anti-Anthropomorphisms of the Greek Pentateuch, (Princeton, 1943); G. van der Leeuw, "Anthropomorphismus," RAC, (Stuttgart, 1950) 1, cols 446-450; H.A. Wolfson, Philo, 1, 56-60; 2, 127-128.

19) E. Stein, Die allegorische Exegese, 7-11; N. Walter, Der Thoraausleger, esp. pp. 58-86; 141-149.

CHAPTER TWO
PHILO'S WRITINGS

Introduction

A large number of Philo's writing have been preserved, and they give us a comprehensive knowledge of his exegesis, his philosophical and theological outlook, and his place within Alexandrian Judaism and Hellenism. The writings are, moreover, a treasure house for a broader knowledge of Judaism, and of philosophy, education and history in the Graeco-Roman world in the first century A.D. Finally, they are important sources for background knowledge of the New Testament and of Patristic literature. Philo's impact on the Christian Church was so extensive that his writings were preserved by the Church, and not by the Synagogue. (1)

This chapter on Philo's writings may serve as a convenient aid for those who wish to acquaint themselves with him and Alexandrian Judaism. The aim is also to contribute to the debate on the classification of his writings, and to survey recent research on the relative dating of the treatises internally.

As for the classification of Philo's writings, there has long been general agreement among scholars on the understanding of the expository treatises. These fall into two main groups: 1. The exposition of the Law of Moses. These writings are but parts of one comprehensive rewriting of the Law of Moses. 2. The exegetical commentaries, which fall into two subordinate series: a) Questions and Answers on Genesis and Exodus which is a brief commentary in the form of questions and answers on parts of the first two books of the Pentateuch. b) The Allegory of the Laws. This series covers the main part of Gen 2-41.

There has been more uncertainty about the classification of the remaining writings. In general they have been divided into purely philosophical writings (On the Eternity of the World; On Providence; Alexander, or Whether the Animals have Reason; Every Good Man is Free) and historical and apologetic treatises (Flaccus; On the Embassy to Gaius; On the Contemplative Life; Apology for the Jews; On the Life of Moses). (2)

The classification of these writings as philosophical and apologetic is also rather unsatisfactory. The main weakness of these labels is that it fails to integrate these treatises with the other works of Philo. It therefore seems pertinent here to start from the fact that Philo was an exegete. His writings are therefore classified under the headings of "The Pentateuch in re-written form". "The Exegetical commentaries", and "Pentateuchal principles applied to contemporary issues and events".

A) THE PENTATEUCH IN RE-WRITTEN FORM

The Exposition of the Laws and On the Life of Moses

The following writings are but parts of one comprehensive re-writing of the Law of Moses: On the Creation of the World (De opificio mundi), On Abraham (De Abrahamo), On Isaac (De Isaaco), On Jacob (De Iacobo), On Joseph (De Iosepho), On the Decalogue (De Decalogo), On the Special Laws (De specialibus legibus), On the Virtues (De virtutibus), and On Rewards and Punishments (De praemiis et poeniis). All these books are preserved except De Isaaco and De Iacobo. As a designation for all these books together, the name "The Exposition of the Laws of Moses" has been used. (3) In addition to these books, Philo's On the Life of Moses (De vita Mosis) also falls into the same category.

On the Life of Moses was formerly classed in a group of miscellaneous writings, but E.R. Goodenough has shown that this treatise and the Exposition of the Law, while independent writings, were companion pieces. (4) The conclusion follows that both works are to be examined together as regards sources, Philo's own contribution, and the purpose of the works.

On the Life of Moses I and II (5)

The two treatises cover most of the story of Moses given in the Pentateuch, the most important omission being that of the theophany on Sinai, which is dealt with in On the Decalogue (32 ff). (6)

The first treatise covers, as Philo states at the beginning of the second, the early life and education of Moses and the main facts of his work as king, that is, as the leader of the Israelites in their escape from Egypt and their adventures in the wilderness. The second treatise deals with the character of Moses under three heads, the legislative, 12-65, the high priestly, 66-186, and the prophetic, 181-292.

The offices of Moses are fundamental to the Jewish people and their divine call in the world. As for kingship, Moses was the king of a nation destined to be consecrated above all others to offer prayers for ever on behalf of the human race that it might be delivered from evil and participate in what is good (Mos I:149).

As for his office as law-giver, Moses was best of all law-givers in all countries, and his laws are most excellent: they are firm and secure and will endure as long as the universe exists; and every other people honors the laws of the Jews, such as the sabbath and the day of atonement. And the supreme proof of the universal acceptance of the laws of Moses is the Septuagint translation of them into Greek, ordered by king Ptolemy Philadelphus himself, an occasion celebrated annually on the island of Pharos, where both Jews an Gentiles participate (II:12-186).

As for his office as high priest, Moses established the priesthood in Israel, and the priestly tribe was the nucleus of all mankind as regards the blessed eschatological life to come (II : 186). Finally, his office of prophet particularly applied to the defence of the Jewish religion, and to prophecies about the things which were to come to pass for Israel (II: 187-291).

Philo's purpose in writing On the Life of Moses is therefore to show the divine calling of Moses and the Jewish people to worship God, keep the Sabbath and serve the whole world. Philo expects that the new (eschatological) era might come when all nations will throw overboard their ancestral customs and honour the laws of Moses alone (II : 43-44).

Thus the book is written for gentile readers to tell them about the supreme law-giver whose laws they are to accept and honour. At the same time it was to strengthen the Jews for their universal role. (7) This dual purpose fits well in to the situation of the Jewish community of Alexandria in the period preceding the time of Gaius Caligula. At that time the Jews were actively penetrating into the Greek community, even by infiltration into its center in the Gymnasium. Philo's work offers an ideological basis for pursuing this goal as Jews.

The form of Vita Mosis is determined by the idea of these four offices of Moses. In Judaism the three offices of King, priest and prophet could be united in one person. Thus, Josephus, Antiq XIII:299 f. says that John Hyrcanus possessed all three. And the office of the law-giver had also to be ascribed to Moses since the Torah was given by him. (8) To these Jewish formative elements Philo has added features which resemble a Greek Bios, or a Greek biographical and historical Novel. He has, thus, taken his presentation of Moses out of its Pentateuchal context of the creation and the patriarchs, and written a life of Moses from his birth to death. (9)

The Exposition of the Laws of Moses

On the basis of Philo's own terminology and outline, as stated in Praem 1-3 and Mos II:45 ff. (10) the book of Philo's Exposition of the Laws of Moses can be listed in this way:

The story of the creation: On the Creation of the World.

The historical part: On Abraham, On Isaac, On Jacob, On Joseph.

The legislative part: On the Decalogue (The ten heads or summaries): On the Special Laws I-IV; On the Virtues of Peace and War; On Rewards and Punishments.

In the "Exposition of the Law" Philo follows in general the chronological outline of the pentateuchal narrative, but modifies it on the basis of systematic interest in some of the subject matters as in On the Life of Moses. The systematic and philosophical effort not withstanding, the closest parallels to this comprehensive work by Philo are other books which re-write the Pentateuch in parts or as a whole: the Book of Jubilees, the Genesis Apocryphon and Pseudo-Philo's Biblical Antiquities. (11)

The story of the creation. "On the Creation of the World" is the first treatise in the Exposition of the Laws of Moses. It covers Gen 1-3 and deals with the creation and the sin committed by Adam and Eve. After an introductory section (1-12) Philo tells the creation story, following the scheme of six days (*hexaemeron*), Gen 1:1-31, and then adding the story of the seventh day, Gen 2:1-3, and using Gen 2:4-5 as a concluding summary (13-130). Subsequent points from Gen 2 and 3 are then elaborated upon (131-170a), including an interpretation of the sin of Adam and Eve and their punishment. The conclusion of the treatise (170a-172) makes explicit the teachings drawn from the creation story.

Philo's scheme of *hexaemeron* is derived, of course, from the biblical story. He develops the pattern into an expanding paraphrase, as is also done in other *hexaemerons* in Jewish writings, such as 4 Ezra 6:38-59; the Book of Jubilees 2:2-21;

2 Enoch 24-30, etc. (12) Philo considers that the creation story serves as necessary background to the actual Laws of Moses given at Mount Sinai. This view is expressed in Mos II:45-52 and is repeated in Opif 3. Moreover, the creation story points to the corresponding eschatological possibility: the first father of the race spent his days without toil or trouble surrounded by lavish abundance. And these glorious times will return - in spite of the punishment of Adam and Eve for their disobedience - if the religious and ethical conditions are met (79 ff.).

In spite of this Jewish character as to form and content the book is adopted to the form and aim of the philosophical treatise. These philosophical interests are in particular evident in paragraphs 170-171, where Philo concludes his version of the creation story with criticisms of the Sceptic view that God's existence is doubtful, the Aristotelian view that the world is without beginning, the Epicurean idea of a plurality of worlds, and the Epicurean denial of Providence. (13)

Philo's presentation has, moreover, many points in common with Plato's Timaeus, as well as with Stoic ideas. (14) Some of the concepts held in common with the Timaeus are: an intelligible world (of 'forms') transcending the visible world (16, etc.; Timaeus 30C; 33B); the Goodness of the Father and Maker of all things (21; Timaeus 29E); the simultaneity of time and the world (26; Timaeus 38B). Some of the Stoic ideas are: the world as a city (3 and 19); time as measured space (26); the fourfold hierarchical order of creatures (66-68). Since Philo thinks that these and other Greek ideas were already present in the writings of Moses, he makes claim on them for his Jewish religion and for the high self-understanding of the Jews as the chief nation in the world. The Jew who observes the Laws of Moses is a cosmopolitan ("citizen of the world"), since these laws are universal and cosmic (3).

In this situation Philo had both Jews and Gentiles in mind when he wrote this treatise and brought the Jewish creation story into the international debate on the philosophy of religion. E.R. Goodenough has rightly argued against the widespread theory that "On the Creation" and the rest of the Exposition of the Law of Moses were written for Jews. Philo addresses himself to Jews as well, however, as can be seen for example from the use of first person plural in § 170: "By his account of the creation of the world of which we have spoken, Moses teaches us (ἡμᾶς ἀναδιδάσκει) ..... (15)

<u>The historical part</u>. <u>On Abraham</u>. The historical part of the Exposition of the Laws of Moses covers the Pentateuchal story from the events after Adam and Eve to the death of Joseph. The title of the first treatise, On Abraham, is somewhat inadequate, since the treatise actually contains the stories of Enos, Enoch, Noah and Abraham. Thus, it draws on parts of Gen 4-26.

After placing Abr within the framework of his Exposition of the Laws of Moses (1-6), Philo interprets Enos as "hope" (7-16) especially based on LXX Gen 4:26, Enoch as "repentance" (17-26), especially based on Gen 5:24, and Noah as "justice" (27-46), especially based on Gen 6:9. (16) These three are wise in a preparatory way, like children, while the triad Abraham, Isaac and Jacob resemble the exercises of full-grown athletes (48).

The outline of Abraham's life follows in part the chronology of the biblical narrative. However, the main principle of organization is systematic, so that the events illustrate the subject matter concerned, piety, hospitality, tact and kindness, courage and self-control. In every case, except the last, which describes Abraham's resignation at the death of Sarah, the narrative of particular events in Abraham's life is followed by the deeper, allegorical interpretation. (17)

Although the treatises on Isaac and Jacob are lost, Philo's basic interpretation of the three patriarchs is summed up in On Joseph 1: Abraham means wisdom or virtue acquired by teaching, Isaac acquired by nature, and Jacob by practice. (18) At this point Philo draws upon a broad Greek tradition about education, in which instruction, nature and practice are discussed in relation to virtue. Plutarch associates the triad with Pythagoras, Socrates and Plato in a way similar to Philo's association of them with the three patriarchs. (19) Philo, however, finds these aspects of learning to be a main characteristic of the Jewish people and the Jewish religion. This understanding is supported by On Abraham 56, where this triad of Abraham/teaching, Isaac/nature and Jacob/practice is seen as parent of the species called "royal" and "priesthood" and "holy nation" (Exod 19:6). (20)

Philo interprets the patriarchs both in relation to creation, and to the giving of the Laws on Mt Sinai. The patriarchs are living laws (ἔμψυχοι νόμοι), that is, they are an embodiment of the divine cosmic laws. The specific and concrete laws given on Mt Sinai are then memorials of the life of the ancients, and commentaries on their words and deeds (Abr 5).

Jewish and Platonizing motifs are here woven together. The Jewish motif is expressed in the correlation between the practices of the patriarchs and the Mosaic Law given on Mt Sinai. For example, according to the Book of the Jubilees, Noah, Abraham etc. observed and enjoined the laws inscribed on heavenly tables, which were later given to Moses. (21) A corresponding correlation is found in Philo, but here the platonizing distinction between archetype and copy is applied in such a way that the lives and words of the patriarchs are the originals and the particular Mosaic laws are copies. (22)

On Joseph. The outline of On Joseph further illustrates the tension seen in On Abraham, and especially in On the Life of Moses, between a chronological principle of organization as found in the biblical narrative, and a systematic and subject-centered form of presentation. Philo has a systematic exposition of Gen 37:2-41:46 in On Joseph 2-156, and then in 157-270 the story, based on Gen 41-47 (with some omissions), runs continuously as it appears in Genesis, with some amplifications. In the systematic part the exposition is developed on two levels, literal and allegorical, as in On Abraham 60-244. (23)

Also in On Joseph the relationship between Jews and the gentile surroundings of Philo's own time is reflected. In paragraphs 42 ff. and in 56-57 the difference is stated between the Hebrew nation and other nations in sexual ethics and marriage laws. The Hebrews have strict customs and strict laws on marital matters, while licentiousness has destroyed the youth of the Greek race and the barbarians also. And in Egypt it is easy for Jewish youth to leave the ancestral way of life and change to alien ways, because the Egyptians deify things created and mortal, and are blind to the true God (254).

Another area of tension was that of table fellowship. Joseph gave a feast both for his own family and for Egyptians together with them. Joseph feasted each party according to its ancestral practice. Surprisingly, the Egyptians followed the same seating order as the Hebrews, which indicated that in older times the style of life in their country was less civilized, until Joseph introduced good order (202-6). (24) Against this background, it is clear that Joseph's free and noble birth must mean Joseph's membership in the Jewish nation. (25) And his authority as govenor yes, actually as the king, of Egypt, was the royal authority bestowed upon him by God, the Creator, who had the Jewish nation as His own loyal people (107 and 119). (26)

The purpose of On Joseph has been stated by E.R. Goodenough in this way: "De Iosepho seems to me, then, to have been written from first to last with a single purpose, namely to ... suggest that the real source for the highest political ideal of the East, the ideal of a divinely appointed and guided ruler, had had its truest presentation in Jewish literature, and highest exemplification at a time when a Jew was, in contemporary language, prefect of Egypt." (27)

Although On Abraham and On Joseph are to be understood as parts of Philo's comprehensive work, the Exposition of the Laws of Moses, the treatises betray features which indicate some influence from the forms of Hellenistic biography. (28) Thus, On Abraham contains certain topics of the genre rhetorical panegyric: eudaimonismus (115); - synkrisis (178-199). It omits things which might darken the outstanding character of Abraham (Sara and Hagar, Gen 16 and 21; Abimelech, Gen 20 and 21: 22-33). The allegorical sections show affinities with the religio-philosophical biography written for edifying purpose.

On Joseph on the other hand, combines elements of a narrative eulogy and a rhetorical panegyric which concentrate on the persons virtues. In a lesser degree the allegorical sections have features in common with the edifying biography.

The legislative part. The combination observed in previous treatises of the chronological biblical order and systematic principles of organization, is also present in the treatises which belong to this part of the Exposition of the Law of Moses. The biblical order is followed in the basic point that the actual giving of the laws at Mt Sinai follows after the story about creation and about the patriarchs. At other points Philo also follows the biblical narrative, but on the whole his systematic interest dominates the presentation to a large extent. In these treatises Philo gives an exposition of large parts of Exodus, Leviticus, Numbers and Deuteronomy. At times also points from Genesis are included if they are relevant to the subject matter discussed. As already seen, parts of the Pentateuch are also covered by Philo's On the Life of Moses, which supplements the treatises presently under discussion, particularly as it chiefly contains narrative material, and only some of the laws.

The laws are set forth in On the Decalogue and On the Special Laws I-IV. The Decalogue serves as a basis for both a summary and an outline of the specific laws.

On the Decalogue. On the Special Laws

The outline of the treatise On the Decalogue is:

1 : Transition.

2-17 : Questions related to the exodus into the desert, see especially Exod 12-19.

18-50 : Preliminary questions on the Decalogue and on the scene at Sinai. See especially Exod 19-20.

51-153: The Decalogue itself. See Exod 20:3-17.

- 50-51 : Summary. Cf. Exod 20:19.
- 52-120: The first table. The first five commandments.
    - 52-65 : The first commandment, against idolatry.
    - 66-81 : The second commandment, against idols. (29)
    - 82-95 : The third commandment on not taking God's name in vain.
    - 96-105: The fourth commandment, the sacred seventh day.
    - 106-120: The fifth commandment, the honour due to parents.
- 121-153: The second table. The second five commandments.
    - 121-131: The first commandment, against adultery.
    - 132-134: The second commandment, to do no murder.
    - 135-137: The third commandment, against stealing.
    - 138-141: The fourth commandment, against false witness.
    - 142-153: The fifth commandment, against covetousness.
- 154-175: General characteristic of the Decalogue as summary to the special laws, see Exod 20:19.
- 176-178: A concluding problem: Why are not penalties mentioned?

In On the Special Laws I-IV the usual treatment of each commandment is to begin with an elaboration on the commandment itself, similar to, though fuller than, that in On the Decalogue, and the exposition then proceeds to a discussion of the particular enactments which Philo thinks may be set under it.

On the Special Laws I interprets the first and second commandments against idolatry and idols and gives specifics on the knowledge of God and reverence for Him and consequently on worship. Book II covers all laws which can be assigned to the next three commandments, that on not taking God's name in vain (regulations on oaths and vows), on keeping the Sabbath (special laws on various feasts), on honouring the parents (the duties of parents and children to each other).

In book III Philo first gives a personal word of introduction (1-6) and then the first and second commandments of the second table are interpreted: the commandments against adultery (special laws on sexual irregularities), and against murder, and specifics involved. Book IV treats the last three commandments, the one against stealing (various forms of dishonesty), the one against false witness and specifics involved, and finally the one against covetousness and the corresponding particular rules.

What is the basis for Philo's presentation of the laws of Moses, especially for the distinction drawn between the Decalogue and the Special Laws? Philo himself gives the clue when he says that the Decalogue was given by God himself directly, and the other laws by Moses (Mos II:188 ff.; Dec 18 and 175, and Praem 2).

H.A. Wolfson has noted that "in rabbinic literature, it is similarly said that the Ten Commandments contain all the laws of the Torah. This last method of classification is adopted by Philo in his direct discussion of the laws of Moses. First, in his De Decalogo he enumerates and discusses the Ten Commandments. Then, in his De Specialibus Legibus, he discusses the special laws which he arranges under the Ten Commandments." Wolfson bases his view on Cant Rab 5, 14:2, where it is stated that the 613 commandments are implied by the Decalogue. (30)

E. Urbach has argued against Wolfson's view. According to him, in Cant Rab and corresponding passages "it is not asserted that the Ten Commandments incorporated all precepts of the Torah; only that each commandment forms the basis of interpretations ... all the Halakha originated in the Oral Law was, as it were, written beside each commandment."

R.D. Hecht points out that Urbach has overlooked the evidence of the Targums, especially the one found in Targum Pseudo-Jonathan Exod 24:12: "And the Lord said to Moses, come up before me to the mountain and be there and I will give you the tablets of stone upon which are hinted the rest of the law and the six hundred and thirteen commandments which I have written for their instruction."

On the basis of this debate among Wolfson, Urbach and Hecht, the conclusion can be drawn, that Philo seems to develop systematically a notion also found in Palestinian tradition, that the Decalogue contained in nuce all the commandments of the Mosaic law. (31)

On the Virtues. On Rewards and Punishments

The connection between On the Decalogue, On the Special Laws and On the Virtues is already given in Spec IV:133-135, where Philo says that the virtues are common to all commandments, and do not fit in with anyone particular number in the Decalogue. The virtue justice is presented in Spec IV:136-238, while the remaining four virtues, courage, philanthropy, repentance and nobility, are treated in On the Virtues.

In the opening paragraph of On Rewards and Punishments Philo surveys the whole scheme of the laws of Moses, from creation and onwards, i.e. the scheme which he has employed for his whole "Exposition". He also defines the relationship between the virtues and the rewards and punishments: those who are schooled in the laws and exhortations are called into the sacred arena to be tested. Then the true athletes of virtue will gain victory and rewards while the unmanly will suffer defeat and punishments. Already Mos II:52-65 presents this understanding of rewards and punishments, and serves as a brief anticipatory survey. (32)

The treatise On the Virtues is organized according to subject matter, but the subjects are not treated in an abstract or analytical way. The virtues of courage (1-50), humanity or philanthropy (51-174), repentance (175-186) and nobility (187-227) serve rather as key words and are illustrated from the Pentateuch. (33)

The virtues of courage and nobility, as well as the virtue of justice, treated in Spec IV:136-238, reflect Greek (Platonic and Stoic) terminology and ideas. To Philo, however, these virtues are biblical, as he shows by examples from the Pentateuch. This means that they characterize the Jewish nation. On this basis, Philo maintains that they have their source in God and His laws. Philo also lifts up repentance as a virtue in a way in which the Greeks did not, and it is in particular applied to the conversion by proselytes from atheism and polytheism to the Jewish religion.

The treatise On Rewards and Punishments falls into two main parts: After the transitional statement, which summarized the whole Exposition (1-6), the first main part deals with rewards and punishments, 7-78. Then the second part follows on blessings and curses, 79-172. Between the two parts a transitional passage is missing, to conclude the discussion of rewards and punishments and to introduce the presentation of blessings and curses. (34)

The work is largely based on Genesis. The paragraphs 7-66, especially 7-56, are almost a short form of the earlier treatise On Abraham, the lost On Jacob and On Isaac, and On the Life of Moses.

In Philo's treatment of the rewards given to Jacob's children, his central interest in the Jews as a nation is emphasized. Moreover, he makes it explicit that both the literal and the allegorical meanings of the Pentateuchal stories serve as characterization of the Jewish nation: "This is the household, which kept safe from harm, perfected and united both in the literal history and in the allegorical interpretation, received for its reward, as I have said, the chieftaincy of the tribes of the nation. From this household, increased in the course of time to a great multitude, were founded flourishing and orderly cities, schools of wisdom, justice and religion, where also the rest of virtue and how to acquire it is the sublime subject of their research" (Praem 65-66).

The second part of the treatise (79-172), which sets forth blessings and curses, follows more the main sequence of the Exposition as a whole. While On the Decalogue and On the Special Laws give an exposition of laws in Exodus, Leviticus, Numbers and Deuteronomy, the blessings and curses cover other sections in these books, with main emphasis on Lev 26 and 28, and Deut 28. These observations tell against Goodenough's attempt to separate the section on blessings and curses from Philo's larger work, the Exposition of the Laws of Moses. (35)

Goodenough, who believed that the Exposition was addressed to Gentiles, thought that the section on blessings and curses could not have been a part of it, since it is so clearly Jewish in feelings and eschatological outlook. Against Goodenough it can be maintained that Philo here only offers more details on points which have been treated throughout the Exposition. (36)

It is essential for the understanding of Philo's eschatology to realize that he relates it to his concept of a God-given cosmic moral law which is made manifest in the Laws of Moses. Thus, his eschatology is conditional upon man's obedience or disobedience to these laws, and he therefore has to develop the eschatological alternatives of blessings and curses, Praem 126.

The blessings are victory over enemies (wild beasts and men), wealth, long life and happiness (79-126). The curses are famine, cannibalism, enslavement, business failures, diseases, wars (127-151). Throughout the whole, the Jewish nation is in the center, but as the center of all nations. Alternatives indicated are: peaceful alliances between Jews and others, with the Jews as head nation (93, 114, 125; cf. On the Life of Moses, II:44), or successful defensive war. If the Jewish nation itself for a while is rejected proselytes will take over its role.

Thus Philo in On Rewards and Punishments, as in the rest of the Exposition of the Laws, has a double aim; to equip the Jews for their God-given call to serve as the center and chief of mankind, and to bring gentiles to join them and thus usher in the new era of heaven on the whole earth.

The main forms employed in On Rewards and Punishments follow the line of Jewish traditions. Philo's blessings and curses develop categories already used in Deuteronomy. And in the Bible and other Jewish writings there are several examples of similar lists of heroes from the biblical story to illustrate rewards or punishments. (37) Nevertheless, throughout the treatise Greek (Platonic and Stoic) ideas and phrases are also seen, as could be expected. (38)

B) THE EXEGETICAL COMMENTARIES

Questions and Answers on Genesis and Exodus

While Philo retells the Pentateuch in an interpretative way in the Exposition of the Laws of Moses, he quotes the Pentateuchal text in several treatises and adds the exposition so as to make the interpretation into an exegetical commentary. These commentaries fall into two series: a) Questions and answers on Genesis and Exodus (Quaestiones et solutiones in Genesin et Exodum) and b) The Allegory of the Laws (Legum Allegoriae).

As the name indicates, Philo's Quaestiones et solutiones in Genesin et Exodum is a brief commentary in the form of questions and answers on the first two books of the Pentateuch. The original work may have taken in other books of the Pentateuch, but Eusebius knew only the sections on Genesis and Exodus. (39) All but a small protion of the Greek original has been lost and for the bulk of the work we must depend upon the ancient Armenian version published by J.B. Aucher in 1826, translated into English by R. Marcus in 1953. (40) According to R. Marcus the Armenian version has faithfully preserved Philo's meaning except in a few cases where the Greek text used by the translator was corrupt or ambiguous or unusually obscure. (41)

The Questions and Answers Commentary has been compared with Philo's other commentary series, The Allegory of the Laws, since both have the form of running commentary based on verse(s) which are quoted from Pentateuchal books. Some scholars have then suggested that Questions and Answers is a catechetical work of questions and answers, while The Allegory of the Laws is Philo's scholarly work. (42) This hypothesis cannot be upheld, however, since several passages in The Allegory of the Laws betray the same form, method and problems, as those found in Questions and Answers. Such passages of questions and answers are even built into the Exposition of the Laws of Moses, although that work does not in general have the formal structure of an exegetical commentary. (43)

Among the passages which have the same form of Questions and Answers in the Exposition are Opif 72-75 (what reason there could be for ascribing the creation of man, not to one Creator, but, as the words would suggest, to several;), Opif 77-88 (why man comes last in the worlds creation) and Dec 36-43 (why, when all these many thousands were collected in one spot, He thought good in proclaiming His ten oracles to address each as to one). (44) In Opif 77, as for example also in Quaes Gen I:43, the problem is that of an unexpected order and rank in the Pentateuchal story. In Opif 72 and Dec 36, as in Quaes Gen I:15, the problems discussed are those of unexpected plural or singular forms of the verb.

Some examples should also be given on the employment of such questions and answers in The Allegory of the Laws: In Leg all I:101-104 (God first addresses the command to a single person, then he speaks to more than one) the very same question is raised as in Quaes Gen I:15, with reference to Gen 2:16-17; in Leg all I:85-87 and in Quaes Gen I:13 almost the same question is asked on the basis of surprising omissions in the text of Gen 2:10-14. In general it should be added that there is no difference of substance where the Commentary on Questions and Answers overlaps with parts of the Allegory of the Laws. (45)

The form of questions and answers is found extensively also in other parts of the Allegory of the Laws. For example, in On the Giants 1, Philo quotes Gen 6:1 "And it came to pass when men began to wax many on the earth and daughters were born into them," and then raises the question: "It is, I think, a problem worth inquiring, why our race began to grow so numerous after the birth of Noah and his Sons." Then the answer follows in Gig 1-5. The form of questions and answers is explicitly used also in §§ 55-57. In the subsequent treatise, On the Unchangeableness of God, the Old Testament quotation from Gen 6:4 is immediately followed by a question in Quod Deus 1, and the answer is given in §§ 1-19. Questions and answer occur throughout the treatise. It is, therefore, worth considering the possibility that the form of questions and answer partly serves as the "mother-cell" of Philo's exegetical developments in his Allegory of the Laws, and also in parts of his Exposition on the Laws of Moses. As it seems, the Allegory of the Laws is to some extent a combination of a running commentary with direct explanatory exegesis and such questions and answers. Similarily, the Exposition of the Laws of Moses is partly a combination of a retelling of the Pentateuch and questions and answers. It may be added that Philo's report on the expository activity on the Sabbath suggests a combination of direct exposition and questions and answers (Vit Cont 31 and 75-79; Quod Omn 82; Somn II:127).

Scholars have observed that Philo's Questions and Answers in their form resemble Greek commentaries on the Homeric poems. (46) This form, however, seems to have been common to Greek commentaries on Homer and both Philo's and rabbinic expositions of the Laws of Moses. (47) A close parallell both in form an content exists between Philo's Opif 77-78 and rabbinic exposition in Tosephta, Sanhedrin 8:7-9. (48) In both places the problem raised is the biblical statement that Adam was created last. In both passages the problem is formulated as a question. Moreover, in both the answers are partly the same: the comparison is drawn between God and a human host, who invites the guest when the meal is made ready. Likewise God made man after the world had been created. Although the agreements do not prove that Tosephta's version is the source, Philo and the rabbinic Tosephta here are clearly rendering two versions of the same tradition. This conclusion is supported by the fact that in Opif 77 Philo explicitly states that he has received the tradition from others, "those, then who have studied more deeply than others the laws of Moses and who examine their contents with all possible minuteness..."

The Questions and Answers Commentary develops mostly into a two-level exposition, the literal and the allegorical. The Questions and Answers Commentary in this respect builds a bridge between the Exposition of the Laws of Moses and the Allegorical Commentary. The same two-level exposition often occurs in the Exposition, while the Allegorical Commentary has mainly allegorical expositions. At the same time, however, the Questions and Answers Commentary is closer to the Allegory of Laws because both follow the form of a running commentary.

As for the original extent of the Questions and Answers Commentary, (49) Massebieau and Schürer (50) have called attention to a passage (Quaes Gen IV:123) in which Philo says, "the principle of these things will be explained when we inquire into the blessings". This may be a reference either to Genesis 49 or to Deuteronomy 33 or to both. It is likely, however, that Philo refers only to the passage on blessings in Genesis, since Eusebius knew only of Questions and Answers on Genesis and Exodus (Ecclesiastical History 2,18:1 and 5) and also because the Greek fragments preserved by Byzantine writings are, with two doubtful exceptions, all ascribed either to Genesis or Exodus. (51) We shall probably be safe in assuming either that Philo never wrote similar commentaries on the last three books of the Pentateuch or that if he did, they were lost before the time of Eusebius.

As for the original book-divisions of the Questions and Answers in Genesis, it is clear that there were originally six books instead of the four indicated in the Armenian version. (52)

But it is also clear that the Armenian version has preserved all six books of the original treatise. As Wendland (53) and other scholars have pointed out, book IV of the Armenian Questions and Answers in Genesis is about as long as books I, II and III together. It therefore probably contains books IV, V and VI of the original Commentary. Since the end of book IV reaches only Gen 28:9, it seems that Philo did not intend to treat the whole of Genesis. (54)

Somewhat similar but more complicated is the problem of the original extent and the book-divisions of the commentary on Exodus. The Armenian version has two books of unequal size. Book I covers Exod 12:2-23 in 25 pages of Aucher's edition, while book II (aside from the first section on Exod 20:25) covers Exod 22:21-28:34 (with the omission of several verses) in 80 pages. If we suppose that the Questions and Answers in Exodus Commentary was divided into books of about the same length as those of

Questions and Answers in Genesis, we must conclude that the present book I is less than half of an original book I or book II, and that the present book II is either a complete book or else contains parts of several of the original books.

The Allegory of the Laws

a) Survey

Several of Philo's treatises have the form of a commentary where the Pentateuchal text is cited and the expository commentary then follows. Among the writings preserved the following fall into this category:

Commentary on Gen 2:1-17	Allegorical Interpretations (Legum Allegoriae) I
" " " 2:18-3:1	(Legum Allegoriae) II
" " " 3:8b-19	(Legum Allegoriae) III
" " " 3:24-4:1	On the Cherubim (De Cherubim)
" " " 4:2-4	On the Sacrifices of Abel and Cain (De Sacrificiis Abelis et Caini)
" " " 4:8-15	That the Worse Attacks the Better (Quod Deterius Potiori Insidiari Soleat)
" " " 4:16-25	(in parts) On the Posterity and Exile of Cain (De Posteritate Caini)
" " " 6:1-4a	On the Giants (De Gigantibus)
" " " 6:4b-12	(in parts) On the Unchangeableness of God (Quod Deus Sit Immutabilis)
" " " 9:20-21	On Husbandry (De Agricultura)
" " " 9:20-21	On Noah's Work as a Planter (De Plantatione)
" " " 9:20-21	On Drunkenness (De Ebrietate)
" " " 9:24-27	On Sobriety (De Sobrietate)
" " " 11:1-9	On the Confusion of Tongues (De Confusione Linguarum)
" " " 12:1-6	(in parts) On the Migration of Abraham (De Migratione Abrahami)
" " " 15:2-18	Who Is the Heir of Divine Things (Quis Rerum Divinarum Heres)
" " " 16:1-6	On Mating with the Preliminary Studies (De Congressu Quaerendae Eruditionis Gratia)

Commentary on Gen 16:6b-14	On Flight and Finding (De Fuga et Inventione)
" " " 17:1-5. 16-22	On the Change of Names (De Mutatione Nominum)
(" " " 18	(in parts) On God (De Deo) Fragment)
" " " 28:10-22	On Dreams
" " " 31:10-13	(De Somniis) I
" " " 37:8-11	
" " " 40:9-11. 16-17	De Somniis II
" " " 41:17-24	

There is some evidence and several indications that Philo wrote other treatises of this nature. The clearest evidence is found in Heres 1, where Philo refers to a lost treatise on Gen 15:1; likewise Somn I:1 is an introduction of a second treatise on dreams, the first one being lost. Still other treatises may have interpreted parts of Genesis which are not covered by the extant writings. (55)

Originally the title of all these commentaries seems to have been Legum Allegoriae. This name is now given only to the first three treatises, while the others have received individual names. The basic structure for these treatises is the form of a running commentary on parts of Gen 2:1-41:24. In this respect they are similar to Philo's Questions on Genesis and Exodus, commentaries in the Dead Sea Scrolls, and several midrashim. (56) The expositions in the allegorical commentaries vary in length and are more complex than those found in Philo's Questions on Genesis and Exodus and the commentaries in the Dead Sea Scrolls. (57) On the other hand, the employment of "questions and answers" in the allegorical commentaries brings them closer to the midrashim, where problems are often discussed in the form of questions and answers. Such problem-solving exegesis is not characteristic of the Qumran writings. (58)

b) Allegorical Interpretations I-III

According to the manuscripts treatises I and II are but parts of a single treatise interpreting Gen 2:1-3:1a. (59) Treatise III is called number two in the manuscripts. (60) This treatise contains an exposition of Gen 3:8b-19. Philo may also have written commentaries on Gen 3:1b-8a and 3:20-23 (61), but it is not possible to be certain of this.

Philo has built up these treatises in such a way that the expositions in Leg all III are more complex than those in Leg all I, while Leg all II has an intermediate place. The exposition of seventeen verses (Gen 2:1-17) in Leg all I fills 28 pages, the exposition of eight verses (Gen 2:18-3:1) in Leg all II covers 22 pages, and the exposition of eleven verses (Gen 3:8b-19) in Leg all III fills 56 pages, all pages in the Cohn-Wendland text edition. (62)

In Leg all III, and to a lesser degree also in Leg all I and II, Philo has used the running commentary on the verses from Genesis as heads for related expositions on other parts of the Pentateuch. Thus, the commentary on Gen 2:8 in Leg all III: 1-48, (Adam hiding himself), leads into a lengthy expositions of other Pentateuchal verses dealing with the theme of hiding and flight. Similarly, God's cursing of the serpent, Gen 3:14, is quoted in Leg all III: 65 and 107 and this leads into a broad exposition on the subject of pleasure based on passages from various parts of the Pentateuch. Such extensive expositions on interrelated passages are quite common in the other treatises of the Allegory of the Laws as well.

Leg all I-III does not serve one main theme, but is rather a running commentary on man and Paradise, which expresses various topics and concerns. In his exposition Philo deduces cosmic and religious/ethical principles from the Laws of Moses in such a way that they can be applied to the situation of Philo and the other Jews in Alexandria. Among the areas reflected are the dangers of luxurious living, specified as temptations at banquets and from wealth in general; furthermore, the temptation to use education only for making a political career in governmental positions regardless of the Jewish values and commitments. (63)

Other Allegorical Treatises

1. On the Cherubim; On the Sacrifices of Abel and Cain; The Worse Attacks the Better; On the Posterity and Exile of Cain; On the Giants; On the Unchangeableness of God

In Leg all I-III a tension was found betwen the structure of a running commentary and a topical and subject-centered collection of expositions. The structure of running commentary formed the basic outline, but is, particularly in Leg all III, interrupted by lengthy topical elaborations. In the other allegorical commentaries, which are here treated in four groups, the topical and subject-centered thread is even stronger. Here we find lengthy elaborations of a topical nature, with Pentateuchal words as the starting point. (64)

The treatise On the Cherubim, is a commentary on two verses, Gen 3:24 and 4:1. In On the Sacrifices the running commentary covers three verses, Gen 4:2-4. In The Worse Attacks the Better, eight verses give the treatise its structure, Gen 4:8-15. Gen 4:16-25, omitting 4:23-4, is the basis for the commentary On the Posterity. On the Giants is a running commentary on Gen 6:1-4a, and On the Unchangeableness of God continues and deals with 6:4b-12 (6:10 is omitted).

The themes discussed in On the Cherubim, On the Sacrifices, The Worse Attacks the Better, On the Posterity, On the Giants and On the Unchangeableness of God are developed on the basis of the Pentateuchal stories about Adam and Eve, Cain and Abel and the appearance of the giants on earth.

Some of the themes are banishment and testing (Cher 1 ff.), the mistaken idea that what we have is our own and not God's (40 ff.), the contrasting ideas of man's mind as master and God as master (Sacr 1 ff.), the precedence of virtue (11 ff.), the danger of tardiness and postponement (52 ff.), the stable and firm life of virtue (88 ff.); the opposing principles of love of self and love of God, with only the apparent victory of the false view of self-love (Quod Det 1 ff.); further characterizations of the impious person who does not recognize God and His gifts, and of the pious person (Post 1 ff.), (sensual) pleasure and, by contrast, the God-born life (Gig 1 ff.), and God's constancy and unchangeableness (Quod Deus).

2. <u>On Husbandry; On Noah's Work as Planter; On Drunkenness; On Sobriety</u>

Philo wrote these treatises as parts of a single composition, as can be seen from the transitional statements. Thus Plant 1 draws the connection with On Husbandry in this way: "We have said in the former book ... (all that the occasion called for regarding the husbandman's art in general). In this book ... (we shall give such an account as we can of the art of a vine-dresser in particular). Ebr. 1 says correspondingly: "The views ... (expressed by the other philosophers on drunkenness) have been stated by me ... (to the best of my ability) in the preceding book. Let us now consider ... (what the great lawgiver in his never-failing wisdom holds on this subject)." And finally Sobr 1 reads: "Having in the foregoing pages dealt fully with the words of the lawgiver on ... (drunkenness and the nakedness which followed it,) let us proceed to carry on the thread of our discussion ... (by treating of the topic which comes next in order, 'And Noah returned to soberness ...')."

The unity is also evident from the fact that the same text, Gen 9:20-21, dealing with Noah who began to be a husbandman, and drank of the wine, serves as the starting point for the treatises On Husbandry, On Noahs Work as Planter, and On Drunkenness, and On Sobriety (65) moves on to Gen 9:24-27, and the related theme of soberness. The last of the four treatises, On Sobriety, follows the structure of a running commentary while the other three have all the same text and are well organized lectures on themes suggested by words in the text.

The Pentateuchal story about Noah, who began to be a husbandman, and drank of the wine and woke up sober, leads to a discussion of the following themes: the contrast between the uncultivated and cultivated approaches to life (Agr), God as Planter, and copies of His planting (Plant 1-139), a survey of what the philosophical schools say about drunkenness (incompletely preserved in Plant 140-77); wine and drunkenness as symbol of folly, stupor and greediness (Ebr); the theme of God's goodness, furthermore the curse on evil and on the other hand the moral and bodily virtues (Sobr).

3. <u>On the Confusion of Tongues; On the Migration of Abraham; Who is the Heir of Divine Things: On Mating with the Preliminary Studies; On Flight and Finding; On the Change of Names; On God</u>

These treatises do not form a united group of writings, although some of them are closely linked together, as we shall see. However, they continue the running commentary on parts of Genesis, while at the same time Philo's topical and systematic interest has influenced their structure. As a result, these treatises on parts of Genesis contain expositions on other parts of the Pentateuch as well as on other books.

The various parts of On the Confusion of Tongues are brought together at the beginning, where the pericope Gen 11:1-9 is rendered in full in 1, and a running commentary follows. In On the Migration of Abraham Gen 12:1-4 and 6 are covered in the form of a (topical and) running commentary on small parts of the verses. The exposition of Gen 12:1-3 are brought together by the "umbrella" quotation in Migr 1, and the running commentary follows, which also covers vv 4 and 6. The long treatise of Who is the Heir is a running commentary on Gen 15:1-18 and On Mating with the Preliminary Studies brings a running exposition of Gen 16:1-6. On Flight and Finding follows at once (both as to theme and structure) on On Mating and interprets Gen 16:6b-14. The whole text is cited in Fug 1, and again a running commentaries of varied lengths follows. Finally, On the Change of Names gives a running exposition of Gen 17:1-5 and 16-22.

On the Confusion of Tongues and On the Change of Names 1-129 serve as defence of the Laws of Moses and the Jewish institutions against scoffers who are on the borderline between the Jewish community and its Gentile surroundings. (66) On mating with the Preliminary Studies is also focused upon questions relating to the borderline between Jews and Gentiles, namely the encyclical education.

The last paragraphs of On the Preliminary Studies (158-180) discuss (Sarah's) Wisdom's rebuke and the discipling of the person engaged in preliminary education (Hagar). On Flight and Finding moves on from this idea, referred to in Fug 2, to a discussion of Hagar as an example of fugitives, Gen 16:9 ff. The idea refers to various attitudes to secular life and the materialistic creed, and then to service of God and the monotheistic creed.

The two treatises, On the Migration of Abraham and Who is the Heir, seem to a great extent to focus the attention on the understanding of the self and the life of man within the Jewish religion, although seen against a background of pagan temptations and surroundings.

The fragment of On God is extant only in Armenian. It concerns the revelation to Abraham at the oak of Mamre recorded in Gen 18. The main point is the idea that God is in control of the world. It is uncertain whether this treatise is to be included in Philo's commentary series called Allegory of the Laws. (67)

4. On Dreams

In these two treatises the form of running commentary only serves as a subordinate element in expositions of various Pentateuchal examples on dreams. The thematic interests are thus predominant, and various Scriptural material serves as examples. In this way the form approaches the forms of On the Virtues and On Rewards and Punishments. It is therefore doubtful whether On Dreams I-II should be listed in the allegorical commentary, where the form of a running commentary is basic to its structure in spite of all modifications.

The topical principle which Philo employs in On Dreams is seen in Somn I:1-2 and Somn II:1-2. Somn II:1b-2 reads: "... This third kind of dreams arises whenever the soul in sleep, setting itself in motion and agitation of its own accord, becomes frenzied, and with the prescient power due to such inspiration foretells the future. The first kind of dreams we saw to be those in which God originates the movement and invisibly suggests things obscure to us but patent to Himself: while the second kind consisted of dreams in which the understanding moves in concert with a divinely induced madness, which is permitted to foretell many coming events."

Corresponding to these three kinds of dreams in Philo's classification, there is the view of Posidonius that "there are three ways in which men dream as the result of divine impulse: first, the soul is clairvoyant of itself because of its kinship with the gods; second, the air is full of immortal souls (i.e. demons), already clearly stamped, as it were, with the marks of truth; and third, the gods in person converse with men when they are asleep." (68) Philo seems, then, to have applied such a classification as found in Posidonius on dreams recorded in Genesis.

The treatise for Philo's first class of dreams is lost. The first treatise extant deals with the two dreams of Jacob, the ladder at Bethel (Gen 28:10-22 in Somn I:3-188), and the flock with varied markings (Gen 31:10-13 in Somn I:189-256). These dreams are characterized by the interplay between man's understanding and the soul of the universe, and they are also said to be caused by angels (Somn I:157 and I:230 and I:189-190). The second treatise preserved deals with the dreams of Joseph (Gen 37:8-11 in Somn II:6-154), the dreams of Pharaoh's chief baker and chief butler (Gen 40:9-11 in Somn II:155-204 and Gen 40:16-17 in II:205-214) and finally the dream of Pharaoh (Gen 41:17-24 in II:215-302). These dreams are caused by man's soul when asleep.

On Dreams I develops the principles for man's (i.e. the Jew's) communication with God, especially his confidence in God. The Pentateuchal principles serve as a "prophecy" which tells about human and social matters, and criticizes the luxury and gluttony of those who during the day are busy in law courts, council chambers and theatres. None such is a disciple of the Holy Word (Somn I:120-124). In the same way, the sophists of Egypt - augurers, ventriloquists, soothsayers, etc. are evils in the political world (Somn I:220 ff.). The universal role of the Jewish nation is also expressed in the Biblical dreams (175-176; 215); so also the weaving together of various elements of education (205). Philo moreover touches on what lies in the future, ahead of his own time, when he writes about the pupils of Jacob: "For so shalt thou be able also to return to thy father's house, and be quit of that long endless distress which besets thee in a foreign land" (255-256).

In On Dreams II, the dream about the sun and the moon and the eleven stars making obeisance to Joseph reveals the principle of vainglory which leads a person to exalt himself not only above men, but above the world of nature. (69) Some people are so brimful of folly that they are aggrieved if the whole world does not follow their wishes. The examples Philo then gives are Xerxes, the king of the Persians, and the Germans. Philo also applies the Pentateuchal principle to his own time: "Not long ago I knew one of the ruling class who, when he had Egypt in his charge and under his authority purposed to disturb our ancestral customs and in particular to do away with the law of the Seventh Day which we regard with most reverence and awe." (Somn II:123). In several other places in On Dreams II Philo also deals with contemporary matters, both political and cultural-social, partly in a direct way, partly in code. (70)

C) PENTATEUCHAL PRINCIPLES APPLIED TO CONTEMPORARY ISSUES AND EVENTS

Introduction

In the remaining writings of Philo contemporary issues and conditions are more in the foreground than in his other works. They are, however, interpreted on the basis of the Pentateuchal principles which Philo has set forth in his interpretation of the Laws of Moses. They therefore, presuppose his exegetical works.

These writings fall into three groups: 1. Writings in which Pentateuchal material, in the form of literal narrative or/and of deeper principles, is applied to socio-religious factors in the Jewish community. Apology for the Jews (Apologia pro Iudaeis) and On the Contemplative life (De vita contemplativa) fall into this category. 2. Writings in which Pentateuchal principles are applied to, or are developed in dialogue with contemporary philosophical issues and religious phenomena: Every Good Man is Free (Quod omnis probus liber sit), On the Eternity of the World (De aeternitate mundi), On Providence (De providentia), and Alexander, or Whether the Animals have Reason (Alexander, sive de eo quod rationem babeant bruta animalia). 3. Writings in which Pentateuchal principles are applied to specific historical events and persons: To Flaccus (In Flaccum) and On the Embassy to Gaius (De legatione ad Gaium).

Pentateuchal basis of the Jewish community

a) Apology for the Jews

Only fragments of this work have been preserved. They were found in Eusebius, Preparation for the Gospel 8,6:1-7:19 and 8,11:1-18. The first extract is taken from a treatise which Philo, according to Eusebius, entitled Hypothetica, and the second comes from the Apology for the Jews, again according to Eusebius. In his Ecclesiastical History 2,18:6 Eusebius, when giving a list of the works of Philo, mentions one treatise on the Jews. These three titles are probably used as designations for the same treatise, which is here called Apology for the Jews. (71)

The treatise could have been discussed together with On the Life of Moses and the Exposition of the Laws of Moses, since Philo in Apology for the Jews rewrites parts of the Pentateuch and Joshua. The preserved fragments of Apology for the Jews deal with events and laws which cover parts of the Pentateuch from Jacob (Gen 25) to the conquest of Palestine in the books of Joshua and Judges.

The emphasis in Apology for the Jews is placed on a characterization of Judaism in Philo's own time, and it can therefore be listed among Philo's writings on contemporary issues. Aspects of this characterization are: the nation has existed from Jacob to the present day and is exceedingly populous (6:1); for more than two thousand years they have not changed a single word of what Moses wrote but would even endure dying a thousand deaths sooner than accept anything contrary to the laws and customs which he ordained (6:9); in contrast to the laxity of the gentile laws and practices, the laws and practices of the Jews are severe (7:1-9); the Sabbath plays a central role, since it provides opportunity for studying the laws, and since it influences all mankind and even animals and nature (7:10-20); finally, the Essenes are trained by Moses for the life of fellowship (11:9-18). The presentation of the Jewish people in this way serves as a defence against criticism by Gentiles who seem to wish to reduce the uniqueness of its history and practice. (72)

Certain differences between Apology for the Jews and other of Philo's writings have caused some to doubt its authenticity. Basic agreements however, also exist for example in the description of the Sabbath in Apology for the Jews and elsewhere (Mos II:215; Somn II:127; Omn 80 ff.; Spec II:61-62) with the result that the doubts are not decisive, particularly since unevenness and differences also exist among passages in the other writings of Philo. (73) The variations are thus probably due in part to differences in the traditions employed and partly to the exegetical method used, a method which attempts to find several shades of meanings in one text.

b) <u>On the Contemplative Life</u>

The opening paragraph of this treatise shows that it is the second part of a larger work: "I have discussed the Essenes, who persistently pursued the active life and excelled in all or, to put it more moderately, in most of its departments. I will now proceed at once in accordance with the sequence required by the subject to say what is needed about those who embraced the life of contemplation." (Vita Cont 1). The reference to the Essenes may point to Omn 75-91 or to Apol Jud VIII:11:1-8, but more probably it presupposes a lost treatise on the theme of the practical life, illustrated by the Essenes, in the same way that the contemplative life is exemplified by the Therapeutae. (74)

Philo'a positive interest in the Essenes and the Therapeutae may at first seem surprising, since he himself belonged to the Jewish majority who had the actual Temple in Jerusalem as their center, while the Essenes did not participate in the present worship in the temple of Jerusalem, and it is also doubtful whether the Therapeutae did. (75) There are two reasons why the Essenes and the Therapeutae are nevertheless important to Philo. The first reason is that these two groups offer model examples of two central aspects of Philo's interpretation of Judaism, the aspect of the heavenly ascent and the aspect of the active and practical life according to the laws of God. In this way Philo attempts to show the viability of his interpretation of Abraham/Isaac, the virtues of learning and intuitive vision, and Jacob, the virtue of practice. (76) The Therapeutae illustrate the aspect of heavenly ascent (Vita Cont 11) and they are citizens of Heaven even in this life in the world (Vita Cont 90). They are in this way model Jews, since to be a true Jew is to be a citizen of heaven, and a proselyte receives a place in Heaven when he becomes a Jew (see for instance Praem 152). Correspondingly, the Essenes exemplify the aspect of practice. Philo often links both contemplation and theory together with practice, as in Leg all I:58: "the theory of virtue is perfect in beauty, and the practice and exercise of it is a prize to be striven for." (77)

The second reason is that these two communities serve as signs and models for the universal (eschatological) community when evil shall be overcome and all will serve God as made manifest in the Laws of Moses. This universal aspect is expressed in several ways, partly by contrasting the Essenes and the Therapeutae with the religious and social life of the pagan world (Vita Cont 40 ff.; Quod Omn 76 ff.), partly by showing the superiority of these Jewish communities to similar phenomena outside Judaism (Vita Cont 14-16; cf. Omn 91), and partly by showing the universal context of the Therapeutae and the Essenes, according to Philo. The Therapeutae represent in Philo's view perfect goodness both in the Greek and the barbarian halves of the world. The community outside Alexandria is the center of this universal movement, as their fatherland (Vita Cont 22). And the Essenes live a life so highly to be praised that not only commoners but also great kings look upon them with admiration (Apol Jud 11:18, Omn 88-91).

Philo's Pentateuchal principles applied to, or used in dialogue with, contemporary philosophical issues and religious phenomena

Introduction

L. Cohn and other scholars (as Colson) think that Philo's philosophical writings belonged to his period as young man. This hypothesis is built on the doubtful assumption that Philo had less interest in philosophy after he began to interpret the Pentateuch. But his expositions betray that all the time he was drawinq on Greek philosophy and philosophical works. Some of the philosophical writings points to a later period than that of youth: Alexander, sive de eo quod rationem habeant bruta animalia, must have been written some time after the year 12 C.E., and in it Philo even refers to a journey of his own to the Temple in Jerusalem to offer sacrifice. And if, as it seems, his own nephew Alexander was old enough to be his dialogue partner, Philo was most probably of mature age.

It is also doubtful whether Philo's life should be divided into the philosophical period of young man and his exegetical period as a mature and old man. He lived all his life in the double contexts of he Jewish community and the Alexandrian Greek community. A. Terian draws the attention to Philo's own statement to this respect in Prov II:115: "I always have time to philosophize, to which field of knowledge I have devoted my life..." (78)

a) Every Good Man is Free (79)

It is not the aim of this survey of Philo's writings to discuss extensively Philo's so-called philosophical writings. It is relevant to raise one question, however: How does Philo use his interpretation of the Laws of Moses in evaluating and developing philosophical notions?

The treatise Every Good Man is Free too is the second part of a larger work: "Our former treatise, Theodotus, had for its theme "Every Bad Man is a Slave" and established this by many reasonable and indisputable arguments. The present treatise is closely akin to that, ... its full brother, indeed, we may say its twin, and in it we shall show that every man of worth is free" (Omn 1).

There are some clear allusions to or quotations from the Pentateuch. Thus, in 42 ff. Philo uses a gradual argument from lower to higher (from friends of kings, friends of celestial gods and) to the extreme freedom "of him who was possessed by love of the divine and worshipped the Self-existent only, as having passed from a man into a god, though, indeed, a god to men..." This text from Exod 7:1 is interpreted elsewhere several times, and the exposition here in Omn 43 f. indicates one important aspect of Philo's way of argumentation: the various levels of freedom of the worthy man receives their full dimension and true expression in Moses and in those who follow him in worshipping the Self-existent only.

Among the Jews, the Essenes are set forth as exemplary models of persons who produce high moral excellence and are free, Quod Omn 75-91. They are characterized by their love of God, love of virtue and love of men, and they base their understanding of God and their ethical way of life on the study of the laws of their fathers which they interpret particularly on the Seventh Day.

Another line of Scriptural argumentation is seen in Quod Omn 53-57, where it is said that Zeno, who lived under the direction of virtue to an unsurpassed degree, drew his thought from the Laws of Moses when he said: "Shall not the bad rue it if he gainsay the good?" Zeno learned this principle from the story about Jacob and Esau where it was said that Esau, the fool, should be his brother's slave (Gen 27:40, cf. Congr 176).

When Philo uses such Pentateuchal passages here, he presupposes the kind of exegesis which he has developed in his various expository works. Every Good Man is Free therefore presupposes Philo's work as an exegete, and does not belong to a period of his life before he had settled down to interpret the Laws of Moses. (79)

The treatise seems to serve as a broad ideological exhortation to the Jews and as an ideological attack on those who ascribe citizenship of freedom to the possessors of civil rights and slavery to servants. According to Philo, freedom is not possessed by the political and social elite of the Alexandrian full citizens who are state officials. They are slaves and exiles. The good man, who is not on the burgess rolls, is rather to be called citizen. (80) Such an ideological exhortation addressed itself to the burning question of the Jews in Alexandria, where they themselves fought for citizenship (and claimed to be even the chief nation in the world), while the Alexandrian full citizens attempted to classify them as a slave nation on the same inferior level as the native Egyptians. (81)

b) On the Eternity of the World (82)

In his various interpretations of the Laws of Moses Philo maintains that the world is created (Opif 7;171; Conf 114; Somn II:283), is in itself perishable (Dec 58), but imperishable by the will and power of the Creator (Dec 58). The same view is expressed by Philo in Aet 13-19, attributed by him to Plato and Hesiod, but first of all stated by Moses, the lawgiver of the Jews.

Then in §§ 20-149 the main point is the opposite doctrine of the indestructibility of the world. In § 150 Philo makes it clear that this view is presented to be refuted in the subsequent section of the treatise: "We have described to the best of our abilities the arguments transmitted to us to maintain the indestructibulity of the world. In what follows we have to expound the answers given in opposition to each point." Philo's answers on these points do not however, follow. Thus, the treatise is incomplete and the last section is probably lost. (83)

The treatise is structured on the Greek literary form of thesis. The essential feature of this genre is its disputatory character. A parallel use of this genre is also found in one of Philo's exegetical treatises, On Noah's Work as Planter 140-175. Here Philo presents to his readers the various views of the Greek philosophers on the subject "will the wise man get drunk."

c) On Providence (84)

The treatise On Providence is preserved as a whole in an Armenian translation, while Greek fragments are found in Eusebius. The treatise consists of two books, both cast in the form of a dialogue between Philo, who maintains the belief that the world is governed by providence, and Alexander, who puts forth his doubts and difficulties. This Alexander is probably Philo's nephew Tiberius Julius Alexander, who afterwards apostatized from Judaism. The first book has been worked over by a person who has destroyed the dialogue form and inserted interpolations.

The theme of the dialogue, providence, was central in Greek philosophy, especially in Stoic polemic against Epicurean views. Nevertheless, Philo maintains that these principles are drawn from the Laws of Moses, as he has disclosed them in his expositions. The main notions are God as the good Creator, Father and Sustainer of the world, and as Judge (Provid I:35). And even in his discussion of the existence of matter prior to creation, he can refer to the existence of water, darkness and chaos before the creation, according to Gen 1:1 ff. (Provid I:22). And in Provid I:34 f. Philo refers to circumcision, Sabbath and purity laws as he rejects the use of astrology and horoscopes. Elsewhere in the treatise Philo also uses the ideas and phraseology which he employs in his exegetical works, and which, according to him, therefore have their authentic expression in the Laws of Moses. (85) As Philo saw it, On Providence formulated Pentateuchal principles as a criticism of false views.

d) Alexander, or Whether the Animals have Reason (86)

This treatise is preserved in an Armenian translation. In § 27 there is a reference to the year when Germanus was consul, 12 C. E. The treatise must have been written after that time. It takes the form of a dialogue between Philo and Lysimachos, a relative of his, about a dissertation written by Philo's nephew, Julius Tiberius Alexander. Since the nephew must have been a young student at that time, Philo had probably reached mature years when he wrote the treatise. (87) Since the embassy mentioned in Anim 54 is presumably the Alexandrian Jewish embassy to Gaius Caligula in A.D. 39/40, the treatise seems written close to 50 A.D. (88)

Leisegang says that nothing in the dialogue betrays that the persons taking part were Jews. (89) Leisegang does not, however, define his criteria for recognizing a Jew in it. The criteria should be: Is the selection of philosophical ideas influenced by a Jewish attitude? Can these ideas be combined with Philo's views expressed elsewhere? And finally, maybe some of the philosophical points expressed were principles which Philo found in the laws of Moses, and which, therefore, occur in his expositions?

The view expressed by Philo in the treatise seems to be selected on the basis of his Jewish attitude, and can be combined with ideas which he puts forward in other writings: the animals know nothing of God, cosmos, law, ancestral customs, state and political life. These attributes are exclusive to man. Some of these Stoic notions are part of Philo's exposition of the Laws of Moses. Thus Philo, in saying that the animals know nothing about man's conscious and purposeful art, gives in Congr 141 the full Stoic definition of art, as part of the exposition of Gen 16:5. And the ideas of God, cosmos, ancestral customs, state and political life are points which are central to Philo's interpretation of the Pentateuch. The conclusion is that Philo's views stated in Alexander or Whether the Animals have Reason are influenced by his attitudes and views as a Jew in the sense in which he himself defines these in his writings.

Pentateuchal principles and practices at work in specific historical events

Flaccus and On the Embassy to Gaius (90)

Philo had applied Pentateuchal principles to historical events and persons already in his expository works on the laws of Moses. Thus as an example of persons who (as seen in Gen 37:9-11) exalt themselves above men and the world of nature, he lists Xerxes, who was punished by insanity. Another example was a governor over Egypt who attempted to disturb the ancestral customs of the Jews (Somn II:123 ff.). (91)

In Flaccus and On the Embassy to Gaius the same approach is followed, in such a way that the Pentateuchal principles, - as understood by Philo, - are used as interpretative keys, and the actual Biblical pasages are presupposed as background. In the foreground the historical events and persons are presented so that the treatises are important historical sources narrated and interpreted by an eyewitness.

Since On the Embassy to Gaius tells about events which happened to the Jewish nation and not just to one individual person, this treatise gives decisive support to our understanding that Philo's works are to be seen within the context of the relationship between the Jewish community and the Gentiles. In Gaium the ideas of "he that sees God" and of the soul's visionary ascent above all created things are even used in such a way that they characterize the Jewish race in the concrete sense.

The glimpses given of this nation include worship in the Temple of Jerusalem (Flacc 44-46; Gaium 231), assemblies in the synagogues, (Flacc 13; Gaium 132) observation of the rules and regulations in the Laws of Moses, (Flacc 74; 83; 96; Gaium 361, etc.). They are even willing to die rather than to give up these loyalties (Flacc 48, etc.). Gaium 3-7 gives a summary of the main points from Philo's interpretation of the Laws of Moses and thus of the Jewish religion. He places emphasis here, as elsewhere, on God's creative, kingly, providential powers and such of the other powers which serve both beneficial and punitive purposes. (92)

This nation, whose God is the Creator, is according to Philo the race of suppliants (§ 3) in the sense that they serve as link between God and man. God's care for all men is in a sense the outcome of His care for the Jews. (93)

Philo then tells how Flaccus and Gaius Caligula proved to be enemies of the Jews (Flacc 24 etc. Gaium 373), but were in reality enemies of God himself: Flaccus was puffed up with arrogance (Flacc 124; 152), and Gaius even overstepped the bounds of human nature and claimed to be god (Gaium 75; 367 f. etc.).

As for Gaius, the part of the treatise has been lost where his fate is told. In the case of Flaccus, however, the section is preserved where Philo tells about the punishment he suffered. Philo's Pentateuchal interpretation runs through the whole story of the punishment and death which Flaccus suffered, Flacc 107-191. The exposition in Virt 171-174 of Num 15:30, about him who provokes God with presumptousness, thus shows features which are also found in Flaccus and On the Embassy to Gaius. (94)

According to Philo's interpretation of the fate of Flaccus, Flaccus himself recognized that the Pentateuchal principles of the Jews were true: "King of gods and men," he cried, 'so then

Thou dost not disregard the nation of the Jew, nor do they misreport Thy Providence, but all who say that they do not find in Thee a Champion and Defender, go astray from the true creed. I am a clear proof of this, for all the acts which I madly committed against the Jews I have suffered myself...'" (Flacc 170).

As for the situation of the Alexandrian Jews, the picture given in Flaccus and On the Embassy to Gaius support our understanding of Philo's other treatises: the environment around the gymnasium, with clubs and religious associations was, as could be expected, the center of the attacks against the Jewish colony. This environment was, according to Philo, characterized by excess, gluttony and political intrigues. And the glimpses given of the situation as to the civil rights, the Greeks were privileged beyond the Jews, though the Jews in turn were here better off than the native Egyptians (Flacc 78-80).

What kind of writings are Flaccus and On the Embassy to Gaius? Philo here narrates theologicaly interpreted history. (95) In this respect these treatises show a similarity to history writing in the Old Testament, in Judaism and in the New Testament. As for Philo's specific point about rulers being punished for their blasphemous arrogance, the brief story in Acts 12:20-23 applies this principle to the same king Herod who aided the Alexandrian Jews: "And the people shouted, 'The voice of a god, and not of a man!' Immediately an angel of the Lord smote him, because he did not give God the glory; and he was eaten by worms and died." (96)

Philo develops his Jewish kind of history writings, however, under the influence of contemporary literary forms. Thus from a literary point of view, the section in Flaccus about Flaccus' journey into exile on the island Andros is in the form of the Greek historical essay-writing, since it seems largely fictitious. Philo tells about this journey in some detail, although he probably had very vague knowledge of it from where he lived in Alexandria. Elements such as the lament of the central figure, his looking back on post misfortunes, his despair, repentance and fear of approaching death, are common topics regularly found in historical fiction, especially in essays of travel. According to Gaium 373, the events described in the treatise reveal Gaius' character, a motif which belongs to moral tales which hold out examples. (97)

The ending of On the Embassy to Gaius, "One must tell the palinode," raises problems. This indicates a recantation to follow. Presumably it told of Gaius' death and his successor Claudius' new policy, which was more favourable to the Jews. But if, as is more probable, Philo meant that history itself brought about the change, no additional writing need be supposed. (98)

NOTES

1) See P. Borgen, "A Critical and Synthetical Survey of Research since World War II," in H. Temporini and W. Haase (ed), ANRW, II: Principat, 21:1, (Berlin, 1984) 98-154; id., "Philo of Alexandria," in M. Stone (ed), Jewish Writings of the Second Temple period, CRINT, II:2 (Assen, 1984) 233-282.

2) See especially L. Cohn, "Einteilung und Chronologie des Schriften Philo's," Philologus, Suppl. 7, (Berlin, 1894) 385-435, and the recent survey in S. Sandmel, "Philo Judaeus: An Introduction to the Man, his Writings, and his Significance," in ANRW, II:21:1, (1984) 6-13.

3) See for example E.R. Goodenough, "Philo's Exposition of the Law and his De vita Mosis," HTR, 26, (1933) 109-125.

4) ibid. Goodenough points to Virt 52 and Praem 53 ff., where Philo makes a reference to De vita Mosis. Moreover, Philo envisages in Mos II:45 ff. the Exposition, and its scheme.

5) On the Life of Moses is treated as three treatises by all manuscripts and all editions before the Cohn-Wendland edition. (L. Cohn and P. Wendland, Philonis Alexandrini opera quae supersunt, 1-7, (Berlin, 1896-1930, repr 1962)). The second treatise ended at § 65. This can hardly be correct, since Philo himself in Virt 52 speaks of two books. Cohn's division of On the Life of Moses into two treatises is therefore followed by F.H. Colson and R. Arnaldez, et al, in their editions and translations. See L. Cohn, et al (ed), Philonis Alexandrini opera quae supersunt, 4, (Berlin, 1902) XXX sq; F.H. Colson et al (ed trans), Philo, with an English Translation, (Loeb Classical Library), 6, (London, 1959) VII and 274; R. Arnaldez, et al (ed trans), Les Oeuvres de Philon d'Alexandrie, 22, (Paris, 1967) 11-12.

6) See F.H. Colson, PLCL, 6, 274-5.

7) Scholars used to understand On the Life of Moses to be an apologetic presentation of Judaism to the Gentiles. See L. Cohn, Philologus, Suppl. 7, (Berlin, 1899) 415 f. - E.R. Goodenough, HTR, 26, 1933, 110 f., regards it as an introduction to Judaism, written for gentiles. R. Arnaldez, Les Oeuvres, 22, 19-20, thinks that the purpose is to give a justification for the Jewish faith on the basis of God's action towards his people by means of Moses. At the same time the book gives the basic justification for Philo's own

expository enterprise. B. Badt, in L. Cohn, Philo Deutsch, 1, 218, has seen the importance which Judaism's universal calling has for the background and the purpose of the book.

8) See G. Delling, "Wunder - Allegorie - Mythus bei Philon von Alexandreia", in Studien zum Neuen Testament und zum hellenistischen Judentum. Gesammelte Aufsätze, (Göttingen, 1970) 73-4.

9) A. Priessnig, "Die literarische Form der Patriarchenbiographien des Philon von Alexandrien," MGWJ, 73, N.F. 37, (1929). 143-155, points out the similarity to Suetonius' imperial biographies, and the Alexandrian scholarly biographies as found in Plutarch. Like On the Life of Moses, these biographies consist of a chronological life history from the person's birth to the main period of his life. Then follows his public work, organized by topics, as also is the case in On the Life of Moses. The next point in such a biography, a presentation of the person's private life, is, however, lacking in On the Life of Moses. Instead, Philo characterizes the Jewish people, whose founder Moses was. Finally, as in the biographies, Philo tells about the death of Moses. Elements of panegyric, of aretalogies, and of edificatory biography are also present. Cf. also P. Wendland, Die hellenistisch-römische Kultur, Handbuch NT I:2, (Tübingen, 1912) 205, n. 2; W. von Christ, O. Stählin and W. Schmid, Geschichte der griechischen Literatur, (6. ed) II:1, (München, 1920, repr 1959) 645 f.; H. Leisegang, "Philon", PW, XX:1, cols. 30-31; R. Arnaldez, Les Oeuvres, 22, 14 ff. (historical novel). G. Delling, Studien, 73-4.

10) In Praem 1-3 Philo divides the Exposition of the Laws of Moses into three main points, - the story of the creation, the historical part and the legislative part. In Mos II:45 ff. two parts are mentioned, the historical and the legislative. The historical part mentioned in On the Life of Moses is, however, divided into the creation story and the genealogical part, in accordance with the first two points of the outline given in Praem 1-3.

11) See L. Rost, Einleitung in die alttestamentlichen Apokryphen und Pseudepigraphen einschliesslich der grossen Qumran-Handschriften, (Heidelberg, 1971) 98-101; 136-139; 146-148.
Philo covers the Biblical story from creation to Joshua's succession of Moses; the Book of Jubilees narrates the story from creation to the giving of the Law on Mount Sinai; the Genesis Apocryphon is only preserved in parts, covering the story of Genesis from the birth of Noah to Gen 15:4; finally, the Biblical Antiquities contain an abstract of the biblical story from Gen 5 to the death of Saul.

12) See R.H. Charles, The Apocalypse of Baruch, (London, 1896) 53, and G.H. Box, The Ezra-Apocalypse, (London, 1912) 83 ff.

13) See F.H. Colson, PLCL, 1, 476.

14) See especially W. Theiler, Forschungen zum Neuplatonismus, (Berlin, 1965); idem, "Philo von Alexandria und der Beginn des Keiserzeitlichen Platonismus" in Parusia. Festgabe für Johannes Hirschberger, (Frankfurt a.M., 1965). 199-217; idem, "Philo von Alexandria und der Hellenisierte Timaeus", in

Philomathes. Studies and Essays in the Humanities in Memory of Philip Merlan, (The Hague, 1971) 25-35; D. Runia, Philo of Alexandria and the Timaeus of Plato, 1-2, (Amsterdam, 1983). E.I. Grumach,, "Zur Quellenfrage von Philos De opificio mundi § 1-3", MGWJ, 83, N. F. 47, (1939), 126-131; See notes in L. Cohn, Philo Deutsch, 1, 25-89; F.H. Colson, PLCL, 1, 2-137 and 475-6. Many Pythagorean features are found in Opif as well, see K. Staehle, Die Zahlenmystik bei Philon von Alexandreia, (Leipzig, 1931). U. Früchtel, Die kosmologischen Vorstellungen bei Philo von Alexandrien, (Leiden, 1968).

15) E.R. Goodenough, HTR, 26, (1933), 113-125. - With regard to Opif 170, it seems artificial to understand the first person plural ἡμᾶς as referring only to Moses' teaching of the Jews, teachings which now are passed on to the Gentiles for information. Philo rather spells out what he and his readers can learn from Moses' account of creation, the readers either being Jews or man in general, the Jews included. Philo's own situation suggests that the latter interpretation is the most probable.

16) See the similar exposition in Praem 11-27.

17) Literal exposition of parts of Gen 11:31-12:9 in 60-7 and allegorical in 68-89; literal exposition of Gen 12:10-20 in 90-8 and allegorical in 99-106; literal exposition of Gen 18 in 107-18 and allegorical in 119-32; literal exposition of Gen 19 in 133-46 and allegorical in 147-66; literal exposition of Gen 22 in 167-77 and allegorical in 200-07; literal exposition of Gen 13:5-11 in 208-16 and allegorical in 217-24; literal exposition of Gen 14 in 225-35 and allegorical in 236-44; and finally literal exposition of Gen 16:1-6, Gen 23, etc in 245-61. Philo sums up Abraham's life in his faith (Gen 15:6) and in his characterization as presbyter. (Gen 26:5), 262-76.

18) See also Mos I:76, etc.

19) See P. Hadot, "Etre, Vie, Pensée chez Plotin et avant Plotin," in Les sources de Plotin, Entretiens 5, (Vandeuvres - Geneve, 1960) 125-6; P. Borgen, Bread from Heaven. Nov T Sup 10, (Leiden, 1965, repr 1981) 103 ff. See Plutarch, De liberis educandis 2A-C.

20) In Abr 98 Philo writes about the marriage of Abraham and Sara: "That marriage from which was to issue not a family of a few sons and daughters, but a whole nation, and that the nation dearest of all to God, which, as I hold, has received the gift of priesthood and prophecy on behalf of all mankind." The same national view of the patriarchs is also expressed in Dec 1, where Philo characterizes them as "founders of our nation."

21) Jubilees 6:17; 15:1; 16-28, etc; See W. Bousset, Die Religion des Judentums in späthellenistischen Zeitalter, 3. ed. by H. Gressmann, (Tübingen, 1926) 125, n. 3 and 126, n. 1.

22) S. Sandmel, Philo's Place in Judaism, (New York, 1956; 2. ed 1971) 49. Cf. p. 108: "The rabbis say that Abraham observed the Law; Philo says that the Law sets forth as legislation those things which Abraham did." Sandmel is correct in his understanding of Philo's view. It should be emphasized,

however, that Philo's interpretation is a modification of the view of those who would state that Abraham obeyed the law probably meaning the Law of Moses: "Such was the life of the first, the founder of the nation, one who obeyed the law, some will say, but rather, as our discourse has shown, himself a law and an unwritten statute." (Abr 276).

23) The literal exposition of Gen 37:2-36 is given in 2-27, followed by the allegorical in 28-36; the literal exposition of Gen 39:1-20 occurs in 37-53, and the allegorical in 54-79; the literal exposition of Gen 39:21-41:46 is found in 80-124, and two allegorical interpretations are given, one in 125-50, another in 151-6.

24) Jos 202-6.

25) Jos 69 and 106.

26) Jos 107; 119. For a full discussion of Philo's political theology, and in this connection also of Jos, see E.R. Goodenough, The Politics of Philo Judaeus, (New Haven, Conn., 1938), especially pp. 43-63.

27) ibid., 62.

28) See A. Priessnig, MGWJ, 73, N.F. 37, (1929) 145-150. A brief summary in English is given in R.G. Hamerton Kelly, "Sources and Traditions in Philo Judaeus", Studia Philonica, 1, (1972) 11-13. See also R. Marcus, "Recent Literature on Philo (1924-34)," in S.W. Baron and A. Marx (ed), Jewish Studies in Memory of G.A. Kohut, (New York, 1935) 473-474.

29) The first and second commandment here are in the usual rabbinic counting held as the second "word".

30) For the discussion among Wolfson, Urbach, Hecht and others, see R.D. Hecht, "Preliminary Issues in the Analysis of Philo's De Specialibus Legibus," Studia Philonica, 5, (1978) 3-17; H.A. Wolfson, Philo, 2, 201; N. Bentwich, Philo Judaeus of Alexandria, (Philadelphia, 1940) 117; E.E. Urbach, The Sages: Their Concepts and Beliefs, (Jerusalem, 1975) 1, 361; Y. Amir, "Philo and the Bible," Studia Philonica, 2, (1973) 1-8, also printed in id., Die hellenistische Gestalt des Judentums bei Philon von Alexandrien, (Neukirchen-Vluyn, 1983) 67-76.

31) Cf. P. Borgen, "Philo of Alexandria. A critical and synthetical survey of research since World War II," ANRW II:21:1, (1984) 126.

32) E.R. Goodenough, HTR, 26, (1933) 112.

33) Courage, from parts of Num 25 and 30, and of Deut 20, 22, and 28; humanity, from Num 27 and various laws in Exod, Lev and Deut; repentance, from parts of Deut 26 and 30 and on Pentateuchal ideas about proselytes; nobility, from passages about Adam - Cain, Noah - Ham, sons of Abraham, Tamar, etc. in Genesis.

34) See F.H. Colson, in PLCL, 8, 455.

35) E.R. Goodenough, HTR, 26, 1933, 118 ff.

36) See Mos II:43-44, 186; Opif 79 ff., etc.

37) See Ps 78; 105; 106; 135; 136; Ezek 20; Sir 44-50; Wis 10; 1 Macc 2:52-61; Hebr 10; cf. Acts 7.

38) See A. Beckaert in R. Arnaldez, Les Oeuvres, 27, especially p. 16.

39) Eusebius. Ecclesiastical History, 2:18, 1 and 5.

40) R. Marcus, (trans) PLCL, Sup 1, (Cambridge, Mass., 1953) V; IX. See the Armenian and Latin translations in J.B. Aucher (ed trans), Philonis Iudaei Paralipomena Armena ... nunc primum in Latium fideliter translata, (Venice, 1826).

41) See R. Marcus PLCL, Sup 1, V-VI and id., "The Armenian Translation of Philo's Quaestiones in Genesin et Exodum", JBL, 49, 1930, 61-64; id., "An Armenian - Greek Index to Philo's Quaestiones and De Vita Contemplativa," JAOS, 53, (1933) 251-282.

42) E. Schürer, Geschichte des Jüdischen Volkes im Zeitalter Jesu Christi, (1886) 2, 836 and 838; and 4. ed 3 (1909) 644 and 648; C. Colpe, "Philo," RGG, 3. ed., 5, (1961) cols 341-6.

43) For the following discussion of Quaestiones in Genesin et Exodum, see P. Borgen and R. Skarsten "Quaestiones et solutiones. Some observations on the form of Philo's exegesis", Studia Philonica, 3 (1975) 1-15; cf S. Sandmel, "Philo's Environment and Philo's Exegesis," JBR, 22, (1954) 249, who thinks that the verse by verse exposition in Quaes were preliminary notes on the basis of which Philo in part got around to composing connected treatises and in part did not. See further H. Hegstad, Synagogen, sted for skriftlesning og utleggelse på sabbaten, (typewritten dissertation), (Trondheim 1977), 59-76; V. Nikiprowetzky, "L'Exégèse de Philon d'Alexandrie dans le De Gigantibus et le Quod Deus," in D. Winston and J. Dillon (ed contr), Two Treatises of Philo of Alexandria, BJS 25, (Chico, Ca, 1983) 5-75; D. Runia, "The Structure of Philo's Allegorical Treatises," VC, 38, (1984) 226-255; P. Borgen, ANRW, II:21:1 (1984) 134-138; id., CRINT II:2, 242 and 262-264.

44) See also Dec 2-17; 176-178, etc.

45) Se S. Sandmel, JBR, 22 (1954) 249, who points to the overlapping and agreement between a section of Quaes and Congr.

46) L. Cohn, Philologus, Sup VII:3, (Berlin, 1899) 402 f.; R. Marcus, PLCL, Sup 1, IX. See examples of Homeric commentary in H. Schrader, Porphyrii Quaestionum Homericarum ad Iliadem pertinentium reliquias, Fasc 1, (Leipzig, 1880).

47) Cf. E.E. Hallewy, "Biblical Midrash and Homeric Exegesis," Tarbiz, 31, (December 1961), 157-169, with English summary on pp. III-IV.

48) See M.S. Zuckermandel (ed), Tosefta, (Pasewalk, 1880) ad loc. Cf. Jer. Talmud, Sanhedrin IV:9. A. Schlatter, Geschichte Israels, 3. rev. ed, (Stuttgart, 1925), 203 f., wrongly believed that the place of Adam in the story of the creation would only become a problem of those who, like Aristobul and Philo, did not think in terms of days of creation, but only in terms of value and rank.

49) The following is taken from R. Marcus, PLCL, Sup 1, X-XII.

50) M.L. Massebieau, "Le classement des oeuvres de Philon", Bibliothèque de l' École des Hautes Études ... Sciences religieuses, 1 (Paris, 1889), 1-91; E. Schürer, Geschichte, 3, 3rd ed, (Leipzig, 1898) 497, n. 33.

51) J. Rendel Harris, Fragments of Philo Judaeus (Cambridge, 1886) 75, labels two fragments as "from the lost book of Questions on Leviticus," but only one of the two in the ms is said to be questions on Leviticus. See also Schürer, Geschichte, 3, 3rd ed, 497, n. 34."

52) See L. Cohn in Cohn-Wendland, Philonis opera, 1, XXXVI.

53) P. Wendland, Neu entdeckte Fragmente Philos (Berlin, 1891) 92; see also Schürer, Geschichte, 3, 3rd ed, 498, n. 35.

54) In the Armenian version book I covers Gen 2:4-6:13; book II covers Gen 6:14-10:9; book III covers Gen 15:7-17:27; book IV covers Gen 18:1-20:18 and 23:1-28:9. Thus, beside the omission of single verses in all four books, the following entire chapters are omitted: 1; 11-14; 21-22; 29-50.

55) See discussion for example in L. Cohn, Philologus, Sup VII:3, (Berlin, 1899) 393, 402.

56) See the Qumran commentary on Habakuk (1QpH) and the midrashim Mekilta de-Rabbi Ishmael and Genesis Rabba, etc.

57) Cf. L. Cohn Philologus Sup VII:3, 392; in the translation by E.R. Goodenough, An Introduction to Philo Judaeus, (New Haven, 1940), 56: "Philo attaches his lucubrations to the Biblical text, which he for the most part follows verse by verse; yet he never confines himself to the passages he is explaining, but wanders off, adduces related passages, and spreads himself out in the greatest detail over these and everything else connected with them, so that he seems in the process to have lost his thread."

58) Some examples of quaestiones et solutiones are: Leg all I:33-41; 48-52; 70-71; 85-87; 90: 91-92a; 101-104; 105-108; II:19-21; 42-43; 44-45; 68-70; 80-81; III:18-19; 49 ff.; 66-68; 77-78; 184-185; 188. See especially the close agreements between Leg all I:85 and Quaes Gen I:13; Leg all I:101 and Quaes Gen I:15; Cher 21 f. and 55 ff.; Sacr 11 ff. and 128 ff.; Quod Det 57 ff. and 80 ff.; Post 33 ff., 40 ff. and 153; Gig 55 ff; Quod Deus 11 f., 60 ff., 70 ff., 86 ff., 104 and 122. Somn I: 5 ff.; 12 f.; 14 ff.; 41 f., and Somn II: 300 ff.
Cf. N.A. Dahl, "Motsigelser i Skriften", STK, 45, (1969) 27-28. Thus, in "Geschichterfarhung und Schriftauslegung - Zur Hermeneutik des frühen Judentums", Die hermeneutische Frage in der Theologie, (Freiburg, 1968) 320-321, the viewpoint of R. Mayer is inadequate, when he writes: "Die Methode gleicht formal bis in die Einzelheiten dem Pesherverfahren der Essener und Therapeuten: ein kurzer Bibeltext wird zitiert, dann folgt nach einem Wort der Überleitung (etwa "das bedeutet") die ausführliche Deutung."

59) See L. Cohn and P. Wendland, Philonis Opera, 1, LXXXVI.

60) ibid., 1, 113, note.

61) See the discussion in E. Schürer, Geschichte des Jüdischen Volkes, 4th ed. 3, (Leipzig, 1909) 650-651, with references to Sacra parallela, and Sacr. 51: "But what is meant by a tiller of the soil I have shown in earlier books." Schürer believes that Sacr 51 refers to a lost treatise on Gen 3:23, but scholars such as L. Cohn, Philo, Deutsch, 3, 235, n. 4, and F.H. Colson and G.H. Whitaker, PLCL, 2, 490-491, find other suggestions probable.

62) Cf. M. Adler, Studien zu Philon von Alexandreia, (Breslau, 1929) 8-24.

63) Leg all I:75 f.; II:17; 29; II:107; III:155-6; 167; 220-1.

64) Cf. M. Adler, Studien, 8 and 66-67.

65) See F.H. Colson, PLCL, 3, 104.

66) See especially Conf 2-3, and Mut 60-62.

67) See Aucher's book referred to in foot note 40.

68) Cicero, De Divinatione, I:30, 64. Translation taken from H.A. Wolfson, Philo, II, 57. See also F.H. Colson, PLCL, 5, 593 and L. Cohn, Philo, Deutsch, 6, 173, n. 2.

69) See Somn II:110-38. See E.R. Goodenough, Politics, 29-30. Goodenough rightly doubts that Somn II:123 ff. refers to Flaccus.

70) See E.R. Goodenough, Politics, 21-32.

71) See F.H. Colson in PLCL, 9, 407.

72) Cf. Apol Jud 6:2; 7:1, 11, 14, etc.

73) See I. Heinemann, Bildung, 353 and 516 ff.

74) So also L. Cohn ed, Philonis Opera, 6, IX; K. Bormann in L. Cohn, Philo, Deutsch, 7, 44, n. 1, and seemingly also F.H. Colson, PLCL, 9, 104. Different views are held by P. Geoltrain, Le traite de la Vie Contemplative de Philon d'Alexandrie, Semitica 10, (Paris, 1960) 14-15 (Quod omn); and E.R. Goodenough. An Introduction, 36 (Apol Jud) and F. Daumas in R. Arnaldez (ed), Les Oeuvres 29, 11-12 (Apol Jud).

75) See Josephus, Ant XVIII:1, 5; cf. Omn 75, concerning the Essenes. The Therapeutae stressed contemplation, exegesis and liturgical life, hymnsinging and meals included. They seemed to follow liturgical practices also found in the Book of Jubilees. See K. Bormann, in L. Cohn, Philo, Deutsch, 7, 44-46.

76) See the discussion of agreements between on the one hand the Essenes and the Therapeutae and on the other hand Jacob and Abraham in S. Sandmel, Philo's Place, 194-6.

77) See further H.A. Wolfson, Philo, 2, 264 ff.

78) L. Cohn, Philologus Sup 7, 389; F.H. Colson, PLCL, 9, 2; A. Terian, Philonis Alexandrini De Animalibus, (Chico, Ca, 1981) 33-34, id., "A Critical Introduction to Philo's Dialogues," ANRW, II:21:1, (1984) 272-294; D.T. Runia, "Philo's De Aeternitate Mundi: The Problem of its Interpretation," VC, 35 (1981) 105-109; 140.

79) On the various introductory questions, such as authenticity, etc., see K. Bormann in L. Cohn (trans), Philo, Deutsch, 7, 1-2 and references given there.

80) See especially Quod Omn 6-7 and 158. The emphasis on the paradox that good man is citizen and bad man is exile seems to be a particular Philonic version of the Stoic notion that the good man is free. Cf. F.H. Colson, PLCL, 9, 14, n.a. -As for the problem of Omn 6 ff., where Philo seems to refer to the views of others, without stating this explicitly, see PLCL, 9, 13, n.e.

81) Since the problem of citizenship was a burning issue for the Jews in Alexandria in the time before Gaius Caligula and Claudius, and the issue seems reflected in Quod Omn, Philo may have written this any time before the outburst of the pogrom in year 38 C.E.

82) For a discussion of authenticity, etc., see the introductions by K. Bormann in L. Cohn, Philo, Deutsch, 7, 71 ff. and 166 ff., with references.

83) See O. Stählin in W. von Christ, Geschichte der Griechischen Literatur, 6, ed by O. Stählin and W. Schmid, Part II:1, (München, 1959) 627 f.; D.T. Runia, VC, 35 (1981) 105-151.

84) For introductory questions, see L. Früchtel, in L. Cohn, (trans), Philo Deutsch, 7, 267-271; F.H. Colson, PLCL, 9, 447 ff.; and especially, A. Terian, De Animalibus, 1-64.

85) See the footnotes in L. Früchtel, op.cit., 280- 316.

86) See H. Leisegang, Pauly-Wissowa, 20, cols. 6-8.

87) Against L. Cohn, Philologus Sup 7, 390-391, who ranks the treatise among those written by Philo as a young man.

88) A. Terian, De Animalibus, 30-34.

89) H. Leisegang, Pauly-Wissowa, 20, col. 8.

90) For introductory questions, especially the question whether the two treatises were parts of a larger number of writings, see for example E.M. Smallwood, Philonis Alexandrini Legatio ad Gaium, (Leiden, 1961); F.H. Colson, PLCL, 9, 295-301 and H. Box, Philonis Alexandrini in Flaccum, (London, 1939).

91) Cf. 3 Maccabees, which tells of such conflicts between Ptolemy Philopator and Judaism.

92) See Quod Deus 77-78 and Plant. 50. Cf. E.M. Smallwood, Legatio ad Gaium, 156-157.

93) See E.R. Goodenough, Politics, 13; and E.M. Smallwood, Legatio ad Gaium, 152. Concerning the Biblical background for the phrase, see Praem 44.

94) Virt 171: men of windy pride, see Flacc 124: 152: Virt 172: overstep limits of human nature, see Gaium 75, etc.

95) Cf. F.W. Kohnke, in L. Cohn, Philo, Deutsch 7, 168.

96) Cf. Josephus, Ant 19:20-23.

97) See K.H. Gerschmann and F.W. Kohnke in L. Cohn, Philo, Deutsch 7, 125-6 and 168-9.

98) See F.H. Colson, PLCL, 10, 187, n. a, and F.W. Kohnke, in L. Cohn, Philo, Deutsch, 7, 169.

CHAPTER THREE
DEBATES ON CIRCUMCISION

Introduction

Judaism was - and is - a religion which places special emphasis on ethics and on observance. All since Old Testament times there has been interplay and tension between these two aspects. In this chapter the discussion will be focused on some passages in the writings of Philo of Alexandria, and the relationship between circumcision and ethics will be examined. Also this particular topic had a long history back to Old Testament times, where the protest over against one-sided reliance on bodily circumcision led to the formation of the phrase "circumcision of the heart", by which the ethical aspect was stressed (Deut 10:16; 30:6; Jer 4:4; etc.). (1)

An examination of the debates on circumcision in Philo has significance in many ways.

1) It can illustrate how Old Testament traditions and topics are interpreted in a later and different time.

2) It will illustrate how Philo's writings do not only reflect a variety of ideas, but reflect actual debates and conflicts which existed in the Alexandrian Jewish community.

3) In particular, such an examination will throw light upon the understanding of the position of the proselytes, and define at what point a person was given the status of being a proselyte.

4) It will throw light upon the various practices and views on circumcision within the Jewish community itself, and show how social pressures might be applied to secure conformity of observance.

5) An analysis of the material in Philo has special importance for the study of the New Testament, since Philo belonged to the same period. The debates and conflicts in the Diaspora-center of Alexandria may throw light upon similar debates and conflicts reflected in Paul's letters and in the Acts of the Apostles, since these writings also come from Diaspora-settings. This last point will only be indicated briefly in this chapter and will be discussed more fully in the chapters eleven, twelve, and thirteen.

<u>Ethics and circumcision, and the case of the proselytes. Quaestiones in Exodum II:2</u>

The text of Questions and Answers on Exodus II:2 is preserved both in Greek and in Armenian translation, with only minor variations. Our comments will be based on the Greek fragment. Philo interprets Exod 22:21, which in accordance with Septuagint can be translated as follows: "and a proselyte (προσήλυτος) you shall not mistreat, nor shall you oppress him. For you were proselytes in the land of Egypt."

The term προσήλυτος in Exod 22:21 is given this interpretation by Philo: "προσήλυτος is no the one who has circumcised his uncircumcision, but the one who (has circumcised) his desires and sensual pleasures and the other passions of the soul. For in Egypt the Hebrew nation was not circumcised, but, being mistreated with all mistreatments of the cruelty shown by the inhabitants against strangers, it lived with them in self-restraint and endurance, not by necessity, but rather of free choice, because it took refuge in the Saviour, God, Who sent His beneficent power and delivered the suppliants from their difficult and hopeless situation."

Wolfson suggests that Philo here speaks of a "spiritual proselyte", as distinct from the full proselyte, who was bodily circumcised, and from the resident alien, who still was a practising idolator. (2)

> Unlike the proselyte who has adopted all the practices and beliefs of Judaism and is a full member of the "congregation of the Lord", this new kind of proselyte is like the <u>ger toshab</u> of the rabbis, who, while he has not undergone circumcision and has not adopted all the Jewish practices and beliefs, has renounced polytheism and idolatry and has given up certain other heathen practices. We shall refer to this kind of proselyte as the "spiritual proselyte" instead of the more common name "semi-proselyte" to which objection has been raised. A reference to such spiritual proselytes is found by Philo in the verses which in the Septuagint are translated 'A proselyte (<u>ger</u>) shall you not wrong, neither shall you oppress him, for you were proselytes (<u>gerim</u>) in the land of Egypt' and 'A proselyte (<u>ger</u>) shall you not oppress, for you know the soul of a proselyte (<u>ger</u>), for you were proselytes (<u>gerim</u>) in the land of Egypt.' Commenting upon these verses, Philo tries to show that the term proselyte in them does not refer to a proselyte in the technical sense of the term, namely, one who is circumcised and follows all the laws. His reason for this interpretation of the term 'proselyte' in these verses is its comparison to the term 'proselytes' applied to the Jews in Egypt. According to Philo, the Jews, during their servitude in Egypt, did not practice circumcision, and consequently, he

> argues, the proselyte who is not to be wronged must also refer to one who has not undergone circumcision. Still, while not circumcised, the 'proselyte' in question is assumed by Philo to have accepted certain principles of Judaism. What those principles are he does not specify. He only describes them as (a) a circumcision of 'the pleasures and the desires and the other passions of the soul' and (b) 'an estrangement (ἀλλοτρίωσις) from the opinions of the worshipers of many gods, and establishing a relationship (οἰκείωσις with those who honor the one God, the Father of the universe.' ... This reference to what we have called spiritual proselytes reflects the actual existence at his time of a class of gentiles who, while uncircumcised, had renounced idolatry and otherwise led a virtuous life. In the literature of a time shortly after Philo there are specific references to the existence of such spiritual proselytes in all parts of the Jewish world. They are called by the name of 'God-fearers'(οἱ φοβούμενοι or σεβόμενοι τὸν θεόν)

There is one serious objection to be made against this interpretation given by Wolfson. Wolfson must himself admit that Philo's use elsewhere of the term προσήλυτος (and synonyms) does not support his view, since it there refers to full proselytes. (3) Thus nothing in Philo's writings speaks against also understanding the proselyte in Quaes Exod II:2 to mean a full proselyte. The usage of the term elsewhere rather supports the view that a full proselyte is meant. Actually, Philo does not anywhere state explicitly that bodily circumcision is required for becoming a proselyte.

S. Belkin, like Wolfson, thinks that Philo here refers to a semi-convert. N.J. McEleney rightly states that Belkin's view has no basis in the passage itself. McEleney himself interprets the passage to mean that Philo did not insist on the fulfilment of the precept of circumcision. (4)

J. Nolland objects to McEleney's understanding of the passage by referring to Philo's theory about attuning the body to the soul. This theory would seem to apply to the proselytes as well as to the Jews in general. Nolland then rephrases the intention of Philo in this way: 'what deeper sense to proselyte (than one who has entered Judaism by circumcision) can be discovered from the juxtaposition in the text of the mention of proselytes with the mention of the israelites as proselytes in Egypt?' 'As Philo saw it, in a unique historical situation, things which normally belong together are separated so that it becomes apparent where the greater part of the reality of circumcision lies - not in the physical but in the spiritual. (5)

Nolland is right in stating that to Philo spiritual circumcision and physical circumcision belong together. His own interpretation seems forced, however, and does not explain why Philo defines 'proselyte' as one who has received ethical circumcision, and not physical circumcision.

How is then Philo's view to be defined? Philo here gives an answer to the question: When does a person receive status as a proselyte in the Jewish Community and cease to be a heathen? This problem was of great importance both at the ideological and practical level, and in different ways it is discussed later in rabbinic literature, also by using similar form: (6)

> Philo, Quaestiones on Exod II,2:
>
> a) προσήλυτος is b) not the one who has circumcised his uncircumcision c) but the one who (has circumcised) his desires and sensual pleasures and the other passions of the soul.For in Egypt the Hebrew nation....
>
> B Talmud Yebamot 46 a:
>
> c) Is he baptized b) and not circumcised a) such a person is a proselyte d) for this we find regarding our (fore-)mothers, who were baptized and not circumcised.

Both texts deal with the definition of the proselyte (a); one criterion is rejected (b), and another criterion is accepted (c). Finally, as support for this decisive criterion, reference is given to the Pentateuchal history of the Israelites (d).

The alternatives given differ, however. Philo discusses ethical circumcision versus bodily circumcision, while Rabbi Joshua in b. Yeb 46 a lists two different observances as alternative criterions, baptism versus circumcision. Still, in both cases the same question is discussed: When does a convert become a proselyte? One should not interpret the difference between Philo and Rabbi Joshua to mean that Joshua here represents the view of Palestinian Judaism with an emphasis on observance, in distinction from a Hellenistic Diaspora Judaism that showed more interest in Jewish ethical life. The ethical criterion for deciding who has the status of a proselyte within the Jewish community was also employed by Jews in Palestine. Thus, according to b. Sabb 31 a Hillel gave the status of proselyte to a heathen who came to him and accepted the Golden Rule as summary of the Torah. (7) Such ethical conversion of the heathen also meant a sociological change from a pagan context to a Jewish one, (8) a fact which is emphasized by Philo in several passages on proselytes. Philo and Hillel's understanding has thus been that bodily circumcision was not the requirement for entering the Jewish community, i.e. for receiving the status as a Jew.

Since Philo states this view in a polemic way, he presupposes and criticizes others who maintained that converts received the status of proselytes on the basis of circumcision.

When Philo did not regard bodily circumcision to be a requirement for entering the Jewish community and becoming a proselyte, what was then his understanding of bodily circumcision? Was it necessary to practise this observance at all? Here another passage is very illuminating, namely On the Migration of Abraham 86-93.

Different attitudes and practices. On the Migration of Abraham 86-93

In On the Migration of Abraham 86-93, Philo shows how such ethical interpretation of circumcision might lead to different attitudes and practices among the Jews.

In De Migratione 86 ff. he gives an exposition of the word to Abrahm in Gen 12:2, "I will make thy name great." Philo stresses then the importance for a man to have high reputation among his fellow Jews for obedience to the Laws of Moses. Against this background he criticizes some Jews who, although they have the right understanding of the meaning of the feasts and circumcision, nevertheless ignore the external observance.

The outline of the passage is as follows: The direct exposition of Gen 12:2, "I will make thy name great," is given in §§ 86-88. The phrase is repeated in §§ 86 and 88 by the word μεγαλώνυμος , with a great name. In conclusion of the exposition Philo applies the thought to a specific situation: "And this fair fame is won as a rule by all who cheerfully take things as they find them and interfere with no established customs, cut maintain with care the constitution of their country."

Then Philo in §§ 89-90 presents a negative example to this application. He tells about some who do not take things as they find them and who in practice interfere with established customs. In the subsequent paragraphs, §§ 91-93 Philo renders specific points made by these non-conformists, and makes corrective exhortations, not only to them, but to all, in first person plural: "but let us not":

> "It is quite true that the Seventh Day is meant to teach the power of the Unoriginate and the non-action of created beings. But let us not for this reason abrogate the laws laid down for its observance, and

> light fires or till the ground or carry loads or institute proceedings in court or act as jurors or demand the restoration of deposits or recover loans, or do all else that we are permitted to do as well on days that are not festival seasons.
>
> It is true also that the keeping of festivals is a symbol of gladness of soul and of thankfulness to God, but we should not for this reason turn our backs on the general gatherings of the year's seasons.
>
> It is true that receiving circumcision does indeed portray the excision of pleasure and all passions, and the putting away of the impious conceit, under which the mind supposed that it was capable of begetting by its own power: but let us not on this account repeal the law laid down for circumcising.
>
> Why, we shall be ignoring the sanctity of the Temple and a thousand other things, if we are going to pay heed to nothing except what is shown us by the inner meaning of things."

Philo's criticism is clothed in Platonic terminology: these Jews err, he says, by regarding the laws in their literal sense only as symbols for noetic realities. Therefore, scholars often call these Jews philosophical spiritualists. (9) If we take a closer look at the views they held, according to Philo, these were Jewish, although influenced by Hellenistic thoughts: The Sabbath expressed the idea that God was the active creator and creation was passive in relation to him. (10) The cultic feasts represented man's joy and thanksgiving to God. (11) And the meaning of circumcision was that it portrayed the excision of pleasure and all passions, and the putting away of the impious conceit under which the mind supposed that it was capable of begetting by its own power. (12)

Philo argues on the basis both of agreement and disagreement with the non-conformists. He makes clear that he and they agree on the theological and ethical meaning of Sabbath, feasts and circumcision: the Sabbath gives a clue to the right understanding of the rlationship between the Creator and the created beings; the keeping of the festivals means spiritual joy and thankfulness to God; and finally, they agree that circumcision portrays the excision of pleasure and the removal of impious opinions about man's own creative power. In spite of this broad area of agreement, Philo and the non-conformists drew opposite consequences when it came to the question whether the external observances were to be practiced or not. The non-conformists argued that the idea of Creator and created beings, expressed in the Sabbath, should be made manifest in their daily pursuit, but with no distinction made between the Sabbath and other days. Likewise, joy and thankfulness should always be the attitude, so that the specific festivals were superfluous. And the ethical conduct and self-understanding portrayed by circumcision should determine their way of life as Jews, without the external observance being needed.

Philo, on the other hand, drew the opposite consequences of the same ideas. He stressed that the ideas and the external observance belonged together. At each of the points he therefore exhorts the non-conformists not to ignore the laws in their outward meaning. In this way Philo argues in favour of loyal observance on the basis of his ideological agreements with the others.

When we relate the observations made here in On the Migration of Abraham 86-93 to the points drawn from Questions on Exod II:2, the following picture emerges: Three different streams within Judaism in Alexandria are reflected in these two passages.

1) Some held the view that bodily circumcision was the basic criterion for deciding when a converted heathen was given the status of a proselyte, a Jew. Philo disagrees with this line of thinking, as stated in Quaes Exod II:2.

2) Philo uses an ethical criterion for deciding who has the status of a proselyte within the Jewish community, Quaes Exod II:2. This ethical conversion of the heathen also meant a sociological change from a pagan context to a Jewish one. From On the Migration of Abraham 86-93 we learn that his (as also was Hillel's) understanding has been that although bodily circumcision was not the requirement for entering the Jewish community as such, it was one of the commandments which they had to obey upon receiving status as a Jew.

3) The non-conformists whom Philo cirticizes in On the Migration of Abraham 86-93, based their view on the Laws of Moses, but ignored the external observance of feasts and circumcision. Only the religious ideas and attitudes and ethical behaviour associated with the feasts and circumcision were of significance, not the external observances themselves.

M. Friedländer thought that these Jews who rejected the external observance of feasts and circumcision were a strong and numerous religious party, with a similar group also in Palestina. Friedländer refers here to the saying attributed to R. Eleazar from Modin, in which Rabbi Eleazar condemns Jews who, although they recognize the Torah and do good works, neglect and reject the observance of feasts and circumcision. (13)

This idea of a numerous religious party cannot be substantiated by the sources. But the sources allow us to say that there were parallel phenomena which took place in Alexandria and Palestine (either at the same time or at different times), where individual Jews or groups ignored the external observance, but kept other parts of the Torah.

Community action against the non-conformists

As stated, Philo's criticism of these non-conformists is in On the Migration of Abraham 86-93 presented as a negative example to the exposition of Gen 12:2, "I will make thy name great." He connects his criticism with the idea of reputation in this way: "These men are taught by the sacred word to have thought for good repute, and let go nothing that is part of the customs fixed by divinely empowered men greater than those of our time." H.A. Wolfson has rightly seen that Philo here appeals to the non-conformists that they should remain loyal to Judaism and the Jewish community. (14)

Although Philo elsewhere offers sharp criticism of boasting, praise and arrogance, (15) he here gives a highly positive view of the related concept of fame and reputation. And there seems even to be an element of opportunism in his treatment of fame here in Migr 88 ff., since he appeals to conformity with the established condition of the Jewish community. Nevertheless, Philo defines the concept on a religious basis: the conformity to the established Jewish customs meant adjustment to customs fixed by divinely empowered men; it meant therefore conformity to the Laws of God, which were the constitution of the nation and were the social norms of the community.

What was then, according to Philo, the reaction of the community against the non-conformists? On the Migration of Abraham 93 he says indirectly that they incur the censure of the many and the charges they bring against them: "If we keep and observe these (outward observances) ... we shall not incur the censure of the many and the charges they are sure to bring against us."

Another term is used in Migr 86, when he writes: "For very many ... through paying no regard to the general opinion have become the objects of hostility (ἐπεβουλεύθησαν)." This verb ἐπιβουλεύω means to plot against in a hostile manner, and often the plotting for murder. (16)

Philo here sketches a situation which is akin to what happened in the Christian missionary work, according to the Acts of the Apostles. The Church in Jerusalem, and missionaries as Paul and Barnabas - who were themselves Jews - were understood by the Jewish communities to interfere dangerously with established customs. As a result they were plotted against by the other Jews. (17)

The plot against Paul's life when he visited Jerusalem and the Temple, Acts 21:27-23:22, can serve as an example. The accusation against Paul was that he everywhere taught everyone against the people of Israel, the Law of Moses, and the Temple, and that he now even had brought some gentiles uncircumcised persons into the temple and defiled the holy place. It is evident from Acts that circumcision was a central question in this conflict, and that tension existed among Jewish Christians on these matters. As a result the people of Jerusalem tried to kill Paul. He was rescued by the Roman army, and then some plotted against his life: "The next morning some Jews met together and made a plan. They took a vow that they would not eat or drink anything until they had killed Paul" (Acts 23:12).

This example from the Acts of the Apostles illustrates how debates and conflicts reflected in Philo's writings can throw light upon aspects of the New Testament, just as the New Testament can illuminate aspects of Philo's writings.

The debates on circumcision and ethics, on the proselytes, and on conformity and conflict with Jewish community customs, are of interest as comparative material for the situations reflected in Paul's letters, especially in Paul's letter to the Galatians. This subject is pursued further below in the chapters eleven, twelve and thirteen.

It should be added, however, that a study of Philo is not only of interest for the understanding of the New Testament. It gives important information on Judaism in the first century, a fact which is of importance in itself. The variety of views and practices in Alexandrian Judaism, as well as parallell phenomena also elsewhere (Palestine included), has been illustrated by our investigation.

Special emphasis might here be placed on the discussion of the various criteria employed to give an answer to the question: When does a heathen convert become a proselyte, and thus receive legal and social status as a Jew? Some obviously maintained that the social and ethical break with the heathen community and the joining of the Jewish community gave a person status as a Jew. Others claimed that bodily circumcision was the decisive criterion. - It is obvious that such a debate in the Jewish communities must be taken into account also in the discussion of whether or not there was a group of heathen "God-fearers" attached to the Jewish communities around in the

Diaspora. To some, such people qualify as being proselytes, while to others, they were not yet to be regarded as members of the Jewish community. (18)

NOTES

1) R. Meyer, περιτέμνω, TWNT, 6, 77.

2) H.A. Wolfson, Philo, 2, 369-73.

3) H.A. Wolfson, 2, 370, n. 329: "The reasoning employed by Philo to show that the term 'proselyte' in the two verses in question is to be taken in the sense of a 'spiritual proselyte' because of its comparison to the Jews who were 'proselytes' in Egypt, is not followed out by him in his interpretation of the term 'proselyte' in two other similar verses. In the verse 'The proselyte who cometh to you shall be as the native-born among you, and thou shalt love him as thyself' (Lev. 19:34), the term 'proselyte' is taken by him, as by the rabbis, to refer to a full proselyte (Spec I:9;52; Virt 20,103; cf. Sipra, Kedoshim, Perek 8, p. 91a), though the verse concludes with the clause 'for you were proselytes in the land of Egypt.' Similarly in the verse 'He administereth justice to the proselyte and the orphan and the widow, and loveth the proselyte in giving him food and raiment (Deut 10:18), the term 'proselyte' is taken by him to refer to the full proselyte (Spec I:57;308-309; Virt 20; 104)..."

4) N.J. McEleney, "Conversion, Circumcision and the Law, NTS, 20, (1974) 328-329.

5) J. Nolland, "Uncircumcised Proselytes?" JSJ, 12, 173-179.

6) See B.J. Bamberger, Proselytism in the Talmudic Period (repr of 1. ed 1939), (New York, 1968) 38-52.

7) The problem is formulated in a similar way by S. Bialoblocki, Die Beziehungen des Judentums zu Proselyten und Proselytentum, (Berlin, 1930) 15 ff.

8) See D. Daube, "Jewish Missionary Maxims in Paul," Studia theologica, 1, (1947) 159.

9) J. Drummond, Philo Judaeus, 1, (Amsterdam, 1969, repr. of ed. London 1888) 20; E.R. Goodenough, By Light, 83-84, etc.

10) See Leg all I:6;18; Cher 87; Joh 5:17; Exod R 30:6.

11) Cf. Hillel's view that the Sabbath joy applied to every day, b Beṣa 16 a. In the Old Testament joy and thanksgiving were already central features of the feasts: Neh 8:12; Jes 16:10; 9:2; 22:13;Zech 8:19; Neh 12:43; Ps 50:14,23 etc.

12) Cf. the ethical interpretation of circumcision in the OT (Deut 10:16; 30:6; Jes 4:4; etc.) and in Qumran (I Qp Hab 11:13; I QS 5:5-6).

13) M. Friedländer, Die religiösen Bewegungen innerhalb des Judentums im Zeitalter Jesu, (repr. Amsterdam, 1974 of 1. ed, Berlin, 1905) 81, etc.

14) H.A. Wolfson, Philo, 1,67.

15) See Spec I:311, etc.

16) Migr 208; Quod Det 45; 69; Spec III:94; 141; 180; 204, etc.

17) Acts 6:8-7:60; 9:22-23; 18:12-15; cf. 20:3;19.

18) See especially K. Lake, "Proselytes and God-fearers", in F. Foakes Jackson and K. Lake, The Beginnings of Christianity, I, The Acts of the Apostles, 5, (London, 1933) 74-96; A.T. Kraabel, "The Disappearance of the 'God-fearers'," Numen, 28:2, (1981) 113-126.

PART II: JOHN

CHAPTER FOUR

THE PROLOGUE OF JOHN - AS EXPOSITION OF THE OLD TESTAMENT

Research standpoints

Analyses of the Prologue of John have concentrated particularly on the question of poetic and prose stylistic forms, and on the question of unity and unevenness in thought, both within the Prologue itself, and the Prologue in relation to the rest of the gospel. As far as form is concerned, several scholars, such as R. Bultmann, E. Käsemann, R. Schnackenburg and R.E. Brown, have suggested that the evangelist has used and supplemented a hymn. (1)

Bultmann's analysis of the Prologue has resulted, amongst other things, in the direct reference to John the Baptist, John 1:6 ff. and v. 15, being considered a secondary addition, as it is prose, thus not belonging to the original poetic hymn. According to Bultmann, the evangelist as a former disciple of the Baptist, added these words about him as a testimony to Jesus, to resolve his problem in leaving the Baptist's sect and becoming a Christian.

Other scholars who interpret John's Prologue as a hymn seem to disagree with several aspects of Bultmann's interpretation of the thoughts piecemeal. Nevertheless, they are in agreement with him in regarding the references to John the Baptist as a secondary addition.

E. Hänchen's study of John 1:1-18 is of particular interest. He believes that the editor who added ch. 21, also added the saying about John the Baptist, 1:6-8, 15. This editor thought that John had to be mentioned first, and then Jesus, and thus undertook the necessary revisions of John's Prologue. Hänchen's study, however, shows that an essential criterion for eliminating vv. 6-8, 15 has been discarded. In fact, he indicates that the difference in style between poetry and prose cannot be utilised with regard to the Prologue, and thereby this criterion is also weakened with regard to vv. 6-8, 15.(2)

With this in mind, it is understandable that W. Eltester completely rejects the hypothesis of a reworked hymn. Eltester maintains that John 1:1-18 is a single entity, and that the gospel narrative begins with v. 1. In fact, each section tells of an epoch in salvation history:

1:1-5 *Das "Wort" als Schöpfungsmittler und als Offenbarer.*

1:6-8 *Johannes als Gottgesandter und als Zeuge des Offenbarers.*

1:9-11 *Der Offenbarer und seine Ablehnung durch Heiden und Juden.*

1:12-13 *Die alttestamentlichen Gotteskinder.*

1:14-17 *Die Fleischwerdung des "Wortes" und der Lobpreis seiner Gemeinde, mit Johannes als Zeugen seiner Pre-existenz und seiner Gnadengaben im Alten Testament und in Jesus.*

1:18 *Der eingeborene Sohn als alleiniger Künder Gottes.* (3)

For Eltester, the statements about John have a central function, but his treatment seems rather schematic and strained. He does not give a satisfactory explanation as to why the statements about John appear as early as vv. 6-8, and not just before the verses on the Incarnation, vv. 14 ff. Another objection to Eltester is that it is difficult not to interpret vv. 9 and 11 as referring to the Incarnation, as much as v. 14.

At the same time, there are two points of Eltester's which seem to be value. When the distinction between poetry and prose is dismissed, it is natural to consider John 1:1-18 as a unity.

And even if Eltester's salvation history epochs are overschematically presented, but nonetheless one ought to investigate whether or not the salvation history motif is present in the passage. Various studies (among others A. Fridrichsen's (4) and N.A. Dahl's (5)) show that there are, in fact, elements of salvation history within the gospel. Therefore one can expect to find such elements in the opening of the gospel as well.

Thus there is a need to investigate John 1:1-18 anew, with regard to both form and content.

The Evangelist and Jewish Exegesis

It is the hypothesis of this study that the Prologue's basic structure is not primarily dependent on whether the style is prose or poetry, but on its character as an exposition of Gen 1:1 ff. Thus the question arises: What is the structure of the Prologue if it is approached as an exposition of the Old Testament? Furthermore, does this expository structure point towards a solution of the problem of disunity and unity in the thought of the Prologue?

It is commonly recognized that the phrase ἐν ἀρχῇ in John 1:1-2 renders בראשית in Gen 1:1. (6) The term (ὁ) θεός in John 1:1-2 also alludes to Gen 1:1. This term is found in John 1:6, 13 as well, but here the direct dependence on Gen 1:1 is less certain. The use of the term θεός in John 1:18 seems, however, to point back to 1:1, since in both places the word occurs with reference to God (the Father) and Logos (cf. v. 14). (7)

The central terms φῶς and σκοτία in John 1:4-5 are taken from Gen 1:2-5, אור and חשך. The term φῶς is repeated in John 1:7,8,9.

These words from Gen 1:1-5 are in John 1:1 ff. interpreted by means of paraphrasing expansions. (8) The question then arises: Do some of the words and phrases in the expansion replace and interpret words and phrases in Gen 1:1 ff? The answer is in the affirmative. In John 1:1 and 18 the term ὁ λόγος is probably an interpretation and replacement of the phrase εἶπεν ὁ θεός in Gen 1:3. The following points support the hypothesis: (1) In addition to the fact that John 1:1-5 clearly draws on Gen 1:1-5, it is significant that John 1:9 makes an explicit identification of Logos and light. (9) This identification suggests Gen 1:3 as exegetical basis, since there εἶπε is connected with light. (2) In Jewish exegesis Gen 1:3 serves as a basis for the idea of λόγος דבר and its identification with light.

In Gen Rab 3:3, Prov 15:23 'A man hath joy in the answer of his mouth, and a word in season, how good it is' is interpreted. The phrase 'the answer of his mouth' (במענה פיו) is understood as the creative utterance of God in Gen 1:3. And the exposition makes clear that this creative 'answer of his mouth' is דבר a word which, as in John 1: 9, is identified with light: 'And a word (דבר) in season, how good it is: And God saw the light, that it was good' (Gen 1:4). (10)

Against the interpretation that ὁ λόγος in John 1 is based on such Jewish exegesis, it may be objected that in Gen Rab 3:3 the 'word' is the uttered word of God and not a hypostasis; also it is not used in the absolute way we find in John 1. (11) This objection, however, disregards the fact that Philo in his interpretation of Gen 1:3 moves from the uttered word of God to the concept of Logos in an absolute sense: 'For the model was the Word of His (God's) fullness-(namely) light, for he says "God said, let there be light"' (τὸ μὲν γὰρ παράδειγμα ὁ πληρέστατος ἦν αὐτοῦ λόγος, φῶς - 'εἶπε' γάρ φησιν 'ὁ θεός' γενέσθω φῶς' Somn. I:75). (12) At times, Philo even attributes to Logos quite personal features, as in Conf. 146, where he associates Logos with concepts from the story of the creation, as 'God's First-Born, the Logos'. 'He is called "the Beginning"-"Logos"'-"the Man after His (God's) Image".' (13)

The conclusion is, therefore, that the use of the term Logos in John 1:1, 18 presupposes an exposition of Gen 1:3 like the one evidenced in Philo, Somn I:75.

The method of replacing words from the Old Testament with interpretative words is used also in John 1:3. The words ברא את השמים ואת הארץ in Gen 1:1 are, in John 1:3, replaced by a formula for the creation: πάντα δι' αὐτοῦ ἐγένετο, καὶ χωρὶς αὐτοῦ ἐγένετο οὐδὲ ἓν ὃ γέγονεν (14) A variant of the formula is found in v. 10 ὁ κόσμος δι' αὐτοῦ ἐγένετο.

Parallels in Jewish literature, and elsewhere in the N.T., suggest that the formula used in John 1:3 f. was traditional and widespread. Such parallels are: Ἰησοῦς Χριστός, δι' οὗ τὰ πάντα (1 Cor 8:6); τὰ πάντα δι' αὐτοῦ...ἔκτισται (Col 1:16); ἐν υἱῷ...δι' οὗ καὶ ἐποίησεν τοὺς αἰῶνας (Hebr 1:2); δι' ἧς τὰ ὅλα (Philo, Fug. 109); בדבר יהוה שמים נעשו (Ps. 33:6), (15) ὁ ποιήσας τὰ πάντα ἐν λόγῳ σου (Wisd 9:1).

Two further observations can be made on the basis of this analysis: (I) John 1:1-18 draws heavily on Gen 1:1-5, the verses which complete the first day of creation. (16) (2) No material from Gen 1:1-5 is used in John 1:6 ff., apart from repetition of terms and interpretative phrases already utilized in John 1:1-5. Thus John 1:1-5 is the basic exposition of Gen 1:1-5, while John 1:6 ff. elaborates upon terms and phrases from John 1:1-5.

The relationship between the basic exposition in John 1:1-5 and the elaboration in vv. 6 ff needs further examination.

In John 1:7-9 the term τὸ φῶς refers back to the introduction of the term in vv. 4-5. In v. 10 the creation formula ὁ κόσμος δι' αὐτοῦ ἐγένετο points back to the introduction of the fuller formula in v. 3, and finally in vv. 14-18 the terms ὁ λόγος and θεός are repeated from vv. 1-2.

It is significant to note that the elaboration in vv. 6 ff. follows exactly the opposite order of that in which the terms and phrases occur in vv. 1-5:

Basic exposition: (a) vv. 1-2 ὁ λόγος-(ὁ) θεός ; (b) v. 3 πάντα δι' αὐτοῦ ἐγένετο; (c) vv. 4-5 τὸ φῶς.

Elaboration: (c) vv. 7-9 τὸ φῶς ; (b) v. 10 ὁ κόσμος δι' αὐτοῦ ἐγένετο ; (a) vv. 14-18 ὁ λόγος - θεός.

Point (c) in the elaboration clearly belongs to the section which begins in v. 6 with the statement about John the Baptist Ἐγένετο ἄνθρωπος . Point (a) in the elaboration introduces the last section of the prologue, vv. 14-18 with the sentence καὶ ὁ λόγος σὰρξ ἐγένετο.

The section to which point (b) in the elaboration belongs is more difficult to identify. Verse 10, in which the creation formula occurs, is closely tied to v.9, since the term ὁ κόσμος occurs in both verses. On the other hand v. 9 belongs to the preceding discussion of τὸ φῶς since its stress on the true light picks up the theme of the Baptist not being the light, but a witness to the light, v. 8. Thus v. 9 is the transition from one section to the other, from vv. 6-9 to vv. 10-13 in which point (b), the creation formula, occurs. (17)

The structure of John 1:1-18 is therefore as follows (the verbal agreements between the points (a), (b), (c) in the basic exposition and the points (c), (b), (a) in the elaboration are underlined):

1. Basic exposition of Gen 1:1-5:

(a) Ἐν ἀρχῇ ἦν ὁ λόγος, καὶ ὁ λόγος ἦν πρὸς τὸν θεόν, καὶ θεὸς ἦν ὁ λόγος. οὗτος ἦν ἐν ἀρχῇ πρὸς τὸν θεόν.

(b) πάντα δι' αὐτοῦ ἐγένετο, καὶ χωρὶς αὐτοῦ ἐγένετο οὐδὲ ἓν ὃ γέγονεν.

(c) ἐν αὐτῷ ζωὴ ἦν, καὶ ζωὴ ἦν τὸ φῶς τῶν ἀνθρώπων. καὶ τὸ φῶς ἐν τῇ σκοτίᾳ φαίνει, καὶ ἡ σκοτία αὐτὸ οὐ κατέλαβεν.

2. Elaboration:

(c) vv. 6-9. Ἐγένετο ἄνθρωπος, ἀπεσταλμένος παρὰ θεοῦ, ὄνομα αὐτῷ Ἰωάννης· οὗτος ἦλθεν εἰς μαρτυρίαν, ἵνα μαρτυρήσῃ περὶ τοῦ φωτός, ἵνα πάντες πιστεύσωσιν δι' αὐτοῦ. οὐκ ἦν ἐκεῖνος τὸ φῶς, ἀλλ' ἵνα μαρτυρήσῃ περὶ τοῦ φωτός. ἦν τὸ φῶς τὸ ἀληθινόν, ὃ φωτίζει πάντα ἄνθρωπον, ἐρχόμενον εἰς τὸν κόσμον.

(b) vv. 10-13. ἐν τῷ κόσμῳ ἦν, καὶ ὁ κόσμος δι' αὐτοῦ ἐγένετο, καὶ ὁ κόσμος αὐτὸν οὐκ ἔγνω. εἰς τὰ ἴδια ἦλθεν, καὶ οἱ ἴδιοι αὐτὸν οὐ παρέλαβον. ὅσοι δὲ ἔλαβεν αὐτόν, ἔδωκεν αὐτοῖς ἐξουσίαν τέκνα θεοῦ γενέσθαι, τοῖς πιστεύουσιν εἰς τὸ ὄνομα αὐτοῦ, οἳ οὐκ ἐξ αἱμάτων οὐδὲ ἐκ θελήματος σαρκὸς οὐδὲ ἐκ θελήματος ἀνδρὸς ἀλλ' ἐκ θεοῦ ἐγεννήθησαν.

(a) vv. 14-18. Καὶ ὁ λόγος σὰρξ ἐγένετο καὶ ἐσκήνωσεν ἐν ἡμῖν, καὶ ἐθεασάμεθα τὴν δόξαν αὐτοῦ, δόξαν ὡς μονογενοῦς παρὰ πατρός, πλήρης χάριτος καὶ ἀληθείας Ἰωάννης μαρτυρεῖ περὶ αὐτοῦ καὶ κέκραγεν λέγων· οὗτος ἦν ὃν εἶπον· ὁ ὀπίσω μου ἐρχόμενος ἔμπροσθέν μου γέγονεν, ὅτι πρῶτός μου ἦν. ὅτι ἐκ τοῦ πληρώματος αὐτοῦ ἡμεῖς πάντες ἐλάβομεν, καὶ χάριν ἀντὶ χάριτος· ὅτι ὁ νόμος διὰ Μωϋσέως ἐδόθη, ἡ χάρις καὶ ἡ ἀλήθεια διὰ Ἰησοῦ Χριστοῦ ἐγένετο. θεὸν οὐδεὶς ἑώρακεν πώποτε· μονογενὴς θεὸς ὁ ὢν εἰς τὸν κόλπον τοῦ πατρός, ἐκεῖνος ἐξηγήσατο.

The section classified as elaboration is more precisely an application to a specific event. That is, each part of the basic exposition (1:1-5) is applied to the event of the appearance of Jesus Christ (vv. 6-9, 10-13 and 14-18).

In vv. 6-9 the light, τὸ φῶς of vv. 4-5 is understood from the viewpoint of the appearance of Jesus Christ: The light was coming into the world, (18) and John the Baptist served as its witness. In vv. 9-13 the creation formula in v. 3 is interpreted within the thought-pattern of an owner and his property. The creator is the owner of his creation and the appearance of Jesus Christ means that the owner comes to his property: 'He came to his own.' (19) The concepts of Logos and God in vv. 1-2 are in vv. 14-18 applied to the appearance of Jesus Christ within the thought-pattern of epiphany. The ideas used are those of the presence of the Logos in flesh, the characterization of him and his blessings and the idea of the vision of God through him. Recent studies on vv. 14-18 have shown that John draws heavily on ideas from the epiphany at Mount Sinai. (20)

From this analysis it is seen that the Prologue of John deals with creation and before, in the form of an exposition of Gen 1:1-5, applying these ideas to the appearance of Jesus Christ. It is therefore probable that John reflects a Jewish thought-pattern in which that which came into being, at creation or before, was regarded as a preparation for a later time. (21) And the structure of a basic exposition which is followed by application explains why the appearance of Jesus Christ is mentioned both in John 1:9, 11 and 14. In this way the three parts of the exposition (vv. 1-5) are each applied to the appearance of Jesus Christ. Moreover, in this structure the references to John the Baptist in vv. 6 ff. and 15 are natural since he is closely tied to this event, the appearance of Jesus Christ, and can even point to the connection between the beginning and this event (v. 15).

In Jewish sources there is quite a strong exegetical tradition that interprets Gen 1:1 ff. as not only referring to the creation of the world but what preceded it. (22) The exegetical basis for this is expressed in John 1:1-2 in the light of v. 3: ἐν ἀρχῇ בראשית in Gen 1:1 is understood as a reference to the time before the creation of the world. This exegesis of Gen 1:1 could be developed in Judaism within the thought-category of existence at creation and before, with subsequent revelation.

The tradition found in the Jerusalem Targum on Genesis 3:24 is of special interest as a parallel to the Prologue of John (the verbal agreements between the points (a), (b), (c) and the points (c), (b), (a) are in italics).

Two thousand years before (קדם עד לא) He had created the world,

(a) He created (ברא) *the Law*; (b) and *prepared Gehinnom*; (c) and *the garden of Eden*.

(c) He prepared (ואתקין) *the garden of Eden* for the righteous that they should eat and delight themselves with the fruit of the tree, because they had kept the commandments of the Law in this world.

(b) He *prepared* (אתקן) *Gehinnom*, for the wicked, which is like the sharp, consuming sword with two edges. He prepared in the depth of it flakes of fire and burning coals for the wicked for their punishment for ever in the world to come, who have not kept the commandments of the Law in this world.

(a) For (ארום) *the Law* is (הוא) the tree of life; whoever keepeth it in this life, liveth and subsideth as the tree of life. *The Law* is good to keep in this world as the fruit of the tree of life in the world that cometh. (23)

Just as in John 1:1 ff. so here as well, a term from Genesis 1 is built into a paraphrasing exposition, namely the word ברא in Gen 1:1. And just as in John 1:1 ff., terms from Gen 1 are replaced by interpretative terms. The word בראשית in Gen 1:1 is replaced in the Targum by the interpretative phrase קדם עד לא , (24) since the term is understood as referring to the time before the creation of the world. In the light of John 1:3 this also is the meaning of ἐν ἀρχῇ in vv. 1 and 2. And the words את השמים ואת הארץ in Gen 1:1 are replaced in the Targum by the term עלמא , just as the same words in John 1:3 and 10 are replaced by πάντα and ὁ κόσμος , respectively.

In the Jerusalem Targum on Gen 3:24 the words which refer back to Gen 1:1 are interpreted by means of a paraphrase which also mentions the Law, the Gehinnom, and the Garden of Eden. Also in the Targum on Gen 3:24, as in John 1:1-18, the basic exposition of Gen 1 is followed by an elaboration of each point of the exposition. In both cases the order followed is (a), (b), (c), and (c), (b), (a).

Moreover, both in John 1:6 ff., and in the Jerusalem Targum on Gen 3:24 two of the elaborating sections have marked beginnings: John 1:6:ʼΕγένετο ἄνθρωποςand 1:14:καὶ ὁ λόγος σὰρξ ἐγένετο and in the Jerusalem Targum: ואתקין and again:אתקן . In both places the beginning of one section is closely tied to the preceding clause. In John 1:10 ἐν τῷ κόσμῳ refers back to εἰς τὸν κόσμον in the preceding clause in v. 9, and in Targum Jerusalem ארום אילן חייא הוא אורייתא refers back to מצוותא דאורייתא in the preceding clause.

With regard to the meaning, important parallels are also to be found. Both John and the Jerusalem Targum deal with the pattern of existence at creation and before with the subsequent event of revelation. In both places each of the three parts of the basic exposition is in the corresponding part of the elaboration applied to a subsequent event.

The present analysis has shown that the structure and outline of John 1:1-18 are determined by the fact that the passage is meant to be an exposition of Gen 1:1 ff. Thus, the question og prose or poetic style as such is not basic for the understanding of the composition, although it is, of course, important for the further analysis.

The exposition of Gen 1:1-5 in John 1:1-5 follows the pattern of (a) ὁ λόγος-θεός (vv. 1-2); (b) δι᾽ αὐτοῦ ἐγένετο (v.3); and (c) τὸ φῶς (vv. 4-5). Then follows the elaboration (vv. 6-18) of the same points in the reverse order, (c) τὸ φῶς (vv. 6-9); (b) δι᾽ αὐτοῦ ἐγένετο (vv. 10-13); and (a) ὁ λόγος-θεός (vv. 14-18).

There is a parallel to this pattern of (a), (b), (c) / (c), (b), (a) found in the Jerusalem Targum on Gen 3:24, and similar patterns of the form (a), (b), (c), etc. followed by (a), (b), (c) are found in other Jewish sources. (25) These parallels deal, as does John 1:1-18, with what originated at creation and before and was revealed at a later time. In the prologue of John the points from creation and before in (a), (b), and (c) in vv. 1-5 are correspondingly applied (vv. 6-18) to the appearance of Jesus Christ in each of the corresponding points, (c), (b), and (a). Thus, the present analysis explains why the appearance of Jesus Christ is referred to three times (v. 9, v. 11, and v. 14), and it makes possible a fresh approach to other aspects of the Prologue.

Logos and Light

It would be possible to relate this structure in the Prologue of John to a source analysis. On this basis one could advance the hypothesis that a source has been reworked and supplemented by the evangelist. In this study, however, we shall put the question: can John 1:1-18 be considered a unit, composed by the evangelist? The question could be formulated in another way: does the exegesis compel us to reckon with a reworked and supplemented source?

If we regard John 1:1-18 as a unit, composed by the evangelist, its arrangement can be presented thus:

(a) vv. 1-2 and vv. 14-18 Logos and God before the creation, and the Epiphany with the coming of Jesus.

(b) v. 3 and vv. 10-13: Logos which creates in primordial time, and which claims its possession by the coming of Jesus.

(c) vv. 4-5 and vv. 6-9: Light and nightfall in primordial time, and the coming of Light with Jesus' coming, with the Baptist as a witness.

On the basis of this structure it is clear, therefore, that vv. 1-2 must be interpreted first and foremost together with vv. 14-18; likewise v. 3 with vv. 10-13; and particularly vv. 4-5 together with vv. 6-9. In the most essential points in this study we shall concentrate the discussion of vv. 4-5 and vv. 6-9 on Light. We shall see if these verses can be understood as a unity, or if their exegesis leads us to consider vv. 6-8 as a secondary supplement. These interests coincide particularly on the issue of how far Jewish traditions of interpreting Gen 1, and other Jewish traditions, illuminate the train of thought, and partially the terminology, og John 1:4-9.

It can be considered very probable that the evangelist has not only reproduced words from Gen 1 such as ἐν ἀρχῇ בראשית θεός אלהים and τὸ φῶς-ἡ σκοτία אור–חשך and substituted the words ברא את השמים ואת הארץ in Gen 1 with a creation formula δι' αὐτοῦ ἐγένετο (vv. 3 and 11), but that he has also drawn on learned Jewish exegesis.

The term ὁ λόγος is particularly interesting in this connection. It occurs explicitly in vv. 1 and 14, and is referred to in many other verses in the passage. Vv. 4-9 contain important factors towards an understanding of the background to the phrase.

This becomes clear when one considers more closely the suggestion that Gen 1:3 forms the background for the term: ויאמר אלהים יהי אור LXX καὶ εἶπεν ὁ θεός Γενηθήτω φῶς (26) Haenchen raised this objection to interpreting ὁ λόγος so: "Aber Judentum hat jenes 'und Gott sprach' von Gen 1 eben gerade nicht zu einer von Gott unterschiedenen Person hypostasiert". (27)

There are several points immediately contradicting Haenchen's rejection of this interpretation. For example, it can be asserted that since Logos seems to be identified with light in John 1:9, (28) Gen 1:3 provides the natural basis, since εἶπε there can be understood as light. This occurs in Jewish exegesis, in Gen Rab 3:3 for example, where דבר is interpreted as light. In a quotation from Proverbs 15:23, "A man hath joy in the answer of His mouth; a word in season, how good it is", the expression "the answer of His mouth" במענה-פיו is understood as God's creative word in Gen 1:3. Thus it is explicit that "the reply of His mouth" is דבר , and דבר is, as in John 1:9, identified with light: "and a word דבר in season, how good it is; And God saw light, that it was good" (Gen 1:4) (29)

Haenchen's objection has som validity all the same, for in Gen Rab 3 דבר is in fact not personified, and is not a greatness independent of God, but is God's spoken word. At the same time Haenchen's objection here overlooks the fact that Philo in Somn I:75 interprets Gen 1:3, and moves from the spoken word, to Logos as the model behind the work of creation: τὸ μὲν γὰρ παράδειγμα ὁ πληρέστατος ἦν αὐτοῦ λόγος, φῶς, 'εἶπε' γάρ φησιν, 'ὁ θεός· γενέσθω φῶς', "for the model was the Word of His (God's) fullness, namely light, for He says "God said, 'Let there be light'". Philo can then on other places add the personal aspect of Logos as a hypostasis, precisely with reference to Gen 1. Thus in Conf 148, of "God's first-born", "Logos"; He is called "The Beginning", "Logos", "the Man after His (God's) image". For additional support from Philo it can be mentioned that in Opif 31 Logos is also characterised as light, against a background of the creation account, that is, the background of Gen 1:3. In the study "God's Agent in the Fourth Gospel", (See chapter ten below).

I have attempted to show that Philo, in "De Confusione Linguarum" and in other places, reworks common Jewish traditions, amongst other ways, within Jewish mysticism. (30) In the light of all this, it must be concluded that Haenchen's objection is untenable. Gen 1:3, therefore, presents the most probable foundation for the term Logos in the Prologue of John.

For further support in thus understanding Logos, one can refer to the fact that John builds upon and expands Jewish exegesis also in other places, for example in John 5. Against the background of Jesus healing a lame man on the sabbath, and the Jewish sabbath rule against work, John 5:17 expresses God's attitude to the sabbath: ὁ πατήρ μου ἕως ἄρτι ἐργάζεται.

The evangelist here presupposes the exegetical traditions, which, based on Gen 2:2-3 raised the question of whether or not God could rest on the sabbath. The conclusion was that God is always active, at least with regard to certain definite functions. (31) There are also other places in John where it is plain that learned exegesis is either taken up or presupposed by the evangelist. (32) Therefore we have reached the probable conclusion, that the term ὁ λόγος in John 1:1 ff. builds upon an exegesis of Gen 1:3 such as we find in Gen Rab 3:1-3 and in Philo in Somn I:75.

Thus the question is, can Jewish traditions in connection with Gen 1:3 and other traditions, throw light upon John 1:4-9 as an entity? Of interest here are the traditions which depict primordial light and dark in primordial time, and thereafter a later revelation of light again. There are several examples of such a tradition. In Ḥag 12a are the following points: (a) Primordial light (Gen 1:3) which gave Adam universal sight and the removal of light because of the sin of the generation in primordial time; (b) light's coming in the next age. (33)

This conception can be given various formulation. The coming of light can be directly connected with the Messiah's coming, or it can be connected with events which have already occured in Israel's history, particularly Abraham, and Moses' lawgiving. (34)

Against this background, the theme for 1:4-9 can be presented thus: primordial light and nightfall in primordial time, vv. 4-5, and light's entry into history, prepared by the coming of John. It would be practical to begin with vv. 6-9 the coming of light into history, prepared by the coming of John.

vv. 6-9: The Entry of Light into History, prepared by the Coming of John

V.6 Ἐγένετο ἄνθρωπος, ἀπεσταλμένος παρὰ θεοῦ,ὄνομα αὐτῷ Ἰωάννης has a style characteristic of historical narrative in the O.T., for example Judges 13:2, (ויהי איש אחד מצרעה ממשפחת הדני ושמו מנוח) 19:1, 1 Sam 1:1. (35) Bultmann underlines the fact that it is the O.T. prose style which is used and therefore he reckons vv. 6-8 as an interpolation in a Logos-hymn, as stated. (36) In addition to the objections already expressed to this conclusion, we are now in a position to see that the Jewish traditions of primordial light can readily be connected with the advent of light in history, and more particularly, in Israel's history.

In accordance with the expression of John's appearance in history in v. 6, a statement follows in v. 7 of his task, to witness to the light. Our hypothesis of a Jewish background is borne out by the fact that John here has expressions characteristic of Rabbinical usage, as ἦλθεν εἰς μαρτυρίαν בא לעדות (37)

Then, vv. 8-9 characterizes John in relation to Jesus: v. 8, οὐκ ἦν ἐκεῖνος τὸ φῶς which states that John was not the primordial light of Gen 1:3, whereas v. 9 ἦν τὸ φῶς τὸ ἀληθινόν states that Logos was.

V. 9 needs closer consideration. As for the question of the subject of ἦν, it could be understood in the verb: he, namely Logos; or it could be τὸ φῶς τὸ ἀληθινόν,the true light was.... Bultmann asserts, rightly, that it is ὁ λόγος , mentioned in vv. 1:4. In support of this interpretation he cites vv. 10 and 11 where the verbs ἦν and ἦλθεν also have Logos as the subject, due to the fact that the pronoun αὐτόν in v. 10b is masculine and must refer back to ὁ λόγος (38)

The term τὸ φῶς connects v. 9 to the preceding, where the same term is used. This fact counts against taking v. 9 together with the following verse, even though the term ὁ κόσμος provides a link with v. 10. (39)

In v. 9, light is identified as the true Light,τὸ φῶς το ἀληθινόν.There is a sharp contrast between this genuine, actual light, and John as the supposed light, v. 8. Again, an observation which speaks for the idea that vv. 6-9 belong together. If vv. 6-8 are removed as an interpolation, it is in fact not so clear what it is that provides the contrast to the true light, despite the fact that the true light may be understood as a more exact precision of Light in v. 4. (40) The most difficult grammatical problem remains in vv. 6-9, that is the participle ἐρχόμενον in v. 9. The seemingly obvious is to take the participle in connection with the preceding πάντα ἄνθρωπον . Even though a Rabbinical formula about becoming man seems to lend support to this approach, it is not satisfactory. The context, and John 3:19 and 12:46, show that it concerns the coming of light, and not the birth of every man. (41)

This problem disappears if ἐρχόμενον is taken as a periphrastic form together with ἦν : "the true light was about to come into the world". Otherwise, ἐρχόμενον can be understood as a loosely connected participle construction to τὸ φῶς "he was the true light which enlightens and which is coming". But even these interpretations are not without difficulties. It is rather unusual that a whole relative clause separates ἦν from the participle in its periphrastic form, and in the case of a loosely connected participle construction, one would hav expected the article to have been positioned before the participle. (42)

On the other hand, there is another alternative which is grammatically defensible and which renders good sense. The participle ἐρχόμενον can refer back to the subject of φωτίζει, i.e. to τὸ φῶς, represented by the relative pronoun ὅ . The participle without the article thus expresses what happens simultaneously with the action of the verb, and how the action occurs. In Blass-Debrunner this is called an adverbial use of the participle, (43) and the translation is thus: "He (i.e. Logos) was the true light, which enlightens every man when it (light) enters the world". Freely rendered the verse goes thus: Logos was the true light, which enlightens every man by coming into the world.

This grammatical interpretation of v. 9 has significance in determining the thought content. Thus it is impossible here to separate light's enlightening work from its coming. (44) In other words, both φωτίζει and ἐρχόμενον characterize the coming of Jesus. (45)

What provides the thought-model for this coming of light? It would be natural to interpret light against the background of ideas of Messiah's light. Since Logos in John is the light, it is more probable that the thought-model behind v. 9 is the coming of the primordial light, with the lawgiving of Moses.

Several references in John support this view. In John 10:35 f. the term ὁ λόγος τοῦ θεοῦ seems to be used of the Torah given at Sinai, and this idea provide the background for the saying regarding Jesus' being sent into the world. (46) And in John 12:46 ff. it is stated that Jesus' coming as light brings ὁ λόγος and ἐντολή from God. These expressions are also understood easiest in the light of Torah. (47) And in several other places, John transfers the Torah's function to Jesus, and uses terminology which usually belongs together with the Torah. For example, it is stated in Jewish sources that the Torah gives life to the world, and thus in John 6:33 that Jesus as the bread from heaven gives life to the world. (48) On this basis it is sensible to understand Logos' and light's coming in v. 9 against the background of the lawgiving of Moses as a thought-model.

In addition, there are several likenesses between the ideas bound up in the Torah in Judaism and ideas in John 1:4-9. It has already been shown that Jewish texts where primordial light from the creation (Gen 1:3) came into appearance at the lawgiving, are a thought-parallel to primordial light in John 1:4-5, which appeared with the coming of Jesus v. 9. Also, as stated, the word דבר is identified with the light and the Torah in Jewish texts, and even with the Torah as a creative instrument. (49) Thus in John, Logos is identified with light, and Logos is the creative instrument, John 1:3 ff. Furthermore, the Torah is life (50) and accordingly in John 1:4, life is in Logos. Further, ideas directly connected with the lawgiving at Sinai illuminate John 1:9. At the lawgiving, Moses brought the primordial light down from heaven (51), and according to John 1:9 primordial light makes its appearance at the coming of Jesus. As the lawgiving of Moses was for all men, (52) so in John 1:9 the light shines for every man when it comes. Of particular note here is Sap. Sal. 18:4, where it says that the law's light will be given to the world: τὸ..νόμου φῶς τῷ αἰῶνι δίδοσθαι . (53) It is also noteworthy that according to Jewish thought, the coming of the Torah made possible walking in the light. (54) In similar way we find that Jesus' coming as the light makes it possible for men to walk in the light, John 8:12 f., 12:35 ff., cf. 12:46 ff.

Thus there are very good grounds for concluding that the conception of logos-light's coming in John 1:9 has as a model the conception of Torah-light's coming with Moses

However, in John 1:6-9 weight is laid on John's coming. Thus we find the aorist forms ἐγένετο and ἦλθεν referring to John in vv. 6-7, whereas the present φωτίζει is used of light's enlightening function. Since φωτίζει and the participle ἐρχόμενον both refer to the incarnation, it is therefore the actual enlightening function which the incarnation effects that is in mind, and not the punctual aspect of the event in itself.

John's appearance signified a marked event in salvation-history. Thus it is understandable that it must be made clear that he is not the light itself. It is therefore possible, but unnecessary, to see any polemic against a baptism-sect in v. 8. (55) In contrast to the fact that John was not the light, the true light's singularity stands out: it was Logos-light of Gen 1:3, "and God said, 'Let there be light'".

Jewish source-material is also of interest with regard to John's function. In John 5:33 ff., it is John's service as a witness which is more closely defined. He was the kindled lamp which burnt and lit up. As background one can refer to the idea that Moses lit a lamp for Israel and took light from the law's light, Syr. Baruch 17:1-18:2. (56) And without actually referring to the creation account, in Midr. Ps.36 § 6 it is stated that the many men from Moses down to the sons of the Hasmoneans who saved Israel, were as lamps which had been extinguished again. Therefore one ought to pray that God Himself would give light. (57) Seen against this background, it is understandable that John's witness to the light had a significance in salvation history: he was the lamp, not the light itself.

Primordial Light and Nightfall in Primordial Time: John 1:4-5.

Having considered John's and primordial light's entry into history, John 1:6-9, we can turn to primordial light and nightfall in primordial time, vv. 4-5. Once again we are up against grammatical problems. This time it is the sentence division between vv. 3-4. Here we shall follow Nestle's text which begins a new sentence with ἐν αὐτῷ in v. 4. Among the many considerations of this problem, we can rely upon that of K. Haacker. He demonstrates that creation formulas of a similar type to that in John 1:3 emerge, if the full stop is placed before ἐν αὐτῷ , v. 4. (58) Verse 4 therefore deals with the ideas of Life and light in relation to Logos and mankind from the creation onwards (v.3). Verse 5a gives a general depiction in the present of the relation between light and darkness, and thereafter in v. 5b, a description of an event in the past in aorist form, that is the assault of darkness against light.

Verse 5b καὶ ἡ σκοτία αὐτὸ οὐ κατέλαβεν provides a good point of departure for a consideration of the thoughts contained in the verses. The debate among scholars has centered around the term καταλαμβάνειν , "grasp", either (a) to accept or (b) to seize with power and overcome in an undesirable or hostile manner. Scholars such as Bultmann, Wikenhauser and Haenchen think that καταλαμβάνειν here means to grasp in the sense of receiving and accepting: "and the darkness did not receive it (light)". They stress particularly that the thought here is parallel to that expressed in the phrase οὐκ ἔγνω , v. 10, and οὐ παρέλαβον in v. 11. All these give expression to the idea that wisdom is not accepted by men. (59) On the other hand, scholars have argued that the verb καταλαμβάνειν in 1:5 must be understood in the same sense as in 12:35. (60) In 12:35 it is clear that the term is taken from daily life and describe nightfall which comes upon man by surprise. The verb therefore means to seize or surprise one in an undesirable or hostile manner. In support of this interpretation it could also be noted that the expression in John 1:5 and 12:35 presents a common formula for an unexpected and undesired nightfall, a formula which is well attested outside the New Testament. (61)

In the light of our analysis of John 1:1-18 an additional factor can be used to strengthen this interpretation. The structure used for John 1:1-18 makes it natural to divide vv. 4-9 into two parts: vv. 4-5, light in primordial time, and vv. 6-9, what happened at John's and light's entries into history. Thus, the phrases used in connection with the coming of Jesus οὐκ ἔγνω v. 10, and ου παρέλαβον , v. 11, are not parallels to v. 5b, which refers to primordial time, not the later entry of light in history.

The event to which v. 5b refers, seems to be the Fall, either connected with Adam, or with Adam and the sin of the first generations. In Jewish sources there are three particular lines of thought on the Fall which are of interest in understanding John 1.

The first line of thought maintains that primordial light became removed, concealed or weakened, because of sin. So it is stated in Hag. 12a that God let primordial light shine in Adam but then concealed in (גנז, reserve, conceal) because of the sinful Flood and Babel-building generations. (62) Also in place here is the idea that sunshine and length of days were lessened because of Adam's Fall.

The second line of thought, in a similar way maintains that the sins of Adam and the first generations led directly to darkness and night. The idea here can be developed to the extent that darkness and night grew, but the eventuality of complete darkness was averted by God's goodness and Adam's repentance. (63)

Generally speaking, these two lines of thought see the darkness as a consequence of sin and thereby a punishment. (64)

The third line of thought does not regard the darkness only as a punishment, but identifies sin and darkness. This identification is found particularly in the Dead Sea Scrolls where the spirits of light and darkness, and the children of light and darkness are mentioned. The idea is also found without this mythological dualism in Syr. Baruch 17-18, where Adam's darkness is contrasted to the light of the law. (65)

In John there are places where darkness can be understood as a result of disbelief and sin, for example in 12:35, but there are also places where sin and darkness are closely connected or identified, John 3:19 ff. In John 1:5b it is stated that nightfall seeks to overcome the light of day, and darkness here seems to be identified with man's sin. (66) Jewish texts support the hypothesis that John here is referring to Adam's Fall, and eventually the first generation's Fall as well, particularly as we find sin and darkness identified in Syr. Baruch 17:18, where Adam's darkness is mentioned.

According to John 1:5b light was not overcome by darkness-but nightfall must have led to a new situation. Since John 1:9 and 12:46 talk about the coming of light with the coming of Jesus, it follows by virtue of the fact, that primordial light, which mankind had according to John 1:4, was removed from them. And since light's coming brought back life, 8:12, it follows that the original life, mentioned in John 1:4, was lost. Thereby the train of thought in John follows precisely that of Jewish interpretative traditions, which consider light and life among the things lost at the Fall, brought back at a later moment of time in history, or in the coming aeon. (67)

Thus we have already touched on the interpretation of John 1:4 and 5a, but some points must be added. One could attempt an understanding of the general saying in v. 5a, καὶ τὸ φῶς ἐν τῇ σκοτίᾳ φαίνει, against the background of ideas in the Dead Sea Scrolls: how God created man, and the spirits of light and darkness are depicted there. (68) In John, however light and darkness are not two equal religious-ethical powers. In fact, in John 1:4 it is said only of light that it was with men in the beginning. (69) On this essential point, John follows the traditions which let Adam, and thereby mankind, have light as their original possession, with the ensuing Fall and darkness. The general saying in v. 5a, that light shines in the darkness, tells thereby of the possibility of the Fall in primordial time as well as in the later coming of light, but does not state that light and darkness are equal powers in men.

Conclusion

(I) We attempted to show that the structure of the Prologue of John must primarily be understood on the basis that it is meant to be an exposition of Gen 1:1 ff. The question of poetry or prose is therefore of subordinate significance.

(2) John 1:1-8 seems to draw on learned Jewish exegesis, wherein Logos, דבר and light, אור are connected on the basis of Gen 1:3.

(3) John 1:4-9 should be understood against the background of Jewish traditions of primordial light which was followed by darkness in primordial time, thus to reappear later in history, or in the coming aeon.

(4) The participle ἐρχόμενον in John 1:9 seems to refer back to the subject for φωτίζει , and both words depict light's, i.e. Jesus' coming.

(5) Since Logos in John is the light, the lawgiving at Sinai seems to provide a thought-model behind the coming of light in John 1:9. With the lawgiving, the light of the Law shone upon all men, just as light in John 1:9 enlightens every man.

(6) Therefore it is possible to understand vv. 6 ff. in terms of John, as a witness and lamp, introducing the salvation-history situation which prepared the coming of light in history.

(7) καταλαμβάνειν in John 1:5b means "seize", "overcome", in an undesirable or hostile manner. The conception of nightfall in this verse can be understood against the background of Jewish conceptions of the removal of light, and the coming of the darkness of night with Adam's and the first generation's sin. John seems to say implicity that light and life were removed at the Fall, in order to be brought back into the world by the coming of Jesus.

(8) Even though an understanding of the Targum schema a), b), c)/c), b), a) in John 1:1-18 can be attempted on the basis of theories of a source reworked and supplemented by the evangelist, we have tried to show that Jewish traditions and a closer analysis of the Prologue of John make such analysis unnecessary,

at least in verses 4-9. Therefore it would seem to be a viable hypothesis that John 1:1-18 in entirety can be treated as a composition of the evangelist himself, wherein elements from different traditions are woven together.

ATTACHED NOTE

In the article "The Pivot of John's Prologue", NTS, 27, (1980) 1-31, R. Alan Culpepper suggests that the Prologue of John has an elaborate chiastic structure. He notices that the structure analysed by me (a, b, c, and c, b, a) has a chiastic structure, although less detailed than that maintained by himself. Culpepper writes:

> Borgen has recently produced two helpful articles on the prologue in which he argues that in a manner comparable to the Jerusalem Targum on Genesis, the prologue contains a targumic exposition of Gen. I. I-5. Borgen argues that 'John i. I-5 is the basic exposition of Gen. i. I-5, while John i. 6 ff. elaborates upon terms and phrases from John i. I-5'. The basic exposition contains three main terms or phrases which are repeated in reverse order in the elaboration: (a) vv. I-2 ὁ λόγος-(ὁ) θεός; (b) v. 3 πάντα δι' αὐτοῦ ἐγένετο ; (c) vv. 4-5 τὸ φῶς ; (c') vv. 7-9 τὸ φῶς (b') vv. 10-13 δι' αὐτοῦ ἐγένετο ; (a') vv. 14-18 ὁ λόγος -θεός. Thus, while Borgen does not call this structure 'chiastic', it is at least roughly so. Borgen's discussion of the relationship between the prologue and Gen. I. 1-5 constructively augments previous research on the subject, but our interest focuses on his proposal regarding the structure of the prologue. By implication, the analysis which follows will show that Borgen's proposal is weak at the following points: (I) it is based on only three key terms or phrases while the prologue contains several other equally important terms which when taken into account alter the structure of the text; (2) vv. I-2 are not balanced by the entirety of vv. 14-18, but only by v. 18; (3) v. 17 with its reference to that which διὰ Ἰησοῦ Χριστοῦ has on the surface at least as strong a claim to balancing v. 3, and on the basis of other correspondences in the prologue it has a stronger claim; and (4) the two references to John the Baptist (vv. 6-8 and v. 15) distort Borgen's proposed structure, since both lie in the second half.

Culpepper's points of criticism call for some brief comments to be added to this chapter. His last point ("the two references to John the Baptist (vv. 6-8 and v. 15) distort Borgen's proposed structure, since both lie in the second half") demonstrates that he applies the theory of chiastic structure in a theoretical and mechanical way, without drawing on historical material in his analysis. Thus, he overlooks that in the chiastic form used in the Jerusalem Targum on Gen 3:24 the references to "this world" and "in the world to come" occur only in the second half. The reason for this unevenness is that the concepts introduced in the first half, "the Law", "prepared Gehinnom", and "the Garden of Eden", are in the second half applied to the schema of "this world" and "the world to come". Correspondingly, in the first half, John I:I-5, the concepts of "Logos" and "God", of "every thing came into being by him" and "light"/"darkness" were introduced, and then in the second half, I:6-18, these ideas are applied to the appearance of Jesus Christ. The references to John the Baptist in vv. 6-8 and v. 15 are tied to this appearance of Jesus. Culpepper's remark that there are references to John the Baptist in only two out of the three parts of the second half, has no weight, since in the same way the term "in the world to come" as also the term "tree", only occurs in two out of the three parts of the second half in the Jerusalem Targum on Gen 3:24.

Culpepper's objection in point (2) above, that vv. 1-2 are not balanced by the entirety of vv. 14-18, but only by v. 18, is not substantiated by a closer analysis. Several features run counter to Culpepper's point among which the following can be listed here: a) just as in the other parts of the second half, so also here in vv. 14-18, terms and ideas from the first half (vv. 1-2) are applied to the appearance of Jesus. This appearance of Jesus has the focus all through vv. 14-18; b) in addition to the explicit repetition in v. 14 and v. 18 of the terms "Logos" and "God" from vv. 1-2, the phrase "in the beginning" (v. 1) is referred to in v. 15, "because he was before me", just as the pre-existence is implied in the formulation of v. 18. c) In John 1:1-2 the relationship between "Logos" and "God" is characterized: Logos is God and is with God. This understanding of the relationship is presupposed and is interpreted in vv. 14-18 by formulations such as "glory as of the only Son from the Father" (v. 14), "fullness" (v. 16), "grace and truth" (v. 17), and "in the bosom of the Father" (v. 18).

In his point (3) above, Culpepper states that the phrase διὰ 'Ιησοῦ Χριστοῦ ἐγένετο has on the surface at least as strong a claim to balancing v. 3, πάντα δι'αὐτοῦ ἐγένετο , as has v. 10, ὁ κόσμος δι'αὐτοῦ ἐγένετο. By saying "on the surface" Culpepper himself indicates that the observation has its weaknesses. And against Culpepper, it must be emphasized that the phrase in v. 10, ὁ κόσμος δι'αὐτοῦ ἐγένετο , in a direct way repeats the other phrase about creation, πάντα δι'αὐτοῦ ἐγένετο in v. 3. The phrase in v. 17, διὰ Ἰησοῦ Χριστοῦ ἐγένετο, is parallel to the phrase διὰ Μωϋσέως in the very same verse.

Finally, it is not correct when Culpepper in his point (1) states that my proposal is based on only three key terms or phrases. The basis for my proposal is much broader: First, the Prologue is an exposition of Gen 1:1-5. Words from this Old Testament Section are either quoted, replaced or alluded to in the Prologue. Second, no material from Gen 1:1-5 is used in John 1:6-18 apart from repetition of the terms and the interprative phrases already utilized in John 1:1-5. Thus, John 1:1-18 is to be divided into two main parts which are interrelated, 1:1-5 and 1:6-18. John 1:1-5 is the basic exposition of Gen 1:1-5, while John 1:6-18 draws upon terms, phrases and ideas from John 1:1-5, and relates them to the appearance of Jesus Christ ("the incarnational event"). Third, the terms "Logos" and "God" tie together John 1:1-2 and 1:14-18. Verses 14-18 about the appearance of Jesus Christ elaborate also on other ideas found in vv. 1-2, such as the <u>relationship</u> between the "Logos" and "God" ("the Son" and "the Father", "glory", "fullness", "truth", etc.), and "in the beginning" (v. 1) referred to by the idea of pre-existence (v. 15 "he was before me"). Fourth, in the phrase "everything was made by him", v. 3, the ideas both of creator and of owner are implied. Both ideas are then interpreted in vv. 10-13, in application to the appearance of Jesus Christ. Fifth, in John 1:4-5 the term "light" is seen both as shining and as having been attacked, but not overcome, by darkness. This attack by darkness forms the logical negative background for the coming of the light to the world, vv. 6-9. Sixth, the proposed structure of a, b, c/c, b, a explains why the incarnation is referred to three times, i.e. in v. 9, v. 11, and v. 14.

Seventh, support for my proposal is produced by parallel material found in targumic and midrashic literature. The parallel in the Jerusalem Targum is of special interest, since it has the same structure of a, b, c/c, b, a. Moreover, the thought-pattern is similar: the first half deals with protology and the second half with eschatology. Another agreement is the lack of balance of length, since the first half in both places is shorter than the longer second half.

The conclusion is that R. Alan Culpepper has not demonstrated that my proposal is inadequate. Furthermore, serious objections can be raised against his own analysis of John 1:1-18 and his proposal as to its structure. Apart from criticism of details two general objections can be made: 1. His approach is too mechanical and too abstract. One reason is that he does not draw on historical parallel material to demonstrate the kind of structures which existed as an empirical fact. 2. Already the opening phrase "In the beginning" shows that Gen 1:1ff is basic for the understanding of John's Prologue. It is a serious weakness that Culpepper does not take this Old Testament background seriously in his analysis of the structure and the content of John 1:1-18.

NOTES

1) See R. Bultmann, Das Evangelium des Johannes, Meyer K. (Göttingen, 1950) 1-5: E. Käsemann, "Aufbau und Anliegen des Johanneischen Prologs", Libertas Christiana (Delekat Festschrift), (München, 1957) 75-99; E. Hänchen, "Probleme des Johanneischen Prologs", ZTK, 60, (1963) 305-34; R. Schnackenburg, Das Johannesevangelium, HTKNT, 4:1, (Freiburg, 1965) 197-207; R.E. Brown, The Gospel according to St. John, I-XII, AB, (Garden City, N.Y., 1966) 1-37. Concerning the earlier stages of this exegetical tradition, see C.K. Barrett, The Prologue of St. John's Gospel, (London, 1971) 6 ff.

2) E. Hänchen, ZTK, 60, (1963), 305-334. Cf. C.K. Barrett, The Prologue, 14 ff. for further criticism of the criterion of poetic and prose styles as applied to the Prologue.

3) W. Eltester, "Der Logos und sein Prophet", Apophoreta (Hänchen-Festschrift), (Berlin, 1964), 109-34, especially 124.

4) A. Fridrichsen, "Missionstanken i Fjärde Evangeliet," SEÅ, 2, (1936), 39-53.

5) N.A. Dahl, "The Johannine Church and History", in Current Issues in New Testament Interpretation, ed. W. Klassen and G.F. Snyder, (New York, 1962), 124-142.

6) R. Bultmann, Johannes, 6.

7) The reading μονογενὴς θεός is supported by evidence of the best Greek manuscripts. The reading μονογενὴς υἱός probably results from a scribal tendency to conform, since the phrase occurs in John 3:16, 18; 1 John 4:9. See R.E. Brown, St. John I-XII, 17.

8) The supplementary words are: ἦν ὁ λόγος καὶ ὁ λόγος ἦν πρὸς-ἦν ὁ λόγος (1:1); οὗτος (1:2); ἐν αὐτῷ ζωὴ ἦν καὶ ἡ ζωὴ ἦν-τῶν ἀν-ἀνθρώπων (1:4); and καὶ-ἐν-φαίνει, καὶ-αὐτὸ οὐ κατέλαβεν (1:5). The whole of 1:3 is supplementary to the text of Genesis 1.

9) See R. Bultmann, Johannes, 31 and n. 6.

10) Hebrew text in מדרש רבה על חמשה הומשי תורה וחמש מגילות, (Jerusalem, 1949), ad. loc. Engl. transl. in H. Freedman and M. Simon (ed.), Midrash Rabbah (London, 1939), vol. 1, ad. loc.

11) See R. Bultmann, Johannes, 6 f., and E. Haenchen, ZTK, 60, (1963), 313.

12) Text in F.H. Colson and G.H. Whitaker (ed. and trans.), Philo (London, 1941), vol. 5, ad loc. (translation is mine); cf. Fug. 95.

13) See further P. Borgen, 'God's Agent in the Fourth Gospel', in Religions in Antiquity, Essays in Memory of E.R. Goodenough, ed. J. Neusner (Leiden, 1968), 144 ff. (See chapter ten below).

14) With regard to the division between vv. 3 and 4, see K. Haacker, 'Eine formgeschichtliche Beobachtung zu Joh 1:3 fin', BZ, N.F. 12 (1968), 119-21.

15) Cf. the exegesis of Ps. 33:6 in Jewish sources, as Gen Rab 3:2, Midrash of the Psalms 42:1, etc. Cf. also the Egyptian formulas discussed by K. Haacher. See the reference in the preceding note.

16) John may thus reflect the continued use of the 6/7 days pattern in Jewish paraphrase of Gen 1. Examples of partial use of the pattern are also found. See R.H. Charles, The Apocalypse of Baruch (London, 1896) 53; G.H. Box, The Ezra Apocalypse (London, 1912) 83 ff.

17) See similar analysis in R.E. Brown, St. John, 28.

18) Concerning this interpretation of v. 9, see R.E. Brown, St. John I-XII, 9 ff.

19) The phrase τὰ ἴδια has been understood by some as 'the world' and by others 'Israel as God's people'. See R. Bultmann, Johannes, 34 (the world), R.E. Brown, St. John I-XII, 10 (Israel). The distinction seems to be false since Israel in John is seen as the centre of the world and therefore represents the world. See N.A. Dahl, 'The Johannine Church and History', esp. p. 129, and P. Borgen, Bread, 148 f., 175-9.

20) See M.E. Boismard, St. John's Prologue (Westminster, Md., 1957), 136-40; S. Schulz, Komposition und Herkunft der johanneischen Reden, Beitrage zur Wissenschaft vom Alten und Neuen Testament, Fünfte Folge 1 (Der ganzen Sammlung 81) (Stuttgart, 1960) 40 f.; N.A. Dahl, "The Johannine Church", 132, P. Borgen, Bread, 150 f.

21) See especially N.A. Dahl, 'Formgeschichtliche Beobachtungen zur Christusverkündigung in der Gemeindepredigt', Neutestamentliche Studien für R. Bultmann, ZNW. Beih. 21, (Berlin, 1954) 3-9.

22) See O. Betz, 'Was am Anfang geschah', in Abraham unser Vater, Festschr. f. O. Michel (Leiden, 1963) 35 ff.

23) English translation in J.W. Etheridge, The Targums of Onkelos and Jonathan Ben Uzziel on the Pentateuch with the Fragments of the Jerusalem Targum from the Chaldee, vol. 1, ad loc. The Aramaic text is found in M. Altschüler, Die Aramäischen Bibelversionen (Targumim). Targum Jonathan Ben Uzziel und Targum Jerusalemij. Vol. 1, Genesis (Wien/Leipzig, 1909) ad loc.

24) Cf. that Targum on Prov. 8:23,

25) See for example: Gen Rab 2:5: (a) built (b) destroyed (c) rebuilt and (a) built (b) destroyed (c) rebuilt. So also Pesiqta, Piska 21. Cf. Gen Rab 3:8 ((a) (b), (b) (a), (a) (b), (a) (b), (b) (a)). See especially

Gen Rab 2:5, which has the patterns of (a) (b)/(b) (a): 'From the very beginning of the creation of the World the Holy One, blessed be He, foresaw (a) the deeds of the righteous, (b) and the deeds of the wicked. (b) Thus, "Now the earth was formless and void" alludes to the deeds of the wicked. (a) And God said, "Let there be Light" to the actions of the righteous.' (Engl. transl. in H. Freedman and M. Simon, Midrash Rabba, 1, ad loc.)

26) See E. Haenchen, ZTK, 60, (1963) 305, note 3.

27) ibid.

28) See P. Borgen, "Observations on the Targumic Character of the Prologue og John," NTS, 16, (1970) 289-90. Concerning ὁ λόγος as subject of ἦν in John 1:9, see R. Bultmann, Johannes, 31, note 6.

29) Cf. Midr. Ps. 18 § 26. See C.H. Dodd, The Bible and the Greeks, (London, 1935) 115 ff. with regard to the concept of Logos and the story of creation in Poimandres.

30) P. Borgen, "God's Agent", 137-48. (See chapter ten below).

31) See C.H. Dodd, The Interpretation of the Fourth Gospel, (Cambridge, 1953) 319-23.

32) See P. Borgen, Bread from Heaven, especially 59-98.

33) Str.-Bill., 2, 348, note 2. Cf. Lev Rab 11:7; Esther Rab Proem 11:5; Gen Rab 11:2; Tanchuma Shemine 9; Ruth Rab Proem 7:5.

34) On the light (Gen 1:4) and the Messiah, see Pesiqta R. 36 (161a); and Abraham, cf. Gen Rab 2:3; and Moses, 3 Petirat Mosheh 72; Jalkut Reubeni Ki Tissa IIIa, cf. Sipre Num. §§ 136-37. See B. Murmelstein, "Adam, ein Beitrag zur Messiaslehre", Wiener Zeitschrift für die Kunde des Morgenlandes, 36, (1929) 56. Cf. Syr. Baruch 17-18.

35) See R. Bultmann, Johannes, 29, note 1 and references.

36) ibid., 3 f., 29-31.

37) ibid., 29, note 1.

38) ibid., 31, note 6.

39) See further P. Borgen, NTS, 16, (1970) 291 and 294.

40) R. Bultmann, Johannes, 32, maintains that in the original hymn the true light was contrasted with the earthly light. Against this point of view it can be said that vv. 1-5,9 which belonged to the hymn, does not make this contrast clear. R. Schnackenburg, Johannesevangelium, 229, gives a more precise characterization of the light in v. 4 by saying that it is of unique kind. Again it can be stated that the most obvious contrast found in the context is that between the preparatory light of John and the true light of Jesus.

41) Thus R.E. Brown, John I-XII, 9-10, with criticism of Burney, Schlatter, Bultmann, Wikenhauser.

42) See especially R. Schnackenburg, Das Johannesevangelium, 1, (Freiburg, 1965) 230-31.

43) F. Blass and A. Debrunner, Grammatik des neutestamentlichen Griechisch, 11. Aufl., (Göttingen, 1961) 260, especially 418,5.

44) Cf. that C.H. Dodd, The Interpretation, 201 f., thinks that φωτίζει refers to the general revelation as background for the special revelation in the coming of Christ.

45) Cf. R.E. Brown, John I-XII, 28, who refers to the Messianic passage of Isaiah 9:2.

46) N.A. Dahl, "The Johannine Church", 133 f.

47) E. Hirsch, Studien zum vierten Evangelium, (Tübingen, 1936) 99, sees that John 12:49-50 alludes to the lawgiving at Sinai, but he draws the wrong conclusion that the words from οἶδα to ἐστιν for this reason are an added gloss. Cf. R. Bultmann, Johannes, 263, note 7. R.E. Brown, John I-XII, 491-92 finds Deuteronomic ideas and terminology in John 12:48-50.

48) See P. Borgen, Bread from Heaven, 148-54.

49) Gen Rab 1:7, 3:1-3.

50) See references in A. Schlatter, Der Evangelist Johannes, (Stuttgart, 1930) 158-59, commenting upon John 5:39. Cf. P. Borgen, Bread from Heaven, 148-49, 165 ff.

51) Cf. S. Aalen, "Licht und "Finsterniss", 273, note 3.

52) S. Aalen, "Licht" und "Finsterniss", 295 f.

53) S. Aalen, ibid., 194. One version of Test. Levi 14:4 has even a close phraseological parallell to the words of John 1:9.

54) Mek. Ex. 13:18; cf. Sipre Num. 6:25, § 41; Ex. Rab 36:3; Midr. Ps. 27, §§ 1-3. Concerning Torah as the light of the world, see S. Aalen, "Licht" und "Finsterniss", 289. In John 3:19 ff. we find the thought that the coming of the light unmasks men. Cf. S. Aalen, "Licht" und "Finsterniss", 233-36; 321-24.

55) R. Bultmann, Johannes, 29 and R.E. Brown, John, 28 find polemic against a baptism-sect, so also R. Schnackenburg, Johannesevangelium, 1, 226 ("warscheinlich"); John 1:6 is interpreted differently by C.K. Barrett, The Gospel according to St. John, (London, 1958) 132 f; E. Haenchen, ZTK, 60 (1963) 328 f.

56) See also 3 Petirat Mosheh, 71 ff.

57) See S. Aalen, "Licht" und "Finsterniss", 186-87 and reference to John 5:35 on page 187, note 1. Such a subordinate lamp is John also according to F. Neugebauer, "Miszelle zu Joh v, 35", ZNW, 52, (1961) 130, who interprets John 5:35 against the background of LXX Ps. 132:17, as the lamp of Messiah.

58) See survey of research in R. Schnackenburg, Johannesevangelium, 1, 215-17; K. Haacker, BZ, N.F. 12, (1968) 119-21.

59) R. Bultmann, Johannes, 28 ("die Finsternis hat es nicht erfasst"); Cf. E. Käsemann, "Aufbau", 79; E. Haenchen, ZTK, 60, (1963) 322.

60) A. Schlatter, Johannes, 9; C.H. Dodd, The Interpretation, 36. 107; R.E. Brown, John I-XII, 8.

61) See especially A. Schlatter, Johannes, 9.

62) Cf. Lev Rab 11:7. Cf. that sin gradually caused the Shekina to be removed, Gen Rab 19:7.

63) Gen Rab 11:2 and 12:6. Abodah Zarah 8a. E. Preuschen, Die apokryphen gnostischen Adamschriften, (Giessen, 1900) 30-32. Cf. S. Aalen, "Licht" und "Finsterniss", 199. 265-66.

64) Gen Rab 2:3 identifies the sinful generations with the primordial chaos in Gen 1:2. Cf. Apocryphon Johannis 73:16-18, where the Deluge is depicted as darkness. See O. Betz, "Was am Anfang geschah", 38.

65) See for example I QS 3:25; Test. Napht. 2:10; 1 Enoch 108:1; Philo, Quaes, Gen II:82. Cf. S. Aalen, "Licht" und "Finsterniss", 178 ff. and N.A. Dahl, "Begrepene 'Lys' og 'mørke' i jødedommen", NTT, 53, (1952) 80 f.

66) Concerning light and darkness in John, see for example R. Schnackenburg, Johannesevangelium, 1, 223 ff.

67) Gen Rab 6; Tanchuma B. Bereshit 18. See also Chag 12a.

68) I QS 3.

69) Detailed discussion of light and darkness in the Dead Sea Scrolls and in the Johannine writings in R.E. Brown, "The Qumran Scrolls and the Johannine Gospel and Epistles", CBQ, 17, (1955) 403-419; 559-574.

CHAPTER FIVE

THE SON OF MAN-SAYING IN JOHN 3:13-14

From ascent to descent

In recent research it has been pointed out that Jesus' dialogue with Nicodemus in John 3 does not only reflect the Old Testament stories of the brazen serpent (John 3:14/Num 21:9) and Abraham's sacrifice of his son (John 3:16/Gen 22) but also draws on ideas from the revelation on Mt Sinai. (1) Thus in John 3:11 the words... ὃ οἴδαμεν ...καὶ ὃ ἑωράκαμεν ... seem to be but a variation of the terms ἀκούειν and ὁρᾶν used in John 3:32; 5:37 and 6:45-46. The hearing and seeing were central features in the theophany on Mt Sinai, and John 5:37, in particular, makes it evident that the Johannine usage draws on this background.(2)

Scholars have seen, moreover, that there is in John 3:13 a polemic against the ascents of Moses and all others who are said to have ascended into heaven. (3) This view is supported by the central role which the term "ascend" (ἀναβαίνειν עלה) plays both in John 3; 13 and in the story about the revelation on Mt Sinai, Exod 19:20.23; 24:1.2.9.13.18. And in Jewish exegesis it is frequently said that Moses entered into heaven when ascended. Such exegesis is evidenced as early as in the first century. Philo Mos I:158 f., cf. Josephus, Antiq. III:96; Pseudo-Philo Antiq. Bibl. 12:1 and Rev. 4:1. (4) Against this background it is significant that the same kind of polemic as in John 3, 13 is found in the old tannaitic midrash Mek on Exod 19:20: (5)

Mek Exod 19:20 — לא עלה משה ואליהו למעלה
ולא ירד הכבוד למטה

οὐκ ἀνέβη Μωϋσῆς καὶ Ἠλίας ἄνω
καὶ οὐ κατέβη ἡ δόξα κάτω (6)

John 3:13 — καὶ οὐδεὶς ἀναβέβηκεν εἰς τὸν οὐρανὸν
εἰ μὴ ὁ ἐκ τοῦ οὐρανοῦ καταβάς...

It is important to note that Moses' ascent in Mek on Exod 19:20 is linked with that of Elijah. John 3:13, therefore, probably serves as a polemic both against the idea of Moses' ascent and against any similar claims of or for other human beings. John 3:13 may thus imply a polemic against persons in the Johannine environment who maintained that they were visionaries like Moses. Philo gives an example of this kind of <u>imitatio Mosis</u>, in Mos I:158: "For he was named god and king of the whole nation, and entered, we are told, into the darkness where God was, that is, into the unseen, invisible, incorporeal and archetypal essence of existing things. Thus he beheld what is hidden from the sight of mortal nature, and, in himself and his life displayed for all to see, he has set before us, like som well-wrought picture, a piece of work beautiful and godlike, a model for those who are willing to copy it." (7)

In one respect, however, Mek on Exod 19: 20 goes beyond John 3:13, since it even rejects the notion of the descent of the heavenly doxa, while John makes one exception, "except he who has descended from heaven, the Son of Man".

As an isolated statement, John 3:13 might have been interpreted as referring to Moses as the exception: He both ascended (Exod 19:20.23; 24:1.2.9.13.18; 34:2.3.4) and descended (Exod 19:14.21.24-25; 34:29). This interpretation could receive some support from Jewish exegesis where Moses takes the role of an angel, on the basis of Gen 28:12, and ascends and descends as intermediary between God and man. This interpretation is as early as i Philo, Somn I:140-143, as well as it occurs in a different version in the much later Gen Rab 68:12. (8) In John, however, the exclusive claim is made for Jesus, as a polemic against any similar claims made for Moses. (9)

Against this background the question has to be raised: Are there further features from the revelation on Mt Sinai which are woven together with other Old Testament features into the Gospel material of John 3:3 ff? (10) The following theses will be discussed and substantiated in the present study:

1. Against the background of the polemic against the idea of man's (Moses', etc.) ascent to heaven, John claims that the historical Jesus represents the reverse phenomenon of descent from heaven and subsequent exaltation. Thus the background ideas move from Moses' ascent (and descent) to God's descent on Mt Sinai (and return). The latter thought model (God's descent and return) is then applied to Jesus.

2. Several observations in John imply that a pre-existent ascent has taken place before the descent and the exaltation: (1) this pre-existent ascent means installation "in office" and is followed by (2) the descent to execute a charge and then (3) the return as exaltation and re-enthronement in glory. Here also Sinaitic ideas influence John.

3. The concept of the Son of Man, which was already a part of the received Gospel tradition, caused the ideas of the coming to God of the one like a son of man (from Dan 7:13) and His exaltation (from Is 52:13) to be associated respectively with the idea of the ascent at Mt Sinai and the story of the brazen serpent in the desert.

4. Drawing on the assumption that Moses and Israel experienced rebirth at Mt Sinai, Jesus states that birth from above is a condition for entry into heaven. This birth from above does not take place by man's ascent into heaven. It is brought about by the descent and exaltation of the divine and royal Son of Man.

Having stated the hypothesis, we return to the discussion of the ascent/descent. Although the notion of ascent has quite frequently been explained on the basis of Jewish ideas, the notion of descent has been found hard to understand against this same background. Thus Schulz thinks that the descent expresses a gnostic motif. Meeks also finds it hard to avoid such a conclusion. (11) It is surprising, however, that Meeks, who stresses Sinaitic ideas, does not give an extensive discussion of the idea of descent against the background of the revelation at Mt Sinai.

Since the ascent in John 3:13-14 is denied to Moses, but applied to Jesus, the point of departure is not that of a human, but of a divine being. Thus, the concept of the Sinaitic ascent and descent is turned upside down, and is changed into the idea of descent and ascent.

A corresponding movement of thought is even applied to Moses by Philo in Sacr 8-10. Here the idea that Moses drew near to God at Mt Sinai, Deut 5:(27).31 ("stand here with Me"), changes into the idea that God has lent Moses to the earthly things and appointed him as a god, putting all the region of the body and its dominating mind in subjection to him (Exod 7:1 "god to Pharaoh"). The reason for this shift is the idea that Moses, as a god, represents God himself. Therefore the movement goes from God and "down" to earth and back (Sacr 10, with reference to Deut 34:6). (12)

It is important that in Eph 4:7 ff. similar kind of expository comments are made, probably also with the thought passing from Moses' ascent and descent, to Christ's descent and ascent, which correspond to the Son of Man's descent and exaltation in John 3:13-14. The quotation is taken from Ps 68(67):19. (13)

> Ἑνὶ δὲ ἑκάστῳ ἡμῶν ἐδόθη ἡ χάρις κατὰ τὸ μέτρον τῆς δωρεᾶς τοῦ χριστοῦ. διὸ λέγει· ἀναβὰς εἰς ὕψος ἠχμαλώτευσεν αἰχμαλωσίαν, ἔδωκεν δόματα τοῖς ἀνθρώποις (Ps 68(67):19) τὸ δὲ ἀνέβη τί ἐστιν εἰ μὴ ὅτι καὶ κατέβη εἰς τὰ κατώτερα μέρη τῆς γῆς; ὁ καταβὰς αὐτός ἐστιν καὶ ὁ ἀναβὰς ὑπεράνω πάντων τῶν οὐρανῶν, ἵνα πληρώσῃ τὰ πάντα καὶ αὐτὸς ἔδωκεν τοὺς μὲν ἀποστόλους...

(The words from Ps 68(67): 19 are underscored).

The most important variant is the reading of ἔδωκεν instead of TM לקחת LXX: ἔλαβες. This change is in agreement with the Targum, where the word is applied to Moses' ascent on Mt Sinai.

Thus the thought seems to pass from Moses' ascent and descent at the giving of the Law to Christ's descent (incarnation) and ascension at the resurrection. (14) As in John 3:13-14, the application of (Moses') ascent and descent to Jesus of Nazareth forced the thought to be turned upside down, since Jesus was a divine being on earth, and thus had God as his point of departure.

Against this background the two basic concepts are (1) man's ascent (and descent) and (2) God's descent (and ascent) with reference to the revelation in the Exodus events, especially the revelation at Mt Sinai. God's descent is mentioned in Exod 19:20; 34; 5, and the implicit idea of His subsequent return is explicitly stated in Exod Rab 42:5. In Sac 8-10, then, the idea of God's descent and return has been transferred to Moses, and in John 3:13-14 to Jesus (cf. Eph 4:7 ff).

The concept of descent in John 3:13 is expressed by the term καταβαίνειν , while the notion of the subsequent return is in v. 14 characterized as an exaltation, by the use of the verb ὑψοῦν :ὑψωθῆναι δεῖ τὸν υἱὸν τοῦ ἀνθρώπου . This phrase is an independent traditional expression, since it occurs in different contexts in John 8:28 and 12:34, cf. 12:32. The expression draws on the reference in Is 52, 13 to the exaltation of the servant, (15) here in John 3; 14 applied on the historical person Jesus.

Ascent, Descent and Return

The connection between John 3:13 and 14 and between the ideas of ascent and descent within v. 13 needs further discussion. Verse 13 is a shortened exception clause. In such cases the parts, which are the same as in the main clause, are omitted in the conditional clause. (16) This means that the completed formulation of the verse should be:

καὶ οὐδεὶς ἀναβέβηκεν εἰς τὸν οὐρανὸν
εἰ μὴ ὁ ἐκ τοῦ οὐρανοῦ καταβάς, ὁ υἱὸς τοῦ ἀνθρώπου,
(ἀναβέβηκεν εἰς τὸν οὐρανόν)

The perfect tense, ἀναβέβηκεν , is puzzling since it seems to imply that the Son of Man (=Jesus) had at the moment of speaking already ascended into heaven. Several scholars think that the ascent here refers to Jesus' death and resurrection, seen from the standpoint of the church. (17) The situation of the church is reflected and included in John, but this interpretation seems nevertheless too forced, and makes it difficult to understand why the saying is rendered as a word from the mouth of Jesus.

It has been suggested therefore that the perfect tense here should be understood as expressing a timeless and general state of affairs. The meaning is then that whereas no one has ascended, <u>he</u> has come down. (18) In this case the words from the main clause (καὶ οὐδεὶς ἀναβέβηκεν εἰς τὸν οὐρανόν) are not to be repeated in the exception clause (εἰ μὴ... κτλ) to complete its meaning.

Against this interpretation it must be stated that the formal parallel in John 17:12 definitely speaks in favor of the usual supplements to be made also in the exception clause of 3; 13 by means of the verb from the main clause.

John 17:12 οὐδεὶς ἐξ αὐτῶν ἀπώλετο
εἰ μὴ ὁ υἱὸς τῆς ἀπωλείας..
(to be added: ἀπώλετο)

With regard to the perfect tense used in John 3:13, it is fortunate that this also occurs in the parallel in John 6:46, where the exception clause is complete: (19)

οὐχ ὅτι τὸν πατέρα ἑώρακέν τις
εἰ μὴ ὁ ὢν παρὰ τοῦ θεοῦ,

οὗτος ἑώρακεν τὸν πατέρα

Here the verbal phrase τὸν πατέρα ἑώρακεν is repeated in the exception clause, and the verbal form is perfect tense with the meaning of a completed action which is lasting in its effect. (20)

Thus, the parallels in John 6:46 and 17:12 show that the exception clause in 3:13 has the same verb as in the main clause, and that the perfect tense has the usual meaning of a completed action:

καὶ οὐδεὶς ἀναβέβηκεν εἰς τὸν οὐρανὸν
εἰ μὴ ὁ ἐκ τοῦ οὐρανοῦ καταβάς, ὁ υἱὸς τοῦ ἀνθρώπου,
(οὗτος ἀναβέβηκεν εἰς τὸν οὐρανόν)

The parallel statement in John 6:46 also suggests that the ascent of the Son of Man expressed in 3:13 refers to an event which is prior to the descent, and serves as its pre-condition: John 6:46 has the corresponding idea that the Son has seen the Father prior to being sent by him to mediate this vision to men.

What kind of "event" then does the ascent of the Son of Man in John 3:13 refer to? (21) Several observations in John show that a pre-existent installing in office is meant:

1) John 17:2 draws on ideas and terms from the passage about the Son of Man in Dan 7:13f and applies them to such a pre-existent installing of the Son: (22) John 17:2 ...ἔδωκας αὐτῷ ἐξουσίαν πάσης σαρκός .../Dan 7:14 LXX ...ἐδόθη αὐτῷ ἐξουσία, , καὶ πάντα τὰ ἔθνη... (23) This installing in office is then followed by the execution of the charge: "... to give eternal life to all whom thou hast given him" (17:2).

2) The central idea in John that Jesus is sent by the Father, implies the commissioning as an event prior to the incarnation. At several places John refers to such a commissioning: (24) "I came not of my own accord, but he sent me" (John 8:42); "For I have not spoken of my own authority; the Father who sent me has himself given me commandment what to say and what to speak" (John 12:49); "For he whom God has sent utters the words of God" (3:34); "My teaching is not mine, but his who sent me" (7:16), "... he who sent me is true, and I declare to the world what I have heard from him" (8:26); "... the word which you hear is not mine, but the Father's who sent me" (14:24). The transfer of the Father's property (i.e. the men who belonged to him) to

the Son, also points back to this commissioning: "... thine they were, and thou gavest them to me" (17:6). Moreover the ideas of commissioning and sending are followed by the concept of Jesus reporting back to the sender, John 13:3; 17:4 ff.

3) The concept of the glorification of the Son follows a line of thought which corresponds to the ideas of a) ascent (as the installing in office), b) descent (execution of the charge) and c) return (return to the position of the pre-existent enthronement). The points about glorification are: a) "... the glory which I had with thee before the world was made" (17:5); "... my glory which thou hast given me because thou didst love me before the creation of the world" (17:24) (25); b) "I glorified thee on earth, having accomplished the work which thou gavest me to do" (17:4); c) "... and now, Father, glorify thou me with the glory which I had with thee before the world was made" (17:5). Against this background the ascent of the Son of Man in 6:62 means his re-ascent to the place of office originally bestowed at the pre-existent ascent 3:13.

On this basis John 3:13 states that Moses at Mt Sinai and others did not ascend heaven to be installed in an office of glory, but Jesus, as the Son of Man had been installed in office before his descent (in the incarnation).

This interpretation raises the problem that the pre-existent Son of Man did not ascend from earth, as would be the case for Moses and the others. The first observation to be made is the fact that the point of departure for the ascent in 3:13 is not given. Since the word functions on two levels, that of human beings and that of a divine being, the ascent of human beings from earth to heaven is denied, while the ascent of the divine Son of Man is affirmed.

Secondly, within Hebrew-Jewish categories of thought, the concept of "ascent into heaven", can refer to a heavenly being, God, and His enthronement. In this case "heaven" or corresponding terms mean the place of the throne of God, and there is no need to think of earth as the point of departure for the ascent. The Old Testament references are

1 Sam 2:10f (26) LXX: κύριος ἀνέβη εἰς οὐρανούς
(TM: יהוה...עלו בשמים)
Ps 47:6 (27) עלה אלהים בתרועה
LXX 46:6: ἀνέβη ὁ θεὸς ἐν ἀλαλαγμῷ
Ps 68:19 (28) עליו: למרום

LXX 67:19 ἀνεβὴς (S ἀνέβη B ἀναβάς) εἰς ὕψος

These Old Testament passages offer support for the understanding that the idea of God's heavenly enthronement is in John 3:13 applied to the heavenly ascent of the Son of Man as an installing in office prior to his descent to carry out his charge. Further support for this interpretation is found in Num Rab 12:11, where God's ascent into heaven is followed by His descent on Mt Sinai: 'Who hath ascended up into heaven' (Prov 30:4) alludes to the Holy One, blessed by He, of whom it is written, 'God is gone up amidst shouting, etc,' (Ps 47:6). 'And descended' (Prov 30:4) bears on 'And the Lord descended upon Mount Sinai' (Exod 29:20)." (29)

These words about God's ascent in the Old Testament and in Jewish exegesis show that the "spatial" movement of ascent expresses a change in role and office and not a change in degree of divinity nor a change of a being's nature from an existence that is not divine into that of divinity. The pre-existent ascent of the divine Son of Man, correspondingly, means his commissioning, and does not conflict with the idea that the Logos was God and was with God in the beginning, John 1:1-2.

From this discussion, John 3:13 can be paraphrased in this way: No person, not even Moses on Mt Sinai, has ascended into heaven, except the heavenly being who descended to execute his office; by his ascent into heaven he was installed and empowered for his descent.

The Son of Man

John 3:14-15 offer a convenient starting point for a discussion of the phrase ὁ υἱὸς τοῦ ἀνθρώπου . The words ὑψωθῆναι δεῖ τὸν υἱὸν τοῦ ἀνθρώπου are an independent traditional expression, since they occur in different contexts in John 8:28 and 12:34, cf. 12:32.

It has been pointed out by several scholars that the expression draws on Is 52:13. (30) The word ὑψωθῆναι (John 3:14 and 12:34; ὑψώσητε in 8:28) is a key term in Is 52:13, ירום /LXX ὑψωθήσεται , and is in John 3:14 combined with the central phrase ὁ υἱὸς τοῦ ἀνθρώπου which renders a similar phrase in Dan 7:13, LXX: ὡς υἱὸς ἀνθρώπου . Since the exaltation in this way is understood from Dan 7:13f., it means installation in a royal office.

This interpretation receives support from rabbinic exegesis, although evidenced in written form at a later time. In Midr. Ps 2 § 9, where Ps 2:7 ("Thou art my son") is interpreted, Is 52:13 and Dan 7:13-14 are quoted together as parallel words. (31) This shows that the word "servant" in Is 52:13 and "one like a son of man" in Dan 7:13f were interchangeable, and the exaltation in Is 52:13 means enthronement. A corresponding Messianic interpretation of Is 52:13 is found in the targum, where "the servant" is defined as the Messiah. (32)

John 3:14 shows how the application of these elements from Is 52:13 and Dan 7:13-14 to the historical persons Jesus - whose death on the cross was central - caused the exaltation to be woven together with points about the brazen serpent, Num 21:9. This application to Jesus' death is made explicit in John 12:32-33 by the comment: "He said this to show by what death he was to die."

Thus John 3:14 is a paralles saying to the synoptic Son of Man sayings which refer to the passion. Even verbal agreements are found, since the words ...δεῖ τὸν υἱὸν τοῦ ἀνθρώπου in John 3:14 and 12:34 are also found in Mark 9:31 and Luke 9:22. (33) The Johannine saying, therefore, builds on elements from the Gospel tradition, elements which are elaborated upon by means of Old Testament ideas and exegesis. (34)

The use of the phrase "the Son of Man" in John 3:13 seems to be due to a fusion of ideas from the Sinaitic ascent and Dan 7:13-14. The Background of John 3:13 in Dan 7:13-14 is seen both in John's use of the terms ὁ υἱὸς τοῦ ἀνθρώπου and ὁ οὐρανός, and in the employment of words from Dan 7:14 in John 17:2, where the pre-existent installations in office is mentioned.

On the basis, it is probable that John 3:13 presupposes the idea in Dan 7:13 that the one like a son of man came, with/on the clouds of heaven to God's throne: "with (עם ,cf. LXX ἐπί , on) the clouds of heaven there came (אתה הוה , LXX ἤρχετο , Theod. ἐρχόμενος ἦν) one like a son of man, and he came (מטה , LXX παρῆν , Theod. ἔφθασε) to the Ancient of Days" (cf. Dan 7:9). (35)

The close agreements are seen when John 3:13 and 17:2 are given in a synopsis together with Dan 7:13-14 (verbal agreements are underscored):

	John:		Dan LXX:
3:13	... ἀναβέβηκεν εἰς τὸν οὐρανόν ὁ υἱὸς τοῦ ἀνθρώπου	7:13	ἐπὶ τῶν νεφελῶν τοῦ οὐρανοῦ ὡς υἱὸς ἀνθρώπου ἤρχετο
17:2	ἔδωκας αὐτῷ ἐξουσίαν πάσης σαρκός	7:14	ἐδόθη αὐτῷ ἐξουσία καὶ πάντα τὰ ἔθνη τῆς γῆς

The hypothesis that(ὁ υἱὸς τοῦ ἀνθρώπου) ἀναβέβηκεν (εἰς τὸν οὐρανόν) in John 3:13 is an expository rendering of אתה or מטה in Dan 7:13 is supported by the observation that in Exod 24:18 an equivalent Hebrew word "to come" (בוא) alternates with "ascend" (עלה) in describing Moses' ascent/coming to God on Mt Sinai.

Moreover, both elsewhere in the New Testament and in rabbinic exegesis ideas of the Son of Man's coming to God draw on Dan 7:13. See Acts 7:56, (36) 1 Thess 4:14 (37) and Midr Ps 21 § 5. (38)

It is thus probable that John 3:13 combines elements from Dan 7:13 and from Exod 19:20.23; 24:1.2.9.13; 34:2.3.4 in a way which corresponds to the fusion of elements from Dan 7:13 and Ps 110:1 in Acts 7:56. In a corresponding way John 3; 14 weaves together elements from Dan 7:13f, Is 52:13 and Num 21:9.

To the paraphrase of John 3:13-14 previously given (no person, not even Moses on Mt Sinai, has ascended into heaven) the following can be added: only he who descended from heaven to execute his office, the divine being, the Son of Man, has ascended to heaven for the installing in office prior to his descent. The subsequent return of the Son of Man to his prior place of glory (John 6:46; 17:5.24) must take place as an exaltation through the death on the cross, to mediate life to those who believe.

Birth from Above

In the present study John 3:13 has to a large extent been interpreted on the basis of ideas which are associated with revelation at Mt Sinai.

Is also the birth from above, John 3:3 ff, to be understood against the background of the Sinai happening?

There are exegetical traditions which give basis for an affirmative answer to this question. Thus, Philo says in Quaes Exod II:46 that Moses' Sinaitic ascent was a second birth, different from the first. Philo interprets Exod 24; 16 (39): "But the calling above (Greek fragment: ἀνάκλησις) of the prophet is a second birth (Greek fragment: δεύτερα γένεσις) better than the first. For the latter is mixed with body and had corruptible parents, while the former is an unmixed and simple soul of the sovereign, being changed from a productive to an unproductive form having no mother, but only a father, who is (the Father) of all. Wherefore, the 'calling above' or, as we have said, the divine birth, happened to come about for him in accordance with the ever-virginal nature of the hebdomad. For he 'is called on the seventh day', in this (respect) differing from the earth-born first moulded man, for the latter came into being from the earth and with a body, while the former (came) from ether and without a body. Wherefore the most appropriate number, six, was assigned to the earth-born man, while the one differently born (was assigned) the higher nature of the hebdomad."

There are several agreements between the Philonic passage and John 3:3 ff and 1:13 (40): a) the ascent at Mt Sinai is interpreted as birth (John 3:5.13); b) this birth is from above (John 3:3, etc; Philo: calling above; from ether); c) it is a birth with God as Father, without a mother (John 1:13); d) it is a second birth, different from the birth from a woman (John 3:3ff); e) there is some correspondence between John's distinction σάρξ - πνεῦμα and Philo's σῶμα - νοῦς . (41)

The question can be raised whether Philo's idea of second birth here depends entirely on Hellenistic ideas of rebirth such as those found in Hermetic teachings? (42) Even so, Philo gives evidence for the employment of such ideas within Judaism as early as the beginning of the first century, and John 3 might therefore have received them via Jewish traditions.

It is important to notice, however, that Moses' rebirth is identified with his experience at Mt Sinai. Why? The implication is that Philo draws on Jewish exegetical traditions which he develops further in his interpretation. This understanding is supported by the fact that the experience of the burning bush and the revelation at Sinai are interpreted as birth also in rabbinic traditions, as E. Stein and E. Sjøberg have shown. (43)

Cant Rab 8:2 reads:"I WOULD LEAD THEE; AND BRING THEE: I would lead Thee from the upper world to the lower. I WOULD BRING THEE INTO MY MOTHER'S HOUSE: this is Sinai. R. Berekiah said: Why is Sinai called MY MOTHER'S HOUSE? Because there Israel became like a new-born child..." (44)

Sjøberg points to these words of R. Berekiah and states that the Israelites at Mt Sinai came into a completely new situation. Their relationship to God was rebuilt upon a completely new foundation and their earlier existence had no value any more.

A totally new beginning had taken place. The connection between R. Berekiah's words and the text of Cant 8:2 makes it evident that the picture of a birth is meant here. (45)

Other parallels also exist, as Exod Rab 30;5, where it seems to be implied that Torah conceived Israel at Mt Sinai.

And E. Stein has drawn attention to Exod Rab 3:15 on Exod 4:12 and Tanchuma, ed Buber, Shemoth 18. According to this piece of tradition, God's relationship to Moses is compared with that of a mother who conceives and gives birth to a child, when God dedicated Moses and commissioned him to his high charge. The exegetical basis for characterizing God as Moses' second mother is the word והוריתיך in Exod 4:12. Instead of understanding the word as a form of ירה show, teach, it is read as a form of הרה , conceive, be pregnant, and interpreted from Exod 2:2 where this term is used: "The woman conceived..."

As the result of his divine birth Moses has from that time the right to speak in the name of God, as said in the subsequent words in Exod 4:12, "so that you may speak" (אשר הדבר). In the midrashic exposition, therefore, this verse does not deal with a physical healing of Moses' organ of speech. (46)

Although the dates of the written forms of Cant Rab 8; 2; Exod Rab 30;5; Exod Rab 3; 15 and Tanchuma, ed Buber, Shemoth 18 are late, these passages and Philo, Quaes Exod II:46 mutually illuminate each other: the rabbinic passages support the hypothesis that Philo relies on Jewish exegesis as a basis for his understanding of the Sinaitic ascent as rebirth, and Philo supports the hypothesis that the core of the rabbinic passages goes back to the beginning of the first century or earlier. (47)

Moreover, Philo's Jewish background is also seen in the fact that in Quaes Exod II:46, both kinds of birth (bodily and noetic) are interpreted as caused by God's activity. And to Philo, Moses' ascent of mind also encompassed his body. (48) Thus to Philo Moses has significance as a person in history as well as a symbol of the mind.

The conclusion is: There is basis for interpreting birth from above in John 1:13 and 3:3 ff against the background of Moses' and Israel's rebirth at the Sinai-event. This concept of rebirth has in John been combined with the word from the Gospel tradition about being like a child as a condition for entry into heaven. (49) This understanding of John 3:3 ff gives point to Jesus' rebuke of Nicodemus: "Are you the teacher of Israel, and yet you do not understand this?"

The main line of thinking in John 3:3-15 can thus be summed up in the following points:

1. Drawing on the tradition that Moses and Israel experienced rebirth at Mt Sinai, Jesus states that rebirth from above is a condition for entry/ascent into heaven.

2. Nicodemus is a literalist and misunderstands rebirth to mean physical rebirth, and he does not understand how spiritual birth can happen. (50)

3. Jesus rebukes Nicodemus: As the teacher of Israel he ought to know the real meaning for the revelation at Mt Sinai, John 3:10-12, cf. 5:37.

4. Jesus and the witnessing disciples ("we") (51) have the knowledge and the vision of the heavenly things, to which the revelation at Mt Sinai was a pointer, John 3:11-12.

5. The birth from above and the entry into the kingdom of God does not (as one might think) take place by means of man's ascent into heaven: No one, not even Moses, has ascended into heaven. No, the birth from above is brought about by the descent and exaltation of the kingly and divine Son of Man. (52) He was first installed in office and empowered in heaven, and descended to execute his office, and returned. Through faith in him (birth from above) men have eternal life (cf, the kingdom of God), John 3:13-15.

This interpretation of John 3:3-15 makes clear that various ideas from the revelation at Mt Sinai are presupposed and employed in the passage. Step by step the Evangelist develops the aspects, such as birth from above, ascent and enthronement, descent and execution of the charge. This view has the advantage that a coherent Jewish background is pictured rather than thinking of several very different background traditions, like those reflected in gnostic and hermetic ideas about regeneration and descent, and Jewish ideas about seeing and hearing, about the brazen serpent, etc. (53)

NOTES

1) Concerning Gen 22 as background for John 3,16, see N.A. Dahl, The Atonement - an adequate reward for the Akeda? (Ro 8:32), in E. Ellis and M. Wilcox (ed.) Neotestamentica et Semitica, (Edinburgh, 1969) 28.

2) See N.A. Dahl, The Johannine Church and History, 133; P. Borgen, Bread from Heaven 150-152; W.A. Meeks, The Prophet-King Sup NT, 14, (Leiden, 1967) 298-301.

3) See H. Odeberg, The Fourth Gospel, (Uppsala, 1929) 72-89; N.A. Dahl, "The Johannine Church and History" 141; P. Borgen, Bread from Heaven, 185, n. 2; W.A. Meeks, The Prophet-King, 141; cf. S. Schulz, Untersuchungen zur Menschensohnchristologie im Johannesevangelium. (Göttingen, 1957) 105.

4) Rabbinic examples of this exegesis are found in Num Rab 12:11, Midr Ps 24§5; 106§2.

5) In its original form Mekilta de Rabbi Ishmael is dated to the 2nd century A.D. in E. Schürer, The History of the Jewish People in the Age of Jesus Christ, New English Version by G. Vermes, F. Millar and M. Black, (Edinburgh, 1973) 90. Concerning the subject matter, cf. the debate whether Moses on Mt Sinai had been taken back to the divinity, according to Josephus, Antiq III:96.

6) Greek translation by A. Schlatter, Der Evangelist Johannes, 93f.

7) English translation in F.H. Colson (ed. trans.), PLCL, 6. (Cambridge, Mass. 1959) 357 and 359. Cf. Quaes Gen I:86.

8) N.A. Dahl, "The Johannine Church and History", 136, has suggested that the expression ὁ υἱὸς τοῦ ἀνθρώπου, ὁ ὢν ἐν τῷ οὐρανῷ, John 3:13 may be original and is to be interpreted together with John 1:51. Dahl writes: "...in the Haggadah, Genesis 28:12, like other visionary texts, is often combined with Daniel 7 and Ezekiel 1, the ascending and descending angels can be taken to refer to the wordly empires and to Israel. In this context appears also the notion of the heavenly image (or model) of Jacob, an idea which must have had its scriptural base in the "human form" seated above the throne (Ezek 1:26). Possibly, the Johannine idea of the Son of Man is also connected with this notion; this could explain the longer text in 3:13: 'the Son of Man who is in heaven' (cf. also 1:18b)."

9) In various Jewish writings exclusive claims are made for Moses, or for the whole of Israel, mostly by showing Moses' and/or Israel's superiority; see Mek on Exod 19:11 (the whole people at Mt Sinai), Pesikta R. Piska 50; Deut Rab 2:2; "Moses' Grösse", in A. Wünsche (trans.) Aus Israels Lehrhallen, 1 (Hildesheim, 1967) 122ff. (=Jellinek, Bet ha-Midrasch, 71ff.) Cf. that Moses is greater than David, because he, but not David, went up to heaven, Midr Ps 24 § 5. Cf. Num Rab 14:21.

10) The idea of light in John 3:19-21 also seems to reflect ideas associated with the giving of the Law at Mt Sinai. Cf. P. Borgen, Logos Was the True Light, NT 14, (1972), 125, especially n. 3, and above p.

11) S. Schulz, Menschensohn-Christologie, 105; W.A. Meeks, The Prophet - King, 297, cf. id., The Man from Heaven in Johannine Sectarianism, JBL 91, (1972) 44-72.

12) See especially E.R. Goodenough, By Light, Light, (New Haven, Conn, 1935) 199.224 ff. in disagreement with H. Leisegang's interpretation. See also W.A. Meeks, The Prophet - King, 104-105, who says that the passage is unique in Philo. B.L. Mack, Imitatio Mosis: Patterns of Cosmology and Soteriology in the Hellenistic Synagogue, in Studia Philonica, (1972) 51, note 81, shows that the notion of descent also occurs elsewhere in Philo, and Sacr 8-10 therefore is not a unique passage, as Meeks thought.

13) See J.St.J. Thackeray, The Relation of St. Paul to Contemporary Jewish Thought, (London, 1900) 182; R.Le Déaut, Pentecôte et tradition juive, in Assemblées du Seigneur 51 (1963) 32-33; id. Liturgie et Nouveau Testament, (Rome, 1965) 46; M. McNamara, The New Testament and the Palestinian Targum to the Pentateuch, (Rome, 1966) 78-81. For other translations which give evidence for the same change, see M. Barth, Ephesians (Anchor Bible), (Garden City N.Y., 1974) 475. The application of Ps 68:19 to Moses was common in rabbinic exegesis, see Str.-Bill. 3:596.

14) Cf. M. Barth, Ephesians, "he applied to Jesus Christ what had been understood to relate to Moses...". - The exposition of Ps 68(67):19 in Eph 4:7 ff. may also draw on Prov 30:4 (LXX) τίς ἀνέβη εἰς τὸν οὐρανὸν καὶ κατέβη ; See especially Eph 4:9-10.

15) C.H. Dodd, The Interpretation of the Fourth Gospel, 247; R. Schnackenburg, Der Menschensohn im Johannesevangelium, NTS 11 (1964-65) 130; G. Reim, Studien zum alttestamentlichen Hintergrund des Johannesevangeliums, (Cambridge, 1974) 174-176; cf. M. Black, The "Son of Man" Passion sayings in the Gospel Tradition, ZNW 60 (1969) 1-8; E.M. Sidebottom, The Christ of the Fourth Gospel, (London,1961) 81.

16) See K. Beyer, Semitische Syntax im Neuen Testament 1:1 (Göttingen, ^{2}1968) 101-134, especially p. 102: "Der voranstehende Hauptsatz nämlich verneinte zunächst einen Tatbestand gänzlich, darauf gab ein verneinter Konditionalsatz an, wo dieser Tatbestand doch gilt. In diesem Konditionalsatz wurden dann alle Satzteile ausgelassen, die mit denen des Hauptsatzes identisch waren." Concerning John 3:13 and similar New Testament examples, see ibid., 109-111.

17) C.K. Barrett, St. John, (London, 1958) ad loc; R.E. Brown, St. John I.XII, R. Schnackenburg, Das Johannesevangelium 1 (Freiburg, 1965) ad loc.

18) See B. Lindars, The Gospel of John, (London,1972) ad loc., cf. R. Bultmann, Johannes, 108, n. 3 with reference to

F. Blass and A. Debrunner, Grammatik des neutestamentlichen Griechisch, (Göttingen, 1943) § 344, cf. also E.M. Sidebottom, The Christ of the Fourth Gospel, 120, and the comments in C.F.D. Moule, The Individualism of the Fourth Gospel, NT 5 (1962) 176, n. 1, and E. Ruckstuhl, Die johanneische Menschensohnforschung 1957-1969, in Theologische Berichte 1, ed. J. Pfammatter and F. Furger, (Zürich, 1972) 209, n. 25.

19) See K. Beyer, Semitische Syntax, 104 n. 109, III n. 3.

20) See F. Blass and A. Debrunner, Grammatik, § 340.

21) Some scholars, such as F.H. Borsch and S. Schulz, think that the idea of ascent applies to the life of Jesus. Borsch (The Johannine Son of Man, The Son of Man in Myth and History, (London, 1967) applies it to Jesus' baptism: after his baptism Jesus was installed as Son of Man. According to Schulz (Menschensohnchristologie, 105 f.) the main point of the saying is the belief that even the earthly Jesus had already been exalted and installed as the Son of Man. Schulz points to 1 Enoch 70 f. as background material, but notes that there Enoch ascended and was exalted, and not the Son of Man. Some comments should be made on these interpretations by Borsch and Schulz: It seems far-fetched to interpret the ascent against the background of the enthronement of the king of Babel, and apply it to the baptism of Jesus, as Borsch does. (See E. Ruckstuhl, Theologische Berichte 1, 25 ff.) The word also seems to refer to a specific ascent of the Son of Man, and Schulz' view that it refers to the earthly Jesus as already the exalted Son of Man, is, therefore, too general. Moreover, John 6:46 speaks against 3:13 referring to the life of Jesus.

22) Cf. C.K. Barrett, St. John, 418: "The aorist may refer to a special empowering for the earthly ministry of the incarnate Son, or to a pre-temporal act proper to the constitution of the Godhead; the Son receives authority from the Father as fons divinitatis." Barrett prefers the former view.

23) Cf. B. Lindars, John, 518.

24) P. Borgen, "God's agent in the Fourth Gospel." 136-148.

25) See R.E. Brown, The Gospel according to John, XIII-XXI, (Garden City N.Y., 1970) 772: "The love of the Father for the Son from before creation is the basis of the glory which the Son possessed before creation (XVII5). This love is also the basis of the earthly mission of Jesus (III 35)."

26) See A. Schlatter, Johannes, 93. Cf. G. Kittel, TWNT, 1, 518.

27) The original setting of the psalm is the cultic worship in the temple. God's ascent to Mt Zion is at the same time His ascent into heaven. See H.-J. Kraus, Psalmen 1, (Neukirchen, [2]1961) 351.

28) *Ibid.*, 474: "In 18-19 wird der 'Aufzug' Jahwes auf den 'höchsten Berg' der mit dem himmlischen Sitz identisch ist, geschilder." Cf. Eph 4:8 ff., where εἰς ὕψος is interpreted as ὑπεράνω πάντων τῶν οὐρανῶν.

29) In Num Rab 12:11 Prov 30:4 is applied to Moses and Elias as well. Cf. that Eph 4:9 may allude to Prov 30:4 in the exposition of Ps 68(67):19 cited in Eph 4:8. See note 14.

30) C.H. Dodd, *The Interpretation of the Fourth Gospel*, 247; R. Schnackenburg, *NTS* 11 (1964-65) 130; G. Reim, *Studien*, 174-176.

31) See S. Buber (ed.) *Midrasch Tehillim*, (New York, 1947 (reprint)) *ad loc*.

32) See John F. Stenning (ed. trans.), *The Targum of Isaiah*, (Oxford, 1949) *ad loc*.

33) See R.E. Brown, *John* I-XII, *ad loc*.

34) The term ὑψοῦν was used in the Christian preaching of Jesus' ascension, as can be seen from Acts 2:33; 5:31; Phil 2:9. This usage may also have influenced the Johannine wording. See S.S. Smalley, *The Johannine Son of Man Sayings, NTS* 15 (1968-69) 291.

35) See L. Hartman, *Prophecy Interpreted*, (Lund, 1966) 186.

36) See N. Perrin, *Rediscovering the Teaching of Jesus* (London, 1967) 177.

37) See L. Hartman, *Prophecy*, 186 f.

38) See N. Perrin, *Rediscovering*, 172.

39) W.A. Meeks, *Moses as God and King*, in *Religions in Antiquity*, ed. J. Neusner, (Leiden, 1968) 354-371, translates the shorter Greek fragment in this way: "But the calling above of the prophet is a second birth better than the former. He was called above on the seventh day, by this differing from the first-formed man, because the latter was composed of earth and with a body, while the former is without a body. Therefore the appropriate number six was assigned to the earthborn, while to the other (was assigned) the most sacred nature of the hebdomad."

40) See P. Borgen, *God's Agent in the Fourth Gospel*, 146; M. De Jonge, "*Nicodemus and Jesus: Some Observations on Misunderstanding and Understanding in the Fourth Gospel*" *BJRL*, 53 (1971), 345.

41) John sees man as a totality, while Philo has a dichotomic anthropology. Philo, however, keeps the Jewish understanding that both body and mind are created, and Moses' ascent included both, as can be seen from Vita Mos II:69-70. See also P. Borgen, *Bread from Heaven*, 182, cf. 118-212.

42) See Corpus Hermeticum XIII, περὶ παλιγγενεσίας. See also R. Bultmann, *Johannes*, 95, n. 5, concerning gnostic ideas, etc.

43) E. Stein, *Der Begriff der Palingenesie im Talmudischen Schrifttum* in *MGWJ* 83, N.F. 47 (1939) 194-205, and E. Sjøberg, *Wiedergeburt und Neuschöpfung im palästinischen Judentum* in *ST* 4 (1951) 44-85.

44) See H. Freedman and M. Simon (trans.), *Midrash Rabba*, 9, *Songs of Songs*, (London, 1961) 303.

45) E. Sjøberg, in *ST* 4 (1951) 51-42.

46) E. Stein, *Der Begriff*, 196-197, in disagreement with the understanding expressed in Strack-Billerbeck, II, 421, and E. Sjøberg, in *ST*, 4 (1957), 60-61, who think in terms of the physical improvement of Moses' speaking ability.

47) The conclusion is also strengthened by parallel traditions about Noah's new birth/new creation in Quaes, Gen II:56, Vita Mos II:65 and Tanchuma, ed. Buber, Noah 12, on Gen 8,1.

48) See for example Vita Mos II:70.

49) See W.A. Meeks, *JBL* 91 (1972), 52-53, especially nn. 33 and 34 about John's mystical interpretation of the notion of entry into heaven. Cf. Wisd 10:10.

50) Concerning Nicodemus' misunderstanding, see H. Leroy, *Rätsel und Missverständnis: Ein Betrag zur Formgeschichte des Johannesevangeliums*, (Bonn, 1968), esp. 124-136; M. De. Jonge. *BJRL* 53 (1971), 348. Concerning the concepts of water and spirit, John 3:5-8, Ezek 36:25-27 seems to give the Biblical foundation. There may also be an allusion to the rebirth brought about by the creative spirit of Gen 1:2 in the form of the wind/spirit experienced by Noah at the end of the Deluge, Tanchuma, ed. Buber, Noah 12, on Gen 8:1. See E. Stein, *Der Begriff*, 200-201.

51) For the discussion of plural, "we", in Jn 3,11, see C.K. Barrett, *St. John, ad loc.*

52) So also the conception and birth of Israel in Cant Rab 8,2, which seemed to be brought about by God's descent on Mt Sinai. W.A. Meeks, *The Prophet - King*, 298, and *JBL*, 91 (1972), 53 incorrectly thinks that Jesus himself, as the Son of Man, is the one born from above.

53) Cf. for example the complex background suggested by C.K. Barrett, *St. John, ad loc*.

CHAPTER SIX
ON THE MIDRASHIC CHARACTER OF JOHN 6

Philological Discussion of Vocalization

For the understanding of the discourse in John 6, it is significant to realize that in a midrashic manner the quotation from the Old Testament cited in v. 31, "He gave them bread from heaven to eat", is obviously paraphrased throughout vv. 32-58, as can be seen from the repeated words: (1)

v. 31[b], (the Old Testament quotation) ἄρτον ἐκ τοῦ οὐρανοῦ ἔδωκεν αὐτοῖς φαγεῖν, v.32, δέδωκεν (ὑμῖν) τὸν ἄρτον ἐκ τοῦ οὐρανοῦ - δίδωσιν (ὑμῖν) τὸν ἄρτον ἐκ τοῦ οὐρανοῦ. v.33, ὁ - ἄρτος - ἐκ τοῦ οὐρανοῦ v.34, δὸς - τὸν ἄρτον v.35, ὁ ἄρτος v.36 (ὑμῖν) v.38, (ἀπὸ) τοῦ οὐρανοῦ v.41, ὁ ἄρτος- ἐκ τοῦ οὐρανοῦ v.42, ἐκ τοῦ οὐρανοῦ v.48, ὁ ἄρτος v.49, ἔφαγον v.50, ὁ ἄρτος - ἐκ τοῦ οὐρανοῦ - φάγῃ v.51, ὁ ἄρτος - ἐκ τοῦ οὐρανοῦ - φάγῃ - τοῦ ἄρτου - ὁ ἄρτος - δώσω v.52, (ἡμῖν) δοῦναι - φαγεῖν v.53, φάγητε v.58, ὁ ἄρτος - ἐξ οὐρανοῦ - ἔφαγον - τὸν ἄρτον.

The systematic structure of this paraphrasing method of Old Testament exegesis becomes evident from the fact that the quotation's final word, φαγεῖν (v. 31[b]), does not occur in vv. 32 -48. In v. 49, however, it is introduced into the exposition, and in the remaining part of the discourse this term has the central position. (2)

Against this background the question arises: Can also other midrashic features be discerned in John 6:31-58? The answer is clearly, "Yes".

The first illustration of a midrashic method and structure is found in John 6:32-33, which is an exposition of the Old Testament quotation cited in v. 31[b]. This exposition is given by a pattern of contrast (v. 32 οὐ - ἀλλ') followed by a sentence introduced by "for" (γάρ, v. 33).

John 6:31-52:

"He gave them bread from heaven to eat".
Jesus then said to them,
Truly, truly, I say to you,
it was not (οὐ) Moses who gave you the bread from heaven;
but (ἀλλ') my Father gives you the true bread from heaven.
For (γὰρ) the bread of God is that which comes down from
heaven and gives life to the world.

A corresponding contrast in the Palestinian midrash gives a philological correction of the Old Testament text, using the formula אל הקרי-אלא (do not read - but -) or similar formulas.(3) Philo uses also this contrast when correcting in the text.

Two examples of correction are Mekilta on Exod. 16:15 and Philo, Quod det 47-48. (As in John, the Old Testament quotations and the words from them in the exposition are underscored). Both places the pattern of contrast is followed by an added clarifying statement.

Mek. on Exod. 16:15: (4)

"Man did eat the bread of strong horses" (Ps 78:25)
Do not read (אל הקרי) "of strong horses" (אבירים).
but (אלא) "of the limbs" (איברים),
that is, bread that is absorbed by the limbs.

Philo, Quod det 47-48: (5)

"Cain rose up against Abel his brother and slew him (αυτον)" (Gen. 4:8)
It must be read in this way (ὥσθ οὕτως ἀναγνωστέον),
"Cain rose up and slew himself (ἑαυτόν)",
not (ἀλλ' οὐχ) someone else.
And this is just what we should expect to befall him. For the soul that has extirpated from itself (αὑτῆς) the principle of the love of virtue and the love of God, has died to the life of virtue.

The exegetical contrast in John 6:31-33 is unquestionably the same as this pattern in the Palestinian midrash and Philo, as the agreements between them prove: 1) In all three cases the Old Testament quotation is followed by an exegetical contrast using the terms אל - אלא (Mekilta), ἀλλ' οὐχ (Philo) and οὐ - ἀλλ' (John). 2) To this contrast an explicative statement can be added, as is done in these examples from Palestinian midrash, Philo, and John 6:33. 3) The determining agreement is, however, that John 6:32 gives a different reading of the Old Testament quotation cited in v. 31b, in accordance with this midrashic method of correcting the Hebrew text.

This third point becomes clear as soon as the verbs in John 6:31-32 are translated back into Hebrew:

v. 31[b], "He gave (ἔδωκεν/ נתן) them bread from heaven to eat".
v. 32, - Truly, truly, I say to you,
not - gave (δέδωκεν(ἔδωκεν) נתן
but - gives (δίδωσιν/ נוֹתֵן

Thus v. 32 shows that the understanding of the Old Testament quotation in v. 31[b] is not based upon the vocalization for perfect tense, נָתַן but upon the vocalization for the participle, נוֹתֵן which in the Greek of v. 32 is rendered by the present tense. This participle may also be rendered in the future tense, as ist supposed in v. 51, δώσω.

This philological exegesis is not an isolated phenomenon in John. Burney and Dahl have shown that John's rendering of Is 6:10 in John 12:40 is based upon a vocalization of the Hebrew text different from that of MT.(6) And it is commonly accepted by scholars since Burney and Odeberg that Gen 28:12 is interpreted in John 1:51 on the basis of Rabbinic exegesis of בו in the Hebrew text. (7)

Exegetical Debate

John 6:41-48 follows a usual pattern of exegetical debate in the Palestinian midrash and in Philo.

John 6:41-48:

(2) v. 41: The Jews then murmured at him, because he said (εἶπεν),
"I am the bread which came down from heaven".

(3) v. 42: They said (καὶ ἔλεγον),
"Is not this (οὐχ οὗτός ἐστιν) Jesus, the Son of Joseph, whose father and mother we know?

(4) How does he now say (πῶς νῦν λέγει ὅτι)
'I have come down from heaven?'"

(5) v. 43: Jesus answered them (ἀπεκρίθη Ἰησοῦς καὶ εἶπεν αὐτοῖς),
"Do not murmur among yourselves.
v. 44: No one can come to me unless the Father who sent me draws him; and I will raise him up at the last day.
v. 45: It is written in the prophets,
'And they shall all be taught by God.'
Every one who has heard and learned from the Father comes to me.
v. 46: Not that any one has seen the Father
except him who is from God; he has seen the Father.
v. 47: Truly, truly, I say to you,
he who believes has eternal life.
v. 48: I am the bread of life".

Mek on Exod 12:2 provides a typical example of such debate. As in the citation of John 6:41-48 the corresponding words in points 2, 4 and 5 are underscored.

Mek on Exod 12:2:

(1) "This new moon shall be unto you" (Exod 12:2)

(3) R. Simon the son of Yohai says (רני שמעון בן יוחאי אומר
Is it not a fact that (והלא) all the words which He spoke to Moses He spoke only in the daytime;

(2) the <u>new moon</u>, of course, He <u>showed him at nighttime</u>.

(4) How then (כיצד) could He, while speaking with him at daytime, <u>show him the new moon, at nighttime</u>?

(5) R. Eliezer says (רבי אליעזר אומר)
He spoke with him at daytime near <u>nightfall</u>,
and then <u>showed him the new moon right after nightfall</u>.

Gen 17:16 is interpreted in Philo, De mutatione nominum 141a. 142b-144.

Philo, Mut 141a, 142b-144: (8)

(1) 141a: So much for the phrase "I will give to thee".
We must now explain "from her" (Gen 17:16)

(2) 142b: There is a third class (τρίτοι δέ εἰσιν) who says (λέγοντες) that virtue is <u>the mother</u> of any good that has come into being, receiving the seeds of that being from nothing that is mortal.

(3) 143: Some ask, however, whether (πρὸς δὲ τοὺς ζητοῦντας, εἰ) the barren can bear children, since the oracles (οἱ χρησμοὶ) earlier describe Sarah as barren,

(4) and now admit that (νῦν ὅτι-ὁμολογοῦσι) she will become <u>a mother</u>.

(5) Our answer to this must be that (λεκτέον ἐκεῖνο,ὅτι)
it is not in the nature of a barren woman to bear, any more than of the blind to see or of the deaf to hear.
But as for the soul which is sterilized to wickedness and unfruitful of the endless host of passions and vices, scarce any prosper in childbirth as she.
For she bears offspring worthy of love, even the number seven according to the hymn of Hannah, that is. grace, who says, "The barren hath borne seven, but she that is much in children hath languished" (1. Sam 2:5).
144: She applies the word "much" to the mind which is a medley of mixed and confused thoughts, which, because of the multitude of riots and turmoils that surround it, brings forth evils past all remedy.
But the word "barren" she applies to the mind which refuses to accept any mortal sowing as fruitful, the mind which makes away with and brings to abortion all the intimacies and the matings of the wicked,

> but holds fast to the "seventh" and the supreme peace which it gives. This peace she would fain bear in her womb and be called its mother.

These three passages has the same exegetical structure, which consists of the following five points: Point (1) has a quotation from the Old Testament. In the Johannine example, as we have seen, the quotation is cited in John $6:31^{b}$. Point (2) gives the interpretation of the quotation. In John 6:41 this interpretation paraphrases words from the Old Testament quotation. In this way it also combines elements from the exposition in John 6:35 and 38. In Mek on Exod 12:2 only one word from the Old Testament quotation is paraphrased, "the new moon" (החדש). No word from the Old Testament quotation, however, is paraphrased in Mut 142b, but the central term "mother" clearly refers to the phrase "from her" in the quotation cited in 141a.

Point (3), then, introduces the objection against the interpretation. In Mek on Exod 12:2 this point precedes point (2). Point (4) refers to and repeats the interpretation in point (2), which has been questioned. In all three examples this repetition is very free and fragmentary.

Finally, point (5) gives the answer to the objection and the solution of the problem. In all three cases the conclusion of this point refers back to point (2), the interpretation, by paraphrasing parts of it. In John 6:41-48, the conclusion (vv. 47-48) also refers back to the exposition in v. 35, indicating that this pattern of exegetical debate has hardly had an independent existence, but is, rather, an integral part of the larger discourse.

The exegetical and stylistic terminology in these passages show close similarities, as might be expected within the same structure:

The passage	John $6:31^{b}$. 41-48	Mek on Exod 12:2	Mut 141^{a}.142b-144
1	Old Testament quotation	Old Testament quotation	Old Testament quotation
2	εἶπεν	רבי שמעון בן יוחאי אומר	τρίτοι δέ εἰσιν οἱ - λέγοντες
3	καὶ ἔλεγον οὐχ οὗτός ἐστιν	והלא	πρὸς δὲ τοὺς ζητοῦντας, εἰ
4	πῶς νῦν λέγει ὅτι	כיצד	οἱ χρησμοὶ νῦν ὅτι - ὁμολογοῦσι
5	ἀπεκρίθη Ἰησοῦς καὶ εἶπεν αὐτοῖς	רבי אליעזר אומר	λεκτέον ἐκεῖνο, ὅτι

This pattern occurs - with slight variations - elsewhere in the Palestinian midrash and in Philo. (9) No further discussion, however, is necesary to establish the fact that John 6:41-48 utilizes this midrashic structure of debate, which also exists in Palestinian midrash and in Philo.

Some Details

Much attention has been paid to the saying introduced by ἐγώ εἰμι, v. 35[a] (10), but as yet it has not been related to John's midrashic treatment of the Old Testament. The significance of this becomes evident as the parallel statements in vv. 41 and 51 are compared with the one in v. 35[a] and the identical parallel in v. 48: (For convenience the words from the Old Testament quotation in v. 31[b] are underscored).

vv. 35, 48: ἐγώ εἰμι ὁ ἄρτος τῆς ζωῆς

v. 41: ἐγώ εἰμι ὁ ἄρτος ὁ καταβὰς ἐκ τοῦ οὐρανοῦ

v. 51: ἐγώ εἰμι ὁ ἄρτος ὁ ζῶν ὁ ἐκ τοῦ οὐρανοῦ καταβάς.

Thus it is obvious that the phrase "Ego eimi" is a formula to be used when a word from the Old Testament shall be identified with a person or a figure in first person singular.

The most obvious parallel in John is the word of the Baptist in 1:23, who identifies Is 40:3 with himself: ἐγὼ φωνὴ βοῶντος ἐν τῇ ἐρήμῳ, κτλ. ("I am the voice of one crying in the wilderness, etc."). (11)

An objection could be raised against the use of John 1:23 as a parallel. Since it lacks the copula, εἰμι, the fuller formula of ἐγώ εἰμι may seem to be something other than a formula of identifying Old Testament words with a person. The use of the equivalent formula אנא הוא in Lam Rab 1; 16 § 45 to the Lam. 1; 16 serves as a warning against stressing this point. There it is told that the Emperor Trajan came to kill the Jews at the feast of Hanukkah: (12) "On his arrival he found the Jews occupied with this verse":

"The Lord will bring a nation against thee from far, from the end of the earth as the vulture (הנשר) swoopeth down" (Deut 28:49)
He said to them:
"I am the vulture (אנא הוא נשרא)
who planned to come in ten days,
but the wind brought me in five".

Although the date of this story is uncertain, it exemplifies the phrase "Ego eimi" as a midrashic formula of identifying Old Testament words with a person in first person singular, a formula which can thus be used to refer to John the Baptist and Trajan as well as to Jesus Christ.

It would lead us to far afield to discuss all the occurences of "Ego eimi" in John from this point of view. In other contexts it may have a different background. This discussion suffices, however, to show that from the viewpoint of form the phrase "Ego eimi" in John 6:35; 41; 48; 51 is a midrashic formula by which the words of "bread, etc." from the Old Testament quotation cited in v. 31 b can be identified with Jesus in the first person singular.

Finally a detail in John 6:36 must be considered. At first this verse, Ἀλλ' εἶπον ὑμῖν ὅτι καὶ ἑωράκατε (με) καὶ οὐ πιστεύετε, seems to refer to another word which is now repeated here. Scholars have had difficulties, however, in finding the word to which it refers. (13)

New light is thrown upon this problem as soon as it becomes apparent that v. 36 also paraphrases the Old Testament quotation cited in v. 31b. In v. 32 Jesus gives the authoritative meaning of this quotation when he renders "them" (αὐτοῖς) in v. 31b as "you" (ὑμῖν). Thus v. 36 refers back to this interpretation by Jesus in v. 32 and repeats "you" (ὑμῖν). This reference is of the same kind as those in John 10:36 and 1:15:

John 6:36 Ἀλλ' εἶπον "ὑμῖν" ὅτι κτλ.
10:36 εἶπον "υἱὸς τοῦ θεοῦ εἰμι"
1:15 εἶπον "ὁ ὀπίσω μου κτλ."

Thus there is no ὅτι <u>recitativum</u> in John 6:36, but a ὅτι which introduces a motivating causal proposition. And the verse is to be translated in this way: "But I said 'you', because you have seen me and yet do not believe".

Again Philo's exegesis offers a parallel: his interpretation of Gen 2:6 in Leg all I:28. The words from the Old Testament quotation are underscored.

Leg all I:28:

"<u>And a spring</u> (πηγή) <u>went up out of the earth</u> (ἐκ τῆς γῆς) <u>and watered all the face</u> (τὸ πρόσωπον) <u>of the earth</u>" (Gen 2:6). He calls (εἴρηκε) the mind "<u>a spring of the earth</u>" (γῆς πηγήν), and the senses its "<u>face</u>" (πρόσωπον) because (ὅτι) Nature - assigned this place to them -, etc.

Here, as in John 6:36, the exposition refers to (and repeats) words from the Old Testament quotation, and a causal proposition introduced with ὅτι is added as a motivation.

These observations from the discourse in John 6 show that the examination of its midrashic elements is fruitful. This midrashic character also goes beyond the examples outlined above. It is, furthermore, obvious that this understanding of the discourse bears upon the whole structure of John 6:31-58 and its use of traditions and sources.

NOTES

1) For my initial study on this subject, see P. Borgen, "The Unity of the Discourse in John 6", ZNW, 50 (1959), 277f., also published in 'Logos Was the True Light' and other Essays on the Gospel of John, (Trondheim, 1983).

2) In connection with the much discussed problem whether vv. 51b-58 is an interpolation, it is significant to notice that also v. 52 clearly paraphrases words from the Old Testament quotation cited in v. 31b:

v. 31b: ἔδωκεν αὐτοῖς φαγεῖν
v. 52: (ἡμῖν) δοῦναι - φαγεῖν.

This observation among others supports the understanding that vv. 51b-58 is an integral part of the discourse.

3) A. Rosenzweig, "Die Al-tiqri-Deutungen. Ein Beitrag zur talmudischen Schriftdeutung", Festschrift zu I. Levy's siebzigsten Geburtstag, (Breslau, 1911), 204-253; W. Bacher, Die exegetische Terminologie der jüdischen Traditionsliteratur 1: Die Bibelexegetische Terminologie der Tannaiten (Leipzig, 1899) 175-177.

4) Quotations from Mekilta are taken from J.Z. Lauterbach (ed. and trans.), Mekilta de-Rabbi Ishmael, 1-3, (Philadelphia, 1949). Slight modifications are made in the translation.

5) Quotations from Philo are taken from F.H. Colson and G.H. Whitaker (ed. and trans.) PLCL, 1-10 (London, 1929-41). C. Siegfried, Philo von Alexandria als Ausleger des alten Testaments, (Jena, 1875 repr.) 176, has observed that Philo at this place uses the method of אל תקרי

6) C.F. Burney, The Aramaic origin of the Fourth Gospel, Oxford, 1912), 120-21; N.A. Dahl, "Kristus, jödene og verden etter Johannesevangeliet", NTT, 60 (1959), 193.

7) C.F. Burney, The Aramaic origin, 115; H. Odeberg, The Fourth Gospel, (Uppsala, 1929), 35.

8) The English translation in F.H. Colsen and G.H. Whitaker (ed. and trans.), PLCL, 5, 215, is altered to point out the midrashic pattern which Philo is using.

9) See Mek. on Exod. 12:1; 15:5, etc.; Philo, Leg all I:31a. 33b. 42, etc.

10) See especially E. Schweizer, EGO EIMI, FRLANT, 56, 38, (Göttingen, 1939); R. Bultmann, Johannes; 167, n. 2; S. Schulz, Komposition, 70-131.

11) Cf. a similar use of the "Ego eimi"-formula in Rev. 2:23: ἐγώ εἰμι ὁ ἐρευνῶν νεφροὺς καὶ καρδίας, probably interpreting Ps 7:10, and also in Philo, Somn II:222: ἐγὼ γὰρ εἰμι ὁ ἐξαγαγὼν ἐκ πέτρας ἀκροτόμου πηγὴν ὕδατος interpreting Deut 8:15.

12) Text in מדרש רבה על המשה חומשי הורה וחמש מגילות, 5 (Jerusalem, 1949). Translation in H. Freedman and M. Simon (ed.), Midrash Rabbah, 7 (London 1939).

13) It is generally regarded as an allusion to John 6:26. See W. Bauer, Das Johannesevangelium, HNT, 6, 2nd ed., (Tübingen, 1925) 93; C.K. Barrett, St. John, 243; R. Bultmann, Johannes, 173, n. 4.

CHAPTER SEVEN
BREAD FROM HEAVEN
ASPECTS OF DEBATES ON EXPOSITORY METHOD AND FORM

Homiletic style

In the monograph Bread from Heaven, I attempted to show that the Discourse on Bread (John 6:31-58) is an exposition of the Old Testament. This exposition is characterized by midrashic features with parallels found in Philo and in Palestinian midrashim. Among such features is the systematic paraphrase of words from Old Testament quotations interwoven with fragments from haggadic traditions. This understanding of the midrashic character of John 6:31-58 has received broad acceptance, as can be seen from commentaries on The Gospel of John written by R.E. Brown, C.K. Barrett, B. Lindars and R. Schnackenburg. (1)

Also G. Richter accepts my understanding of John 6:31-58 as a midrashic exposition of an Old Testament quotation. (2)

Richter attempts, however, to show that my analysis at some points may be used as a boomerang. He suggests that my approach supports the hypothesis that John 6:51-58 is an interpolation, instead of disproving it. The discussion in this chapter will be limited mainly to the article of G. Richter, and in the final section on pure and applied exegesis the viewpoints of other scholars are brought to the center of the discussion.

Richter's main point is the question whether John 6:51b-58 is an interpolation or not, but several of his viewpoints are also of interest for the broader discussion of homiletic style. Richter accepts my analysis to a large extent: He renders with approval the observation that a paraphrasing and systematic exposition of an Old Testament text is found in Leg all III: 162-168, Mut 253-263, John 6:31ff., with close similarities also in Exod Rab 25:1.2.6. Richter also approves of the observation that subordinate Old Testament quotations are woven into the exposition of the main Old Testament quotation, the text. He also agrees that a homiletic pattern can be found in the passages. He concludes that he has discussed a work "die trotz aller geübten Kritik eine hervorragende Leistung ist". (3)

In spite of all details in Richter's study, and in spite of thoroughness, he at times criticizes me for viewpoints which I do not hold, nor have written in Bread from Heaven. One such example is that he projects on me that I stress the independence of the Jewish homily over against the hellenistic diatribe. Richter writes: "Auch mit der Eigenständigkeit der jüdischen Homilie scheint es nicht ganz so weit her zu sein, wie Borgen meint, denn andere Forscher meinen, dass sie von der kynisch-stoischen Diatribe gelernt hat, und zwar auch in formaler Hinsicht". The footnote on this section reads: "Dieser Meinung ist z.B. der jüdische Gelehrte Ed. Stein (Warschau), 'Die homiletische Peroratio im Midrash', in Hebrew Union College Annual (Cincinnati) VIII/IX (1931/1932), 318.370, zusammen mit Arthur Marmorstein (1882-1946), einem anderen jüdischen Gelehrten". (4)

There is here no reference to any page in my book, only to my name, "wie Borgen meint". The reason is that Richter attributes to me viewpoints not found in my book. I have stated just the opposite of the viewpoints he attributes to me. In discussing the contrast drawn by some scholars between midrashic style and terminology and the Greek style of diatribe, I give reasons for not making such a contrast, and continue: "This contrast is also weakened by some studies which demonstrate close points of agreements between the Greek and rabbinic style and method of exegesis. Therefore, it is possible to analyse Greek elements both in the Palestinian midrash and in Philo. The more limited undertaking to investigate the midrashic method in John 6:31-58 and draw upon Palestinian midrash and Philo for comparative material, therefore, does not exclude the possibility of an influence from Greek exegetical method". My footnote on this section reads: "With regard to style, cf. A. Marmorstein, HUCA VI, 1920, pp.183-204, and E. Stein, HUCA VIII-IX, 1931-32, pp. 370-371, who trace the diatribe in Palestinian sources. Concerning Greek and rabbinic exegetical method, see S. Liebermann, Hellenism in Jewish Palestine. Studies in the Literary Transmission, Beliefs and Manners of Palestine in the I Century B.C.E-IV Century, C.E. TStJThS XVIII, New York 1950, pp. 47-82; and D. Daube, "Rabbinic Methods of Interpretation and Hellenistic Rhetoric, "HUCA XXXII, 1949, pp. 239-264; "Alexandrian Methods of Interpretation and the Rabbis", Festschrift Hans Lewald, Basel 1953, pp. 27-44, and A. Kaminka, "Bibel VII, Bibelexegese", EJ IV, Berlin 1929, col. 622; M. Hadas, "Plato in Hellenistic Fusion, JHI XIX, 1958, pp. 11-12". (5)

The unity of the Discourse on Bread, John 6.

Richter puts emphasis on the observation in my book that the closing statements in Leg all III:162-168, Mut 253-263, John 6:31ff. and Exod Rab 25 show many similarities with the opening statements and sum up points from the exposition. He then finds that there are agreements between the opening in John 6:31-33 and 6:51a, which to him confirm the theory that vv. 51b-58 is an interpolation. (6)

In reply to Richter it must be said that since the Old Testament text is paraphrased in the exposition there are, of course, agreements with the opening throughout the passage. Thus, vv. 48-49 might serve as a close, if Richter's approach is to be followed:

John 6:31-33: οἱ πατέρες ἡμῶν τὸ μάννα ἔφαγον ἐν τῇ ἐρήμῳ, καθώς ἐστιν γεγραμμένον: ἄρτον ἐκ τοῦ οὐρανοῦ ἔδωκεν αὐτοῖς φαγεῖν.

32. Εἶπεν οὖν αὐτοῖς ὁ Ἰησοῦς: ἀμὴν ἀμὴν λέγω ὑμῖν, οὐ Μωϋσῆς δέδωκεν ὑμῖν τὸν ἄρτον ἐκ τοῦ οὐρανοῦ, ἀλλ' ὁ πατήρ μου δίδωσιν ὑμῖν τὸν ἄρτον ἐκ τοῦ οὐρανοῦ τὸν ἀληθινόν.

33. ὁ γὰρ ἄρτος τοῦ θεοῦ ἐστιν ὁ καταβαίνων ἐκ τοῦ οὐρανοῦ καὶ ζωὴν διδοὺς τῷ κόσμῳ.

John 6:48-49: Ἐγώ εἰμι ὁ ἄρτος τῆς ζωῆς.
49. οἱ πατέρες ὑμῶν ἔφαγον ἐν τῇ ἐρήμῳ τὸ μάννα καὶ ἀπέθανον.

The underscoring shows the agreements in wording between John 6:48-49 and the opening in John 6:31-33, and proves that there is no need to continue further to v. 51a, as Richter suggests. Also in Leg all III:162-168 there are corresponding agreements between the opening statement in § 162 and various parts of the passage.

In spite of such agreements throughout the passage it is still relevant to analyse agreements between opening and closing statements. Richter ignores one important point: The closing statements in Leg all III:162-168, Mut 253-263 and John 6:31-58 come at the point when the paraphrase of the quotation from the Old Testament ends as stated in my study: "The unit which belongs to a quotation from the Old Testament may be traced by examining the extent to which the paraphrase of that quotation goes..." (7)

"No paraphrase of the Old Testament texts is found outside the homiles, apart from certain traces in the transitional sections which introduce them... There is no paraphrase in John 6 vv. 60 ff. of the Old Testament text of the homily (cited in v. 31b)". (8)

From this it becomes clear that John 6:51a cannot, as Richter maintains, be shown to be a closing statement by using my method of analysis since the paraphrase of the Old Testament quotation in 31 continues in vv. 51b-58. (9)

In a recent study J.D.G. Dunn rightly puts emphasis on the aspect of paraphrase: "...Borgen's well-argued thesis that 6:31-58 forms an exegetical paraphrase of the OT quotation (v. 31) strongly reaffirms the coherence and unity of the whole passage, and makes much less plausible any attempt to isolate vv. 51c-58 as a later interpolation". (10)

Dunn also correctly adds another point: "...v. 58 has as much if not more right than v. 51a-b in terms of correspondence to v. 31 to be considered as the closing statement of the homily". (11)

A pattern?

One further point of general interest from Richter's article should be mentioned. He touches the question of a stricter and freer use of the word "pattern": "Damit soll jedoch nicht behauptet werden, dass in Joh. 6:31 ff. das homiletic pattern nicht vorliegt. Nur dürfte es der Evangelist viel freier - vielleicht ohne bewusste Anlehnung? - verwendet, als Borgen meint". (12)

Nowhere in Bread from Heaven is it stated that the Evangelist was conscious of employing a certain pattern as a pattern. The Evangelist expressed the ideas in traditional forms, and had hardly any independent interest in form as such. Therefore, the forms were not applied in a mechanical way. The view is indicated in Bread from Heaven: "The exegetical paraphrase fuses together words and fragments from different traditions into traditional forms and patterns. This method of exegetical paraphrase, then, leads to a dynamic process of new combinations within the framework of tradition". (13) A similar view is held by Le Déaut: "The authors were conscious of writing in a tradition rather than in a certain form". (14)

Since Richter thinks that the Evangelist used the homiletic pattern in a free way, it is surprising that he at points criticizes me on the basis of a stricter and more narrow use of the term "pattern" than my use of it in Bread from Heaven. In my analysis the exegetical paraphrase was regarded as one main characteristic of the homiletic pattern under discussion. The outline of the paraphrase could vary, however: Sometimes, as i Leg all III:162-168, Mut 253-263, John 6:31-58, etc., the Old Testament quotation is divided in parts and paraphrased in a successive sequence, in other passages, as in Leg all III:169-174, most of the words and phrases are paraphrased in the same sequence as they are given in the Old Testament quotation, and again other places, as in Leg all III:65-75a, Rom 4:1-22, etc., the paraphrase does not follow the sequence in which words occur in the quotation. Rather the words are here drawn upon as they can throw light upon the problem which is discussed. (15)

Thus, the freer use of the word pattern, - which Richter suggests, - can be found in Bread from Heaven itself, while the too narrow use is found in Richter's summary of my views, as when he states: "Die Erklärung erfolgt nach einem bestimmten System. Das Zitat wird in mehrere Teile oder Abschnitte zerlegt, die dann der Reihe nach interpretiert werden". "... in einer Aufgliederung und Reihenfolge, wie sie für das von Borgen aufgezeigte common homiletic pattern charakteristisch sind". (16)

In my analysis I use, at points, expressions as "the systematizing work of the exegetes", "in a systematic way the words, ... are paraphrassed", etc. (17) but I do not think of "ein bestimmtes System" of paraphrase as a general characteristic of the homiletic pattern concerned. In Bread from Heaven, therefore, it was not argued against the interpolation of John 6:51b-58 on the basis of the proportional lengths of the two parts, vv. 31-48 and vv. 49-58. One of the points made, however, was: "In vv. 51b-58 the discussion of the eating is at the center. This fact ties the section closely to the exposition from v. 49 onwards, where the word "to eat" is the main subject for the exegesis". (18) Richter's report on this point lacks precision: "Die Tatsache, dass der Teil b mit v. 49 beginnt und in den vv. 51-58 seinen Höhepunkt erreicht, ist nach der Meinung von Borgen ein Beweis für die enge Zusammengehörigkeit der vv. 51b-58 mit den vorhergehenden Versen und spricht gegen ihre Interpolation". (19) I argue on the basis that the concept of eating is in the center, while Richter attributes to me a mechanical characterization of "Teil b".

Richter counts the lines and concludes: "In der Homilie Joh. 6 - so wie sie Borgen annimmt - wäre das Zeilenverhältnis zwischen dem Teil a (= vv. 31-48) und dem Teil b (= vv. 49-58) 36:24, der Unterschied würde also nur das Eineinhalbfache betragen, während er bei Philo immerhin das Dreifache, Vierfache, Viereinhalbfache, Sechsfache und sogar das Achtzehnfache ausmachen kann". (20) In this summary Richter does not include all the data, since he does not mention the proportion in Leg all III:65-75a, which according to his own counting is 18:38, that is, approximately "das Zweifache", which comes quite close to "das Eineinhalbfache" in John 6. The natural conclusion which can be drawn from Richter's counting is that the proportional length among the parts vary so that no argument for or against the interpolation of John 6:51b-58 can be based on this.

Still another point can be mentioned to illustrate how Richter applies a stricter use of the term pattern than I did, - although he himself calls for a freer use. While my hypothesis is that various midrashic methods, patterns, terminology and ideas are utilized in the homilies, he seems to be critical or reserved to parallel material drawn from sources outside the homilies listed. Thus Richter criticizes a reference to an exegetical phrase in Leg all II:86 ("for the flinty rock is the Wisdom of God") since it does not occur in a context which follows the homiletic pattern. (21) In my study the many midrashic features analysed are of primary importance, while the theory of a homiletic pattern is of secondary interest for my thesis.

Richter's too strict use of the term "pattern" causes him to require that the various interpretations on the bread of life which Richter finds in John 6 itself, must have a parallel in the other homilies listed. Such differences are, according to Richter, the idea in John 6:31-51, that the Father gives the bread, and in vv. 51b-58, that Jesus gives it; another difference is the shift from φαγεῖν to τρώγειν (22)

These differences can be explained within John's gospel itself, however. John's christology makes the alternative use of the Father and the Son natural, since they are one in action, confer a similar variation between John 6:44 and 12:32. (23) The word τρώγειν is used also in John 13:18, and probably reflects eucharistic traditions utilized by the Evangelist. (24) It is to be noted that Richter himself regards John 13:18 as part of the original Gospel, and not as an interpolation. (25) In this way Richter contradicts his own conclusion about John 6:51b-58 that it is an interpolation.

Even if one here should compare John with parallel homilies in Philo, there are parallel features to be found. Also in Leg all III:162-168 there are terminological variations: The word οἱ ἄρτοι (Exod 16:4) in § 162 is later in the same paragraph rendered as οἱ λόγοι , and in § 168 as ἐπίστημαι In this way the thought moves in the exposition from the heavenly principles (οἱ λόγοι) to the actual perception of these principles (ἐπίστημαι). (26)

A movement of thought from one shade of meaning to another, and from the spiritual to the concrete, is also found in the same passage. Thus the phrase εἰς ἡμέραν (Exod 16:4) receives various interpretations: In Leg all III:163 the phrase τὸ τῆς ἡμέρας εἰς ἡμέραν means that the soul should gather knowledge, not all at once, but gradually. In § 167 εἰς ἡμέραν is interpreted in the concrete sense as day and light, then as light in the soul, which is further specified as the right use of school-education: "Many, then have acquired the lights in the soul for night and darkness, not for day and light".

Thus this homily in Philo presents two or more shades of meanings of the same phrase from the Old Testament, and includes both the spiritual and concrete. Thus, corresponding variations in John 6:31-58 do not support a theory of interpolation. (27)

Comparative midrash

Bread from Heaven has contributed to the discussion of terminology in the field of comparative midrash, as can be seen from Le Déaut's approving reference to my use of the term midrash. (28)

It is essential to the thesis of Bread from Heaven that John 6:31-58, Leg all III:162-168, Mut 253-263 and Exod Rab 25:2.6 are exegetical expositions of the Old Testament, and that these expositions fall within Jewish exegetical traditions and activity. Meeks does justice to this intention when he writes: "P. Borgen (Bread from Heaven, NovTSup, 10; Leiden: Brill, 1965) has demonstrated the midrashic charcter of the discourse and has shown that a number of motifs incorporated in it were already familiar in Alexandrian Judaism and attested somewhat later in haggadah from Palestinian sources". (29)

The terms "homily" and a "homiletic pattern", as such, are therefore not essential to my study, but a term of convenience to account for the structural agreements in the main passages analysed and similar passages. Moreover, John 6:59 says that the preceding discourse was given as teaching in the synagogue at Capernaum.

The term "homily" was chosen because scholars already had used it to characterize passages as Exod Rab 25:2.6 and parts of the works of Philo. Thus S.M. Lehrman writes about Exodus Rabbah: "The first chapters form a running commentary on each verse of Exodus I-XI, keeping at the same time the continuity of the narrative selected in view. The rest of the book (XV-LII) cites only selected verses, as a rule, the first verse in the section of the weekly Sidra. The result is a medley of heterogenous homilies (italics mine) with the first verse only as their text". (30) Among the many scholars who had applied the term to Philo's commentaries, H. Thyen may be cited: "Die These, dass der allegorische Genesiskommentar Philos aus ursprünglich für sich bestehenden Homilien entstanden sei, ist nicht neu". (31)

In his study on the midrash as literary genre, Wright classifies homilies as sub-tradition within the genre, and he refers with approval to the works by Silberman and Borgen as recent studies on the subject. (32) A word of caution is needed, however, in this connection. The terminology should not be based on abstract definitions but all the time on specific observations made in the historical sources, primarily in the midrashim.

In my study I delimited the homily to John 6:31-58, and regarded vv. 26-30 as transition from the narratives to the homily. The transitional verses 26-27a refer back to the multiplication of the bread, while v. 27b ff. point forward to the exposition on the bread from heaven. Meeks disagrees with this understanding and writes: "Though it is a saying of Jesus rather than a scripture text that provides the starting point of the "midrash" (and we should therefore recognize that the form of explication may have had a wider application in rhetoric than only the exposition of sacred texts) that saying already has the manna tradition in mind..." (33)

This view is worth testing, of course, and Meeks would then need to present a number of parallels of form from sources contemporaneous to the New Testament. Meeks makes a comparison with the dramatic style of Berthold Brecht, but this is not satisfactory from a historical point of view. (34)

In a recent article L. Schenke analysed the structure of John 6:26-58, and he finds my hypothesis of a homiletic pattern employed in 6:31-58 to be improbable, since I have not accounted for the dialogue structure of the passage. (35) I admit that the form of dialogue has not been sufficiently analysed in my book, although it was not completely ignored. Thus, the dialogue between "the Jews" and Jesus in John 6:41-48 is discussed in detail. (36)

Moreover, further studies of Jewish expository activity shows that there is hardly any conflict between the form of homily and the form of dialogue. For example, Philo tells that when the Jewish community of the Therapeutae meets, the President at a certain point in the gathering discusses (ζητέω) some questions arising in the Holy Scriptures or solves (ἐπιλύομαι) one that has been proposed by someone else (Vita Cont 75). (37) Furthermore, Philo's commentaries on parts of the Pentateuch give ample evidence for the fact that homiletic exposition comprises the form of questions and answers. (38)

The units of exposition studied in Bread from Heaven were identified by using the following criterion: "The unit which belongs to a quotation from the Old Testament may be traced by examining the extent to which the paraphrase of that quotation goes." (39) The employment of this principle uncovered the following units: Leg all III:162-168; Mut 253-263 and John 6:31-58. In addition to these elements of 1) Old Testament quotation and of 2) its paraphrase, also other similarities were found: 3) Subordinate quotations from the Old Testament were used in the exposition, and 4) when the paraphrase of the basic Old Testament quotation ended, there was a concluding statement referring back to the opening section. 5) The exposition in these passages draws on traditions received, as for example traditions dealing with the giving of the manna in the desert. (40) 6) Various midrashic methods, patterns and terminology are employed in these passages. (41)

All of these characteristics are also found in Palestinian midrashim, as i Exod Rab 25, with the main difference that the fresh and creative paraphrase of words from the Old Testament text together with fragments from the tradition has here been changed into a text being followed by compilation of fixed units from the tradition. Some paraphrase of words from the quotation still remains, however, and the repetition of the quotation marks the end of the exposition. (42)

These observations from Philo, rabbinic writings and the New Testament indicate that the theories of Bacher, Theodor and Vermes are inadequate with regard to the history of exegesis. Bacher pictures the development as that from philological, simple and literal exegesis into the authoritative body of exegetical traditions in the midrashim. (43) A similar viewpoint is expressed by Theodor: "the simple exposition of Scripture is more and more lost in the wide stream of free interpretation". (44)

Vermes is in general agreement with Theodor, since he thinks that "applied exegesis" represents the second stage in the history of exegesis, while "pure exegesis" characterized the first stage: "Whereas at first midrash was primarily required to eliminate obscurities in the biblical text, by the beginning of the Christian era other demands were being made of it. The point of departure was no longer the Torah itself, but contemporary customs and beliefs which the interpreter attempted to connect with scripture and to justify". (45)

Against Vermes' viewpoint, it must be stated that also most of his documentation of the first stage of "pure exegesis" is taken from writings which belong to the beginning of the Christian era or later: Philo, Josephus, Talmud, the midrashim, and Eusebius. Moreover, our analysis suggests that one significant aspect of this developmental process is that a fresh, creative paraphrase of words from the Old Testament text together with fragments from the tradition has changed into a text being followed by compilation of fixed units from the tradition. In many cases, therefore, philological exegesis, harmonization of contradiction, etc. ("pure exegesis") in the earlier stage formed integral part of the creative and contemporizing paraphrase, while they later were preserved mechanically as separate units of tradition.

In this way Philo and John throw light upon earlier stages of the kind of exposition of which the rabbinic midrashim represent a later stage.

NOTES

1) P. Borgen, Bread from Heaven; R.E. Brown, St. John, I-XII, 262-303; C.K. Barrett, St. John, (2nd ed., London, 1978) 279-297; B. Lindars, John, 250-253; R. Schnackenburg, Das Johannesevangelium, 1, 13. 53-87. Cf. U. Wilckens "Der eucharistische Abschnitt der johanneischen Rede vom Lebensbrot (Joh 6:51c-58)," in J. Gnilka (ed.), Neues Testament und Kirche. FS R. Schnackenburg, (Freiburg, 1974) 220-248; J. Dunn, "John VI- a Eucharistic Discourse?" NTS, 17, (1971) 328-338; R. Kysar, The Fourth Evangelist and His Gospel, (Minneapolis, Minn. 1975) 124-125.

2) G. Richter, "Zur Formgeschichte und literarischen Einheit von Joh 6:31-58, ZNW, 60, (1969) 21-55; cf. H. Thyen, "Aus der Literatur zum Johannesevangelium", ThR, NF 44, (1979) 338-359.

3) G. Richter, ZNW, 60, (1969) 54.

4) ibid., 51.

5) P. Borgen, Bread from Heaven, 60-61.

6) G. Richter, ZNW, 60, (1969) 23 f.

7) P. Borgen, Bread from Heaven, 29.

8) ibid., 46.

9) Cf. G. Richter, ZNW, 60, (1969) 54; W.A. Meeks, JBL, 91, (1972) 58, n. 50, is thus mistaken when he writes: "... my chief criticism of Borgen's analysis is ... his fixation on the scripture text so loosely cited in vs. 31. Consequently his work seemed vulnerable to G. Richter's ingenious attempt to show that vvs. 51-58, by Borgen's own method ought to be regarded as a later addition."

10) J. Dunn, NTS, 17, (1971) 330.

11) ibid.

12) G. Richter, ZNW, 60, (1960) 50-51.

13) P. Borgen, Bread from Heaven, 59.

14) R. Le Déaut, Interpretation, 25, 1971, 270-271.

15) P. Borgen, Bread from Heaven, 34.38.42.47.50-51.

16) G. Richter, ZNW, 60, (1969) 21.23.

17) P. Borgen, Bread from Heaven, 34.42.

18) ibid.,35.

19) G. Richter, ZNW, 60, (1969) 22.

20) ibid., 23.

21) ibid., 32.

22) ibid., 24-25.

23) See P. Borgen, Bread from Heaven, 158-164, especially 160-161.

24) ibid., 92-93.

25) G. Richter, Die Fusswaschung im Johannesevangelium, (Regensburg, 1967) 308-309.

26) P. Borgen, Bread from Heaven, 139. Cf. the references to various exegetical interpretations by Paul made by J. Dunn, NTS, 17, (1971) 330.

27) Many other points in Richter's article call for comments, but they belong more to a specific discussion within the area of Johannine studies as such. Two specifically Johannine points from G. Richter, ZNW, 60, (1969) 21-55 may serve as illustrations:
A) Richter uses the statement of purpose in John 20-31 to identify the authentic parts of the Gospel. Richter then writes: "Es ist auf den ersten Blick klar, dass die vv. 31-51a mit dem in 20:31 angegebenen Zweck übereinsstimmen. Nicht nur die gemeinsame Terminologie, sondern auch die gleiche Thematik und die gleiche Tendenz beweisen das." (p. 35). "Das Verhältnis der vv. 51b-58 zu 20:31 sieht ganz anders aus. Es bestehen Unterschiede in der Terminologie, im Inhalt und auch in der Tendenz." (p. 37). In his discussion of terminology, Richter deals with the following from John 20:31:

1) πιστεύειν, which Richter finds in John 6:35.36.40. Against Richter it must be said that this term is not only lacking in John 6:51b-58, but also in vv. 41-51a. Moreover, the question must be asked why Richter interprets φαγεῖν in vv. 49-51a as meaning πιστεύειν , when this term does not occur in these verses at all? Thus Richter has overlooked the fact that the term πιστεύειν is missing in the whole section, vv. 49-58, in which the term and the concept of φαγεῖν are in the center of the exposition. See P. Borgen, Bread from Heaven, 189, n. 3.

2) ζωὴν (αἰώνιον) ἔχειν . Richter admits that this and similar terms occur throughout the discourse, also in John 6:51b-58: vv. 33.35.40.47.48.51a.51b.53.54.57.58. This fact speaks against the view of Richter and in favour of the unity of the discourse as a whole.

3) ὁ χριστὸς ὁ υἱὸς τοῦ θεοῦ . Richter sees that this term does not occur in John 6:31-58. He performs arbitrary exegesis when he accepts synonymous expressions in 6:31-51a (ὁ ὢν παρὰ τοῦ πατρός 46; καταβέβηκα ἀπὸ τοῦ οὐρανοῦ v. 38; ὁ πέμψας με v. 44 cf.v. 39, etc.) but rejects the synonymous expressions in vv. 51b-58 (ἀπέστειλέν με ὁ ζῶν πατήρ v. 57; οὗτός ἐστιν ὁ ἄρτος ὁ ἐξ οὐρανοῦ καταβάς v. 58; ὁ υἱὸς τοῦ ἀνθρώπου v. 53). Thus, Richter's use of John 20:31 - which itself is debatable - offers support for the unity of John 6:31-58 rather than is a defence of the theory of interpolation. Another point made by Richter is that σὰρξ καὶ αἷμα σάρξ alone and αἷμα alone never carries article when it means man as an earthly being (p. 45). Richter overlooks, however, John 3:6 τὸ γεγεννημένον ἐκ τῆς σαρκὸς σάρξ ἐστιν which shows that the article can be used with reference to specific aspects of man as earthly being, as also in John 6:53 ff. Cf. also 6:63. Although the main purpose of Bread from Heaven

was not to argue against the interpolation theory as such, several such points grew out of the analysis. Some of them are referred to by Richter. Both these, and those not discussed by him, remain untouched, however, by his criticism. Observations which speak against the interpolation theory are found in P. Borgen, Bread from Heaven, 25-26.35.37-38.90.95-97.187-192. See also R. Schnackenburg, "Zur Rede vom Brot aus dem Himmel: eine Beobachtung zu Joh 6:52, BZ, N. F. 12, (1968) 248-252 and J.D.G. Dunn, NTS, 17, (1971) 328-338.

28) R.L. Déaut, Interpretation, 25, (1971) 281, n. 82.

29) W.A. Meeks, JBL, 91, (1972) 58, n. 48.

30) M. Lehrman, "Introduction", Midrash Rabbah, ed. by H. Freedman and M. Simon, 3, Exodus, (London, 1961) VII. See P. Borgen, Bread from Heaven, 53, n. 1.

31) H. Thyen, Der Stil der Jüdisch-Hellenistischen Homilie, FRLANT LXV (N.F.XLVII), Göttingen 1955, 7. See also P. Borgen, Bread from Heaven, 29 and note 1.

32) A.G. Wright, CBQ, 28, (1966) 127-128.

33) W.A. Meeks, JBL, 91, (1972) 58, n. 50.

34) ibid., 56 and n. 43. Among the other points to be answered by Meeks here, is the connection between John ch. 5 and ch. 6. The exposition of the Old Testament text in John 6:31-58 serves as example of Jesus' word in 5:39: "You search the scriptures, because you think that in them you have eternal life; and it is they that bear witness to me." The narratives in John 6:1-25 are examples of "the works" mentioned in 5:36. See P. Borgen, Bread from Heaven, 180.

35) L. Schenke, "Die literarische Vorgeschichte von Joh 6, 26-58," BZ, (N.F. 29, 1985) 68-89.

36) P. Borgen, Bread from Heaven.

37) See the dissertation by my student, H. Hegstad, Synagogen, sted for skriftlesning og utleggelse på sabbaten (typewritten), (Trondheim,1977) 65-68.

38) See P. Borgen and R. Skarsten, Studia Philonica, 4 (1976-77) 1-15; P. Borgen, ANRW, II:21,1, (1984) 134-137; ibid., CRINT, II:2, (1984) 263; V. Nikiprowetzky, "L'exégèse de Philon d'Alexandrie dans le De Gigantibus et le Quod Deus sit Immutabilis," in D. Winston and J. Dillon, Two Treatises of Philo of Alexandria, 5-75; D. Runia, VC, (1984) 227-247.

39) P. Borgen, Bread from Heaven, 29.

40) ibid., 29-43; 14-27.54.

41) ibid., 59-98.

42) ibid., 51-54.

43) W. Bacher, Die Jüdische Bibelexegese vom Anfange des zehn-

<u>ten bis zum Ende des fünfzehnten Jahrhunderts</u>, (1892) 1.

44) J. Theodor, "Midrash Haggadah", <u>The Jewish Encyclopedia</u>, 8, (New York, 1904) 554.

45) G. Vermes, "Bible and Midrash: Early Old Testament Exegesis", <u>Cambridge History of the Bible</u>, 1, (Cambridge, 1970) 221.

CHAPTER EIGHT
JOHN'S USE OF THE OLD TESTAMENT, AND THE PROBLEM OF SOURCES AND TRADITIONS

In contemporary research on the Gospel of John there has been a renewed interest in various kinds of source analysis, and also an increasing interest in John's use of the Old Testament. With regard to source analysis the view points vary from the theory that the Evangelist on the one hand has made use of a complete Gospel of narrative material, to the view on the other hand that he has made use of unrelated traditions or several short collections. With regard to the Evangelist's use of the Old Testament, recent studies have been made, in a traditional way, on quotations and allusions. There have also been attepts made to find new approaches by examination of exegetical traditions and exegetical methods presupposed and employed in the Gospel. (1) Within this picture R. Bultmann represents an intermediary position on the source question, but has a rather reluctant or negative view on the importance of the Old Testament for the Gospel.

In 1974 Gunter Reim published a comprehensive study on John's use of the Old Testament and the problem of source analysis. (2) To a large extent G. Reim is dependent on Bultmann's source analysis, but disagrees decidedly with Bultmann's quite reluctant attitude towards the Old Testament element in John. Bultmann's hypothesis on John's sources is well known; The discourses are divided into a Revelatory source ("Offenbarungsreden") and the comments made by the Evangelist. The narrative material consists, according to Bultmann, of a Semeia source which mainly comprised miracle stories, and the Passion narrative. Finally, a church minded editor made som interpolations and added chapter 21. (3)

It is significant that Reim attempts to make his analysis of John's use of the Old Testament fruitful for the discussion of John's sources. Earlier attempts have failed, although there is foundation for new approaches in some recent studies. (4) Reim rightly criticizes Bultmann's use of the Old Testament element, or the absence of the Old Testament background as a criterion for source analysis. Bultmann did not find any significant Old Testament background for ideas in the supposed Revelatory source ("Offenbarungsreden"), which, according to him, came from a gnostic context. Consequently, in the cases where the Old Testament was used, Bultmann saw in such features the commenting hand of the Evangelist at work. Reim stresses that the Old Testament background of Wisdom ideas in John must be taken seriously. As a result Reim finds that the prologue of the Gospel, and other parts, which Bultmann includes in his gnostic Revelatory source, are significantly stamped by the Old Testament. (5) As a result of his view, Reim therefore thinks that the Evangelist has written both the parts which Bultmann classifies as the Revelatory source, as well as what he regards as added comments: "So, wie nach Bultmann die Offenbarungsredenquelle schreibt, schreibt meiner Meinung nach der Evangelist, wenn er, von allgemeinen alttestamentlichen Gedanken herkommend, wie sie ihm in der Weisheit vorlagen, das Christusereignis beschreibt" (281).

Reim does not isolate the traditional elements in the discourses as a clearly defined source; he rather speaks of a stream of Christian tradition, the Wisdom tradition, which was cultivated in the circle to which the Evangelist himself belonged. (6)

Although Reim is right in stressing the Old Testament background of the idea of Wisdom and other ideas in John's discourses, he draws, at times, too sharp a distinction between Wisdom traditions and rabbinic traditions. Thus, since he realizes that John 1:51 reflects rabbinic discussion of the phrase בו in Gen 28:12, this observation falls outside his main thesis, and he does not seem to know how to account for it. According to Reim, John 1:51 does not come from the Semeia-source, (104, n. 15); it is added to the traditional Son of Man material by the Evangelist (255), but it does not come from the Evangelist (274-5), and it is doubtful whether it belonged to the Wisdom tradition (223). (7) Correspondingly, although Reim follows the reviewer's understanding of John 6:31 f., that these verses reflect midrashic method of exegesis (John 6:32 presupposes a change of vocalization from נותן to נותן , etc.), he ignores this rabbinic background in his conclusion, and links this exegesis to the Wisdom tradition and the Wisdom circle, (14-15). In the same way Reim onesidedly interprets the prologue, John 1:1-18, against the background of Wisdom traditions, to the effect that rabbinic background material in targums and midrashim, etc., are not seriously discussed (see especially 276-77). (8)

With regard to the question of distinguishing between traditional material and the hand of the Evangelist, the author several times mentions the characteristics of the Evangelist, but he does not clarify his basis for establishing such characteristics. (9) For example, no statistics of stylistic features are given.

According to Reim the Evangelist has written such discourse material as an addition to a Semeia source which he had received. The definition of this source is more precise than was the source for the discourse material. The main criterion which he follows here, is the use of allusions to the Elijah/Elisha stories in the Old Testament. Reim finds such allusions in the narratives of 2:1 ff.; 4:46 ff.; 6:1 ff.; 9:1 ff.; and 11:1 ff. This criterion leads him also to include John 1:19 ff. and 35 ff. in the same source; and finally, 12:37-41 and 20:30 f. express the purpose of the source. (10)

It is of importance that Reim regards the prophet stories of Elijah and Elisha as background material for the picture of Jesus expressed in the miracle stories, and not Hellenistic ideas about divine men. (11) However, his use of allusions to Elijah and Elisha as a general criterion for a Semeia source is not convincing. First, some of the phraseological allusions are doubtful. Reim finds that the phrase τί ἐμοὶ καὶ σοί in John 2:4 has its background in 1 Kings 17:18. (12) In the latter passage, however, the words are not from the mouth of the prophet - corresponding to <u>Jesus</u>' words in John 2:4 - but in the mouth of the widow from Sarepta. Moreover, in the Old Testament the corresponding phrase occurs also at other places, (Judg 11:12.; 2 Chron 35:21; 2 Kings 3:13; Hos 14:8). - And the phrase in John 2:5 (ὅ τι ἂν λέγῃ ὑμῖν, ποιήσατε) may allude to Gen 41:55 rather than to 1 Kings 17:15. (13) Furthermore, it seems to go too far to regard Jesus' prayer at the raising of Lazarus, John 11:41 f., as a direct allusion to Elijah's prayer at the cultic encounter with Baal's priests on Mt. Carmel, 1 Kings 18:37. (14)

Secondly, Reim's delimitation of the Semeia source leads to improbable consequences, as can be seen from his discussion of John 6:1 ff. Since John 6:9, 10, 13 seems to allude to 2 Kings 4:42 f., Reim includes the feeding miracle in the Semeia source (157 and 208). He has then also to include the story of Jesus' walking on the sea, John 6:16-21, in the Semeia source, although it contains no allusions to the Elijah-Elisha cyclus. Reim's explanation is that the story of Jesus' walking on the sea was tied to the feeding miracle in the tradition. (15)

The same argument provides support, however, for regarding the feeding miracle, the walking on the sea, a speech on bread, and Peter's confession, as a cycle of stories which belonged together in the tradition. Several scholars have pointed to this, from comparison with the Synoptics. (16) This observation speaks against Reim's separation of Peter's confession, John 6:68 f., from the feeding miracle and the walking on the sea, to the effect that he places Peter's confession in a hypothetical 4th Synoptic Gospel, while he puts the other two stories in the Semeia source.

Still another improbable result of Reim's analysis is found in his discussion of John 4. Because of his use of Elijah-Elisha as criterion, he disagrees with Bultmann who included the main part of John 4:5-42 in the Semeia source. Reim states "Ich zähle die Samariageschichte in John 4 nicht zur Semeiaquelle, sondern zu dem synoptischen Material" (p. 209). He cannot point to any synoptic parallels or synoptic features in John 4, however, and he only states: "Zum Material aus dem 4. Synoptiker zähle ich auch John 4:1-42. Es handelt sich ja hier nicht um eine Wundergeschichte, sondern um den Bericht einer Begegnung Jesus mit einer Samaritanerin. Wie an manchen anderen Stellen, die aus dem 4. Synoptiker stammen, so findet sich auch in John 4 ein ausgezeichnete Ortskenntnis" (213). These points, mentioned by Reim, do not justify the inclusion of John 4:1-42 in a 4th Synoptic Gospel.

Moreover, when he argues against John 4:1-42 as part of the Semeia source because it is not a miracle story (213), he himself weakens the force of such a point, when he includes John 1:19 ff., 35 ff., in the Semeia source, although it is not a miracle story. The improbability of Reim's analysis becomes quite evident, when he discusses John 4:1-42 under the heading of material similar to that in the Synoptics, while the stories of the feeding miracle and the walking on the sea - with their many agreements with the Synoptics - are not classified as material similar to that in the Synoptics and are not included in the 4th Synoptic, but in the Semeia source.

Another miracle story which Bultmann included in the Semeia source, but Reim excludes from that source and regards it as part of the 4th Synoptic Gospel, is John 5:1-16, together with 5:27-29, 35 and 7:19-24. According to Reim, ch. 5 was inserted into the Evangelist's first version of his Gospel, and therefore it caused disorder in the geographical scenes of chs. 4 and 6 (158 and 213).

The geographical aporia is obvious, but Reim fails to discuss seriously the continuity which exists in the theological thoughts in the chapters in their present order: John 5 concludes with a discussion of the witness of the works, 5:36, and the witness of the Scriptures, 5:39 ff. It is then quite logical that ch. 6 offers 2 examples of the witness of the works, John 6:1-26, followed by an example of the witness of the Scriptures, 6:31-58. (17) Also in John 4:46-5:47 there are ideas which bind the various parts together. Thus the two healing miracles, John 4:46-54 and 5:1-16, are both loosely tied to the subsequent discourse, 5:17 ff., corresponding to the loose connection between the two stories in John 6:1-26 and the discourse in 6:(27)31-58. And the themes of life (4:46-54) and of Jesus' authority (5:1-16), offer a stepping stone for the ideas in the discourse on Jesus' authority as lifegiver, 5:17 ff. Thus, it is questionable if ch. 5 is to be regarded as a dislocation. For this reason, and because there are only few verbal agreements with the Synoptics, it seems strange that Reim classified it as material similar to that in the synoptics, and did not include it in the suggested Semeia source. (18)

Reim believes, as did Bultmann, that the story of the Baptist formed the beginning of the Semeia source. According to Bultmann, the source began in John 1:35 ff. (19), while Reim also includes 1:19 ff. Although the story of the Baptist is not a miracle story, Reim includes it in the Semeia source because of the reference to Elijah. From this starting point, Reim reaches the following conclusion: "War es das Anliegen dieser Geschichte aus der Tradition, den Täufer nicht als Elia oder als den Propheten gelten zu lassen, so ist doch der Evangelist an dieser Abwehr nicht mehr so interessiert. Ihm geht es, wie wiederholt im Evangelium deutlich wird, darum dass der Täufer nicht der Christus ist. In diesem Sinne hat Johannes dann die Geschichte aus der Tradition mit synoptiker-ähnlichem material für die Darstellung des Verhältnisses des Täufers zu Jesus umgestaltet" (9).

In accordance with this understanding, Reim regards the Old Testament quotation from Isa 40:3 in John 1:23 as one of the insertions from the 4th Synoptic Gospel, and the reference to the Christ, 1:20, 25, as an interpretative gloss by the Evangelist himself. (20)

Several points speak against Reim's view. Reim states himself that Jesus was characterized as king in the Semeia source, John 6:14-15 (196, 248), and it then seems unwarranted to take out the royal term "the Christ" from the suggested Semeia source in 1:20, 25. And Reim seems to hold contradicting views, when he on the one hand says that the Evangelist himself added the phrase "the Christ", and on the other hand expresses the opinion that the Evangelist himself had no special interest in this concept, but received it from tradition (213, 248). Thus it is more probable to think that John 1:19 ff. draws on a list of traditional Jewish eschatological figures, in which the term "the Christ" also occured.

As support for his view that the dialogue in 1:19 ff., except the above mentioned insertions, (21) comes from the Semeia source, Reim uses an argument from style: "Auch der Stil der kurzen Fragen und Antworten (wer bist du? ... Wer dann? ... Ich bin's nicht ... Nein) entspricht nicht dem Stil des Evangelisten, von dem man ganz andere Antworten gewöhnt ist (vgl. nur John 18:37)" (7). Here Reim uses the argument of style in a summary fashion, without basing it on careful documentation and statistical analysis. He only gives a parenthetical reference to John 18:37, to indicate the broader style of the Evangelist, in contrast to the short questions and answers in the suggested Semeia-source in John 1:19 ff. Reim does not discuss, however, the shorter questions and answers in the dialogue at Jesus' arrest, 18:4 ff. Reim's lack of precision here becomes also evident, when he at another place in his study lists 18:37, as well as 18:4 ff., among material which came from the 4th Synoptic Gospel (211), without specifying the impact made on the passages by the Evangelist himself.

According to Reim, the Evangelist's first version of his Gospel consisted of the Semeia source with interpretative additions and expansions drawn from ideas in the Christian Wisdom circle to which the Evangelist belonged. The final form of the Gospel was then written by the Evangelist himself, when he worked parts of the 4th Synoptic Gospel into the first version of his Gospel, thus making disturbing insertions into the order of the first version, and adding the passion narrative. (22)

Reim's hypothesis, that the Evangelist himself is responsible for both versions of the Gospel, implies that he also is responsible for the disorder caused by the insertion of the cleansing of the temple, the insertion of ch. 5, etc., when the second version was produced. This understanding weakens, however, the source analysis which Reim bases on aporias, such as disorder and unevenness in the run of the Gospel. Since the Evangelist himself was responsible for bringing disorder into the final form of the Gospel, why should that same person have followed smooth order and consistency in his first version? Thus there seems to be no need to develop a two version theory to account for dislocations and other aporias.

The conclusion is that Reim's theory of a Semeia source, interpreted and expanded on by the Evangelist's Wisdom-ideas, and given its final form by insertions and additions from a 4th Synoptic Gospel, is not convincing. His study has important merits at several points nevertheless: a) He shows that Bultmann's attempt to use the Old Testament ideas or lack of Old Testament background as criterion for source criticism, is not valid. (23) b) He points to the fact that in John, the gospel traditions have been penetrated and influenced by traditions and ideas based on the Old Testament. c) He thus raises again the important question of the relationship between the Evangelist's use of the Old Testament and his use of various sources. d) He thinks that the Evangelist was positively connected with a Christian community, and, that its ideas gave him the basis for his own interpretative activity. Reim even lists this community as one of the sources of the Gospel (189).

These points can be built into another hypothesis on the sources behind John's Gospel. In the form of theses, it might consist of the following points:

A. In the Johannine community a dual activity took place: 1) Oral and written traditions were received and handed on, and 2) they were subject to interpretative activity. (24) In John's Gospel there are indications that a deposit of traditions is presupposed: the baptism of Jesus is presupposed in John 1:33, (25) the imprisonment of John the Baptist is referred to in 3:24, (26) the institution of the Lord's Supper is presupposed in 6:51-58, (27) and Jesus' prayer in Gethsemane is alluded to in 18:11b, etc., (28) cf. also the reference to the many signs, 20:30-31.

B. The Evangelist is a representative of the interpretative activity which took place in his community. This means that the Gospel is a result of a process, rather than a result of the reshaping of fixed sources by the Evangelist. It is possible to trace back certain aspects of the history of tradition that preceded the composition of the Gospel, but the continuous interpreting activity makes it impossible to reconstruct comprehensive prejohannine theology of the sources. The interpreting activity of the community behind the Gospel, has caused aporias to develop in the Gospel tradition, so that aporias as inconsistencies, etc., are of little help for making distinctions between the hand of the Evangelist (or an Editor) and his sources.

C. The oral and written traditions behind the Gospel, belonged to a specific Gospel tradition, and they were not a collecting basin for other traditions from the non-Christian surroundings of the Johannine community. These oral and written sources seem to fall into two groups of relatively independent material, the narrative material and the discourse material. Some interplay between the narrative material and the discourse material already took place in the interpretative activity in the Johannine community. The Evangelist continued this tendency towards bringing narratives and discourses together. On the whole, the oral/written traditions are independent of the Synoptics: John has some of them in common with traditions behind the Synoptics, and at points influence from the Synoptics is probable. (29)

D. In the oral and written traditions behind the Gospel, some events were lifted up as points of orientation, which influenced the place and perspective given to other parts. The end of Jesus'ministry, i.e. the passion narrative was such a point of orientation. In a lesser degree also the beginning of Jesus' ministry, tied to John the Baptist, was lifted up as another point of orientation. Various oral and written cycles of traditions, various outlines and selections would then develop at different times and in different situations, but they were all understood within the context of these two points of orientation.

E. These two points of orientation, the passion narrative at the end, and John the Baptist at the beginning of Jesus' ministry, were lifted up in this way in the early church in general. This circumstance gave basis for two mutually independent manifestations of the gospel form, that of Mark and that of John. (30) In John's Gospel the narrative and discourse material are written out with the passion traditions and traditions on John the Baptist as the beginning and end. To some extent the end forms the backbone of the Gospel as a whole, since traditions from the passion are scattered in its different parts: John 2:13 ff.; 6:51-58;

11:47-12:19; 13:1-38, and then chs. 18-20. Correspondingly, traditions about John the Baptist are stretched out from the beginning into a large part of the Gospel: John 1 (in parts) 3:22-4:3; 5:30-36; 10:40-41.

F. The interpretative techniques employed by the Evangelist and his community are complex. Sometimes stories and sayings are written mainly as received, with only some new interpretative elements in the rendering itself (for example John 6:3-13, 16-21; 13:20, cf. the synoptic parallels). The Evangelist and his community have also formed new stories and new sayings on the basis of fragments and key terms from traditions, or by replacing parts of a tradition with other phrases (in John 1:40 ff. fragments from different stories have been reshaped together: the calling of the disiples, the naming of Peter, Jesus as son of Joseph, etc.; and interpretative variants of John 13:20 are found in 12:44-45, etc.). Such reshaped stories and sayings seem to have been given traditional forms. (31)

G. The interpretative activity of the Evangelist and his community was largely based on exegetical traditions from Old Testament exposition: Old Testament quotation can be followed by a systematic exposition (as in John 6:31-58) or the Evangelist can employ targumic elaborations on Old Testament passages (as in John 1:1-18), or he can develop arguments which are based on exegetical traditions which are presupposed (as John 5:17 presupposes exegetical debates on Gen 2:1 ff.). The use of the Old Testament in the Gospel indicates that learned expository methods and techniques have been employed. To a large extent Gospel traditions have been woven together with such expositions of the Old Testament. Such methods and techniques can also throw light upon methods and techniques which the Evangelist and his community have used in the interpretations of the Gospel traditions. (32)

H. Specific historical persons, events and situations have influenced the interpretations, such as the historical fact of Jesus himself, and his conflict leading up to the cross, and problems in the Christian community in general, and in the Johannine community in particular (the break with the synagogue, John 9:1 ff., different views on miracles as signs, 4:48, docetic tendencies, 1:14, 3:13; 6:46, 52 ff.; 19:17, etc.).

I. The Gospel represents a cross-section of such rendering and interpretation of traditions at that particular point in the process, when the Evangelist wrote it. The combination of unity and inconsistencies belonged to this Gospel from the time it was written down. Traces of the continuing handling of Gospel traditions in John's community after the Gospel was written down, are found in John 21. It gives support to the unity of the Gospel that such later developments were added at the end, and not interpolated into the Gospel itself.

NOTES

1) R.T. Fortna, The Gospel of Signs, (Cambridge, 1970), who attempts to reconstruct a comprehensive narrative source, which formed a complete gospel, while he is rather pessimistic about the possibility of reconstructing a corresponding source of sayings. Cf. W. Nicol, The Semeia in the Fourth Gospel, (Leiden, 1972), and J. Becker, "Wunder und Christologie: zum literarkritischen und christologischen Problem der Wunder im Johannesevangelium, NTS, 16, (1970) 130-48. - B. Lindars, Behind the Fourth Gospel, (London, 1971), holds the view that the Evangelist drew on various traditions, not only one or two comprehensive sources.

   E.D. Freed, Old Testament Quotations in the Gospel of John, Nov T Sup, 11, (Leiden, 1965), concentrates, as the title says, on the Old Testament quotations, while N.A. Dahl, "Der Erstgeborene Satans und der Vater des Teufels (Polyk. 7.1 und Joh. 8.44)" in Apophoreta: Festschrift für Ernst Haenchen, ed W. Eltester, (Berlin, 1964), 70-84; id. "The Johannine Church", 124-142, and W.A. Meeks, The Prophet-King, explore Jewish exegetical traditions used in the Gospel. This is also done by P. Borgen, Bread from Heaven.

2) G. Reim, Studien zum alttestamentlichen Hintergrund des Johannesevangeliums, (Cambridge, 1974).

3) See R. Bultmann, Johannes. Cf. E. Ruckstuhl, Die literarische Einheit des Johannesevangeliums, (Freiburg in Switzerland, 1951) 20. 34, and G. Reim, op.cit., 269-82.

4) See especially A. Faure: "Die alttestamentlichen Zitate im 4. Evangelium und die Quellenscheidungshypothese", ZNW, 21, (1922) 99-121, with the subsequent criticism by F. Smend, "Die Behandlung alttestamentlicher Zitate als Ausgangspunkt der Quellenscheidung im 4. Evangelium", ZNW, 24, (1925) 147-50. - Too pessimistic is Charles Goodwin, "How did John treat his sources", JBL, 73, (1954) 61-75, when he says that John's free and inexact use of the Old Testament makes it unlikely that he would have treated other sources with greater respect. Therefore "we must despair", he held, "of any attempt to reconstruct them from his text" (73). See the discussion and criticism of Goodwin's view by R.T. Fortna, op.cit., 12. With regard to recent studies, see references in note 1.

5) See R. Bultmann, Johannes, for example in his comment on the use of the Old Testament in John 3:12 f.: "V. 14 f. ist eine Bildung des Evangelisten, denn seiner Quelle lag eine positive Beziehung auf das AT fern..." (109, n. 1). G. Reim, op.cit., 273-4.

6) G. Reim, op.cit., 273.

On page 189 Reims uses the term "source" also in connection with the Wisdom traditions, but does not indicate that this source was written down in a document. He defines rather the source sociologically, as the Wisdom circle, with which the Evangelist was connected.

7) It is strange that Reim on page 223 does not include the preposition ἐπί in the words which in John 1:51 come from Gen 28:12. Reim concludes that it cannot be decided what the background of John's wording is, since he differs both from LXX and MT. If Reim here also had included a discussion of ἐπί against the background of בו , the background in MT had received strong support. Cf. p. 101: "Man konnte auf Grund des MT, in dem das בו zweideutig ist, so verschieden exegieren."

8) In the bibliography The Babylonian Talmud and Midrash Rabbah are listed, but only in translations. On Mekilta de Rabbi Ishmael on Exodus, no text nor any translation are given, nor on Siphre Numeri or on Tanḥuma. Moreover, some inconsistencies are found in the references. The listings of Deut Rab and Exod Rab are followed by Midr Lev, instead of Lev Rab. And the listing of Mek Exod varies with the more specified Mek Baḥodesh. Also the use of Roman and Arabic numerals is inconsistent in the references to rabbinic literature. Such observations indicate that the rabbinic material would need to be more thoroughly examined. Thus, the author seems too easily to discard rabbinic ideas and methods of argumentation in John (115-16, etc.).

9) See page 7, etc.

10) The theory of a Semeia source has had a long history. Especially important was A. Faure's study, ZNW, (1922), 99-121, where he uses the Old Testament quotation in 12:37-41 as key for the identification of the source. As mentioned above, Bultmann accepted this hypothesis, and Fortna, op.cit., and W. Nicol, op.cit., have in different ways based their studies on it.

11) See for example J. Becker's use of the idea of the divine man in NTS, 16, (1970), 130-48. Cf. the criticism of Becker's view by B. Lindars, Behind the Fourth Gospel, 36 ff.

12) Reim, op.cit., 156 f.

13) ibid.

14) ibid.

15) ibid., 158, n. 89: "Nur die Erzählung vom Seewandeln (Joh 6:16-21) ist in der Semeia-quelle nicht auf dem Elia/Elisa-Hintergrund gezeigt worden. Diese Erzählung war aber in der von Johannes übernommenen Tradition fest mit dem Speisungswunder, in dem auf Elisa angespielt wird, verbunden."

16) See B. Gärtner, John 6 and the Jewish Passover, (Lund, 1969), 6-12; J. Jeremias, "Johanneische Literaturkritik," TBl, 20, (1941), cols. 42-3; N.A. Dahl, Matteusevangeliet, 1, (Oslo, 1949), 205; R.E. Brown, St. John, I-XII, ad.loc., and P. Borgen, Bread from Heaven, 45.

17) See P. Borgen, Bread from Heaven, 152, n. 2.

18) In structure, John 5:1-16 shows many similarities with 9:1 ff., a passage which Reim includes in his Semeia source.

19) See E. Ruckstuhl, op.cit., 31.

20) The following points are classified as material of synoptic character by Reim: the quotation of Isa 40:3 in John 1:23, and 1:26 f., 33, cf. 1:15; 30 and 1:34. As a result of these insertions, the Evangelist, according to Reim, added the phrase "the Christ" 1:20; 25, and mentioned Jesus' baptizing activity, 3:26 and 4:1. Reim does not give convincing reasons why the Evangelist had to make these additions as a result of his use of elements from the suggested 4th Synoptic Gospel.

21) Reim says that the call for repentance implied in the quotation from Isa 40:3 in John 1:23, does not fit into the ideas found in the context, but points to the context in the 4th Synoptic Gospel. - It is not necessary to connect the idea of "the voice" in 1:23 with a call for repentance, however, but rather with the idea of "witness", 1:23 etc. It is a weakness, that Reim does not discuss this possibility, nor does he give a thorough discussion of the central idea of witness in John and the (rabbinic) background material.

22) Reim, op.cit., 238-46.

23) Cf. Reim, op.cit., 273 ff., etc.

24) An example of such dual activity of handing on tradition and interpreting it, is found in 1 Cor 10 and 11. In 1 Cor 11:23-26 Paul renders the traditional unit of the institution of the Lord's Supper. In 11:27 ff. a paraphrasing interpretation follows. Moreover, in 10:16-21, a paraphrasing interpretation of words from the institution (the cup, the bread, the blood and body) is given, with the tradition on the institution presupposed, but not rendered.

25) Cf. B. Lindars, John, 100.

26) ibid., 165.

27) See P. Borgen, Bread from Heaven, 91 ff.

28) See P. Borgen, "John and the Synoptics in the Passion Narrativ", NTS, 5, (1959), 249-50, also in 'Logos was the True Light' and Other Essays on the Gospel of John, (Trondheim, 1983) 67-80.

29) P. Borgen, NTS, 5, (1959), 246-59. See also the same hypothesis developed in A. Dauer, Die Passionsgeschichte im Johannesevangelium; eine traditionsgeschichtliche und theologische Untersuchung zu John 18.1-19.30, (München, 1972).

30) Cf. C.H. Dodd, The Apostolic Preaching and Its Developments, (repr., London, 1939) 104 ff., and 164 ff., and id., The Interpretation of the Fourth Gospel, 6 f.

31) This way of analyzing John's Gospel is especially found in A. Fridrichsen, "Jesus avskedstal i fjärde evangeliet", SEÅ, 3, (1938) 1-16; P. Borgen, Bread; and id., NT, 14, (1972) 115-30, and B. Lindars, Behind the Fourth Gospel; and id. John.

32) Se the works mentioned in note 31, and also W.A. Meeks, The Prophet-King; N.A. Dahl, "The Johannine Church", 124-42, and id., Der Erstgeborene Satan, 70-84.

CHAPTER NINE
THE OLD TESTAMENT IN THE FORMATION OF NEW TESTAMENT THEOLOGY

The topic of the role of the Old Testament in New Testament theology is so comprehensive that only some aspects can be treated in this chapter. In spite of the extensive nature of the subject, it is surprising to note that the Old Testament has been drawn into major books on New Testament theology only to a limited degree. For example, in his book The Theology of the New Testament (London, 1973), W.G. Kümmel stresses that there must be separate presentations of Old Testament theology and New Testament theology. R. Bultmann, Theology of the New Testament, 1-2 (New York, 1951-1955) draws the same distinction. As a result, the Old Testament is brought into the discussion of New Testament theology mainly as subordinate points, such as: Jesus and Jewish piety: the relationship between the Church and Judaism; Paul's teaching on freedom from the Law (Bultmann); Jesus' preaching of God's will and the Jewish tradition; Paul's understanding of the history of Israel in relation to the Christ-event; and his understanding of the Law, etc. (Kümmel).

In this way, the relatively independent developments of Old and New Testaments as two different disciplines have had the effect that the role of the Ole Testament in New Testament theology has not been given a broad enough treatment. Thus, more attention should be paid to this subject. Moreover, the use of the Old Testament in the New Testament can throw light upon theological agreements and differences among its various parts. In the following some points relative to the Gospel of John, Pauline letters, and the Synoptic Gospels will be taken up.

In New Testament Studies, 23, (1976) 59-66, B. Lindars published an article on "The Place of the Old Testament in the Formation of New Testament Theology". This essay may serve as a convenient point of departure for our discussion. Lindars here stresses the fact that besides quotations and literary allusions to the Old Testament, there are also major Old Testament themes, such as creation, exodus, Israel, covenant, righteousness, life etc. Thus, the Old Testament is the greatest single influence in the formation of New Testament theology. Moreover, Lindar's rightly states that contemporary Jewish exegesis is the proper background to the church's use of the Old

Testament. He mentions exegesis found in liturgical forms, in rabbinic literature, in the targumim, in the Qumran writings, and in apocalyptic literature. The writings of Philo of Alexandria should be added to Lindar's list.

Philo of Alexandria and his writings are much debated and it may therefore be difficult to relate him to the present topic. His writings are, nevertheless, an extensive source for Judaism during the first half of the first century. Most of his writings are exegetical commentaries, and his interpretation of the Pentateuch also influence his other writings. (1)

In New Testament research Philonic exegesis has especially been utilized to throw light upon the concept of Logos in John's Gospel and upon the platonizing exegesis and thoughts in the Epistle to the Hebrews. (2) It has been pointed out that Philo's exegesis can illuminate other New Testament ideas as well, and his use of exegetical techniques and forms produces comparative material of interest. Moreover, when Philo - or the other exegetes to whom he refers - can be shown to draw on common Jewish exegetical traditions, also preserved for example in the later rabbinic writings, then he can give support for the understanding that these traditions existed in New Testament times. (3)

When Lindars refers to the Qumran sect and apocalyptic writers and their application of the Old Testament to their own generation, Philo seems to offer another parallel to the New Testament at this point. He can apply his exposition of the Old Testament to the life of the Jewish community and the treatises To Flaccus and The Embassy to Gaius contain theologically interpreted history. They can be classified as passion narratives, and Philo's exposition of the Pentateuch serves as interpretative key. (4)

Guiding the Process

Professor Lindars rightly stresses that the role of the Old Testament in the New Testament is to be seen relative to God's 'declaration in Christ'. This fact leads him to state both that the Old Testament has authority and at the same time takes the place of a servant:

> The scriptures are, then, an agreed basis for discussion. They have an authority which is unquestioned...
>
> The place of the Old Testament in the formation of New Testament theology is that of a servant, ready to run to the

aid of the gospel whenever it is required, bolstering up arguments, and filling out meaning through evocative allusions, but never acting as the master or leading the way, nor even guiding the process of thought behind the scenes.

There seems to be some tension between the view that 'the scriptures have an authority which is unquestioned' and the definition of their role as "that of a servant ... (not) even guiding the process of thought behind the scenes'. In my comments I shall be more in agreement with the stress on authority, since the symbol of a servant does not seem to do justice to the historical data about the role played by the Old Testament in the formation of New Testament theology. Since the Old Testament was the thought-world in which Jesus, the disciples and the other first Christians lived, and since the Old Testament was woven into the very fabric of Jewish institutions and Jewish ways of life, it therefore determined the theological issues raised to a large extent, either negatively or positively.

It may prove fruitful to begin the discussion with a characterization of Judaism. Since the term 'the Old Testament' is itself an interpretative designation, the more neutral term 'the scriptures' will be used. In Judaism the scriptures - primarily the Pentateuchal Law - served as the centre of revelation and devotion. As they were interpreted, they had the function of being religious, civil, criminal and ethical law, and they formed the constitution of the nation. As such they were recognized (5) by the Roman authorities, although within limits. From the viewpoint of the Jews, the scriptures were the Law which all nations ought to have accepted, but which, nevertheless, became the distinctive mark of the Jewish nation. (6) Thus the scriptures, especially the Pentateuch as the Torah, should determine all aspects of the life of the Jews. (7)

In this way, the institutions and other aspects of the life of the Jewish people served as a functional exegesis of the scriptures: the Temple worship and the Temple tax, the keeping of the Sabbath, the synagogal activities, the functions of the teachers, the purity laws regarding meals, the understanding of the land of Israel, the ethical behaviour, and so on.

The scriptures served in this way as centre for the revelation of God's will, and as a focus of loyalty for the Jewish people, whether in Palestine or in the Diaspora. They were the centre of devotion and enthusiasm to such a degree that they even called forth willingness to martyrdom. Philo wrote:

at any rate for more than two thousand (years) they have not changed a single word of what he (Moses) wrote but would even endure dying a thousand deaths sooner than accept anything contrary to the laws and customs which he had ordained. (8)

Indeed, a variety of views and movements existed within Judaism and a variety of exegetical traditions. And hellenistic influences were absorbed by the Jews, in Palestine and to a larger degree in the Diaspora; but, on the whole, they were adapted to the basic structures and basic loyalities of Judaism, with its centre in God's will revealed in the scriptures, the prescribed Temple worship and Temple tax included.

Jesus, the disciples, Paul, and the other first Christians, were Jews who lived within the context of Judaism. The comprehensive role of the scriptures and their exegetical applications to the daily life of individuals and society, served therefore as an important factor for the formation of New Testament theology, since they created many of the issues to be taken up on its 'agenda'.

Some of these scriptural issues were: the keeping of the Sabbath, the question of divorce and other halakhic problems, the authority of Jesus as teacher, purity laws applied to table fellowship, and then circumcision. In this way New Testament theology may partly be characterized as a theology of encounters and confrontations, a theology of yes and no to Jewish interpretations and applications of the scriptures. This Christian theological and exegetical activity also challenged the basic and actual structure of Judaism, where the scriptures, as the divine Law of the people, served as foundation.

Paul illustrates this confrontation when in Phil. 3: 5 ff. he looks back upon his own conversion from persecutor to apostle. As a Pharisee he had dedicated himself to scriptures (and oral tradition) as the centre of revelation and loyalty. In Phil 3:9 he tells about the shift which took place.

be found in him (Christ), not having a righteousness of my own based on law but that which is through faith in Christ, the righteousness from God that depends on faith.

Paul's binding to the scriptures as law is replaced by the binding to Christ. There is therefore some truth in the understanding that Christ here has taken over the place and role of the scriptures as the Law. (9) Furthermore, the scriptures as the Law have formulated the theological issue and problem at stake, that of righteousness. Paul's doctrine of justification by faith in Christ means the reversal of the position he held when he lived within the structure of Pharisaic Judaism with its binding to the Pentateuchal Law of Moses. (10)

In conclusion it must be said that the scriptures to a large extent guided the process of thought, and created many of the theological issues which were taken up in the New Testament.

Authoritative Witness

Professor Lindars emphasizes the fact that contemporary Jewish exegesis is the proper background to the church's use of the scriptures. It may thus be of interest to show how Jewish exegesis can serve as background by using as illustration the theological issue of righteousness. As shown above, this topic was 'placed on the New Testament agenda' because of the role the concept played within the Jewish religion of the Law.

Although Paul reversed the position which he held as a Pharisaic Jew, he nevertheless formulated this theological problem of righteousness and its solution by means of scriptural exegesis. And the scriptures were re-evaluated from his new centre of allegiance, Jesus Christ, but still had a role beyond that of being 'a servant, ready to run to the aid of the gospel whenever it is required', as Professor Lindars stated. The scriptures rather served the function of a legal witness to justification through faith. Paul's exegesis then showed that this doctrine had the authoritative and proper scriptural basis.

The exegetical discussion along this line is developed in Rom 4 and Gal 3. Some selected points from Gal 3 can serve as examples of the way in which Paul follows Jewish hermeneutical method in his reinterpretation. N.A. Dahl has shown in a study how Paul in Gal 3 employs the same hermeneutical method as is also found in Philo and in rabbinic exegesis. (11) In their problem-solving exegesis one problem discussed is the occurrence of contradictions within the scriptures. The regular hermeneutical principle then was the view that both contradictory words were to be maintained in their different contexts, but usually one was to be given the priority. In this way Philo solves the contradiction between Num 23:19 that God is not like a man and Deut 8:5 that he is like a man. Philo defends both statements and solves the problem by saying that Num 23:19 - God is not like a man - is the basic principle - while Deut 8:5 - God is like a man - expresses the subordinate pedagogical approach needed in presenting God, since revelation is to be grasped by men.

Correspondingly, Paul in Gal 3 formulated the theological problem of faith and works by discussing the contradiction he sees between Hab 2:4 'He who through faith is righteous shall live' and Lev 18:5 'He who does them shall live by them'. Paul's solution is the view that Hab 2:4 gives the basic principle of justification by faith in Christ, while Lev 18:5, about the works of the law, has a subordinate place within the context of the Law of Moses, seen as an interim arrangement until the coming of Christ.

Moreover, the Epistle to the Galatians shows how such scriptural and theological debate was occasioned by very specific points of confrontation, such as circumcision (5:2, 6:12 f.). Paul's opponents were advocates of a Jewish legalism which attempted to integrate Christianity into the basic structure of Judaism, cf. 2:16, 3:21 b, 4:21, 5:4. (12) Paul then relates his exegesis of the scriptures to this situation in the Galatian church, to show that such an integration was not scriptural at all.

Transferred Ideas

The reason Professor Lindars characterizes the role of the scriptures as that of a servant is the central role which Jesus Christ plays in the New Testament. Lindars correctly maintains that Jesus Christ is the interpretative key, and on this basis he stresses the newness of the Gospel in phrases like 'God's new declaration in his Son' and 'God's new word'. Such formulations give rise to two comments: (I) the scriptures have also influenced the interpretative key itself, Jesus Christ, and (2) in spite of the newness of the word of Christ, the same God speaks and acts in the Old and New Testament.

The influence of the scriptures on New Testament christology has been examined by many scholars in recent years. As an example, M. Black's study, 'The Christological use of the Old Testament in the New Testament', (13) can be mentioned. Professor Lindars has also referred to Black's study, but mainly in support of the tremendous impact of the Christ-event itself. The corresponding aspect is also to be emphasized, however, namely the impact made by the scriptures in and on the Christ-event. The way in which ideas from the scriptures have been transferred to Jesus Christ can for example be illustrated by the giving of the Law on Mt Sinai.

The central place of the Law of Moses in Judaism brought

into the foreground the revelation of God's will on Mt Sinai. In this way the receiving of the Torah by Moses and the people, and also the notions of Moses' ascent to God, and of God's theophanic descent, became important features. The Jewish scholar S.E. Karff expresses this in the following way; 'The Covenant at Sinai provides the context for a Jewish understanding of the divine-human encounter in History' ... it is 'a paradigm of the rabbinic understanding of God's relation to man'. (14)

In this way the scriptures, from the place given them in Judaism, put the Sinai-event on the agenda of New Testament theology. One way of meeting this challenge was to reduce the importance of the revelation on Mt Sinai by moving it into the background. Paul gives such an interpretation when he says that the Law, given by God through the mediation of angels and Moses on Mt Sinai, came in 'on the side' and had a special function for a limited period, until Christ, Gal 3:19; Rom 5:20.

Another response is given in the Gospel of John, especially in John 5:37-8: 'His voice you have never heard, his form you have never seen; and you do not have his word abiding in you.' From the context the meaning becomes clear: the Jews, who refuse to interpret the scriptures christologically and do not 'come to' Jesus, prove that they have no share in the revelation at Mt Sinai. Since John 6:46 declares that there is no vision of God apart from the Son, then it is even probable that God's 'form' appearing at Mt Sinai, 5:37, is identified with the Son of God. (15) In John's interpretation here the Sinai-revelation is exclusively claimed for the disciples who believe in Jesus Christ. The 'Jews', who disbelieve, are denied any share in it.

John's Gospel can, moreover, illustrate Karff's statement that the Sinai-event served as a paradigm of the understanding of God's revelation to man, but with the decisive modification that here it is understood christologically: For example, the lawgiving of Moses, as it was developed as a paradigm in Judaism, served as the conceptual model behind the Prologue. Several scholars have shown that John 1:14; 17-18 draw on the theophany at Mt Sinai, where the law was given and Moses wanted to see God's glory. These ideas are in John transferred to Jesus Christ, and transformed on this basis (16) the disciples were now given the vision of God's glory which was denied Moses. When such a concept is employed, ideas from other theophanies may be fused into the composition. Thus, ideas about God's presence in the Temple, and Wisdom taking up residence in Israel, may also have been transferred to Jesus in John 1:14, and transformed on that basis. (17) In this way I share Professor Lindars' reservation about the typological method as such, and rather prefer the more flexible concept and method of scriptural thought-models employed in the New Testament.

The transfer of the role of the scriptures and related ideas to Jesus can also be seen where the revelation at Mt Sinai is not the primary model. For example, the study of the scriptures in Judaism may form the background and the model. In Matt 18:20 'For where two or three are gathered in my name, there am I in the midst of them', both the idea of the study of the scriptures and the idea of the presence of the Shechinah seem to be transferred to Jesus, as is suggested by the parallel in Abot 3:3: "When two sit and there are between them the words of Torah the Schechinah rests between them." (18)

Correspondingly, according to John 5:39-40, Jesus takes over the role given to the scriptures in Judaism: "You search the scriptures, because you think that in them you have eternal life; and it is they that bear witness to me; yet you refuse to come to me that you may have life." John's rendering here of the view of the Jews is supported for instance by Abot 2:8: "He who has acquired words of Torah has acquired for himself the life of the world to come." (18)

In John 5:39-40 the coming to Jesus takes over the role played by the Jews' searching of the scriptures, and Jesus is the giver of eternal life in the place of the scriptures. Again we find that ideas about the scriptures were transferred to Jesus and were reinterpreted on that very basis. This process meant criticism of the basic structure of Judaism, where they searched for life in the scriptures themselves. It also implied that the scriptures served as witness to Jesus Christ, (19) and to a large extent influenced the christological concepts themselves.

The other comment which needed to be made was the statement that in spite of the newness of the word of Christ, the same God speaks and acts in the Old and the New Testament. In the New Testament a selection is made of Old Testament quotations, allusions and ideas. The selection is not, however, meant to exclude other parts of the Old Testament or replace the Old Testament itself. Consequently, the New Testament presupposes and relies on the Old Testament in such a way that the understanding of God and his actions would be incomplete if the New Testament only had been kept. The New Testament does not teach a new God, but sees God as the Creator and as the God of Abraham, Isaac and Jacob, just as the Old Testament does. The Old Testament is therefore an integral part of God's revelation, centred as it is in the works and words of Jesus Christ.

A final question has to be raised. Is the Old Testament only an integral part of New Testament theology as this theology developed on the basis of the resurrection belief, or did Jesus in his self-understanding, and in his works and message also employ this kind of Old Testament exegesis? Professor Lindars indicates that some of the exegetical intuitions in the New Testament are to be traced back to Jesus himself.

This question needs to be developed further. Jesus lived within an environment which was permeated by the scriptures and by scriptural ideas. The scriptures, therefore, as they were applied to institutions and to daily life, constituted Jesus' frame of reference as well as being a source for direct reference. Jesus drew on the scriptural view of God, (20) referred to the patriarchs, (21) the scriptural ideas of the twelve tribes of Israel, (22) and of repentance, etc. (23) And the confrontations with other Jews concerning the Sabbath implied an exegesis of the Old Testament.

The fact of Jesus' execution, moreover, makes it evident that Jesus' contemporaries raised questions about his role and authority, and that his own understanding of himself made him willing to allow this conflict of authority to be brought to its ultimate end, death. This conflict implied a challenge to the prevailing understanding of the authority of the Law of Moses, but at the same time exegetical ideas with regard to Jesus' person and role were brought into play both by his surroundings and by Jesus himself. (24)

In this presentation we have attempted to illustrate and, at some points, to elaborate upon aspects of Professor Lindars' paper. At the same time questions have been raised as to the adequacy of the metaphor of 'servant' to characterize the role of the Old Testament in the formation of New Testament theology. Other of Lindars' formulations do not seem to do justice either to the fundamental role played by the Old Testament: for example, the role is more than to be a mere mode of expression used in an ad hoc way. The Old Testament is rather a necessary and integral part of New Testament theology, just as Jesus Christ was a Jew and cannot be understood severed from Israel and its history, interpreted as revelation. (25) These comments offer support for the thesis which Professor Lindars formulated in this way: 'The scriptures are, then, an agreed basis for discussion. They have an authority which is unquestioned.'

NOTES

1) See the surveys in L. Cohn, Philologus, Sup 7, 385-435; E. Schürer, Geschichte des jüdischen Volkes, 4. ed., 3, 633-95; P. Borgen, CRINT, II:2, 233-282.

2) See P. Feine, J. Behm and W.G. Kümmel, Introduction to the New Testament (New York, 1966), 155 and 277f.

3) See P. Borgen, Bread from Heaven; idem, NT, 14 (1972), 115-30. W.A. Meeks, The Prophet King.

4) The Pentateuchal interpretation is evident in the following way. (1) In Philo's interpretation of the Jewish people as Israel, the one who sees God, and as the people under God's special care, where the scriptural basis is Gen 32 in particular. See Gaium 4, together with Leg all II:34; Quod Deus 144; Conf 146, etc. (2) In his interpretation of God's governing function through beneficent powers and punitive powers, where the scriptural basis is in particular the Pentateuchal terms for God, θεός and κύριος. See Gaium 6-7, together with Quod Deus 77-8; Plant 50; Conf 171, etc. (3) In his interpretation of Flaccus' sin of arrogance and Gaius' sin of overstepping the bounds of human nature and claiming to be god - ideas which Philo in his exegesis finds to be expressed in Num 15:30. See Gaium 75 and 367 f; Flacc 152, together with Virt 171-5. (4) In his interpretation of the punishment of Flaccus, where he draws on words from Deut 28:(15-)67. See Flacc 167.

5) See S. Safrai et al. CRINT, I:1, 308-503.

6) See Pesiq Rab Kah 103b and 186a; cf. Philo, Mos. II:44; I Macc 2:67; II Baruch 48:24; Abot 3:15. F. Weber, Jüdische Theologie, 2 ed. (Leipzig, 1857), 57 ff.; R. Asting, 'Nomismens innflytelse på hellighetsbegrepet i jødedommen', NTT, 29, 43-70.

7) For this characterization of the place of Torah in Judaism, see especially R. Asting, NTT, 29, 43-70.

8) Apol Iud 6:9. Concerning martyrdom for the sake of the Law of Moses, see I Macc. 13:14; Gaium 232 ff.; b. Abod Zar, 18a, etc.

9) See U. Wilckens, "Die Bekehrung des Paulus als religionsgeschichtliches Problem", ZTK, 41, (1959) 273-293.

10) K. Haacker, "Die Berufung des Verfolgers und die Rechtfertigung des Gottlosen", Theologische Beiträge, 6, (1975) 12ff.

11) N.A. Dahl, STK, 45, (1969), 22-36; in German: 'Widersprüche in der Bibel, ein altes hermeneutisches Problem', ST, 25, (1971) 1-19.

12) P. Feine, J. Behm and W.G. Kümmel, Introduction, 193-5.

13) NTS, 18, (1971) 1-14.

14) S.E. Karff, "The Agadah as Source of Contemporary Jewish Theology", The Central Conference of American Rabbis' Yearbook, 73, (1965), 193.

15) See P. Borgen, Bread from Heaven, 151-2; cf. N.A. Dahl, 'The Johannine Church, 132-133; W.A. Meeks, The Prophet-King, 299-300.

16) M.-E. Boismard, St. John's Prologue, 136-40; N.A. Dahl, "The Johannine Church", 132-3, and n. 13; P. Borgen, Bread from Heaven, 150 f., idem, NT, 14, (1972) 115-30.

17) See for example B. Lindars, John, ad loc.

18) Translation is taken from R. Travers Herford, The Ethics of the Talmud: Sayings of the Fathers, (New York, 1962, repr.) ad loc.

19) Cf. that in John 5:46 it is said that Moses wrote of Jesus. On this basis the following hypothesis can be formulated as to the formation of the Johannine tradition: Since Moses wrote about Jesus, the Evangelist and the Johannine community regarded the scriptures as valid sources to the words and works of Jesus, together with the Gospel-tradition received from his disciples. If so, then in John Gospel-traditions are interpreted and recast from exegetical insights into the Old Testament.

20) Cf. Luke 10:21/Matt 11:25.

21) Cf. Mark 12:26 par.

22) Cf. Mark 3:14 par; Matt 19:28, etc.; I Cor 15:5.

23) Cf. Mark 1:15 par.

24) Cf. Mark 2:23-8 par; 7:15 par; 10:2-9 par; 11:27 ff. par; 12:35-37 a par.

CHAPTER TEN
GOD'S AGENT IN THE FOURTH GOSPEL

The state of research

In his discussion of Christological ideas in the Fourth Gospel, C.H. Dodd finds that the status and function of the Son as God's delegated representative recalls the language of the Old Testament prophets. Certain peculiarities, such as the Son's complete and uninterrupted dependence on the Father, and the dualism between higher and lower spheres, suggest to him that this aspect of Jesus' human career is a projection of the eternal relation of the Son and the Father upon the field of time. (1) This intepretation by Dodd does not take seriously the idea of the Son being commissioned and sent, but rather dissolves the idea of agency into an eternal and "Platonic" idea of relationship.

R. Bultmann, on the other hand, rightly places the commissioning and sending of the Son in the very center of the message of the Gospel. He also finds certain points of contact between the Johannine ideas and the prophets of the Old Testament. But John, according to Bultmann, goes beyond the thought of a prophet and interprets gnostic mythology about divine and pre-existent agents, commissioned by the Father and sent to the world. The Mandean literature is Bultmann's main source for his hypothesis. (2)

Close parallels found in the halakah encourage the investigation of the extent to which John's Christology and soteriology are moulded on Jewish rules for agency. K.H. Rengstorf had made a promising beginning at this point, although he does not think that the idea of agency plays any central role in the Johannine idea of Jesus as the Son of God. (3) Also Théo Preiss and C.K. Barrett draw attention to the similarities between John and the halakah at certain places. Significantly enough, Preiss discusses the idea of the Son as commissioned by the Father within the wider framework of the juridical aspects of Johannnine thought. The importance of judicial ideas in John has been stressed by N.A. Dahl as well. (4) In spite of the work of these scholars, the field is open to examine the degree in which halakhic principles of agent are reflected in the Fourth Gospel.

Principles of agency

(a) The basic principle of the Jewish institution of agency is that "an agent is like the one who sent him." (5) This relationship applied regardless of who was the sender. Thus, for example "the agent of the ruler is like the ruler himself." (6) Consequently, to deal with the agent was the same as dealing with the sender himself:

> With what is the matter to be compared? With a king of flesh and blood who has a consul (agent) in the country. The inhabitants spoke before him. Then said the king to them, you have not spoken concerning my servant but concerning me. (7)

The saying in John 12:44 is a very close parallel to the saying by the king in the quotation from Siphre:

> John: he who believes in me, believes not in me but in him who sent me;
>
> Siphre: you have not spoken concerning my servant but concerning me.

Another saying which expresses the same idea, that dealing with the agent is the same as dealing with the sender himself, is found in all four gospels. (8) The Johannine version occurs in 13:20.

> he who receives any one whom I send receives me;
> he who receives me receives him who sent me.

There are also other similar sayings scattered throughout John:

> 5:23: he who does not honor the Son does not honor the Father who sent him;
> 12:45: he who sees me sees him who sent me;
> 14:9: he who has seen me has seen the Father;
> 15:23: he who hates me hates my Father also.

The halakhic principle that "an agent is like the one who sent him" usually meant that the agent was like his sender as far as the judicial function and effects were concerned. There were, however, rabbis who developed it into a judicial mysticism saying that the agent is a person identical with the sender. (9) Thus not only his authority and his function are derived from the sender, but also his qualities. Qiddushin 43a formulates this mysticism in the following way: the agent ranks as his master's own person. (10)

In the Fourth Gospel the personal identity between the Son and the Father is stated in several different ways. One formula is "I and the Father are one" (10:30) and another formula is "the Father is in me and I am in the Father" (10:38; cf.

14:10-11 and 17:21-23). In 10:36-38 it is explicitly stated that it is the agent, the Son in the capacity of being sent into the world, who is one with the sender. Similarly, in 17: 20-23, the unity between the Son and the Father shall make it possible for the world to recognize the Son as agent of the Father, "so that the world may believe that thou hast sent me". Moreover, in 10:37-38 and in 14:10-11 the oneness between the Son and the Father is made manifest in Jesus' words and works which also are said to be the works of the Father.

(b) Although John interprets the relationship between the Father and the Son in such legalistic terms, it is a legalism that is not seen in contrast to personal "mysticism". Thus Preiss' term "judicial mysticism" is a very apt one, and the personal element is further deepened by the fact that it was the Son who was the agent of the Father. (11) It should be added that the idea of the Son-Father relationship also implies that the Son is subordinate to the Father. This subordination fits very well to the principles of agency, since here the thoughts of unity and identity between agent and sender are modified by an emphasis on the superiority of the sender. The principle is stated in John 13:16 and Gen Rab 78:

John: a servant is not greater than his master; nor is he who is sent greater than him who sent him. (12)

Gen Rab: the sender is greater than the sent.

Matthew 10:24, cf. Luke 6:40, offers a parallel to the first part of John 13:16: "nor (is) a servant above his master." What in Matthew and Luke is said about pupil-teacher and servant-master relationship is in John specifically applied to agency.

(c) Another important area of agency centers around the specific mission of an agent. it was a legal presumption that an agent would carry out his mission in obedience to his sender, (13) as can be seen from Erub 31b-32a, Qidd 2:4 and Ter 4:4:

> It is a legal presumption that an agent will carry out his mission (עושה שליחותו) (14)
>
> I appointed you for my advantage, and not for my disadvantage. (15)
> If a householder said to his agent (לשלוהו), "Go and give heave-offering," the agent should give heave-offering according to the house-holder's mind (כרעתו של בעל הבית), (16)

In accordance with this principle, Christ was an obedient agent who did as the Father had commanded. He said, "I have come down from heaven, not to do my own will but the will of him who sent me" (John 6:38). Likewise, the Christ always did what was pleasing to the one who sent him (8:29).

(d) The Johannine idea of the mission of Christ as God's agent is seen within the context of a lawsuit. The statement in B Qam 70a is of special interest for this question:

> Go forth and take legal action so that you may acquire title to it and secure the claim for yourself.

The principles reflected in this rule are also found in the Fourth Gospel. Although there is no scene of commissioning as pictured in the halakhic statement ("go forth", etc.), the commissioning itself is referred to in these words: "I came not of my own accord, but he sent me" (John 8:42); "For I have not spoken of my own authority; the Father who sent me has himself given me commandment what to say and what to speak" (John 12:49); "For he whom God has sent utters the words of God" (3:34); "My teaching is not mine, but his who sent me" (7:16); "... he who sent me is true, and I declare to the world what I have heard from him" (8:26); "... I do nothing on my own authority but speak thus as the Father taught me. And he who sent me is with me..." (8:28-29); "... the word which you hear is not mine but the Father's who sent me" (14:24).

According to the halakah the sender transferred his own rights and the property concerned to the agent. (17) On this basis the agent might acquire the title in court and secure the claim for himself. The will of the sender, the Father, in John 6:39 makes just this transfer clear: "This is the will of him who sent me, that all that he has given me (πᾶν ὃ δέδωκέν μοι)..." The transfer is even more pointedly stated in 17:6: "thine they were, and thou gavest them to me" (σοὶ ἦσαν κἀμοὶ αὐτοὺς ἔδωκας). (18)

The next step is the actual acquiring of the title in court and the agent's securing of the claim for himself. John 12:31-32 pictures such a court scene:

> Now is the judgment of this world,
> now shall the ruler of this world be cast out;
> and I, when I am lifted up from the earth,
> will draw (ἑλκύσω) all men unto myself (πρὸς ἐμαυτόν).

There is close resemblance between the two phrases "I will draw all men to myself" (John) and "secure the claim for yourself" (halakah). In both cases the agent himself is to take possession of the property since the ownership has been transferred to him. John uses a different verb, "draw" (ελκυσω) and not "secure" (ואפיק), but the Johannine term comes from judicial context. The verb renders with all probability the Hebrew משך , to draw, pull, seize. (19) Thus the Septuagint frequently translates משך by ἑλκύειν . (20) And in the halakah of Judaism משך has received the technical meaning of "to take possession of" (by drawing or seizing an object). (21) Thus the meaning of the phrase in John 12:32 and B Qam 70a is the same.

Moreover, the legal acquiring of the title can be seen in John 12:31-32, although pictured in a negative way. The world and the ruler of this world are judged and cast out from the heavenly court. (22) The ruler of this world is judged not to have any just title to or claim upon God's people. (23) Thus it is implied that God's agent has the title and therefore can secure the claim for himself.

Although the ownership, for sake of the lawsuit, is transferred from the sender to his agent, the agent is, of course, still an agent of the sender. Thus as a matter of fact, the sender takes possession of the property when the agent does. The meaning of John 6:44 is to be understood along this line: "No one can come to me (i.e. the agent) unless the Father who sent me (ὁ πέμψας με . i.e. the sender) draws (ἑλκύσῃ) him." In other words, the coming to the agent, Christ, is the same as being in the possession of the Father, and only those who are included in the Father's claim come to His agent. Against this background it is logical that the rabbis discussed if an agent in such cases is to be characterized as partner to his sender. (24)

(e) As Jesus has completed his mission (John 4:34, 5:36, 17:4, 19:30) he is to report to his sender. John 13ff. is dominated by this theme of Jesus' return to his Father: "Jesus, knowing that the Father had given things into his hand, and that he had come from God and was going to God ..., etc." (13:3). And just as the judgment scene in John 12:31-32 was pictured in a proleptic way before its completion on the cross (19:30), so also is the Son's report given ahead of time in the form of the prayer found in John 17: "I glorified thee on earth, having accomplished the work which thou gavest me to do" (17:4).

It is in accordance with the halakah that an agent who is sent on a mission is to return and report to the sender. The return is mentioned in Y. Hag 76d: "Behold we send to you a great man as our shaliach, and he is equivalent to us until such time as he returns to us." Although a contrast between human and divine agency is drawn in Mek Exod 12:1, the passage illustrates the point of return and report by an agent to his sender: "Thy messengers, O God, are not like the messengers of human beings; for the messengers of human beings must needs return to those who send them before they can report. With thy messengers, however, it is not so, ... withersoever they go they are in thy presence and can report: we have executed thy commission." John does not draw this contrast between human and divine agents but applies rather the human principle of return and report also to God's agent, Jesus Christ.

(f) One question remains, namely, the actual effectuation of Jesus' mission after his return to his Father and beyond the limitation of his work in Israel. John found the solution of this problem in the halakhic rule that "an agent can appoint an agent" (Qidd 41a). (25) Consequently at the completion of his own mission, Jesus said: "As thou didst send me into the world, so I have sent them into the world" (John 17:16).

At the last evening before his departure, Jesus therefore first made clear to the disciples the principles of agency, John 13:16.20, and then in his prayer reported to the Father about the sending (Ch. 17), and then after his resurrection the actual commissioning of the disciples took place: "Peace be with you. As the Father has sent me, even so I send you" (John 20:21). Accordingly, the unity between the Father and His agent, the Son, is extended to these agents of the agent: "... as thou, Father. art in me, and I in thee, that they also may be in us, so that the world may believe that thou hast sent me" (John 17:21).

Thus there are striking similarities between the halakhic principles of agency and ideas in the Fourth Gospel, as (a) the unity between the agent and his sender - (b) although the agent is subordinate, (c) the obedience of the agent to the will of the sender, (d) the task of the agent in the lawsuit, (e) his return and reporting back to the sender, and (f) his appointing of other agents as an extension of his own mission in time and space.

Heavenly agent

On the basis of the analysis of agency in John one might be tempted to draw the conclusion that the Fourth Gospel represents the socalled normative and rabbinic Judaism, (26) and not mystical Judaism which E.R. Goodenough so forcefully championed. (27) Such a conclusion would be premature. the study so far has not explained the fact that Jesus according to John is not just a human and earthly agent but a divine and heavenly agent who has come down among men. Bultmann's hypothesis of gnostic mythology would offer an explanation of this point, since the gnostic agents were divine figures who were sent down to earth. (28)

The close similarities between agency in John and halakhic principles point in another direction. The question can be formulated in this way: Where do we find halakah applied to the heavenly world and man's relation to it? It is the merit of G.D. Scholem to have brought to the foreground the Merkabah mysticism and to have made manifest its halakhic character. Here we find a combination of halakah, heavenly figures and the heavenly world as is the case with the idea of agency in the Fourth Gospel. (29) H. Odeberg, G. Quispel, N.A. Dahl and P. Borgen have suggested that the Fourth Gospel reflects early stages of Merkabah mysticism. (30)

Since Philo also is influenced by early Merkabah mysticism, his writings can throw light upon ideas in John. (31) In connection with the concept of agency, the Johannine idea of the vision of God can serve as a good point of departure for a comparison with Philo. According to John 12:45 God's agent mediates the vision of God: "he who sees me sees him who sent me." Moreover, in John the agent from God is a heavenly figure and the only one who has seen God:

> Not that any one has seen the Father
> except him who is from God:
> he has seen the Father (John 6:46).

John 6:46 as well as 1:18 ("No one has ever seen God; the only God (Son), who is in the bosom of the Father, he has made him known") are an interpretation of the theophany at Sinai. According to Exod 33:20 there was a significant modification made to this theophany. Moses was not allowed to see the face of God; for no man can see God and live. John adds that one heavenly figure has had this full vision of God, namely the divine Son, the one who is from God. (32)

The closest parallel to this heavenly figure is the idea of the heavenly Israel, "he who sees God." The idea is found in Philo, Conf 146 and Leg all. I:43:

> But if there be any as yet unfit to be called a Son of God, let him press to take his place under God's First-born, the Word, who holds the eldership among the angels, their ruler as it were.
> And many names are his, for he is called, "the Beginning", and the Name of God, and His Word, and the Man after His image, and "he that sees", that is Israel.

> ... the sublime and heavenly wisdom is of many names; for he calls it "beginning" and "image" and "vision of God".

Two observations support the theory that there is a connection between the Christ of the Fourth Gospel and the angel Israel. First, although there is no explicit etymological interpretation of the word Israel ("he who sees God") in John, the idea of Israel is tied together with the idea of vision in the interpretation of Jacob's vision, John 1:47-51. Nathanael, the true Israelite is to see what his ancestor, Jacob/Israel saw. And the reference to the Son of Man (John 1:51) probably presupposes the idea of the heavenly model of Jacob/Israel. (33)

Secondly, important parallels can be seen between John and Philo as to the many other names of the heavenly figure. Both John and Philo identify him who sees with Logos (John 1:1,14 and Conf 146, cf. the heavenly wisdom in Leg all I:43). He is furthermore called the Son, in John the only Son (μονογενής John 1: 14; 3:16.18) and in Philo the firstborn Son (πρωτόγονος Conf 146). It should be added that both John and Philo at times characterize the Logos and the Son as God. (34)

Two other parallel terms for the heavenly figure are Philo's "the Man after God's image" (see Conf 146 and Leg all I:43) and John's "the Son of Man." The kinship between these two terms can be seen from the fact that both John and Philo associate this heavenly man with vision, with ascent into heaven, and with the second birth in contrast to the first birth.

At this point the ideas found in Quaes Exod II: 46 are of particular interest. Philo here says that when Moses, at the theophany at Sinai, was called above on the seventh day (Exod 24:16), he was changed from earthly man into the heavenly man, and the change was a second birth in contrast to the first. John's ideas in 3:3-13 seem to be a polemic against the very idea expressed by Philo. John says that the vision of God's kingdom (35) and the second birth from above are not brought about by ascent into heaven to the Son of Man. It is rather the heavenly man's descent which brings about the second birth. (36)

The conclusion is that John and Philo have in common the idea of a heavenly figure as the one who sees God, associate this figure with Israel, and also have in common several of the other terms and concepts which are crystalized around the same heavenly figure.

Although Philo in Conf 146 says that Israel, "he that sees", mediates the vision of God, he does no apply the halakhic principles of agency to the concept. At this point John differs and says that the heavenly figure, the only one who has seen God, is sent as God's agent to mediate the vision. it is of interest to note that John in 8:16-18 applies also another judicial principle to Christ and his mission. Here the Old Testament and halakhic rule of two witnesses has been applied to the idea of Jesus as the Son of the (heavenly) Father: the Father and the Son both witness. (37)

Conclusion and perspective

Thus the ideas of the heavenly figure who sees God (Israel) and ascent/descent are found in both Philo and John. Similarities have also been found between John and the rabbinic halakah about agency. The Fourth Gospel, therefore, shows that no sharp distinction can be drawn between rabbinic and Hellenistic Judaism. (38)

It has been suggested above that the Jewish background reflected in John should be characterized as early stages of Merkabah mysticism, in which we find such a combination of halakah, heavenly figures and the heavenly world. A strong support for this conclusion is found in text from Nag Hammadi: (39)

> But when Sabaoth received the place of repose because of his repentance, Pistis moreover gave him her daughter Zoe with a great authority so that she might inform him about everything that exists in the eighth (heaven). And since he had an authority, he first created a dwelling place for himself. It is a large place which is very excellent, sevenfold (greater) than all those which exist [in the] seven heavens.
>
> Then in front of his dwelling place he created a great throne on a four-faced chariot called "Cherubin". And the Cherubin has eight forms for each of the four corners-lion forms, and bull forms,

> and human forms, and eagle forms - so that all of the forms total sixty-four forms. And seven archangels stand before him. He is the eighth having authority. All of the forms total seventy-two. For from this chariot the seventy-two gods receive a pattern; and they receive a pattern so that they might rule over the seventy-two languages of the nations. And on that throne he created some other dragon-shaped angels called "Seraphin", who glorify him continually.
>
> Afterward he created an angelic church - thousands and myriads, without number, (belong to her) - being like the church which is in the eighth. And a first-born called "Israel", i.e. "the man who sees god", and (also) having another name, "Jesus the Christ", who is like the Savior who is above the eighth, sits at his right upon an excellent throne.

This text shows close parallels to the ideas discussed from Philo and John, such as the heavenly Son, the firstborn who is the same as the heavenly Israel, the man who sees God. (40) It is significant that this heavenly figure has its place in the heavenly palace near the throne erected upon a chariot. Thus the influence of Merkabah traditions is unmistakable, a fact which shows that the same is the case with regard to the ideas discussed in John and Philo. (41)

Furthermore, the text from Nag Hammadi gives clear evidence for the fact that Jewish Merkabah traditions have influenced the gnostic movement. It is therefore quite probable that the ideas of heavenly agents in gnostic/ Mandean literature similarly have been influenced by Jewish principles of agency and Jewish ideas of heavenly figures. In that case the gnostic agents do not explain the background of God's agent in the Fourth Gospel, as Bultmann thinks. (42) The Fourth Gospel rather gives a clue to the Jewish background of the gnostic/Mandean mythology. (43)

NOTES

1) C.H. Dodd, *The Interpretation of the Fourth Gospel*, 254-262.

2) R. Bultmann, *Johannes*, 187-188; and idem, "Die Bedeutung der neuerschlossenen mandäischen Quellen für das Verständniss des Johannesevangeliums," *ZNW*, 24, (1925) 104-109.

3) K.H. Rengstorf, *Theologisches Wörterbuch zum Neuen Testament*, ed. G. Kittel, 1, (Stuttgart, 1933) 403-405; 421-422; 435-436.

4) Théo Preiss, *Life in Christ*. (London, 1954) 9-31; C.K. Barrett, *St. John*, London, 1958, 216, 474; N.A. Dahl, "The Johannine Church, 137-142; See also P. Borgen, *Bread from Heaven*, 158-164.

5) Mek Exod 12:3; 12:6; Ber 5:5; B Mes 96a; Hag 10b; Qidd 42b, 43a; Menah 93b; Nazir 12b, etc.

6) B Qam 113b.

7) Sipre on Num 12:9, cited in K.H. Rengstorf, *Apostleship. Bible Key Words*, 6, translated from Kittel's *Theologisches Wörterbuch* by J.R. Coates, (London, 1952) 16.

8) See Matt 10:40; cf. Matt 18:5; Mark 9:37 and Luke 9:48. The parallels are discussed in C.H. Dodd, "Some Johannine 'Herrnworte' with parallels in the Synoptic Gospels," *NTS*, 2, (1955/1956) 81-85.

9) The phrase of judicial mysticism as clue to central ideas in John is suggested by Théo Preiss, *Life in Christ*, 25.

10) "He ranks as his own person" (הוה ליה כגופיה). Translation in *The Babylonian Talmud*, Nasim 8, ed. by I. Epstein, (London, 1935) 216. Hebrew text in *Der Babylonian Talmud mit Einschluss der vollständigen Mischnah*, by L. Goldschmidt, 5, (Leipzig, 1906) 845.

11) See Théo Preiss, *Life in Christ*, 24-25: "the formulae suggestive of mystical immanence so typical of Johannine language are regularly intermixed with juridical formulae... Jesus reveals himself to be one with the Father as a result of the strict fidelity with which he waits upon him and utters his words and performs his task as ambassador and witness. (The bond between the Father and the Son) *coincides* with the bond formed by the obedience of a witness... Jesus is in the Father and the Father in him because he does the work of the Father (10:30, 37, 38). Inasmuch as he is the Son of Man sent as a witness from the height of heaven, ... Jesus is according to rabbinical law "as he who sends him."

12) See also John 15:20.

13) Cf. K.H. Rengstorf, *Theologisches Wörterbuch*, 1, 415.

14) Erub 31b-32a; cf. Ketub 99b; Nazir 12a.

15) Qidd 42b; cf. B Bat 169b; Ketub 85a; Bek 61b.

16) Ter 4:4. Cf. the Mediaeval collection, Shulhan Aruq, Hoshen Mishpat, 188:5: "Stets wenn der Vertreter (שהשליה) von dem Willen des Vertretenen (מדעת המשלח) abweicht, is das Vertretungsverhältnis gänzlich aufgelöst." See M. Cohn, "Die Stellvertretung im jüdischen Recht," *Zeitschrift für vergleichende Rechtswissenschaft*, 36, (1920) 206.

17) See M. Cohn, *Zeitschrift für vergleichende Rechtswissenschaft*, 36, (1920) 165-167; L. Auerbach, *Das jüdische Obligationsrecht*, 1, (Berlin, 1870) 567-569.

18) Variants of the phrase occur in John 17:2,6,7; cf. 13:3.

19) So also A. Schlatter, *Der Evangelist Johannes*, 176, and R. Bultmann, *Johannes*, 171, n. 7. These scholars have not, however, focused the attention upon משך as a judicial term.

20) Deut 21:3; Neh 9:30; Ps 9:30 (10:9); Eccl 2:3; Cant 1:4, etc.

21) B Meṣ 4:2; B Meṣ 47a; 48a; 49a. Cf. Ph. Blackmann, (ed. and trans.), *Mishnayoth*, 4, (London, 1951) 579.

22) See N.A. Dahl, The Johannine Church, 139; C.K. Barrett, *St. John* (1958) 355-6 ("The devil will be put out of office, out of authority. He will no longer be ἄρχων; men will be freed from his power").

23) Cf. that the children of Abraham have as Father God and not the devil, John 8:39-47.

24) B Qam 70a, from which the above quotation was taken, discusses this very question; "He was surely appointed but a shaliach. Some, however, say that he is made a partner..."

25) There was discussion among the rabbis on this question, and some offered specific qualifications as to circumstances under which an agent could appoint an agent. See Git 3:5-6; Git 29b.

26) The champion of "normative" Judaism is G.F. Moore, *Judaism*, 1-3, (Cambridge, Mass., 1927-1930).

27) See especially E.R. Goodenough, *Jewish Symbols in the Greco-Roman Period*, 1, (New York, 1953) 3-58.

28) See reference in n. 27.

29) G.D. Scholem, *Major Trends in Jewish Mysticism*, 3rd rev. ed., (New York, 1961); idem, *Gnosticism, Merkabah Mysticism and Talmudic Tradition*, (New York, 1960), 9-19.

30) H. Odeberg, The Fourth Gospel; G. Quispel, "L'Évangile de Jean et la Gnose," in L'Évangile de Jean, Rech Bib 3, (Lyon, 1958) 197-208; N.A. Dahl, "The Johannine Church", 124-142; P. Borgen, Bread from Heaven; have especially emphasized Jewish mysticism as background for John.

31) Concerning elements of Merkabah traditions in Philo, see K. Kohler, "Merkabah," The Jewish Encyclopedia, Ed. I. Singer, 8, (New York, 1947) 500.

32) Further discussion of ideas from the theophany at Sinai in the contexts of John 1:18 and 6:46 in M.E. Boismard, St. John's Prologue, 136-140; S. Schulz, Komposition, 40f.; N.A. Dahl, "The Johannine Church," 132; P. Borgen, Bread from Heaven, 150f.

33) See especially N.A. Dahl, "The Johannine Church," 136-137 and foot notes with numerous references. it is even possible that the etymology of Israel meaning "he who sees God," is implied in John 1:47-51. It would be more of pure speculation to try to find allusions to the etymology also in John 1:18, that "No one has seen God" should render Hebrew לא איש ראה אל Concerning other places in which the idea of Israel and the vision of God are associated in John, see P. Borgen, Bread from Heaven, 175-177.

34) John 1:1.18; Somn I:228-230 and Quaes Gen II:62.

35) For the idea of seeing God's kingdom, see Wisd 10:10.

36) This analysis of John 3:3-13 gives support to the interpretation suggested by H. Odeberg, The Fourth Gospel, ad loc., that v. 13 is a polemic against the idea of visionary ascent among Merkabah mystics. So also N.A. Dahl, "The Johannine Church," 141; cf. also E.M. Sidebottom, The Christ of the Fourth Gospel, 120-121.

Commentators have overlooked the importance of Quaes Exod II:46 for the interpretation of John 3:3ff.

37) See C.H. Dodd, The Interpretation of the Fourth Gospel, 77 and H.L. Strack and P. Billerbeck, Kommentar zum Neuen Testament aus Talmud und Midrasch, II, München 1924, ad loc.

38) Also E.R. Goodenough, "John a Primitive Gospel" JBL, 64, (1945) 145-182 rightly stresses the Jewish background of John. He draws, however, too sharp a distinction between legalistic rabbinism and Hellenistic (mystical) Judaism.

39) H.-G. Bethge and O.S. Wintermute (trans), "On the Origin of the World," in J.M. Robinson (ed), The Nag Hammadi Library, (San Francisco, 1977) 166. Cf. J. Doresse, The Secret Books of the Egyptian Gnostics, (New York, 1960) 167. (See also p. 176f.).

40) See N.A. Dahl, Current Issues (ed. W. Klassen and C.F. Snyder), 136, nn. 21, 22; H. Jonas, "The Secret Books of the Egyptian Gnostics," The Journal of Religion XLII, (1962), 264.

41) See references to the works by J. Doresse The Secret Books, and N.A. Dahl, "The Johannine Church,"

42) R. Bultmann, Johannes; idem, ZNW, 24, (1925) 104-109.

43) Jan-A. Bühner, Der Gesandte und sein Weg im 4. Evangelium, (Tübingen, 1977) has further developed this study on the Jewish concept of agency and its importance for the understanding of Johannine christology. See especially pp. 59-62: "Borgen stellt die richtige Frage...: Wo finden wir halachische Regeln in Bezug auf die himmlische Welt und die menschliche Beziehung zum Himmel?" (p. 60) On pp. 71-72 Bühner states: "... so tritt hier eine entscheidende forschungsgeschichtliche Wende mit den Arbeiten von P. Borgen und W.A. Meeks ein."

CHAPTER ELEVEN
THE USE OF TRADITION IN JOHN 12:44-50

Introduction

The point of departure for this study is the hypothesis that the Johannine discourses are composed from oral (and written) traditions. (1) Accordingly, they do not presuppose one or more comprehensive written sources which run throughout the Gospel. The general problem to be analysed can be formulated in this way: How was a unit of tradition used? There is a wide range of possibilities, from a verbatim and complete quotation to the use of small fragments, even just one word. In this paper we shall attempt to distinguish between a "quote", where a self-contained unit of tradition is repeated, and a paraphrastic use, where small fragments, a phrase or a word, are paraphrased into new sentences. (2)

The problem is to find contemporary examples to illustrate such usages of traditions. The most obvious example of citations of traditions and their use in paraphrasing expositions is of course the Talmud. The Talmud is practically a mere interpretation and amplification of the Mishnah by manifold comments and additions, the Gemara. (3) The Talmud cannot give us much help for the understanding of John's use of tradition, however. The Talmud was written down at a much later date than John. Moreover, the interpretative Gemara amplifies the Mishnah, a comprehensive, written text, which already had developed beyond the oral stage.

A much more helpful example is produced by Paul, who in 1 Cor 10 and 11 quotes an oral tradition and employs fragments from it in an interpretative paraphrase. And most important, Paul quotes from the <u>Gospel</u> tradition and renders a version of the institution of the Lord's Supper.

In 1 Cor 11:23-34 the quote of the tradition and the periphrastic use of fragments are presented in the form of a quote followed by an exposition:

1 Cor 11:23-34:

23 Ἐγὼ γὰρ παρέλαβον ἀπὸ τοῦ κυρίου, ὃ καὶ παρέδωκα ὑμῖν, ὅτι
ὁ κύριος Ἰησοῦς ἐν τῇ νυκτὶ ᾗ παρεδίδετο
24 ἔλαβεν ἄρτον καὶ εὐχαριστήσας ἔκλασεν καὶ εἶπεν,
τοῦτό μού ἐστιν τὸ σῶμα τὸ ὑπὲρ ὑμῶν.
τοῦτο ποιεῖτε εἰς τὴν ἐμὴν ἀνάμνησιν.
25 ὡσαύτως καὶ τὸ ποτήριον μετὰ τὸ δειπνῆσαι, λέγων,

τοῦτο τὸ ποτήριον ἡ καινὴ διαθήκη ἐστὶν ἐν τῷ ἐμῷ αἵματι.
τοῦτο ποιεῖτε, ὁσάκις ἐὰν πίνητε, εἰς τὴν ἐμὴν ἀνάμνησιν.
26 ὁσάκις γὰρ ἐὰν ἐσθίητε τὸν ἄρτον τοῦτον
καὶ τὸ ποτήριον πίνητε,
τὸν θάνατον τοῦ κυρίου καταγγέλλετε, ἄχρις οὗ ἔλθῃ.
27 Ὥστε ὃς ἂν ἐσθίῃ τὸν ἄρτον ἢ πίνῃ τὸ ποτήριον τοῦ κυρίου
ἀναξίως, ἔνοχος ἔσται τοῦ σώματος καὶ τοῦ αἵματος τοῦ κυρίου.
28 δοκιμαζέτω δὲ ἄνθρωπος ἑαυτόν,
καὶ οὕτως ἐκ τοῦ ἄρτου ἐσθιέτω
καὶ ἐκ τοῦ ποτηρίου πινέτω.
29 ὁ γὰρ ἐσθίων καὶ πίνων κρίμα ἑαυτῷ ἐσθίει καὶ πίνει
μὴ διακρίνων τὸ σῶμα.
30 διὰ τοῦτο ἐν ὑμῖν πολλοὶ ἀσθενεῖς καὶ ἄρρωστοι
καὶ κοιμῶνται ἱκανοί.
31 εἰ δὲ ἑαυτοὺς διεκρίνομεν, οὐκ ἂν ἐκρινόμεθα.
32 κρινόμενοι δὲ ὑπὸ τοῦ κυρίου παιδευόμεθα,
ἵνα μὴ σὺν τῷ κόσμῳ κατακριθῶμεν.
33 Ὥστε, ἀδελφοί μου,
συνερχόμενοι εἰς τὸ φαγεῖν ἀλλήλους ἐκδέχεσθε.
34 εἴ τις πεινᾷ, ἐν οἴκῳ ἐσθιέτω,
ἵνα μὴ εἰς κρίμα συνέρχησθε.

By using technical terms for the transmission of tradition, παρέλαβον .... παρέδωκα ... Paul introduces in v. 23 a quote of the Institution of the Lord's Supper, vv. 23 b - 25. (4) The version which he renders is very close to the one found in Luke 22:19-20, even in wording. Nevertheless, since we know the approximate date of 1 Cor no one can maintain that 1 Cor 11:23 ff. depends upon the Gospel of Luke which was written at a later time. Thus, we here see how similar a pericope in Luke may be to the oral tradition as it existed decades earlier. (5)

Although Paul quotes this given unit of the tradition about the Lord's Supper, he at the same time brings interpretative elements into his rendering. This interpretative element is especially evident in v. 26. Paul has here formulated a sentence paralell to v. 25b, so that at first Jesus seems still to be speaking:

v.25b ὁσάκις ἐὰν πίνητε ....

v.26a ὁσάκις γὰρ ἐὰν ἐσθίητε ......

In spite of this similarity, v. 26 is clearly Paul's own formulation since he in this sentence refers to Jesus in 3rd person, as the Lord: "For as often as you eat this bread and drink this cup you proclaim the Lord's death until he comes." (6)

Then in vv. 27 ff. Paul gives a paraphrasing commentary on the quoted unit of tradition. From this fact we see that (already) in the middle of the fifties the Jesus-tradition was so fixed that it was quoted and used as basis for an added exposition.

As can be seen from the words underscored with a single line in vv. 27 ff. Paul utilizes fragments - words and phrases - from the quoted tradition and builds them into a paraphrasing exposition which applies it to a case-situation. (7) In Paul's exposition the genitive τοῦ κυρίου v. 27, serves as a clarifying addition to the fragments from the quoted tradition,.. τὸ ποτήριον and .. τοῦ σώματος ... As can be seen from the words underscored by a double line, legal terms are woven together with these fragments from the tradition of the Lord's Supper. Such legal terms are: ἀναξίως, Ἔνοξος ἔσται, v. 27; and κρίμα ... διακρίνων... in v. 29. In vv. 30-32 Paul elaborates upon these legal terms, without drawing on fragments from the eucharistic tradition. Finally, in vv. 33-34 he returns back to the explicit discussion of the eucharistic meal. Here he refers back to the institution of the Lord's Supper, vv. 23 ff., and even back to the situation in Corinth, pictured in vv. 17 ff. In these concluding verses, vv. 33-34, we again, as in vv. 27-29, find terminology from (the eucharistic) meal (τὸ φαγεῖν - ἐσθιέτω) woven together with a legal term (κρίμα).

Although Paul writes the exposition himself and applies the eucharistic tradition to a specific case, he nevertheless uses traditional ethical/legal forms. The form of casuistic legal clauses is especially evident:

v.27: ὃς ἂν ἐσθίῃ ...., ἔνοχος ἔσται ....
v.29: ὁ γὰρ ἐσθίων ... κρίμα ἑαυτῷ ἐσθίει ...

For such casuistic statements, see Matt 5:21.22, etc. See Old Testament examples and examples from the Qumran writings in W. Nauck, Die Tradition und der Charakter des ersten Johannesbriefes, (Tübingen, 1957) 29 ff. Examples from rabbinic writings and Philo are given by P. Borgen, Bread from Heaven, (Leiden, 1965, repr 1981) esp. 88 f.; see further P. Fiebig, Der Erzählungsstil der Evangelien, (Leipzig, 1925) 3-20.

The following sentences give rules for avoiding judgment:
v. 31 εἰ δὲ ἑαυτοὺς διεκρίνομεν, οὐκ ἂν ἐκρινόμεθα
v. 32 κρινόμενοι ... παιδευόμεθα, ἵνα μὴ ...
v. 34 εἴ τις πεινᾷ, ἐν οἴκῳ ἐσθιέτω, ἵνα μὴ ...

The form of v. 31 is similar to that of John 3:18 and Matt 6:14. All these sentences give the condition(in conditional clauses, 1 Cor 11:31 and Matt 6:14, or by a participle John 3:18) for avoiding (1 Cor 11:31 and John 3:18) or gaining (Matt 6:14) what is stated in the main verb.

To the sentences in 1 Cor 11:32 and 34 where the main verb is followed by ἵνα μή, to show what is to be avoided, there are parallel forms in Matt 5:25; John 5:14; Luke 12:58 and Matt 7:1.

The common parenetic imperative is used in 1 Cor 11:28 (δοκιμαζέτω) (cf v. 34), and in v. 33 (ἐκδέχεσθε). Finally, v. 30 has a descriptive sentence by which Paul explains phenomena which exist in the Corinthian Church.

This analysis shows that Paul in his elaboration uses a variety of forms, and he changes style from 3rd person singular to 1st and 2nd person plural, and from indicative to imperative, etc. Paul's style is, moreover, argumentative. He draws logical conclusions, as can be seen from ὥστε in vv. 27 and 33. In v. 29 he gives the reason (γάρ) for the parenetic appeal in v. 28, etc.

After he have analysed 1 Cor 11:23-34, some remarks should be added on 1 Cor 10:16;17 and 21. It is significant that Paul here uses an expository paraphrase of fragments from the eucharistic tradition, without first quoting the tradition itself: (8)

v. 16 <u>τὸ ποτήριον</u> τῆς εὐλογίας, ὃ εὐλογοῦμεν,
οὐχὶ κοινωνία ἐστὶν <u>τοῦ αἵματος</u> τοῦ χριστοῦ;
<u>τὸν ἄρτον</u>, ὃν <u>κλῶμεν</u>, οὐχὶ κοινωνία <u>τοῦ σώματος</u>
τοῦ χριστοῦ ἐστιν;
v.17 ὅτι εἷς <u>ἄρτος</u>, ἓν <u>σῶμα</u> οἱ πολλοί ἐσμεν,
οἱ γὰρ πάντες ἐκ τοῦ ἑνὸς <u>ἄρτου</u> μετέχομεν.
v.21 οὐ δύνασθε <u>ποτήριον</u> κυρίου <u>πίνειν</u>
καὶ ποτήριον δαιμονίων.

The words underscored by a line are taken from the eucharistic tradition, as it later is quoted, in 1 Cor 11:23 ff. The terms underscored with a dotted line, .. τῆς εὐλογίας, ὃ εὐλογοῦμεν , raise the question whether Paul also draws on other versions of the tradition, since the corresponding term in 1 Cor 11:24 is εὐχαριστήσας, just as in Luke 22:17,19. On the other hand, Matt 26:26 and Mark 14:22 have εὐλογήσας.

The relevance of this analysis of 1 Cor 11:23-34 and 10:16; 17;21 for John can be seen from John 6:51-58. In <u>Bread from Heaven</u> I have argued for the hypothesis that John 6:51-58 in a similar way draws on fragments from a presupposed eucharistic tradition, and paraphrases these fragments into new sentences. (9) The new sentences, in turn, followed traditional form and style:

<u>John 6:51</u> καὶ ὁ ἄρτος δὲ ὃν ἐγὼ δώσω ἡ σάρξ μού ἐστιν
ὑπὲρ τῆς τοῦ κόσμου ζωῆς.
Cf. Luke 22:19 ἄρτον - ἔδωκεν - ἐστιν τὸ σῶμά μου τὸ ὑπὲρ -
1 Cor 11:13f ἄρτον - μού ἐστιν τὸ σῶμα τὸ ὑπὲρ
<u>John 6:52</u> πῶς δύναται οὗτος ἡμῖν δοῦναι τὴν σάρκα φαγεῖν;
Cf. Matt 26:26 δοὺς - φάγετε - τὸ σῶμα
Luke 22:19 Ἔδωκεν - τὸ σῶμα -
<u>John 6:53</u> ἐὰν μὴ φάγητε τὴν σάρκα τοῦ υἱοῦ τοῦ ἀνθρώπου
καὶ πίητε αὐτοῦ τὸ αἷμα οὐκ ἔχετε ζωὴν ἐν ἑαυτοῖς.
<u>John 6:54</u> ὁ τρώγων μου τὴν σάρκα καὶ πίνων μου τὸ αἷμα
ἔχει ζωὴν αἰώνιον..
<u>6:56</u> ὁ τρώγων μου τὴν σάρκα καὶ πίνων μου τὸ αἷμα
ἐν ἐμοὶ μένει κἀγὼ ἐν αὐτῷ
<u>6:55</u> ἡ γὰρ σάρξ μου ἀληθής ἐστιν βρῶσις,
καὶ τὸ αἷμα μου ἀληθής ἐστιν πόσις.

Cf. the words quoted above from Matt, Luke and 1 Cor and Matt 26:27-28 πίετε - τὸ αἷμά μου
Mark 14:23-24 ἔπιον - τὸ αἷμά μου
(1 Cor 11:27 ἐσθίῃ, - πίνῃ - τοῦ σώματος καὶ τοῦ αἵματος -)
<u>John 6:57-58</u> ὁ τρώγων με κἀκεῖνος ζήσει δι' ἐμέ
<u>6:58</u> ὁ τρώγων τοῦτον τὸν ἄρτον ζήσει τὸν αἰῶνα
Cf Matt 26:26 ἄρτον - φάγετε -
(1 Cor 11:27 ἐσθίῃ τὸν ἄρτον)

The agreements between John 6:51-58 and the texts about the institution of the Lord's Supper, indicate clearly that John draws upon this tradition in the same way as 1 Cor 10:16;17; 21 and 11:27 ff. use fragments from the institution of the eucharist recorded in 1 Cor 11:23 ff., and possible also from another version.

Conclusion: In 1 Cor 11:23 ff Paul quotes a unit from the Gospel tradition, namely a version of the institution of the Lord's Supper. Then in vv. 27 ff. he gives a commentary on the quoted tradition. He utilizes fragments, -words and phrases- from the quote and builds them into a paraphrasing exposition together with legal terms, etc. In this exposition Paul uses traditional forms as for example the form of legal sentences and for parenetic appeals. At the same time he varies the style employed.

When Paul in 1 Cor 11:23-24 quotes a unit of tradition and adds a paraphrasing exposition, he shows in an embryonic stage the form which in the Talmud is developed into the quoted Mishna followed by the Gemara.

In 1 Cor 10:16-17;21 Paul uses an expository paraphrase of fragments from the eucharistic tradition(s), without first quoting the tradition itself.

John 6:51-58 draws upon the eucharistic tradition(s) in the same way as 1 Cor 10:16-17;21 and 11:27 ff. use fragments from the institution of the eucharist in a paraphrase with other words and phrases. Just as in 1 Cor 10:16-17;21, the tradition about the eucharist also in John 6:51-58 is presupposed known by the readers and is not quoted. A special feature in John 6:51-58 is the fact that this expository paraphrase of the eucharistic tradition is presented as saying in the mouth of Jesus.

John 12:44-50: The hypothesis

The section John 12:44-50 clearly forms a unit of its own. It is introduced by the formula Ἰησοῦς δὲ ἔκραξεν καὶ εἶπεν, (cf. 1:15; 7:28,37), and it serves as the concluding part of Jesus' public ministry according to John. The questions about the misplacement and placement of this paragraph will not be taken up in this paper. (10) Instead our discussion will be concentrated on the way in which traditional material has been used in the paragraph.

The study will attempt to substantiate the following main hypothesis: John 12:44-45 quotes a traditional Jesus-logion in a way which corresponds to Paul's quotation of the eucharistic tradition in 1 Cor 11:23 ff. John 12:46-50 is an expository elaboration of the Jesus-logion corresponding to Paul's paraphrase of eucharistic words in 1 Cor 11:27 ff. and 10:16-27;21. (11)

The Jesus Logion quoted in John 12:44-45

John 12:44-45 renders a Jesus Logion which has a firm place in the Gospel tradition. In various versions it occurs in John 13:20;5:23;8:19;14:7;9 and 15:23. Variants are found in the Synoptics in Matt 10:40; Luke 10:16; Mark 9:37 and Luke 9:48. (12) Moreover, parallels are also found in rabbinic writings, as in Mek on Exod 14:31 and Sipre on Num 12:8. The occurences can be grouped in the following way:

I. Sender, double agency, addressee

Joh 13:20:

a) ὁ λαμβάνων ἄν τινα πέμψω b) ἐμὲ λαμβάνει,
c) ὁ δὲ ἐμὲ λαμβάνων d) ———
e) λαμβάνει τὸν πέμψαντά με.

Matt 10:40:

a) ὁ δεχόμενος ὑμᾶς b) ἐμὲ δέχεται,
c) καὶ ὁ ἐμὲ δεχόμενος d) ———
e) δέχεται τὸν ἀποστείλαντά με

Luke 10:16:

a) καὶ ὁ ἀθετῶν ὑμᾶς b) ἐμὲ ἀθετεῖ
c) ὁ δὲ ἐμὲ ἀθετῶν d) ———
e) ἀθετεῖ τὸν ἀποστείλαντά με,

Mark 9:37:

a) ὃς ἂν ἓν τῶν τοιούτων παιδίων δέξηται ἐπὶ τῷ ὀνόματί μου,
b) ἐμὲ δέχεται, c) καὶ ὃς ἂν ἐμὲ δέχηται
d) οὐκ ἐμὲ δέχεται, e) ἀλλὰ τὸν ἀποστείλαντά με.

Luke 9:48:

a) ὃς ἐὰν δέξηται τοῦτο τὸ παιδίον ἐπὶ τῷ ὀνόματί μου,
b) ἐμὲ δέχεται c) καὶ ὃς ἂν ἐμὲ δέξηται
d) ——— e) δέχεται τὸν ἀποστείλαντα με.

II. Sender, single agency, addressee

Luke 10:16:

a) ὁ ἀκούων ὑμῶν b) ἐμοῦ ἀκούει.
c) ——— d) ——— e) ———

Joh 12:44:

a)——— b)——— c) ὁ πιστεύων εἰς ἐμὲ
d) οὐ πιστεύει εἰς ἐμὲ e) ἀλλὰ εἰς τὸν πέμψαντά με.

Joh 12:45:

a)——— b)——— c) καὶ ὁ θεωρῶν ἐμὲ
d)——— e) θεωρεῖ τὸν πέμψαντά με.

Joh 14:9:

a)——— b)——— c) ὁ ἑωρακὼς ἐμὲ
d)——— e) ἑώρακεν τὸν πατέρα.

Joh 15:23:

a)——— b)——— c) ὁ ἐμὲ μισῶν
d)——— e) καὶ τὸν πατέρα μου μισεῖ.

Joh 5:23:

a)——— b)——— c) ὁ μὴ τιμῶν τὸν υἱὸν
d)——— e) οὐ τιμᾷ τὸν πατέρα τὸν πέμψαντα αὐτόν.

Joh 14:7:

a)——— b)——— c) εἰ ἐγνώκειτέ με,
d)——— e) καὶ τὸν πατέρα μου ἂν ᾔδειτε.

Joh 8:19:

a)——— b)——— c) εἰ ἐμὲ ᾔδειτε,
d)——— e) καὶ τὸν πατέρα μου ἂν ᾔδειτε.

Sipre on Num 12:8 § 103

a)——— b)———
c) (The inhabitents spoke before him [i.e. the agent]).
d) "you have not spoken concerning my servant
e) but concerning me."

Mek on Exod 14:31

a)——— b)——— c)...having faith in the Shepherd of Israel
d)——— e) is the same as having faith in (the word of) Him who spoke and the world came into being.

Mek on Exod 14:31

a)——— b)——— c) ... speaking against the Shepherd of [Israel
d)——— e) is like speaking against Him who spoke ...

The versions fall into two main groups: 1) Those which mention a chain og two agencies, i.e., the sender, 1st agency and 2nd agency, addressee: John 13:20; Matt 10:14; Luke 10:16b; Mark 9:37 and Luke 9:48. 2) Those versions which deal only with a single agency, i.e., the sender, agency, addressee: John 5:23; 8:19; 12:44-45; 14:7:9; 15:23; Luke 10:16a; Mek on Exod 14:31; and Sipre on Num 12:8, §103. Although the versions about a single agency probably reflect the most commonly occuring usage in Judaism (as seen from Mek on Exod 14:31 and Sipre on Num 12:8, § 103), the versions of a chain of two agencies seems to have the firmest place in the Gospel tradition. Their firm place is seen from the fact that they are represented in all four Gospel. Thus, the several versions on single agency occuring in John (and in a different way in Luke 10:16a) are to be regarded as partial renderings of the Logion on a chain of two agencies.

The partial renderings of the Logion in John 12:44-45 form a pair, where the version in v. 44 consists of three parts, and the one in v. 45 has two parts:

John 12:44	John 12:45
c) ὁ πιστεύων εἰς ἐμὲ	c) καὶ ὁ θεωρῶν ἐμὲ
d) οὐ πιστεύει εἰς ἐμὲ	d)
e) ἀλλὰ εἰς τὸν πέμψαντά με	e) θεωρεῖ τὸν πέμψαντά με

Both of these forms are traditional. The form found in v. 45 is the one used in all the listed parallels in the Synoptic Gospels, except the one in Mark 9:37, which has the same structure as the one in John 12:44 (cf. Sipre on Num 12:8, § 103):

Mark 9:37:

c) καὶ ὃς ἂν ἐμὲ δέχηται,

d) οὐκ ἐμὲ δέχηται

e) ἀλλὰ τὸν ἀποστείλαντά με

In John 12:44-45 different verbs are used to characterize the representation given by the agent: in v. 44 the verb is πιστεύειν in v. 45 it is θεωρεῖν. Also in the occurrences of the Logion elsewhere in John the verbs vary: in 5:23 τιμᾶν; in 8:19 εἰδέναι; in 14:7 γινώσκειν/εἰδέναι ; in 14:9 ὁρᾶν; and in 15:23 μισεῖν. It would seem probable to conclude that John here has developed a method of varying the verbs of the basic form of the Logion, found in John 13:20 and Matt 10:14. John 13:20 and Matt 10:14 both use synonyms for the verb "to receive", John λαμβάνειν , Matt δέχεσθαι (as also Mark 9:37 and Luke 9:48). (13) This method of varying these verbs is not John's own, however, but is itself traditional, since such variations are found also in Luke 10:16, (cf. Mek on Exod 14:31 and Sipre on Num 12:9). John then may have brought some of his preferred terminology into the Logion, or he may just have taken over verbs used in the tradition as he received it.

Conclusion: John 12:44-45 are partial renderings of a Jesus-Logion which has a firm place in the Gospel tradition. Parallels are also found in rabbinic writings. The forms used in 12:44-45 (in v. 44, 3 parts, in v. 45, 2 parts) are both exemplified in the Synoptics. So also is the method of varying the verbs which characterize the representation of the agent. Thus, John and Syn give here different examples of tendencies at work in the transmission of the Gospel tradition.

Paraphrastic use of fragments from the Jesus-Logion

John 12:46-50 is an exposition of the Logion rendered as a pair in vv. 44-45. The expository character of vv. 46-50 is seen from the fact that fragments from the Logion are paraphrased in a way which corresponds to Paul's paraphrase of tradition-fragments in 1 Cor 11:27 ff. and 10:16-7.21. In the quotation given below the words and phrases which occur in the Logion, vv. 44-45, and are used in the elaborations, vv. 46-50, are underscored with a single line. The words which probably are fragments from other versions of the Logion than the two rendered in vv. 44-45, are underscored by a dotted line John 12:44-50:

44 Ἰησους δὲ ἔκραξεν καὶ εἶπεν
ὁ πιστεύων εἰς ἐμὲ οὐ πιστεύει εἰς ἐμὲ
ἀλλὰ εἰς τὸν πέμψαντά με,
45 καὶ ὁ θεωρῶν ἐμὲ θεωρεῖ τὸν πέμψαντά με.
46 ἐγὼ φῶς εἰς τὸν κόσμον ἐλήλυθα, ἵνα
ὁ πιστεύων εἰς ἐμὲ ἐν τῇ σκοτίᾳ μὴ μείνῃ.
47 καὶ ἐάν τίς μου ἀκούσῃ τῶν ῥημάτων καὶ μὴ φυλάξῃ,
ἐγὼ οὐ κρίνω αὐτόν.
οὐ γὰρ ἦλθον ἵνα κρίνω τὸν κόσμον,
ἀλλ' ἵνα σώσω τὸν κόσμον.
48 ὁ ἀθετῶν ἐμὲ καὶ μὴ λαμβάνων τὰ ῥήματά μου
ἔχει τὸν κρίνοντα αὐτόν.
ὁ λόγος ὃ ἐλάλησα, ἐκεῖνος κρινεῖ αὐτὸν
ἐν τῇ ἐσχάτῃ ἡμέρᾳ.
49 ὅτι ἐγὼ ἐξ ἐμαυτοῦ οὐκ ἐλάλησα,
ἀλλ' ὁ πέμψας με πατὴρ αὐτός μοι ἐντολὴν δέδωκεν

τί εἴπω καὶ τί λαλήσω.

50 καὶ οἶδα ὅτι
ἡ ἐντολὴ αὐτοῦ ζωὴ αἰώνιός ἐστιν.
ἃ οὖν ἐγὼ λαλῶ,
καθὼς εἴρηκέν μοι ὁ πατήρ, οὕτως λαλῶ.

As indicated by the underscoring in v. 46, the phrase ὁ πιστεύων εἰς ἐμέ is taken verbatim from the Logion in v. 44. In v. 46 then the phrase is paraphrased together with other words. Likewise, the underscored expression in v. 49, ὁ πέμψας με is a fragment taken from the Logion in vv. 44-45, ... τὸν πέμψαντά με. The expository use of the expression in v. 49 is seen from the fact that it is specified by an interpretative gloss, πατήρ. . (It might be added that the word ἐγώ in vv. 46.47.49 and 50 has been underscored as well as the form μοί in vv. 49 and 50. These forms of the personal pronoun are renderings in different cases of the accusative μέ in the phrase τὸν πέμψαντά με , vv. 44-45. Thus this μέ in the Logion, vv. 44-5, receives already in v. 46 an emphatic place since ἐγώ is placed first in the sentence. In this way the "I" is made into a central theme of the exposition).

The underscoring by means of a dotted line indicates the probable use of fragments from other versions of the Logion than the two rendered in vv. 44-5. In v. 48 there are two parallel phrases underscored in this way:

ὁ ἀθετῶν ἐμὲ
καὶ μὴ λαμβάνων τὰ ῥήματά μου ..

The phrase ὁ ἀθετῶν ἐμέ is a negative counter part to the words ὁ πιστεύων εἰς ἐμέ in the Jesus Logion, v. 44. A similar contrast of a positive statement being followed by a negative one is found in Mek on Exod 14:31: the phrase "having faith in the shephard of Israel" is contrasted by the negative statement "speaking against the shephard of Israel". Consequently, ὁ ἀθετῶν ἐμέ in John 12:48 probably comes from a negative version of the Jesus Logion quoted in vv. 44-5. This conclusion receives strong support from Luke 10:16, where such a version is quoted:

Luke 10:16	a)	καὶ ὁ ἀθετῶν ὑμᾶς
	b)	ἐμὲ ἀθετεῖ
	c)	ὁ δὲ ἐμὲ ἀθετῶν
	d)	————
	e)	ἀθετεῖ τὸν ἀποστείλαντά με

The phrase ὁ ἀθετῶν ἐμέ in John 12:48 is therefore the point c) in the Logion used as a fragment. The fact that the verb ἀθετεῖν does not occur elsewhere in John gives added support to this understanding that the phrase comes from a traditional Jesus Logion. (14)

With regard to the parallel phrase in v. 48, καὶ μὴ λαμβάνων τὰ ῥήματά μου it should be noted that the verb λαμβάνειν takes personal object elsewhere in John (1:12; 5:43; 13:20). It is therefore probably that τὰ ῥήματα here in 12:48 is an interpretative specification due to the interest for the word(s) in the context. Thus the phrase (μὴ) λαμβάνων ....μου is probably a fragment taken from the Jesus Logion as it occurs in 13:20, or possible the same version in a negative form.

Since fragments from the Jesus Logion, quoted in John 12:44-5 and elsewhere, are built into a paraphrase, the other elements of the paraphrase must also be analysed.

Legal terminology

a) Judgment and salvation

The underscoring with a double line marks off the legal and eschatological terminology which are woven into the paraphrase, in a way similar to the use of legal terminology by Paul in the expository paraphrase of 1 Cor 11:27 (also underscored with a double line).

The term κρίνειν in John 12:47;48 occurs frequently in John, as well as in Matt and Luke and elsewhere in the NT. (15) The Hebrew equivalents in the Old Testament and in Jewish writings show that this terminology and the ideas expresses, are central Old Testament and Jewish tenets. (16) The immediate background of John's use is the place of the term in the Gospel tradition, but the phrase κρίνειν τὸν κόσμον , John 12:47, cf. 3:17, seems to reflect the wider usage in the early Church, as can be seen from similar expressions in Acts 17:31; Rom 3:6; 1 Cor 6:2; and also 1 Cor 11:32. (17)

In John 12:48 the word spoken by the agent receives the function of the judge, ὁ λόγος, ὃν .., ἐκεῖνος κρινεῖ αὐτόν. This phrase seems to be but a variant of the similar statement about the Law, as found in John 7:51 ..ὁ νόμος ἡμῶν κρίνει τὸν ἄνθρωπον. In similar ways the Law is pictured as an acting person also in Jewish writings, as shown by A. Schlatter, Der Evangelist Johannes, (Stuttgart, 1930) 205.

The term ζωὴ αἰώνιος is in John 12:50 used in an interpretative gloss, by which the term ἡ ἐντολὴ αὐτοῦ is explained: καὶ οἶδα ὅτι "ἡ ἐντολὴ αὐτοῦ" "ζωὴ αἰώνιός" ἐστιν . The term belongs to the eschatological language found elsewhere in John, in the

Synoptics, Paul, Hebrews, Jewish apocalyptic literature and the rabbinic writings. (18) Its immediate background is then the usage within the Gospel tradition.

Likewise, the term σῴζειν, John 12:47, belongs to the eschatological language found elsewhere in John, in the Synoptics, elsewhere in the New Testament and in the Jewish sources. (19) Again, the immediate background of the term is the usage within the Gospel tradition.

Finally, the phrase ἐν τῇ ἐσχάτῃ ἡμέρᾳ, John 12:48 (as well as in John 6:39;40;44;54; 11:24) is also an eschatological term. It has a parallel in Sipre on Deut 34:2, where the biblical expression as far as the Western Sea (עד הימ האחרן) is read as "until the last day" (עד היומ האחרון). The plural form of this phrase in Greek and in Hebrew equivalents is frequently used in the New Testament, Septuagint, apocalyptic and rabbinic traditions and the Qumran literature. (20) This phrase does not occur in the Synoptics, however, and its use in John is, may be, due to the usage of similar phrases in the early Church.

b) <u>Elaborations of the rules of agency, implicit in the Jesus Logion, John 12:44-5</u>

Most of the remaining phrases and words in John 12:46-50 belong to the language of agency. Especially central and typical are the ἦλθον-words in vv. 46-7:

v. 46: ἐγὼ φῶς εἰς τὸν κόσμον ἐλήλυθα ἵνα πᾶς ὁ πιστεύων ...

v. 47: οὐ γὰρ ἦλθον ἵνα κρίνω τὸν κόσμον ἀλλ' ἵνα σώσω τὸν κόσμον.

C H. Dodd has pointed out that the form of pronouncement, ἦλθον with the infinitive of purpose or an equivalent ἵνα-clause, is one of the most widely established forms in which the sayings of Jesus are transmitted. (21) Dodd lists the following examples from the Syn, John, the Gospel according to the Egyptians, the Ebionite Gospel and the "unknown gospel" of Egerton Papyrus 2: (22)

"Luke 19:10: ἦλθεν ὁ υἱὸς τοῦ ἀνθρώπου ζητῆσαι καὶ σῶσαι τὸ ἀπολωλός.
Luke 12:49: πῦρ ἦλθον βαλεῖν ἐπὶ τὴν γῆν.
Matt. 10:35: ἦλθον διχάσαι ἄνθρωπον κατὰ τοῦ πατρὸς αὐτοῦ.
John 10:10: ἐγὼ ἦλθον ἵνα ζωὴν ἔχωσιν.
John 12:46: φῶς εἰς τὸν κόσμον ἐλήλυθα ἵνα πᾶς ὁ πιστεύων εἰς ἐμὲ ἐν τῇ σκοτίᾳ μὴ μείνῃ.
Ev.Ebion. ἦλθον καταλῦσαι τὰς θυσίας.
Ev. Aegypt. ἦλθον καταλῦσαι τὰ ἔργα τῆς θηλείας.
Matt. 5:17: μὴ νομίσητε ὅτι ἦλθον καταλῦσαι τὸν νόμον ἢ τοὺς προφήτας.

Matt. 10:34a: μὴ νομίσητε ὅτι ἦλθον βαλεῖν εἰρήνην ἐπὶ τὴν γῆν.
Pap.Eg.2: μὴ δοκεῖτε ὅτι ἦλθον κατηγορῆσαι ὑμῶν πρὸς τὸν πατέρα μου.
Mark 2:17: οὐκ ἦλθον καλέσαι δικαίους ἀλλὰ ἁμαρτωλούς ...
Mark 10:45: ὁ υἱὸς τοῦ ἀνθρώπου οὐκ ἦλθεν διακονηθῆναι ἀλλὰ διακανῆσαι .....
Mark 10:34b οὐκ ἦλθον βαλεῖν εἰρήνην ἀλλὰ μάχαιραν.
John 12:47: οὐ γὰρ ἦλθον ἵνα κρίνω τὸν κόσμον ἀλλὰ ἵνα σώσω τὸν κόσμον
Luke 9:56: ὁ γὰρ υἱὸς τοῦ ἀνθρώπου οὐκ ἦλθεν ψυχὰς ἀνθρώπων ἀπολέσαι ἀλλὰ σῶσαι.

The last five of these passages, four drawn from the Synoptics and one from the Fourth Gospel, agree in the form οὐκ ἦλθον.. ἀλλά, which was evidently well established in various branches of the tradition. John seems here to have rewritten a traditional saying in his own terms-κρίνειν and κόσμος being among his favorite words."

As seen from Dodd's survey, the sayings occur both in a positive form (ἦλθον, etc. and an infinitive or a ἵνα-clause), and in a negative form (ὀυκ ἦλθον ... ἀλλά Mark 2:17; 10:45; Matt 10:34b; John 12:47 and Luke 9:56). Thus, as a core of his exposition in 12:46-7, John has ἦλθον -logia in the Gospel tradition. He uses the basic structure of such logia and weaves it into his paraphrase. As shown by Jan-A. Bühner in his study and by myself in a study on agency, such ηλθον-words, especially in John, belong to the judical language on agency. (23)

Some observations should be added on John 12:47: καὶ ἐάν τίς μου ἀκούσῃ τῶν ῥημάτον καὶ μὴ φυλάξῃ. The similar phrases in Matt 7:26 and Luke 11:28 seem to suggest that John draws on such a formulation in the Gospel tradition. (24)

John 12:47 ἐάν τίς μου ἀκούσῃ τῶν ῥημάτων καὶ μὴ φηλάξῃ.
Matt 7:26 καὶ πᾶς ὁ ἀκούων μου τοὺς λόγους τούτους καὶ μὴ ποιῶν αὐτούς.
Luke 11:28...οἱ ἀκούοντες τὸν λόγον τοῦ θεοῦ καὶ φυλάσσοντες.

John here draws on Gospel tradition, and employs it within the context of the rejection of the agent's words. If the clause is a parallell to Matt 7:26 or Luke 11:28, then the use in John 12:47 of the verb φυλάσσειν instead of the verb τηρεῖν which John uses elsewhere, is caused by the terminology he found in the Gospel saying at this point. (25)

The halakhic terminology of agency is evident in the phrase ἐξ ἐμαυτοῦ οὐκ..., John 12:49. With variations such phrases are used in 5:19; 30 and 7:28 (cf. 7:18; 18:34). The preposition ἐκ is used in John 12:49, in the other occurrences of the phrase, ἀπό. Similar variation between ἐκ and ἀπό is also found elsewhere in the Gospel, however, as in 6:33.38, etc. Thus, such peculiarity in 12:49 does not mark this verse and its context off from the rest of the Gospel. (26) The parallel phrases in connection with agency in Jewish sources, show that John here utilizes terminology from such halakhic background: Tobit 12:18 (οὐ τῇ ἐμαυτοῦ), b Sabb 87a, etc. (מדעתו , etc.) Exod Rab 5:21, etc. (מעצמי , etc.); cf. Num 16:28.

The positive formulation of "not from myself" is expressed by the formula καθώς ... οὕτως in John 12:50. In both cases the unity between the sender and his agent is stated. (27)

The charge which the sender has given the agent is in John 12:47-50 concentrated on the words/word/commandment which are mediated by the agent. The commissioning is stated explicitly in 12:49 (cf. 7:17; 14:10): (28) ..ἐγὼ ἐξ ἐμαυτοῦ οὐκ ἐλάλησα, ἀλλ' ὁ πέμψας με πατὴρ αὐτός μοι ἐντολὴν δέδωκεν τί εἴπω καὶ τι λαλήσω. In a parallel way Moses according to the midrash has been given the charge to speak on behalf of God: Moses: not of myself do I speak (this) to you, but from the mouth of God do I speak (this) to you, Sipre on Deut 5:9, 12. (29) In John 12:49f., therefore, the term ἐντολή, commandment, is applied to the legal charge received by an agent from his sender. (30)

The use of the Old Testament

The use of the Law of Moses is presupposed by John when he in 12:44-50 and elsewhere draws on Jewish rules of agency. In Judaism these rules of agency developed within the interplay between ideas and events written down on the laws of Moses, and the functions of agency in Jewish society. (31) Thus, in order to understand the rules and functions of agency, one has to examine the Laws of Moses and the other writings in the Old Testament, and also the various forms of their exposition in the Targumim, in Josephus, in the midrashim, etc., as well as more independent halakhic statements. The concept of agency, therefore, developed within the realm of the jurisdiction of the Laws of Moses, as well as having its authoritative source in them. As shown in recent studies, John draws heavily on this Old Testament and halakhic background, so also in 12:44-50, which is dominated by the thought of agency. (32)

There are some indications which point to a specific influence by material from the Old Testament, as interpreted in New Testament times. Thus, it is probable that the giving of the Laws of Moses at Mt. Sinai is the idea behind John 12:49, and that contemporary formulations have influenced John's wording. The close agreements between John 12:49 and Sirach 45:5 support this understanding:

John 12:49-50:	Sirach 45:5:
αὐτός μοι ἐντολὴν δέδωκεν	καὶ ἔδωκεν αὐτῷ
καὶ οἶδα ὅτι ἡ ἐντολὴ αὐτοῦ	ἐντολάς, νόμον ζωῆς
ζωὴ αἰώνιός ἐστιν	

Furthermore, as pointed out by several scholars, the terminology and ideas of Deut 18:18 about a prophet like Moses, seem to have influenced formulations in John 12:44-50. (33)

Finally, the reference to light and darkness, φῶς ... ἐν τῇ σκοτίᾳ, in John 12:46 has its scriptural basis in Gen 1:3-4, as can be seen from the explicit use of Gen 1:1ff. in John 1:1ff., where light and darkness also are central ideas. (34)

How is the use of the Old Testament in John 12:44-50 to be characterized? There is no direct citation, nor should the usage be understood as allusive rendering from memory. The usage rather reflects living exegetical traditions and concepts in contemporary Judaism, adapted (by and) to Jesus and Christology. Sirach 45:5 is one evidence that the giving of the Law at Sinai was a living concept, the Qumran document 4 QTestim 1-8 reflects a living expectation of a prophet like Moses (cf. Joh 1:21-25), and John 1:1ff., as well as the Qumran scroll, testify to the existence of living traditions on dualism between light and darkness. (35)

<u>Conclusions</u>:

Our analysis has shown that John 12:44-50 consists of the following "building material":

1) Two versions in a pair of the Jesus-Logion on agency, vv. 44-5 Fragments from these versions:
   v. 46 ὁ πιστεύων εἰς ἐμέ
   v. 49 ὁ πέμψας με
   Fragments from other versions which are presupposed:
   v. 48 ὁ ἀθετῶν ἐμὲ καὶ μὴ λαμβάνων - μου
2) Legal and eschatological terminology, central to the Gospel tradition (except ἐν τῇ ἐσχάτῃ ἡμέρᾳ) and widely used elsewhere in the NT and in Judaism:
   v. 47 οὐ κρίνω - οὐ - κρίνω τὸν κόσμον - σώσω τὸν κόσμον.
   v. 48 τὸν κρίνοντα - ὁ λόγος - κρινεῖ - ἐν τῇ ἐσχάτῃ ἡμέρᾳ.

v. 50 ζωὴ αἰώνιός -

3) Words from Gospel tradition:

v. 46 ἐγὼ - ἐλήλυθα, ἵνα -

v. 47 οὐ - ἦλθον ἵνα - ἀλλ' ἵνα -

v. 47 (?)ἐάν τίς μου ἀκούσῃ τῶν ῥημάτων καὶ μὴ φυλάξῃ -

4) Terminology on agency:

v. 49 ἐξ ἐμαυτοῦ οὐκ -

v. 50 καθώς - οὕτως

5) Influence from the Old Testament can be seen throughout, but the following words should receive special notice:

v. 49 ἐντολὴν δέδωκεν -

v. 46 φῶς - ἐν τῇ σκοτίᾳ

This "building material" is composed into an exposition (vv. 46-50) of the Jesus Logion in vv. 44-5. Into what kinds of forms have they then been shaped? Just as in our discussion of 1 Cor 11:27-34, so also here in John 12:46-50, we find that the fragments have been paraphrased into statements which have traditional forms. And just as in Paul's exposition so also here in John the form of casuistic legal clauses is especially evident:

v. 46b ... πᾶς ὁ πιστεύων εἰς ἐμὲ ἐν τῇ σκοτίᾳ μὴ μείνῃ.

v. 47 ... ἐάν τίς μου ἀκούσῃ τῶν ῥημάτων καὶ μὴ φυλάξῃ, ἐγὼ οὐ κρίνω αὐτόν ....

v. 48 ὁ ἀθετῶν ἐμὲ καὶ μὴ λαμβάνων τὰ ῥήματά μου ἔχει τὸν κρίνοντα αὐτόν.

In verses 46 and 47 we find two ἦλθον-clauses, to which form there are several parallels in the Gospels, as shown above:

v. 46 ἐγὼ φῶς εἰς τὸν κόσμον ἐλήλυθα, ἵνα ....

v. 47 οὐ γὰρ ἦλθον ἵνα κρίνω τὸν κόσμον ἀλλ' ἵνα σώσω τὸν κόσμον.

Then there are sentences in which the person presents and legitimates himself as agent, vv. 49-50:

v. 49 ὅτι ἐγὼ ἐξ ἐμαυτοῦ οὐκ ἐλάλησα, ἀλλ' ὁ πέμψας με πατὴρ αὐτός μοι ἐντολην δέδωκεν τί εἴπω καὶ τί λαλήσω.

v. 50 ἃ οὖν ἐγὼ λαλῶ, καθὼς εἴρηκεν μοι ὁ πατήρ, οὕτως λαλῶ.

With regard to form, as well as content, these sentences can be compared to Moses' statement of himself according to Sipre on Deut 5:9;12: "not of myself do I speak (this) to you, but from the mouth of God do I speak (this) to you."

In John 12:48 there is a declaration "who" will be the judge on the last day: ὁ λόγος ὃν ἐλάλησα ἐκεῖνος κρινεῖ αὐτὸν ἐν τῇ ἐσχάτῃ ἡμέρα. Finally, verse 50a) has the form of an exegetical gloss, a scholie: καὶ οἶδα ὅτι "ἡ ἐντολὴ αὐτοῦ" "ζωὴ αἰώνιός" ἐστιν.

When these various forms are composed together, a varied style is the result. In verse 46 an ἦλθον-clause is combined with a casuistic clause (πᾶς ὁ πιστεύων -). In verse 47 a casuistic clause (καὶ ἐάν τίς μου ἀκούσῃ-) is explained (γάρ) by an ἦλθον-clause. The declaration about "who" will be the judge on the last day v. 48b (ὁ λόγος - κρινεῖ-) serves as an interpretation of the words τὸν κρίνοντα αὐτόν in the preceding casuistic clause (ὁ ἀθετῶν ἐμὲ κτλ).

The legitimating sentence in v. 49 gives the reason (ὅτι) for the preceding declaration in v. 48b. Then comes the scholie in v. 50a), and finally the legitimating sentence in v. 50b serves as a conclusion (οὖν).

It is not the purpose of this paper to give an exegesis of the content of John 12:44-5. On the basis of the statement on agency, vv. 44-5, the passage contains the message which the agent delivers when he comes to the people to whom he is sent. He explains his mission and its relationship to the judgment on the last day, and he gives the statement about his commissioning, and thereby legitimates his mission.

In this way, John, using Gospel material and halakhic principles, shows how Jesus' mission and his words replace the role of the Torah, and the role of Moses. (36)

NOTES

1) For a recent formulation of such a hypothesis for the sources of John, see B. Lindars, Behind the Fourth Gospel. For the view of the author, see P. Borgen, Bread from Heaven, and the chapters 4-10 in the present book; See also idem, review of "J. Beutler, Martyria, Frankfurt am Main 1972", in Bib, 55, Fasc 4, (1974) 580-3; idem, "John and the Synoptics in the Passion Narrative, NTS, 5, (1959) 246-59; also in idem, 'Logos was the True Light' and other Essays on the Gospel of John, (Trondheim, 1953).

2) It is impossible to draw a sharp line between these two usages, but borderline cases have then to be discussed as part of the analysis.

3) See for example W. Bacher, "Talmud", The Jewish Encyclopedia, 12, (New York, 1906) lff., and introductions to the Talmud.

4) See H. Conzelmann, Der erste Brief an die Korinther, Meyer, K., (Gøttingen, 1969) 230; B. Gerhardsson, Memory and Manuscript, (Uppsala, 1961) 290.

5) See the comparison among the various versions of the Institution of the Lord's Supper made by J. Jeremias, The Eucharistic Words of Jesus, (London, 1964) 101-14; 138-203.

6) Cf. H. Conzelmann, an die Korinthier, 237; J. Jeremias, The Eucharistic Words, 106.

7) In the exposition, vv. 27 ff and in v. 26 ἐσθίω is used, although it does not occur in the quote, vv. 23 ff. The term is used as part of the story of the institution in Matt 26:26; cf. John 6:53.

8) Cf. H. Conzelmann, an die Korinther, 201 f. Cf. J. Hering, Le Royaume de Dieu et sa venu, (Neuchatel, 1959[2]) 224, n.l; J. Jeremias, The Eucharistic Words, 104.

9) P. Borgen, Bread from Heaven, 91 f.

10) See R. Bultman, Johannes, 237; R.E. Brown, John (I-XII), 490.

11) The most specific analysis in recent years on the use of sources in John 12:44-50, as well as in the Johannine discourses in general, is that of R. Bultmann, Johannes. Among the critics of Bultmann's theory of a Revelatory Source (Offenbarungsreden), etc., see R.E. Brown, St. John (I-XII), XXIX-XXXII.

12) See C.H. Dodd, Historical tradition in the Fourth Gospel, (Cambridge, 1965) 343-7; See also chapter 10 in the present book.

13) Cf. C.H. Dodd, Historical Tradition, 344.

14) See f.i. R.E. Brown, St. John (I-XII), 490-1.

15) John 3:17,18; 5:22,30; 7:24,51; 8:15:16:26:60; 16:11; 18:31; Matt 7:1,2; 19:28; Luke 6:37; 22:30. For the usage elsewhere in the NT, see the reference in the next foot note.

16) See F. Büchsel and V. Hentrich, κρίνω , TWNT, 3, 920-42.

17) See also Sipre on Deut, 311. A. Schlatter, Johannes, 98f.

18) John 3:15.35; 4:14.36; etc. Mark 10:30, etc. Gal 1:4, etc. Hebr 6:5, Cf. Syr Baruch 14:13, etc.; Abot 2:7, etc. See P. Borgen, Bread from Heaven, 165, and n. 4.

19) See W. Foerster, σῴζω κτλ , TWNT, 7, 982-99.

20) A. Schlatter, Johannes, 175; P. Borgen, Bread from Heaven, 167.

21) C.H. Dodd, Historical Tradition, 355.

22) ibid., 355-6.

23) J.-A. Bühner, Der Gesandte, and chapter 10 in the present book.

24) See J. Marsh, The Gospel of St. John, (Hammondsworth,1968, reprint 1974), 474; R.E. Brown, St. John I-XII, 491; B. Lindars, John, 440. A. Schlatter, Johannes, 277.

25) Cf. R. Schnackenburg, Das Johannesevangelium, 2, (Freiburg, 1971) 524.

26) Against M.-E. Boismard, "Le caractere adventice de Jo. XII: 45-50", in J. Coppens etal (eds), Sacra Pagina, 2, (Paris, 1959) 190-191.

28) Chapter 5 and 10 above.

29) See A. Schlatter, Die Sprache und Heimat des vierten Evangelisten, (Gütersloh, 1902) 85.

30) See J.-A. Bühner, Des Gesandte, 209.

31) Cf. chapter 9 above.

32) See J.-A. Bühner, Der Gesandte; W.A. Meeks, The Prophet-King, 301-305, P. Borgen, chapter 10 above.

33) See R.E. Brown, St. John I-XII, 492; R. Schnackenburg, Johannesevangelium, 2, 529.

34) See chapter 4 above.

35) See R.E. Brown, St. John I-XII, LXII f, etc.

36) Cf. Deut Rab 8:6, where it is said that another Moses will arise and bring another Torah from heaven.

P A R T III : P A U L

CHAPTER TWELVE
THE EARLY CHURCH AND THE HELLENISTIC SYNAGOGUE

The formulation of the topic is problematic and needs to be analysed and defined.

In the study of the Early church and Judaism one of the distinctions traditionally drawn is that between Palestinian and Hellenistic elements. The basis for this distinction is the division drawn by scholars between Palestinian "normative" Judaism and Hellenistic Judaism. Correspondingly, a distinction has been made between the Palestinian Jewish church with a Palestinian kerygma, and the Hellenistic church with a Hellenistic kerygma. The scheme has even been elaborated through the addition of a transitional phase: the Palestinian Jewish Christianity - Jewish Hellenistic Christianity - Hellenistic Gentile Christianity.

The prevailing trend within research on Judaism is moving away from this understanding. There had been a considerable degree of Hellinization in Palestinian Judaism by the time that the Early church developed. In his survey of the period up to 150 B.C., M. Hengel has shown that the whole of Judaism from the middle of the third century B.C. must be characterized as 'Hellenistic Judaism', and this applies to the Judaism of Palestine as much as any where else. At the same time, the Judaism of the Diaspora was by no means free from the kind of features often labelled 'Palestinian'.

In spite of the fact that Hellenistic Judaism can hardly be defined in contrast to Palestinian Judaism, the terminology may still be useful to distinguish between two different linguistic and cultural settings of Judaism. Thus, on the basis of Gerhard Delling's use of the term "Hellenistic Judaism" the following definition seems helpful: the Hellenistic synagogue means the synagogal communities in the Graeco-Roman world, where Greek is used as the main language. These communities are minority groups in a non-Jewish environment. (1)

One of the crucial issues for Hellenistic synagogue Judaism was the problem of Jewish identity in pagan environment. Within this context the following themes will be analysed in this essay: The transition of converts from paganism to Judaism, and against this background, the different views on the conditions for admission into the Jewish community. At this point, debates on physical circumcision and circumcision of the heart prove to be central. Another theme of importance is the problem of Jewish participation in pagan community life, particularly those involving acts of sacrifice and worship.

The topic of this essay is not just an analysis of the Hellenistic synagogue, however, but a discussion of the Hellenistic synagogue and the Early church. The term "the Early church" is not to be limited to the Jerusalem Church. Rather, it comprises the church from its beginning to the turn of the century. We shall emphasize the Early church within the setting of the Jewish Diaspora. Thus, the question of "the Hellenists" in Jerusalem (Acts 7-8) will not be discussed in the present study.

Our thesis is: The Early church draws on traditions, debates and practices from Jewish proselytism, modifies them, and makes them serve a different kind of community structure. Consequently, the Christian "proselytes" did not leave their national and ethnic society to join the Jewish nation and ethnic community.

In spite of the many similarities between Jewish and Christian forms of proselytism, there developed a basic difference. This difference is particularly evident in connection with debates on physical circumcision and circumcision of the heart. Such religious debates were not only theoretical, but existential, and had social, political and legal ramifications. Thus, even persecution could occur.

Moreover, the Early church took over some of the varied attitudes and practices of the Hellenistic synagogues in relationship to pagan cult and pagan cult-related cummunity life.

Our main sources are The New Testament, Philo and Josephus. To some extent Christian literature from the second century will also be utilized, as well as the implications of archaeological investigations. With due caution Jewish pseudepigraphal and rabbinic writings will be drawn into the discussion. Instead of entering into a detailed examination of each rabbinic tradition and its dating, we will simply formulate the question in this way: Are there agreements and similarities between the sources on Diaspora Judaism and the New Testament on the one hand, and the rabbinic writings on the other? If so, those scholars who attempt do draw the line from the rabbinic sources and back to New Testament times, have no basis for making a sharp distinction between the Judaism of the Diaspora and the Palestinian Judaism. Such a conclusion would, in turn, imply that our sources provide no basis for drawing a sharp distinction between the Palestinian Church and the Church in the Diaspora.

Our study points to the tensions and variations that existed within the Hellenistic synagogue itself. Such observations indicate that debates and conflicts within each Jewish community were even more crucial than the differences between Palestinian Judaism and Hellenistic Judaism.

Conversion from paganism to synagogue/church

Scholars such as N.A. Dahl and P. Tachau have shown that statements which draw a contrast between "once" and "now" form a pattern in parts of the New Testament. (2) In this way the new Christian life in faith is characterized against the background of a pagan past. These scholars maintain that this pattern reflects the preaching in the Early church. Gal 4:8 f. may serve as example: "Formerly, when you did not know God, you were in bondage to beings that by nature are no gods; but now that you have come to know God ..." Further examples are found in Eph 2:11-22; 5:8-9, etc. This understanding of statements exhibiting the once/now pattern must be correct, for they occur in settings of congregational preaching to Christians. Nevertheless, further research is needed in two directions beyond this conclusion; Are there passages where the contrast between past and present forms of existence is expressed without the exact formula of "once" (ποτέ) and "now" (νῦν) being used? For example in 1 Thess 1:9 the verb ἐπιστρέφειν marks the contrast between a pagan past and the Christian present:"... how you turned to God from idols, to serve a living and true God ..." (3) If there are other pasages as this one, they must be drawn into the discussion.

Another question is to be raised. Does this congregational preaching in the Early church have its background in the missionary preaching, which in turn might build on traditions related to Jewish proselytism? Such an understanding has already been suggested by C. Bussmann, and by my student Jonas Beverfjord. (4) This avenue should then be explored further.

In order to identify some of the traditions the following criteria will be used: 1. The content is presented in the form of contrast between aspects of paganism on the one hand and aspects of Judaism/Christianity on the other hand. 2. The contrast outlines two stages in the life of the same persons, namely, persons who were or are heathens, and who are or are to become Jews/Christians.

On the basis of these criteria a comprehensive body of material can be identified, in Philo, The New Testament, Justin and other Christian literature, Joseph and Asenath, Sibylline Oracles, and in Rabbinic writings. (5)

An investigation of this material leads to the following conclusion: This pattern of contrast in the New Testament draws on Jewish traditions on the conversion of heathens to Judaism. In the Early church these traditions have been christianized, a fact which reflects the early Christian adaptation of the Jewish institution of proselytism. At first, the Christian proselytizing activity was part of controversies and debates on proselytism within the Hellenistic synagogue. The church utilizes such traditions on proselytism beyond the New Testament period, as can be seen from the writings of Justin and other christian literature.

Conversion as past event and future goal

In his section on conversion in Virt 178-179 Philo pictures Moses as a teacher who exhorts people to turn away from the many gods to the one God. Thus, the conversion of pagans is content and aim of his instruction: (6) "... when Moses convokes such people and would initiate them into his mysteries, he invites them with conciliatory and amicable offers of instruction, exhorting them to practise sincerity and reject vanity, to embrace truth and simplicity as vital necessaries and the sources of happiness, and to rise in rebellion against the mythical fables impressed on their tender souls from their earliest years by parents and nurses and tutors and the multitude of other familiars, who have caused them to go endlessly astray in their search for the knowledge of the best. And what is the best of all that is but God, whose honours they have assigned to those who were no gods and glorified them beyond measure, while Him in their senseless folly they forgot? So therefore all these who did not at the first acknowledge their duty to reverence the Founder and Father of all, yet afterwards embraced the creed of one instead of a multiplicity of sovereigns, must be held to be our dearest friends and closest kinsmen. They have shown the godliness of heart which above all leads up to friendship and affinity, and we must rejoice with them, as if, though blind at the first they had recovered their sight and had come from the deepest darkness to behold the most radiant light."

In this way we see that the aim of Moses' instruction was that people should practise sincerety and reject vanity, and rise in rebellion against the mythical fables, i.e. against polytheism.

Several observations show that Moses' instruction is a model for the instruction of pagans in Philo's own time: a) The section is part of Philo's presentation of the virtue conversion, μετάνοια (Virt 175-186). The opening statement in Virt 175 shows the application of Moses' teaching to every one everywhere, thus including Philo's own time; b) The content of the section deals with a central theme in statements on proselytism, namely the turning away from polytheism to monotheism. c) This instruction by Moses is by Philo called the first and most essential form of repentance, Virt 180. Then in Virt 180-182 he goes on to deal with the ethical conversion of the proselytes, now, without mentioning Moses as grammatical subject. Thus, Moses' instruction is pictured as the basic step in the conversion of proselytes to Judaism. On this basis we draw the conclusion that Moses here addresses people in Philo's time when he teaches pagans about conversion. Thus, conversion is the aim of Moses' teaching also in the Hellenistic Judaism of Philo's time.

This aim is not limited to Hellenistic Judaism, however. In a factual manner, - without reference to Moses, - conversion is stated as the result of teaching also in rabbinic sources as Cant Rab I:63: When the elder sits and teaches, many proselytes are converted to Judaism.

In accordance with this aim of instruction in Judaism, conversion from the darkness of pagan life to the light is the aim of Paul's work, according to Acts 26:18: Paul was sent to the gentiles "... to open their eyes, that they may turn from darkness to light and from the power of Satan to God ..."

In the material where this contrast occurs, it is more common to look back upon the conversion as an event in the past, or as a fact in the present. Two passages already quoted, Gal 4:8 f. and 1 Thess. 1:9 refer back to conversion and describe the present Christian existense with their pagan past. Among the many parallel passages in Philo, the brief characterization of proselytes in Somn II 273 may be mentioned: "... those who have left their homes and taken refuge (with God) ..."

In Joseph and Asenath 13:11-12 the terms τὸ πρότερον and νῦν are used in a way similar to the formula ποτέ and νῦν in Christian writings; "... all these gods, whom I once in ignorance worshipped, I have now recognized that they were dumb and dead idols ... To you, Lord God, have I taken my refuge ..." (7)

Conclusion: According to Philo, the conversion of pagans is content and aim of Moses' instruction. Philo addresses this teaching of Moses to the conversion of proselytes in his own time and place. Thus, there is basis for supposing that conversion was the aim of (Moses') teaching as it was made present in Hellenistic Judaism. It is worth noticing that the conversion of proselytes is seen as the result of teaching in rabbinic sources.

In the material where the contrast between paganism and Jewish Christian existence occurs it is more common to look back upon the conversion as an event in the past or as a fact in the present.

Our next step is to outline some of the main themes in these traditions, and examine how they are christianized. The following themes are central : a) the transition from many gods to the one God; b) the transition from other peoples and other nations to the people of God; and c) the transition from pagan immorality to Jewish/Christian moral life. (8)

From many gods to the one God

This theme is a central motif in the conversion passages found in Philo and Joseph and Asenath. In Virt 102-104 Philo tells how the proselytes have abandoned their customs and the temples and images of their gods, and the tributes and honours paid to them, and thus turned away from idle fables to the clear vision of truth and the worship of the one and truly existing God within the context of the Jewish law. (9) Similarly, Asenath's conversion meant that she recognized that the pagan gods were dumb and deaf idols, and that the God of the Hebrews was the only true God.

Also in the New Testament and in other Christian writings this motif is a basic element in the conversion of the polytheists Gal 4:8 f.; 1 Thess 1:9; Barn 16:8 and Justin, I Apol 14; 25; 49; Dial 11:4; 30; 21; 83:4; 91:3. Cf. Acts 15:19.

Have any modifications been made in the Christian adaptation of this Jewish proselyte-tradition? The Christian interpretation is evident in 1 Thess 1:9-10, by the fact that the underscored reference to the parusia of Jesus is added: "... how you turned to God from idols, to serve a living and true God, and to wait for his Son from heaven, whom he raised from the dead, Jesus who delivers us from the wrath to come."

There is no Christological statement added to Gal 4:8 f. Paul's Christian interpretation of the Jewish tradition is evident, nevertheless, since he makes clear that the Christian "proselytes" are not to conform to the Jewish cultic calendar. To Philo, on the other hand, the conversion meant that the former pagans entered the Jewish nation and committed themselves to worship God within the context of the observance of the Torah (cf Virt 102-104). Although Philo does not here give specific reference to the cultic feasts, these are implied since he elsewhere treats them extensively (Spec I:39-222, etc.).

From other peoples to the people of God

According to Philo, conversion meant that the proselytes made a social, judicial and ethnic break with pagan society and joined another ethnic group, the Jewish nation. In Virt 102-104 Philo says that the proselytes have left their family (γενεά), their country (πατρίς), their customs (ἔθος). Abraham is the prototype of the proselyte who leaves his home in this way, Virt 214. The proselytes thus have made their kinsfolk (συγγενεῖς) into mortal enemies (Spec IV:178). According to Philo, proselytes have entered the Jewish nation, or πολιτεία, a term which means rights of a citizen, body of citizens, government, constitution of a state, commonwealth. (10) The proselytes have entered a "new and godly commonwealth" (καινῇ καὶ φιλοθέῳ πολιτείᾳ), Spec I:51; "the government of the best laws" (εἰς τὴν εὐνομωτάτη πολιτεία) Virt 180; "a commonwealth full of true life and vitality" (πρὸς ἔμψυχον τῷ ὄντι καὶ ζῶσαν πολιτείαν), Virt 219.

Christian sources draw on these Jewish traditions in their characterization of the Christian "proselytes". The best example is found in Eph 2:11-22. In accordance with the proselyte pattern of contrast, the present is described against the pagan background, when they were uncircumcised gentiles, alienated from the commonwealth of Israel (πολιτεία τοῦ Ἰσραήλ). In the present they are not strangers (ξένοι) nor foreigners (πάροικοι), but fellow citizens (συμπολῖται) and members of the household (οἰκεῖοι of God. In Eph 2:12 the term πολιτεία is used, the term which also is central in Philo's passages on proselytes.

In spite of this use of legal and technical terminology from the realm of state and ethnic communities, (11) the passage in Eph 2:11-22 breaks away from this context. According to Eph 2:11-22 the Christian proselytes are not to make an ethnic and judicial break away from their families, country and nation. thus, the Christian "proselytes" are not to become citizens of the Jewish nation of the Torah. The law of commandments is abolished. In this way the Jewish idea of the people of God has been reshaped to mean the church of Christ into which both Gentiles and Jews are to enter. The atonement in Christ has made this new inclusive community possible. (12)

From pagan immorality to Jewish/Christian morality

The conversion from paganism to Judaism/Christianity meant a change of ethical behaviour and life-style. In the description of this contrast, catalogues of vices and virtues may be used. Philo, Virt 180-182 illustrates this point. First Philo describes the conversion of the proselyte: "For it is excellent and profitable to desert without a backward glance to the ranks of virtue and abandon vice that malignant mistress; and where honour is rendered to the God who is, the whole company of the other virtues must follow in its train as surely as in the sunshine the shadow follows the body" (181).

"The proselyte becomes at once temperate, continent, modest, gentle, kind, humane, serious, just, high-minded, truth-lovers, superior to the desire for money and pleasure..." (182).

In the same way Paul uses a catalogue of virtues to picture the Christian life in connection with the Galatian's conversion from pagan life: "But the fruit of the Spirit is love, joy, peace, patience, kindness, goodness, faithfulness, gentleness, self-control" (Gal 5:22-23).

Also elsewhere in Christian literature catalogues of virtue are used to characterize the new life of the converts. (13) Thus, Justin in Dial 110:3 writes: "... we cultivate piety, justice, brotherly charity, faith and hope ..."

Catalogues may also be used to characterize the pagan life which the proselytes leave behind. Thus, in Virt 180 Philo uses a double catalogue to show what conversion means: "... from mob rule ... into democracy; from ignorance to knowledge ... from senselessness to good sense; from incontinence to continence; from injustice to justice; from timidity to boldness." (14)

In his missionary instruction to the pagan Galatians Paul used a catalogue of vices to show the Jewish/Christian disapproval of polytheistic worship and pagan way of life: "Now the works of the flesh are plain: immorality, impurity, licentiousness, idolatry, sorcery, enmity, strife, jealousy, anger, selfishness, dissension, party spirit, envy, drunkenness, carousing, and the like. I warn you, as I warned you before, that those who do such things shall not inherit the kingdom of God" (Gal 5:19-21). (15)

Again Paul has re-interpreted the Jewish proselyte traditions. He refers to the Christians crucifixion with Christ as basis for the new life. (Gal 5:24), and he understands the virtues as fruits of the spirit and not as a life under the Law of Moses (Gal 5:16-25). (16)

Love of neighbour. The golden Rule

Although the life of proselytes can be described by means of a catalogue of virtues, it may also be characterized by means of general summary statements. Such general statements are given by Philo when he says that the proselytes join the commonwealth of the best laws (Virt 180), the godly commonwealth (Spec I:51), and a commonwealth full of true life and vitality (Virt 219). A proselyte has even secured himself a place in heaven (Praem 152).

Of particular interest is the observation that the commandment of the love of neighbour and the Golden Rule may be used as characterization of the nature of the community into which the proselytes enter. According to b. Šabb 31a Hillel summed up the Law of Moses in the Golden Rule. Hillel made his summary for a heathen whom he accepted as a proselyte. Similarily, the western text of Acts 15:20 and 29 includes the Golden Rule in the basic instruction to be given to the Christian "proselytes". (17)

To Paul, the commandment of love of neighbours, Lev 19: 18, has the same function. Paul uses this commandment as a summary of the Law and as a description of the community life into which the Galatians have been called through his missionary work, Gal 5:13-14.

The love commandment is also used by Philo and in parallel rabbinic tradition with reference to proselytes. Here, however, the commandment has a specific application. it shows the way in which the Jews are to treat the proselytes. The scriptural basis for this use of the commandment is LXX Lev 19:34, which can be translated in this way: "The proselyte that comes to you shall be as the native among you, and you shall love him as yourself." (18)

Both in the synagogue and in the church the love commandment and the Golden Rule were closely knit together. Thus, both are paraphrased together in the Targum Pseudo-Jonathan on Lev 19:18, and in Did 1:1f they are cited together. (19)

To sum up, in the Early church traditions on the conversion of proselytes in the Hellenistic synagogue were taken over and applied to the Christian "proselytes".

The pattern of contrast between paganism and Judaism in the Hellenistic synagogue was applied to the proselytizing activity both as its goal and as an interpretation of the new Jewish existence of the proselytes over against their pagan past. The Early church used this pattern of contrast in the same way.

A number of common themes were also exhibited in the proselyte traditions of the Hellenistic synagogue and the Early church. The Gentiles were called to turn away from the many gods to the one God, to join the people of God, and to leave behind pagan immorality and follow a Jewish/Christian morality. Catalogues of vices and virtues were used to exemplify this moral contrast. Moreover, both in the synagogue and in the church, the love commandment and the Golden Rule were used to characterize in a general way the kind of existence into which the proselytes were to enter.

The Early church gave a Christian interpretation and application to these Jewish proselyte traditions. In the church they were tied to Christology/Soteriology and to the eschatological life of the Spirit. At the same time they were understood in such a way that the Gentile converts did not have to conform to the Jewish cultic calendar. Neither were they expected to leave their legal and ethnic context by becoming citizens of the Jewish ethnic community. Consequently, they should not be obliged to obey the law of the Jewish nation, but be members of the church as the people of God. In this people of God, both Gentiles and Jews were to enter through the atonement brought about in the death of Jesus Christ.

Circumcision of the body and circumcision of the heart

In the Hellenistic synagogue - and probably also in the synagogue in Palestine - the debates and conflicts about the observance of circumcision were continued. This tension has its background in the Old Testament, where circumcized persons received severe criticism because they lacked the circumcision of the heart (Lev 26:41; Deut 10:16; 30:6; Jer 4:4; 6:10; 9:25; Ezek 44:7.9). the Early church participates in these controversies in the Hellenistic synagogue.

Philo's writings reflect these debates and conflicts, although his statements on the conversion of proselytes do not specifically mention circumcision. At other places Philo discusses circumcision, however. Bodily circumcision portrays the excision of pleasure and all passions (Migr 92; Spec I:305; Quaes Gen III:47-52). The foreskin symbolizes sense-pleasures (Quaes Gen III:52). Circumcision is the figure of the excision of excessive and superfluous pleasure (Spec I:9; cf I:305).

Philo is a representative of the Hellenistic synagogue. His ethical interpretation of the circumcision has parallels in Palestinian traditions, however. From New Testament times the Qumran writings provide evidence for the existence of such ideas in Palestine. According to 1 QpHab 11:13 the foreskin of the heart is to be circumcised in addition to the circumcision of the body, which seems assumed. A parallel to the thought of Philo also occurs in 1 QS 5:5-6, where it says that the foreskin of the evil inclination is to be circumcised. (20)

The rabbinic writings place the emphasis on the circumcision as the sign of the covenant. At some places, however, there are close similarities found between Philo and passages in rabbinic writings.

In his interpretation of circumcision in Spec I:9 and I:305 he uses a play on words in Greek. In Spec I:9 it runs as follows: "περιτομὴν περιττῆς ἐκτομὴν καὶ πλεοναζούσες ἡδονῆς," "circumcision, a cutting off of superfluous and excessive pleasure." Similarily, Spec I:305 interprets Deut 10:16 περιτέμνεσθε τὴν σκληροκαρδίαν " in this way "τὰς περιττευούσας φύσεις τοῦ ἡγεμονικοῦ ," prune away the superfluous overgrowths of the ruling mind.

I. Heinemann thinks that the basic wordplay reads περιτομή = περιττοῦ ἐκτομή , and he emphasizes that this is a play on Greek words, and cannot, in his opinion go back to Hebrew. (21)

D. Daube takes issue with Heinemann. (22) Daube shows that according to Gen Rab 46:10 a parallel wordplay is used in the rabbinic exegesis of Gen 17:11: "And you shall be circumcised (u-nemaltem) in the flesh of your foreskin." A mere maltem would have done, so the rabbis treat the ne as conveying a message of its own: nemaltem or, as they seem to read for this purpose, nommaltem means nomi maltem, "the growth you shall cut off" (in the flesh of your foreskin). Thus, by means of play on words in Greek and Hebrew respectively, Philo and the rabbis developed the same interpretation of circumcision. Daube does not believe that Philo and the Midrash hit on the idea independently. Moreover, Gen Rab 46:10 seems to go back to the first century AD, since it refers to Monobaz and Izates of Adiabene by name.

Nomi, "growth", "sore", is a Greek noun. This noun is also used in Sipre Deut 45 on 11:18, "and you shall lay up these my words." (23) Playing on vesamtem "and you shall lay up", the rabbis detect here the message that God's precepts are a sam hayyim or sam tam, a "herb of life" or "perfect herb". They liken him to a king who, having inflicted a terrible blow on his son, puts a compress on it and warns him that, so long as it is there, he can indulge himself without fear - "eat what you enjoy, drink what you enjoy, bathe in warm water or in cold" - but that if he takes it off, "a growth" (nomi) will come up. Just so, God created the evil impulse, with the Torah as antidote: so long as you immerse yourself in the latter, the former has no power over you. Daube believes that the ultimate root of this parable is in teaching concerning circumcision. We may add that Philo offers some support to this view of Daube, since in Spec I:305 he also uses pictures from gardening in his interpretation of circumcision: it means to prune away the superfluous overgrowths of the ruling mind, sown and raised by the immoderate appetites of the passions and planted by folly, the evil husbandman of the soul. Correspondingly, according to Sipre Deut 45 on 11:18 the pleasures of eating, drinking and bathing if not controlled by Torah, will produce "a growth". (24)

Thus, Philo's understanding of circumcision as portraying the excision of excessive and superfluous pleasure finds points of contact with some passages in rabbinic writings.

What then was the situation of the proselytes? Was physical circumcision required? In this connection scholars have discussed Philo, Quaes Exod II:2. (25)

This text is preserved both in Greek and in Armenian translation, with only minor variations. Our comments will be based on the Greek fragment. Philo interprets Exod 22:21, which in accordance with LXX can be translated as follows: "and a proselyte you shall not mistreat, nor shall you oppress him. For you were proselytes in the land of Egypt."

The term προσήλυτος in Exod 22:21 is given this interpretation by Philo: προσήλυτος is not the one who has circumcised his uncircumcision, but the one who (has circumcised) his desires and sensual pleasures and the other passions of the soul. For in Egypt the Hebrew nation was not circumcised, but, being mistreated with all mistreatments of the cruelty shown by the inhabitants against strangers, it lived with them in self-restraint and endurance, not by necessity, but rather of free choice, because it took refuge in the Saviour, God, Who sent His beneficent power and delivered the suppliants from their difficult and hopeless situation.

H.A. Wolfson suggests that Philo here speaks of a "spiritual proselyte", as distinct from the full proselyte, who was bodily circumcised. Wolfson must himself admit, however, that Philo's use of the term προσήλυτος (and synonyms) does not support his view, since it elsewhere refers to full proselytes. (26) Thus nothing in Philo's writings speaks against also understanding the proselyte in Quaes Exod II:2 to mean a full proselyte.

S. Belkin, similarily, thinks that Philo here refers to a semi-convert. N.J. McEleney rightly states that Belkin's view has no basis in the passage itself. McEleney himself interprets the passage to mean that Philo did not insist on the fulfilment of the precept of circumcision. (27)

J. Nolland objects to McEleney's understanding of the passage by referring to Philo's theory about attuning the body to the soul. This theory would seem to apply to the proselytes as well as to the Jews in general. (28) Nolland then rephrases the intention of Philo in this way: "what deeper sense to proselyte (than one who has entered Judaism by circumcision) can be discovered from the juxtaposition in the text of the mention of proselytes with the mention of the Israelites as proselytes in Egypt?" (29) "As Philo saw it, in a unique historical situation, things which normally belong together are separated so that it becomes apparent where the greater part of the reality of circumcision lies - not in the physical but in the spiritual." (30)

Nolland is right in stating that to Philo spiritual circumcision and physical circumcision belong together. His own interpretation seems forced, however, and does not explain why Philo defines "proselyte" as one who has received ethical circumcision, and not physical circumcision.

The most probable view is that Philo here gives an answer to the question: When does a person receive status as a proselyte in the Jewish community and cease to be a heathen? This problem was of great importance both at the ideological and practical level, and in different ways it is also discussed later in rabbinic literature. (31)

Philo uses an ethical criterion for deciding who has the status of a proselyte within the Jewish community. This ethical conversion of the heathen also meant a social change from a pagan context to a Jewish one. (32) It is of interest to note that Philo's view does not represent an isolated attitude among the Jews. According to b. Šabb 31a, Hillel gave the status of proselyte to a heathen who came to him and accepted the Golden Rule as summary of the Torah. (33) Philo's and Hillel's understanding has thus been that bodily circumcision was not the requirement for entering the Jewish community, but was one of the commandments which they had to obey upon receiving status as a Jew.

Circumcision of the heart and not of the body

Philo's writings offer evidence, however, to support the fact that there existed Jews who spiritualized the laws and discarded the external observances of feasts and circumcision, Migr 86-92. Thus, he writes on circumcision: "It is true that receiving circumcision does indeed portray the excision of pleasure and all passions, and the putting away of the impious conceit, under which the mind supposed that it was capable of begetting by its own power; but let us not on this account repeal the law laid down for circumcising" (Migr 92).

M. Friedländer thought that these Jews who rejected the external observance of feasts and circumcision were a strong and numerous religious party, with a similar group also in Palestine. Friedländer refers here to the saying attributed to R. Eleazar from Modin, in which Rabbi Eleazar condemns Jews who, although they recognize the Torah and do good works, neglect and reject the observance of feasts and circumcision. (34) This idea of a numerous religious party cannot be substantiated by the sources. But the sources allow us to say that there were parallel phenomena which took place in Alexandria and Palestine (either at the same time or at different times), where individual Jews or groups ignored the external observance, but kept other parts of the Torah.

It must be admitted that Philo's definition of a proselyte in Quaes Exod II:2 could lead easily to a stress on ethical circumcision to the exclusion of physical circumcision. A comparison with Rom 2:28-29 will illuminate this point: Quaes Exod II:2: "proselyte is not the one who has circumcised his uncircumcision, but the one (who has circumcised) his desires and sensual pleasures and the other passions of the soul ..." Rom 2:28-29: "For he is not a Jew who is one outwardly, nor is circumcision the circumcision outwardly in the flesh. But he is a Jew who is one inwardly; and circumcision is circumcision of the heart, by the spirit and not literal ..."

Philo and Paul agree that the circumcision of the heart is basic, and that this spiritual circumcision is the decisive criterion for deciding who is a Jew, and then also who is a proselyte. Both Philo and Paul can be understood to imply that physical circumcision is not necessary. As we have seen, this was not the view of Philo himself. Both the Jews criticized by Philo in Migr 86-93 and Paul draw that negative conclusion with regard to physical circumcision. Paul says: "So, if a man who is uncircumcised keeps the precepts of the law, will not his uncircumcision be regarded as circumcision?" (Rom 2:26).

Also in other writings hints are found which suggest that there were Jews who ignored physical circumcision: 1. In his letter to the Christians in Philadelphia Ignatius says that it is better to learn Christianity from a circumcised Christian than to learn Judaism from a uncircumcised Jew (Philad 6,1). Several scholars, among others C.K. Barrett, think that Ignatius here refers to an unorthodox Jewish group who did not require physical circumcision, probably due to pressures from the official authorities. (35)

2. When king Izates of Adiabene wanted to convert to Judaism, and thus to be circumcised, his Jewish adviser, the merchant Ananias, thought the king could forgo circumcision in view of his subjects' antipathy to the idea of a fully Jewish king. "The king could, he said, worship God even without being circumcised if indeed he had fully decided to be a devoted adherent of Judaism, for it was this that counted more than

circumcision." In his report on this incident Josephus shows that Jews had different views on this matter. He reports that another Jew, the Galilean Eleazar, "who had a reputation for being extremely strict when it came to the ancestral laws," charged the king with impiety against the Law and God in not carrying out the commandment. So the king had himself circumcised (Josephus, Ant 20:34-48).

Scholars have maintained that since Izates was a monarch his case was a very special case, and that Ananias advised the king not to take curcumcision due to caution, not because of religious belief. (36)

King Izates' situation was hardly so unique, however, since Jewish proselytes elsewhere might face severe dangers from the pagan surroundings also. Thus Philo, Spec IV:178, says: "For the proselyte, because he has turned his kinsfolk ... into irreconcilable enemies ..." In any case the passage in Josephus gives further proof for the existence of different viewpoints on circumcision among Jews. Ananias placed less emphasis on physical circumcision than did Eleazar. (37)

3. A rabbinic tradition should also be included in this list. It occurs in slightly different versions in Abot R Nat 26; Sipre Num § 112 on Num 15:31; Sanh 99a; Abot 3:11; y. Pesah 33b. In all versions, but y. Pesaḥ 33b it is rendered as a saying by rabbi Eleazar from Modin. The version in Abot R Nat 26 is a very close parallel to Philo Migr 89-93. Both places criticism is raised against some who ignore the observance of sabbath, feasts and circumcision, although they nevertheless accept the Law of Moses and do good works.

The agreements between this tradition and Philo, Migr 89-93 give support to the view that the rabbinic saying reflects controversies in Palestine, possibly back to Philo's time. In any case, this rabbinic tradition makes it difficult to defend the view that such controversies on circumcision only occured in the Hellenistic Diaspora. (38) Thus, there existed within the synagogal communities in the Hellenistic world a tendency to emphasize the spiritual circumcision of the heart. The emerging church brought these tendencies to develop into a major movement on a new basis. In this way the Early church participated in debates and conflicts on circumcision in the Hellenistic synagogue. These debates and conflicts are clearly seen in the New Testament. We have already pointed to the fact that Paul in Rom 2:26-29 favours the circumcision of the heart at the expense of physical circumcision. This conflict is even more pointed in the exchange between Paul and his opponents in Gal 5. (39) In Gal 5:11 Paul says: "And I, brethren, if I am still preaching circumcision, why am I despite this fact being persecuted? (40) In that case the stumbling-block of the cross is done away with." The emphatic use of ἐγώ shows that Paul deals with a very personal matter. (41) Paul's opponents had evidently been saying that he himself was still preaching circumcision. The commentators have had difficulties in defining on what basis the opponents made this claim. (42) There is good reason for raising anew the question whether the context of Gal 5:11 can yield more information about Paul's preaching of circumcision. The question may be formulated in this way: Does Paul in the context reiterate ideas from his missionary preaching in Galatia, ideas which the opponents have misunderstood and misused in support for their circumcision campaign?

In Gal 5:19-21 Paul states explicitly that he repeats points from his previous preaching to the Galatians:

"Now the works of the flesh are manifest, such as fornication, etc., respecting which I tell you beforehand, as I already previously told you, that they who do such things will not inherit the Kingdom of God." In his missionary preaching to the pagan Galatians Paul spoke against the works of the flesh. With some variation in wording, Paul repeatedly stresses this point in his missionary preaching in 5:13.16.17.24.

Earlier in this study it has been shown that Philo interprets circumcision to portray the excision of pleasure and passions. The observation has also been made that in Migr 92 Philo shows how such ethical interpretations of circumcision might lead to different attitudes and practices: Philo himself stressed that the ethical ideas were of necessity tied to the external observance of bodily circumcision. Although Philo, according to Quaes Exod II:2, gave heathens the status of proselytes on the basis of ethical circumcision of the pagan pleasures, he meant that the observance of bodily circumcision was to follow. In a similar way Paul's opponents have linked Paul's preaching against (pagan) fleshly desires closely to bodily circumcision: ethical circumcision was to be followed by obedience to the commandment of bodily circumcision.

This idea that the observance of circumcision should follow and complete the ethical circumcision is supported by Gal 3:3, where Paul writes: "Having begun with the Spirit, will you now complete with the flesh?" A. Oepke suggests that Paul's opponents in Galatia have argued that the Galatians needed a supplement, needed a completion by obeying the Law of Moses. (43) Circumcision played a basic role in this complete submission to the Law.

In this way Paul's opponents - who appeared as his followers - said that Paul preached circumcision, Gal 5:11.

In Gal 5:11 there is another point which Paul comments upon, namely the stumbling-block of the cross. In 5:11 Paul formulates an "either-or" between circumcision and the stumbling-block of the cross. (44) If in his preaching against the pagan vices of desire and the passions he has preached bodily circumcision, then the stumblind-block of the cross ceases to exist.

The idea of the cross is elaborated upon in 5:24. Against the background of 5:11, how is this elaboration to be understood? In 5:24 Paul writes: "and they who belong to Christ (Jesus) have crucified the flesh together with the passions and desires". Since Paul in 5:11 formulated an "either-or" between circumcision and the cross, it is probable that Paul in 5:24 has made the believer's crucifixion with Christ replace the function of bodily circumcision: crucifixion with Christ and not bodily circumcision has removed the passions and desires.

The debate on circumcision is also seen in Acts from chapter 15 and onwards. An analysis of this material would go beyond the limits of this article. The main issue was whether gentile converts had to take physical circumcision or not. The corresponding question was also raised with regard to the Jews, when according to Acts 21:20-21 leaders of the Jerusalem church referred to the accusation raised against Paul that he "teaches all the Jews who are among the gentiles to forsake Moses, telling them not to circumcise their children or observe the customs." (45)

Persecutions

Tension was produced when some Jews in a community wanted to ignore physical circumcision. According to the saying attributed to Eleazar from Modin, all those who profane the sabbath, despise the feasts, and annul the covenant of Abraham (i.e. circumcision) will be excluded from the age to come. Philo, on the other hand, shows that the Hellenistic synagogue, at least in some places, made attempts to check such irregularities already here in this world. In Migr 86-93 he tells that those who do not pay heed to external observances incur the censure of the many and charges from them. The Jews should take thought for fair fame, by not interfering with established customs. Persons who do not pay attention to the general opinion have become the objects of hostility. (46)

Against this background, it is understandable that Paul argues against the claim that he still preaches circumcision by referring to the fact that he is being persecuted, Gal 5:11. Likewise, this threat of persecution explains why Paul's Jewish Christian opponents could not accept that the newly won converts in Galatia had not received physical circumcision. If they had accepted this, they would themselves have been subject to persecution. They therefore compelled them to be circumcised in order that they themselves would not be persecuted for the cross of Christ (Gal 6:12). (47)

The relationship between the Hellenistic synagogue and the Early church was one of antagonism which frequently took the form of various degrees of persecution. these conflicts, however, should be seen as intramural controversies within the Jewish communities, in which Paul and other Christian Jews were regarded as threats to institutional stability. (48)

The conflict in Galatia as well as the disagreements which were taken up at the Jerusalem meeting, Acts 15 and Gal 2, prove that there were Jewish Christians who, because of their convictions, conformed to the synagogal community, and who in this way did not suffer persecution. The views and practices of those who did not conform to the synagogal community won out. This group within the Early church became the main stream, and thus a wider and wider separation from the synagogue developed.

The problem of participation in pagan sacrificial cult

This topic is quite comprehensive, and only a couple of points will be dealt with briefly in this context. We shall make some comments on the fact that the Hellenistic Synagogue, as well as the Christian Church, was subject to strong pressures from their pagan surroundings. In both groups there were persons who took part in sacrificial pagan cult. Thus, both within the synagogue and in the church there existed different attitudes and practise on these matters.

Josephus provides us with evidence that such pressures were applied to the Jews in the Hellenistic synagogue. The polytheists in the Ionian areas of Asia Minor "claimed that, if the Jews were to be their fellows, they should worship the Ionian gods ..." (Ant XII:125; cf. XVI:58-59). Similarily, it is stated in Contra Apionem 2:66: "... why, then, if they are citizens, do they not worship the same gods as the Alexandrians?" (49)

There is evidence for the fact that some Jews and Christians took part in polytheistic worship and participated in other aspects of pagan community life. From Cyrene we know from inscriptions that the Jew Eleazar, in the year 60 A.D. is listed among the nomophylakes of the city. The inscription opened with the names of the high priests of Apollo, and it is a dedication to some deity. Moreover, Jews received education in the Greek gymnasia and did not hesitate to permit their names to be engraved on ephebe steles dedicated to the gods Hermes and Heracles. (50) Among the points of relevant information from Asia Minor we may mention the Jerusalemite, Nicetas, who took part in the worship of Dionysos in Jasos. (51)

Philo also provides us with material of interest. (52) Of special interest is his interpretation of Deut 13:1-11 in Spec I:315-317. Here he speaks against anyone cloaking himself under the name and guise of a prophet and claiming to be possessed by inspiration lead Jews to the worship of gods recognized in the different cities. He is not a prophet, but an impostor. Philo directs the criticism against a brother or son or daughter or wife or a housemate or a friend or any one else who urge Jew to fraternize with the multitude, resort to their temples and join in their libation and sacrifices. It is a religious duty to seek his death.

Also rabbinic literature informs us about Jew who took part in pagan cult. Thus, in Tosephta, Hul II:13 (ed Zuckermandel, p. 502) we read with reference to Caesarea Maritima, that if a Jew slaughters an animal in order to sprinkle its blood for idolatrous purposes, such meat is considered as "sacrifices of the dead". Levine dates the saying to 2. century AD and states that it presupposes that Jews in Caesarea actually slaughtered animals for idolatrous purposes. (53)

The problem of participation in pagan cult was also a burning issue in the Early church. According to Rev 2:14-15 there were persons in the church in Pergamum who participated in pagan sacrificial meals. (54) The same was the case in the church in Thyatira, Rev 2:20-21. As in Philo, Spec I:315-317, so also here, persons were encouraged to take part by prophets. The many admonitions against idolatry in The New Testament show that this was a central problem for the Christians in the Hellenistic polytheistic environments. (55)

The impact of pagan cult continued to cause difficulty through the first 3-4 Christian centuries. Attempts at accommodations are documented. A statement about the situation in Egypt in a letter attributed to Hadrian may be quoted, although it is onesided and is of uncertain date: "There those who worship Serapis are, in fact, Christians, and those who call themselves bishops of Christ are, in fact, devotees of Serapis. There is no chief of the Jewish Synagogue, no Samaritan, no Christian presbyter, who is not an astrologer, a soothsayer, or an anointed." (Scriptores Historiae Augustae, trans D. Magie, Loeb Vol 3, 399). (56)

Different attitudes. Different practices

The Early church of the New Testament followed the main stream in the Hellenistic synagogue and avoided participation in pagan cults. Also within this context, different attitudes and practic es were possible. Some examples from a later time can illustrate different approaches followed. Both Tertullian, De Idololatria Ch 2, and Mishna, Sanh 7:6 show that some Jews and some Christians limited the question of idolatry strictly to the direct participation in the cultic ceremonies, such as participation in libations and in sacrificial acts. (57)

Philo seems to have followed this approach. he says that a Jew may pay fees or club subscriptions when the object is to share in prudence, and there is a desire for virtue behind the action. Participation in club life may, however, lead to irregularities and to participation in idolatry (Ebr 20 ff.; 95). Thus, both in the Early church and in the Hellenistic synagogue there were persons who understood idolatry in the restricted sense of direct participation in pagan acts of worship.

This is not the place to consider all aspects of Paul's discussion of these problems in 1 Cor 8-10. Only one point will be touched briefly. Paul also limits idolatry to direct participation in sacrifical acts of worship. (58) Barrett characterizes Paul's view in this way: "Hence (conscientious scruples permitting) the Christian may freely use εἰδωλόθυτα and eat with unbelieving friends. To take part in idolatrous ritual is another matter." (59) Paul likewise makes evident that some christians in Corinth gave a more inclusive definition of sacrificial cult. They do not limit pagan cult only to mean acts of sacrificial worship, but to include the eating of any food which has been connected with pagan cult. Similar differences existed in the synagogue. (60)

In this study we have seen how the Early church emerged within the context of the Hellenistic synagogal communities, especially as a movement related to Jewish proselyte ideas and proselyte practices, and Jewish debates and controversies on proselytism. Such proselyte ideas and practices were christianized and thus the Early church gradually grew into a new form of community which comprised both Jews and Gentiles. As for the problem area of participation in pagan society, there existed corresponding spectrums of thought and practices within both the synagogue and the church.

NOTES

1) H. Marshall, "Palestinian and Hellenistic Christianity: Some critical comments," NTS, 19, (1973) 271-275; P. Borgen, Bread from heaven, (2nd ed., 1981) esp. 59-61; 110; 129-130; 144; and 1-27; G. Delling, "Perspektiven der Erforschung des hellenistischen Judentums," HUCA, 45, (1974) 133-176.

2) N.A. Dahl, "Formgeschichtliche Beobachtungen zur Christusverkündigung, ZNW Beih 21, 3-9 English translation: "Form-critical observations on early Christian preaching," in N.A. Dahl, Jesus in the Memory of the Early Church, (Minneapolis, Minn., 1976) 33-34; P. Tachau, "Einst" und "Jetzt" im NT, (Göttingen, 1972), Jfr. R. Bultmann, Theology of the New Testament, 1, (1951) 105-106; H. Conzelmann, Geschichte des Urchristentums, (Göttingen, 1971) 61.

3) Jfr. Acts 26:17-18; Col 1:13; 2:13.

4) C. Bussmann, Themen der paulinischen Missionspredigt auf dem Hintergrund der spätjüdisch-hellenistischen Missionsliteratur, (Frankfurt am Main, 1971).
J. Beverfjord, ποτέ - νῦν , (typewritten diss.; Trondheim, 1981).
Spec I:51f.; I:308-310; IV:178; Virt 102f.; 178ff.; 212ff.; cf Praem 152.

5) Eph 2: 1-10, and 11-12; 5:8; Gal 4:8f.; Rom 6:17-22; 7:5f.; 11:30; 1 Pet 2:9-10; Titus 3,3-7; 1 Thess 1:9; Col 1:13-14; 1:21f.; 2:13; Acts 26:17-18. Justin, I Apol 14; 16:4; 25; 39; 49,5; II Apol 2:1-2; Dial 11:4; 30:2; 34:8; 83:4; 91:3; 110:2-4; 116:1. 1 Clem 59:2. 2 Clem 1:4-6; Barn 14:5; 16:8. See O. Skarsaune, "The Conversion of Justin Martyr," ST, 20, (1976) 66-67; idem, The Proof from Prophecy, (Oslo, 1982) 469.
Joseph and Asenath 13:11-12; Sibyllan Oracles, Fragment 1, lines 25-27. See R.M. Grant, Theophilus of Antioch, Ad Autolycum, (Oxford, 1970) 89, and O. Skarsaune, The Proof, 467.
C.G. Montefiore and H. Loewe, A Rabbinic Anthology, (New York 1974) 570, quotes the following passage from Tanchuma: "And God says: It is enough that the proselyte has abandoned his idolatry, and come to thee, therefore I urge thee to

love him." See also Sipre Lev 19:33f.; "Yesterday you were an idolator, and today you are under the wings of Shekina."

6) Virt 178-179. Translation in F.H. Colson, PLCL, 8, 273.

7) P. Tachau "Einst" und "Jetzt", 53f.; P. Riessler, Altjüdisches Schrifttum ausserhalb der Bibel, (Augsburg, 1928) 513.

8) For the following discussion of these themes, see J. Beverfjord, ποτέ - νῦν .

9) See also the development of this theme in Spec I:309; IV: 178; Virt 178-179; 212.

10) Concerning the debate on Philo's use of πολιτεία and ἰσοπολιτεία, see P. Borgen, "Philo of Alexandria", ANRW, II:21:1, 108-111.

11) The legal and technical nature of these terms is shown by P. Tachau, "Einst" und "Jetzt", 141.

12) See P. Tachau, "Einst" und "Jetzt", 141; N.A. Dahl, Et kall, (Oslo, 1966) 48ff.;

13) See also Plinius' letter to Trajan 10:96: "they bound themselves with an oath, not for any crime, but not to commit theft or robbery or adultery, not to break their word and not to deny a deposit when demanded."

14) Cf. a similar double catalogue of contrast in the Apostolic Constitutions, cited in K. Berger, "Jüdisch-hellenistisch Missionslitteratur und apokryphe Apostelakten," Kairos, 17, (1975) 233.

15) Cf. the socalled Apostles' Decree in Acts 15,20.29, which is a catalogue of vices from which the new converts should abstain. See F. Siegert, "Gottesfürchtige und Sympathisanten," JSJ, 4, (1973) 135: "Das Aposteldekret galt eben nicht christlichen Gottesfürchtigen, sondern aus den Heiden kommenden getauften Gemeindegliedern - wenn man so will, christlichen Proselyten."

16) Further analysis below in chapter thirteen: "Debates on Circumcision in Paul and Philo."

17) This is not the place for discussing further the very complicated and much discussed problems related to the Apostolic decree. See surveys given in E. Haenchen, Die Apostelgeschichte, (Meyer, K; Göttingen, 1968[6]) 410-414; B.M. Metzger, A Textual Commentary on the Greek New Testament, (London - New York, 1971) 429-434. See further P. Borgen "The Golden Rule, with Emphasis on Its Usage in the Gospels," in P. Borgen, 'Paul Preaches Circumcision and Pleases Men' and Other Essays on Christian Origins, (Trondheim, 1983) 99-114. J. Jeremias, "Paulus als Hillelit", in E.E. Ellis and M. Wilcox (eds), Neotestamentica et Semitica, (in honour of M. Black), (Edinburgh, 1969) 89-90. - See also chapter thirteen below.

18) Virt 102-103; Spec I:52. See further C.G. Montefiore and H. Loewe, A Rabbinic Anthology, (New York, 1974) 570.

19) See P. Borgen, "The Golden Rule".

20) See further chapter thirteen; E. Lohse, Die Texte von Qumran, (Darmstadt, 1971) ad loc. Cf. R. Meyer, "περιτέμνω" TWNT 6, 78-79; J.J. Gunther, St. Paul's Opponents and Their Background, NovT Sup, 35, (Leiden, 1973) 87-78; cf. H.A. Wolfson, Philo, 2, 225-237, who connects the concepts of desire and evil inclination.

21) I. Heinemann, Philons griechische und jüdische Bildung, (repr, Darmstadt, 1962) 177-178; 525.

22) D. Daube, "Jewish Law in the Hellenistic world," in B.S. Jackson (ed), Jewish Law in legal History and the Modern World, The Jewish law Annual, Sup 2, (Leiden, 1980) 45-50.

23) ibid, 48. The tradition is also rendered in Qidd 30b, with slight variations.

24) ibid, 46-47, also discussing Abod Zar 10b and Pesaḥ 87b.

25) See chapter thirteen below.

26) H.A. Wolfson, Philo, 2, 369-71; see especially p. 370, n. 329. Cf. Philo, Cher 108; 119; Somn II:273; Spec I:51; 308.

27) N.J. McEleney, NTS, 20, (1974) 328 329.

28) J. Nolland, JSJ, 12, 173-179.

29) ibid, 177.

30) ibid, 178.

31) See for instance B.J. Bamberger, Proselytism in the Talmudic Period, (repr 1968) 38-52.

32) See D. Daube, ST, 1, (1947) 159.

33) The problem is formulated in a similar way by S. Bialoblocki, Die Beziehungen des Judentums zu Proselyten, 15ff.

34) M. Friedländer, Die religiösen Bewegungen innerhalb des Judentums, (repr 1974) 81 etc.

35) C.K. Barrett, "Jews and Judaizers in the Epistles of Ignatius", in R. Hamerton-Kelly and R. Scroggs (ed), Jews, Greeks and Christians. Essays in honor of W.D. Davies, (Leiden, 1976) 234.242.

36) See J. Nolland, JSJ, 12, 192-194. L. Feldman, Josephus with an English translation, 9 (Loeb), (Cambridge, Mass., 1969) 410-411.

37) N.J. McEleney, NTS, 20, (1974) 328: "Obviously, Ananias thought the precept was dispensable in necessity."

38) For details in the discussion of this rabbinic tradition, see i Str-B, 2, 754; A. Jellinek, "Zur Geschichte der Polemik gegen das Christentum", Orient 10, 1847, 413; G. Kittel, Rabbinica, (Leipzig, 1920) 1-16; J. Klausner, From Jesus to Paul, (London 1946[2]) 600-601; K.G. Kuhn, "Der tannaitische Midrasch Sifre zu Numeri", in G. Kittel

and K.H. Rengstorf (eds, Rabbinische Texte, 2 Reihe, 3, (Stuttgart 1959) esp. pp 806-807; W. Bacher, Die Agada der Tannaiten, 1, (1903) 197f.

39) For the following, see chapter thirteen.

40) See E. De Witt Burton, A Critical and Exegetical Commentary on the Epistle to the Galatians, ICC, (Edinburgh, 1921) 287.

41) G.S. Duncan, The Epistle of Paul to the Galatians, MNTC, (London, 1955[8]) 159; A. Oepke/J. Rohde, Der Brief des Paulus an die Galater, THK NT , (Berlin, 1973[3]) 161; H. Schlier, Der Brief an die Galater, Meyer, K, (Göttingen, 1962[12]) 238; F. Mussner, Der Galaterbrief, HTKNT, (Freiburg, 1974) 358; K. Müller, Anstoss und Gericht, (München, 1968) 114: "Das δέ adversativum distanziert ἐγώ von dem in V 10 genannten part. ὁ ταράσσων . Es belastet ἐγώ mit einem gewichtigen Akzent".

42) Se G.S. Duncan, to the Galatians, 159; A. Oepke/J. Rohde, an die Galater, 161f.; H. Schlier, an die Galater, 239; - F. Mussner, Der Galaterbrief, 359, just takes for granted that Paul has not preached circumcision and writes, - "Doch dass Paulus jemals die Beschneidung 'gepredigt' habe, ist nicht anzunehmen." On the same page, n. 112, he attempts to explain away the fact that the conditional clause has the form of a real case: "Paulus stellt vielmehr aus zorniger Erregung heraus in dem εἰ-Satz einen schlecthin unwirklichen Fall als wirklich hin, um auf die Konsequenzen dieses "Falles" aufmerksam machen zu können."

43) A. Oepke/J. Rohde, an die Galater, 101; so also H. Schlier, an die Galater, 123f.

44) H. Schlier, an die Galater, 239f.: "περιτομή und σταυρός stehen sich für ihn als einander ausschliessende Mittel und Zeichen des Heiles entgegen...".

45) The fact that the issue is raised and debated is significant whether or not the accusation against Paul was true. Cf. H. Conzelmann, Die Apostelgeschichte, (Tübingen, 1963) 121-122.

46) See chapter thirteen.

47) Cf. Martin Hengel, "Erwägungen zum Sprachgebrauch von χριστός bei Paulus und in der 'vorpaulinischen' Überlieferung", in M.D. Hooker and S.G. Wilson (eds), Paul and Paulinism, (London, 1982) 142.

48) Cf. W.D. Davies, "Paul and the Law", in M.D. Hooker and S.G. Wilson (eds), Paul and Paulinism, 6f.

49) Cf. Cant Rab 5:9: "Come and mingle with us." See Y.F. Baer, "Israel, the Christian Church, and the Roman Empire", in A. Fuks and I. Halpern (eds), Scripta Hierosolymitana, 7, Studies in History, (Jerusalem, 1961), 82.

50) S. Applebaum, Jews and Greeks in Ancient Cyrene, (Leiden, 1979) 186ff.; 219.

51) G. Kittel, "Das kleinasiatische Judentum in der hellenistisch-römischen Zeit, ThLZ, 69, (1944) col. 15.

52) Cf. Post 182ff.; Ebr 73ff.; Conf 57; Mos I:295-311; Spec I:54-56; Virt 34ff.

53) L.I. Levine, Caesarea under Roman Rule, SJLA, 7,(Leiden, 1975) 45, 179; cf. p. 72 and p. 200.

54) In recent archeological excavations in Pergamum, a cultic dining room has been uncovered. See W. Radt, Deutsches Archäologisches Institut, Archäologischer Anzeiger 1977, (Berlin, 1977) 307-313. In connection with the reference to adultery in Rev. 2:14.20, it is relevant to mention that according to recent excavations the results of which are not yet published, Pergamum was a center for the production of ceramics with "pornographic" pictures, especially connected with the Dionysos. This information was in Spring 1982 given to the author by the director of The Ephesus Museum, Selahattin Erdemgil. Mr. Erdemgil had himself been in charge of this excavation, and showed me the photograps of the findings.

55) Gal 5:20; 1 Cor 5:10f.; 6:9; 10 : 7.14. Cf. 1 Pet 4:3; 1 John 5:21; Rev 21:8; 22:15.

56) See L.I. Levine, Caesarea under Roman Rule, 200.

57) Y.F. Baer, "Israel, the Christian Church, and the Roman Empire", 89.

58) Cf. W.L. Willis, Paul's Instructions to the Corinthian Church on the Eating of Idol Meat, PhD thesis (microfilm), Southern Methodist University, (Dallas, Texas, 1981) 400-401.

59) C.K. Barrett, "Things Sacrificed to Idols," NTS, 11, (1965) 149.

60) Str-B 3, 377-378; 420-421.

CHAPTER THIRTEEN
DEBATES ON CIRCUMCISION IN PAUL AND PHILO

Introduction

At the congress celebrating the 100th anniversary of the Society of Biblical Literature in December, 1964, professor Johannes Munck, shortly before his death in February 1965, read a paper on "Pauline research since Schweitzer". In this essay Munck emphasized that Paul was a Jew, and that he was to be understood against the background of Judaism and the Old Testament. In this connection Munck referred to the works of W.D. Davies as representing a fruitful approach to Paul. (1)

On the same occasion W.D. Davies gave a presentation on "Paul and Judaism". (2) Davies here criticized the assumption of Schweitzer, and of many other scholars, that it is possible to make a clear distiction between what was Semitic or Palestinian Judaism and Hellenistic or Diaspora Judaism in the first century.

"The Judaism which Schweitzer found fulfilled "in Christ" was an emasculated, apocalyptic Judaism, not the varied Judaism of Pharisaism, Qumran, and other currents. From the essential emphasis of Schweitzer there is no possibility of escape. But this emphasis must be related to aspects of Judaism which he ignored. it is this process that is now going on - the exploitation of the fullness of Judaism, - Hellenistic, Pharisaic, Essene (Qumran), Septuagintal and classically hebraic, - in the interest of a deeper understanding of Paulinism. In short, the rooting of Paul, not only in apocalyptic but in the whole complex of Judaism as an integral part of the ancient Greco-Roman-oriental world, is the way of advance beyond a Schweitzer, who in his rightful concern to emphasize the "strangeness" of primitive Christianity endangered its relations with the continuities of history. (3)

Against this background there are good reasons for drawing afresh on Philo's writings so as to gain a better understanding of Paul also in this way. From the outset it is important to realize that Philo's writings reflect a variety of movements within Judaism. This diversity is not only seen in the richness of ideas used, but also in the direct debates and controversies mentioned. It may thus prove fruitful to compare some of the debates and conflicts in Pauline letters with controversies reflected in Philo's works.

One area that seems relevant is that of the questions raised concerning the observance of feasts and circumcision. This paper will be concentrated on certain aspects of the meaning and observance of circumcision. In a preliminary way the problem can be formulated as follows: tension and controversy between the observance of bodily circumcision on the one hand and on the other, the ethical meaning of circumcision. In Paul we shall center the discussion on Gal 5:11-6:10. From Philo we shall draw on material on circumcision from various places, but pay special attention to the tension and controversy reflected in On the Migration of Abraham 86-93 and Questions and Answers in Exodus II:2, discussed in detail above in chapters three and twelve.

On the Migration of Abraham 86-93 and Questions and Answers in Exodus II:2

Before we analyse Gal 5-6, the two main passages in Philo should be characterized. In On the Migration of Abraham 86ff. Philo gives an exposition of the word to Abraham in Gen 12:2 "I will make thy name great." Philo stresses then the importance for a man to have high reputation among his fellow Jews from one's obedience to the Laws of Moses. Against this background he critcizes some Jews who, although they have the right understanding of the meaning of the feasts and circumcision, nevertheless ignore the external observance.

Philo's criticism is clothed in Platonic terminology: these Jews err by regarding the laws in their literal sense only as symbols for noetic realities. Therefore, scholars often call these Jews philosophical spiritualists. (4) If we take a closer look at the views they held, according to Philo, these were Jewish, although influenced by Hellenistic thoughts: Sabbath expressed the idea that God was the active creator and creation was passive in relation to him. (5) The cultic feasts represented man's joy and thanksgiving to God. (6) And the meaning of circumcision was that it portrayed the excision of pleasure and all passions, and the putting away of the impious conceit under which the mind supposed that it was capable of begetting by its own power. Similar ethical interprelations of circumcision are found in the Qumran writings, IQS V:5 and I Qp Hab XI:13, and in the Old Testament, Lev 26:41; Deut 10:16; Jer 4:4, 9:25; 6:10.

In his controversy with these fellows Jews, Philo expresses his agreement with their views by using 1. pers. plural. Thus, he writes on circumcision: "It is true that receiving circumcision does indeed portray the excision of pleasure and all passions, and the putting away of the impious conceit under which the mind supposed that it was capable begetting by its own power: but let us not on this account repeal the law laid down for circumcising" (Migr 92).

M. Friedländer thought that these Jews who rejected the external observance of feasts and circumcision were a strong and numerous religious party, with a similar group also in Palestine. Friedländer refers here to the saying attributed to R. Eleazar from Modin, in which Rabbi Eleazar condemns Jews who, although they recognize the Torah and do good works, neglect and reject the observance of feasts and circumcision. (7) This idea of a numerous religious party cannot be substantiated by the sources. But the sources allow us to say that there were parallel phenomena which took place in Alexandria and Palestine (either at the same time or at different times), where individual Jews or groups ignored the external observance, but kept other parts of the Torah.

A special problem area in connection with circumcision is the relation between circumcision and the proselytes. In several places Philo deals with the proselytes, but only in one place does he mention circumcision explicitly, in Questions and Answers in Exodus II:2. this text is preserved both in Greek and in Armenian translation, with only minor variations. Our comments will be based on the Greek fragment. Philo interprets Exod 22:21, which in accordance with LXX can be translated as follows: "and a proselyte you shall not mistreat, nor shall you oppress him. For you were proselytes in the land of Egypth."

The term προσήλυτος in Exod 22:21 is given this interpretation by Philo:"προσήλυτος is not the one who has circumcised his uncircumcision, but the one who (has circumcised) his desires and sensual pleasures and the other passions of the soul. For in Egypt the Hebrew nation was not circumcised, but, being mistreated with all mistreatments of the cruelty shown by the inhabitants against strangers, it lived with them in self-restraint and endurance, not by necessity, but rather of free choice, because it took refuge in the Saviour, God, Who sent His beneficent power and delivered the suppliants from their difficult and hopeless situation."

Philo gives here an answer to the question: When does a person receive status as a proselyte in the Jewish Community and cease to be a heathen? This problem was of great importance both at the ideological and practical level, and in different ways it is also discussed later in rabbinic literature. (8)

Philo uses an ethical criterion for deciding who has the status of a proselyte within the Jewish community. This ethical conversion of the heathen also meant a social change from a pagan context to a Jewish one. (9) It is of interest to note that Philo's view does not represent an isolated attitude among the Jews. According to b Shabbath 31a, Hillel gave the status of proselyte to a heathen who came to him and accepted the Golden Rule as summary of the Torah. (10) Philo's and Hillel's understanding has thus been that bodily circumcision was not the requirement for entering the Jewish community, but was one of the commandments which they had to obey upon receiving status as a Jew.

From our analysis of the two Philonic passages, Migr 91-92 and Quaes Exod II:2, the following hypothesis can be formulated for Paul's discussion of the problems in Galatia:

1. As Philo in On the Migration of Abraham 91-2 argues for bodily circumcision based on his agreement with the idea held by the other Jews mentioned, so Paul's opponents in Galatia have also stressed that they agreed with Paul, and that Paul agreed with them: Paul still preached circumcision, Gal 5:11. At this point, at least, Paul's opponents were his venerators. (11)

2. As in Philo, On the Migration of Abraham 92 and Questions and Answers in Exodus II:2, the debate in Gal 5:11-6:10 deals on the one hand with the ethical ideas and way of life associated with circumcision, and on the other hand with the need for performing the external observance of physical circumcision itself.

   When Paul preached that the heathen Galatians should depart from the desires of the flesh and enter the society of those who served and loved each other, then the opponents claimed that this was the ethical meaning of circumcision. This "ethical circumcision" was to be followed by bodily circumcision and a life in accordance with the Law of Moses. In this way they had grounds for claiming that Paul still preached circumcision.

3. In Gal 5:13 - 6:10 Paul repeats points from his missionary preaching in Galatia, together with polemic clarifications so as to remove the misunderstandings made by the opponents. According to Paul, the transition from paganism, and thus from the desires of the flesh, was tied to the believer's crucifixion with Christ, and not bodily circumcision, Gal 5:11, 24, cf. 6:13-14. The new life in the community of service and love was therefore a life under the power of the Spirit, and not a life under the Law, Gal 5:18. It was a life in accordance with the Law of Christ, Gal 6:2.

<u>Paul preaches circumcision</u>

In Gal 5:11 Paul says: "And I, brethren, if I am still preaching circumcision, why am I despite this fact being persecuted? (12) In that case the stubling-block of the cross is done away with." The emphatic use of ἐγώ shows that Paul deals with a very personal matter. (13) Paul's opponents had evidently been saying that he himself was still preaching circumcision. The commentators have had difficulties in defining on what basis the opponents made this claim. (14) There is good reason for raising anew the question whether the context of Gal 5:11 can yield more information about Paul's preaching of circumcision. The question may be formulated in this way: Does Paul in the context reiterate ideas from his missionary preaching in Galatia, ideas which the opponents have misunderstood and misused in support for their circumcision campaign?

In Gal 5:19-21 Paul states explicitly that he repeats points from his previous preaching to the Galatians: "Now the works of the flesh are manifest, such as fornication, etc, respecting which I tell you beforehand, as I have already previously told you, that they who do such things will not inherit the Kingdom of God." In his missionary preaching to the pagan Galatians paul spoke against the works of the flesh. With some variation in wording, Paul repeatedly stresses this point in his missionary preaching:

Gal 5:13 εἰς ἀφορμὴν τῇ σαρκί
5:16 ἐπιθυμίαν σαρκὸς
5:17 ἡ ... σὰρξ ἐπιθυμεῖ ...
κατὰ τῆς σαρκός
5:24 τὴν σάρκα .....
σὺν τοῖς παθήμασιν καὶ ταῖς ἐπιθυμίαις

Paul refers so repeatedly and pointedly to this topic from his previous preaching, because his opponents have claimed that in this way he preached circumcision (as the removal of the passions and desires). On what basis could they make this claim? The reason was that among the Jews of that time circumcision was understood to portray the removal of passions and desires and the evil inclination.

In Philo's works this interpretation of circumcision is very common, and he uses a terminology similar to the one Paul uses in Gal 5:13, 16, 17, 19, 24: Migr 92: τὸ περιτέμνεσθαι ἡδονῆς καὶ παθῶν πάντων ἐκτομὴν ... ἐμφαίνει , (receiving circumcision portrays the excision of pleasure and all passions).

Spec I:9: ἡδονῶν ἐκτομῆς
(excision of pleasures).
Spec I:305: περιτέμνεσθε τὴν σκληροκαρδίαν
(Lev 26:41 cf Deut 10:16), τὸ δέ ἐστι, τὰς περιττευούσας φύσεις τοῦ ἡγεμονικοῦ, ἅς αἱ ἄμετροι τῶν παθῶν ἔσπειράν τε καὶ συνηύξησαν ὁρμαί
("Circumcise the hardness of your hearts", that is, the superfluous overgrowths of the mind, which the immoderate appetites of the passions have sown and raised).

Of special interest is Questions and Answers in Genesis III:52, since here the term "flesh" - central to Paul - symbolizes the passions: "The flesh of the foreskin, symbolizing those sensual pleasures and impulses (= ἡδονὰς καὶ ὁρμάς) which afterwards come to the body." (15)

Although Philo has a dichotomic anthropology, in these passages he does not employ a sharp dualism between body and soul. He applies circumcision at both levels, so that both the body is to be circumcised, and also the soul/mind/heart must be circumcised.

In a similar way we read in the Qumran writings, in I Qp Hab 11:13, that the foreskin of the heart is to be circumcised in addition to the circumcision of the body, which seems assumed. A parallel to the thoughts of Paul and Philo also occurs in I QS 5:5-6, where it says that the foreskin of the evil inclination is to be circumcised. (16) It is of importance that in I Qp Hab 11:13-14 the evil inclination leads to drunkenness, a vice which Paul includes among the works of the flesh in Gal 5:21 (μέθαι, κῶμοι).

In the Migr 92 Philo shows how such ethical interpretations of circumcision might lead to different attitudes and practices:

Philo himself stressed that the ethical ideas were of necessity tied to the external observance of bodily circumcision. Although Philo, according to Quaest in Exod II:2, gave heathens the status of proselytes on the basis of ethical circumcision of the pagan pleasures, he meant that the observance of bodily circumcision was to follow. In a similar way Paul's opponents have linked Paul's preaching against (pagan) fleshly desires closely to bodily circumcision: ethical circumcision was to be followed by obedience to the commandment of bodily circumcision.

This idea that the observance of circumcision should follow and complete the ethical circumcision is supported by Gal 3:3, where Paul writes: "Having begun with the Spirit, will you now complete with the flesh?" A. Oepke suggests that Paul's opponents in Galatia have argued that the Galatians needed a supplement, needed a completion by obeying the Law of Moses. (17) Circumcision played a basic role in this complete submission to the Law.

In this way Paul's opponents - who appeared as his followers, said that Paul preached circumcision, Gal 5:11.

In Gal 5:11 there is another point which Paul comments upon, namely the stumbling-block of the cross. In 5:11 Paul formulates an "either-or" between circumcision and the stumbling-block of the cross. (18) If in his preaching against the pagan vices of desire and the passions he has preached bodily circumcision, then the stumbling-block of the cross ceases to exist.

The idea of the cross is elaborated upon in 5:24. Against the background of 5:11, how is this elaboration to be understood? In 5:24 Paul writes: "and they who belong to Christ (Jesus) have crucified the flesh together with the passions and desires". Since Paul in 5:11 formulated an "either-or" between circumcision and the cross, it is probable that Paul in 5:24 has made the believer's crucifixion with Christ replace the function of bodily circumcision: crucifixion with Christ and not bodily circumcision has removed the passions and desires.

Philo gives support to this understanding, since to him, as we have seen, circumcision has the role of removing the passions and desires, a role which Paul in Gal 5:24 attributes to the crucifixion with Christ. As example, Migr 92 might be quoted again: "... receiving circumcision portrays the excision of pleasure and all passions..." The role of circumcision, removing pleasures and passions, has thus by Paul been transferred to the believer's crucifixion with Christ, to the exclusion of the observance of bodily circumcision itself. (19)

In a similar way the role of circumcision in Col 2:13 is transferred to the believer's resurrection with Christ, and re-interpreted on that basis: "For though you were dead in your trespasses, and in the uncircumcision of your flesh, he made you live with Christ." (20) Moreover, in Col 2:11 we read about the circumcision not made by hands, the circumcision of Christ, ἐν τῇ περιτομῇ τοῦ Χριστοῦ. The meaning is the circumcision which belongs to Christ, and is brought about by union with him. (21)

At this point there is a basic difference between the anti-circumcision-Jews, criticized by Philo in De Migratione 86-93, and Paul. Those Jews accepted and practiced the ethical meaning of circumcision, but ignored the observance of bodily circumcision itself. Paul, on the other hand, transferred the role of circumcision to another event, namely the believer's crucifixion (and resurrection) together with Christ. Paul also rejected the observance of bodily circumcision, but gave the ethical life a new and eschatological foundation in the death and resurrection of Jesus Christ. (22)

In this way we have substantiated part of our hypothesis: When Paul preached that the heathen Galatians should depart from the desires of the flesh and enter the society of those who serve and love each other, then his opponents claimed that this was the ethical meaning of circumcision. Paul still preached circumcision, and their task was to persuade the Galatians to make bodily circumcision follow upon their ethical circumcision. By obedience to the commandment of circumcision they would make evident that they lived under the Law of Moses. Paul objected to this misunderstanding and misuse of his missionary preaching to the Galatians. For him their transition from the (pagan) desires of the flesh to a communal life in love was in an exclusive way tied to the beliver's crucifixion with Christ, and thus not to bodily circumcision and the jurisdiction of the Law of Moses.

Gal 5:12-14 (15) Nomism and libertinism

Our analysis makes it possible to approach from a new angle one of the most discussed problems in research on the Letter to the Galatians, namely the relationship between nomism and libertinism in the Letter. The main positions in this debate may be sketched in the following way: On the one hand there are scholars who in various ways follow the traditional view that

Paul's opponents were Judaizers: i.e. Jewish Christians who were faithful to the Law of Moses. W.G. Kümmel is a representative of this view. As a consequence of this approach, he thinks that Paul in Gal 5:13ff. argues against possible, or actual, libertine misunderstandings of his own Gospel about freedom from the Law of Moses. Paul's polemic against libertinism is then a result of his polemic against nomism. (23)

On the other hand there are scholars who maintain that Paul in Gal 5:13-6:10 continues his polemic against the opponents in a direct way. He criticizes them for being libertinists. (24)

From this standpoint, W. Schmithals for example, suggests that the opponents were gnostics, who practiced circumcision and at the same time cherished libertinistic attitudes. For Schmithals, as well as for the other scholars who follow similar approaches, it is difficult to account for the massive and pointed anti-nomistic polemic Paul develops in other part of the Letter. (25)

These two main approaches to the question of Paul's opponents in Galatia do not seem to have placed in sharp focus the problem which Paul discusses in Gal 5:13-6:10. Paul's polemic addresses itself here neither to the libertinism of his opponents, nor to a libertinistic misunderstanding of Paul's Gospel about freedom from the Law. In this passage Paul continues his polemic against the opponents' campaign for bodily circumcision and thereby for obedience to the Law of Moses.

As we have seen, Paul's missionary preaching and exhortations to the Galatians, - that they should not follow the passions and pagan vices, but serve each other in love, - were tied neither to the specific observance of circumcision nor to the general jurisdiction of the Law of Moses: This preaching against the pagan life was to Paul based in an exclusive way on the believer's crucifixion with Christ: it is a life in the Spirit, and in accordance with the Law of Christ.

From this view point we shall analyse Gal 5:13-14, and then afterwards sketch the interpretation of the other parts of 5:13-6:10. Verse 5:15 will be discussed together with 5:25-6:6. In the analysis we shall attempt to reveal how the opponents have misunderstood Paul's preaching, and then define Paul's view and polemic.

Gal 5:13-14 characterizes the term ἐλευθερία, freedom, and tells what it is not and what it is: (26)

<u>The content and the purpose of the call:</u> ἐλευθερία,

v. 13 a Ὑμεῖς γὰρ ἐπ' "ἐλευθερίᾳ" ἐκλήθητε, ἀδελφοί,
<u>what ἐλευθερία is not:</u>
v. 13 b μόνον μὴ τὴν "ἐλευθερίαν" εἰς ἀφορμὴν τῇ σαρκί,
<u>what ἐλευθερία is:</u>
v. 14 ἀλλὰ διὰ τῆς ἀγάπης "δουλεύετε" ἀλλήλοις,
ὁ γὰρ πᾶς νόμος ἐν ἑνὶ λόγῳ πεπλήρωται, ἐν τῷ
ἀγαπήσεις τὸν πλησίον σου ὡς σεαυτόν

There are two main observations which suggest that in these verses Paul draws on points from his missionary preaching in Galatia: <u>1</u>. The phrase in v. 13 b) εἰς ἀφορμὴν τῇ σαρκί, is, as shown above, a variant to the phrase τὰ ἔργα τῆς σαρκός, v. 19. And this expression in v. 19 forms part of Paul's previous preaching to the Galatians, as seen from the verb προεῖπον in v. 21.
<u>2</u>. The verb in 13 a) ἐκλήθητε is aorist and refers back to the call the heathen Galatians received through Paul's missionary preaching. (27) When Paul in v. 13 a says that freedom was the purpose of his call, ἐπ' ἐλευθερίᾳ ἐκλήθητε, then this implies that freedom was part of the content of Paul's preaching. (28)

In v. 13 b the term ἐλευθερία is given negative definition. Paul tells what it is not. The article τὴν ἐλευθερίαν has demonstrative force, so that the word here refers back in a direct way to ἐλευθερία in the preceeding sentence, v. 13 a). (29)

The verb is lacking in v. 13 b, but a verb is not to be presupposed or added, since similar formulations of an excluding μή without verb occurs elsewhere in Greek. (30)

In this way v. 13 b is given the character of a negative definition of ἐλευθερία in v. 13 a: "For you were called to "freedom", brethren, only not "freedom" to opportunity for the flesh". Since the Galatians were called away from paganism, this negative definition meant primarily "not as opportunity for pagan vices". This understanding is supported by Paul's list of vices in Gal 5:19-21, which contains primarily pagan vices.

In Gal 5:14 Paul states his positive understanding of ἐλευθερία . This positive statement has a paradoxical form, since the term ἐλευθερία here is rendered by its contrast in the verb δουλεύετε : freedom means that they shall serve as slaves to each other, "for the whole Law of Moses is fulfilled in this one word, even this, you shall love your neighbour as yourself." The verb δουλεύετε has the form of present imperative, and states the continous parenetic imperative under which the Galatians live after having left paganism.

When Paul in v. 14 says ὁ γὰρ πᾶς νόμος ἐν ἑνὶ λόγῳ πεπλήρωται he draws here on the formula phrase πληροῦν τὸν νόμον: a person fulfills the Law of Moses by doing the commandments of the Law. (31) At the same time Paul understands the Law of Moses as a totality, with the love commandment of Lev 19:18 as its center. (32) To fulfill therefore also implies the idea of summarizing.

There are several points which show that Paul here draws on a Jewish and Christian tradition in which Lev 19:18 summarizes the Law of Moses. The two main points are:

1. As stated, Paul reiterates in Gal 5:13-14 parts of his missionary preaching to the Galatians. Within this context his use of the love commandment, Lev 19:18, as the center of the Law of Moses, is entirely parallell to the way in which Hillel according to b Šabb 31a summed up the Law of Moses in the Golden Rule. Hillel made this summary for a heathen whom he accepted as a proselyte.

Moreover, in Jewish tradition the Golden Rule was so closely associated with the love commandment of Lev 19:18 that in Jerusalem Targum both are paraphrased together to render Lev 19:18. (33) Thus Paul draws on such traditions from the teaching to gentiles who contemplated joining the Jewish nation.

2. There is also evidence that the Love commandment was used as the basic commandment of the Law of Moses. The evidence within Christian tradition is found in the double commandment of love to God and to neighbour, Matt 22:34-40; Mark 12:30-31; Luke 10:27. (34) Evidence is also found in the commandment of love in John 13:34-5, etc.

In Jewish writings we find the commandment of love, Lev 19:18 designated as the greatest commandment of the Law of Moses in a saying which in Siphre Lev 19:18 is attributed to Rabbi Akiba. (35)

Hence, in Gal 5:14 Paul draws on a Jewish and Christian tradition in which the love commandment, Lev 19:18, sums up the Law of Moses. This statement by Paul therefore fits very well into a nomistic context. Paul's opponents have applied Paul's summary of the Law in the love command, Lev 19:18, to the entering of proselytes into the jurisdiction of the Law of Moses, in a way similar to Hillel's use of the Golden Rule when he received a heathen as proselyte. As for freedom, the term is not extensively used in Jewish sources, but there is sufficient evidence to say that the opponents would agree when

Paul defined freedom as slavery to one another in accordance with the Law of Moses, Gal 5:14. (36)

Our interpretation of Gal 5:13-14 fits into the preceeding context of these verses. Verse 13 is in a direct way connected with v 12, by the motivating γάρ, and by the emphatic place of ὑμεῖς, which is seen together with οἱ ἀναστατοῦντες ὑμᾶς in v 12. This grammatical analysis is not problematic in itself. (37) It has proved difficult, however, to formulate the precise and logical movement of thought from v 12 to v 13. Many commentators therefore find it difficult to keep closely to the grammatical observations. Instead of interpreting v 12 and v 13 together, they suggest a more general and broader background of thought for the motivating γάρ in v 13. (38)

The close grammatical connection between vv 12 and 13 should, however, be taken seriously, and our analysis makes this possible: Paul builds on the views and presuppositions of his opponents, bringing them to their extreme and absurd conclusions. The opponents maintained that the circumcision of the foreskin of the flesh portrayed the excision of the passions and desires, and brought a person into society under the Law of Moses. Along these lines they have interpreted Paul's preaching. Against this background Paul exclaims: I wish they would go all the way, and castrate themselves.

This would express more clearly that the passions are removed. The connection between v 12 and v 13 can be paraphrased in this way: O that those who are upsetting you by preaching that circumcision removes the passions of the flesh, and who claim that I do the same, may go all the way and take the logical consequence of such a view and castrate themselves, and thereby express even more clearly that the passions are removed. For you, it is true, were by my missionary preaching called to "freedom", precisely not as opportunity for the flesh ...

The interpretation of Gal 5: (15)16-6:10. A sketch

In Gal 5:16-6:6 Paul elaborates on the thoughts of 5:13-15; he uncovers the misunderstandings of the opponents and gives a precise definition of his own views. The passage is brought to a close in 6:7-10, in a conclusion where Paul both threatens and exhorts the Galatians. (39)

The beginning of this explanatory section is marked out by λέγω δέ "but I say" v 5:16. By this phrase Paul refers back to his statement in vv 13-15 and indicates that his own explanations and elaborations follow. (40)

The topic ἡ σάρξ and ὁ νόμος in vv 13-14 is discussed by Paul in vv 16-18. In vv 13-14 Paul pictured the community's life as a life in accordance with the Law of Moses, in contrast to (pagan) life according to the flesh. In vv 16-18 these two terms are further defined as "desire of the flesh" v 16: ἐπιθυμία σαρκός, and "under the Law", v 18: ὑπὸ νόμον. The opponents have misunderstood Paul's preaching: he advocates life under the Law of Moses as "freedom" as against the pagan life of the fleshly desires. Gal 4:21 supports this interpretation. There Paul tells that the Galatians, as a result of the work of his opponents, wish to live under the Law of Moses, οἱ ὑπὸ νόμον θέλοντες εἶναι.

As already mentioned, Philo presents views akin to those of Paul's opponents. For example, in Quaes Gen III:48 he presents the view of some other Jews, a view with which he himself agrees. Here also there is a contrast drawn between the life of desire and life in accordance with the Law, and circumcision marks the transition: circumcision is the symbol of the cutting off of excessive desires by exercising continence and endurance in matters of the Law.

In Gal 5:16-18 Paul removes the misunderstanding made by his opponents. He gives a judicial ruling by which the jurisdiction of the Law of Moses is annulled: εἰ δὲ πνεύματι ἄγεσθε, οὐκ ἐστε ὑπὸ νόμον, v 18.
Since the Galatians had received the Spirit (Gal 3:2) and were driven by the Spirit, they belonged to an eschatological reality, and were not under the jurisdiction of the Law of Moses. (41)

In this way we see that Paul has as background the Jewish dualism between a life in (pagan) passions and desires, and a life under the Law of Moses. He replaces this dualism, however, by the dualism between a life in (pagan) passions and desires and a life in the power of the eschatological Spirit.

As a result, if a person in this eschatological situation still claims that one has to live under the Law of Moses, he comes in conflict with the eschatological reality of the Spirit. In this way those who still cling to the works of the Law of Moses are with logical consequence pushed together with those who live in (pagan) passions, since both categories oppose Christ and the life of the Spirit. Thus, Paul's thinking moves from the idea of (pagan) fleshly desires to life under the Law also being flesh, since man in both cases puts his trust in man's effort and boasting (6:12-13), and not in the cross of Christ, 6:14.

In Gal 5:19-24 Paul continues his deliberations on the topic and terms of ἡ σάρξ and ὁ νόμος, vv 13-14 and v 19. 23-24; and he also includes the idea of ἀγάπη, v 13 and 22. Paul draws in vv 19-21 on his previous preaching in Galatia, as explicitly stated in v 21, and he exemplifies here the works of the flesh by a list of vices in which there is an emphasis on the typically pagan vices. (42)

The corresponding list of virtues, vv 22-23 should then give examples of a life lived in accordance with the Law of Moses. In this way, there would be a direct line drawn from vv 13-14, - where the love command of Lev 19:18 sums up the Law of Moses, - and to the virtues of love, etc. in v 22 f. (43)

Here again Philo can illustrate such an understanding as this one, championed by Paul's opponents. In Virt 180 ff Philo pictures the conversion of the heathens from the worship of creation to the worship of the true God, the Creator; from a life in vice to a virtuous life. By means of a list of virtues Philo describes the life of the proselytes (οἱ ἐπηλύται) in contrast to the life of those who rebel against the holy Laws of Moses. The proselyte becomes at once temperate, continent, modest, gentle, kind, a lover of mankind, serious, just, high-minded, superior to the desire for money and pleasure. (44)

In a corresponding way Paul's opponents could claim that the virtues listed by Paul in Gal 5:22-3 portrayed a life under the Law of Moses, in contrast to the pagan life exemplified by the list of vices, vv 19-21. (45)

This understanding of vv 19-21 and of vv 22-23, receives support from vv 23b-24. Thus, in v 23b the Law of Moses is in a direct way brought into the discussion: κατὰ τῶν τοιούτων οὐκ ἔστιν νόμος. This point is not superflous, as F. Mussner and others think. (46) In his polemic against his opponents, - who contrasted the life of fleshly desires and the life under the Law of Moses, - Paul states that the life of love, as fulfillment of the Law of Moses (vv 13-14) is the life of the Spirit outside the jurisdiction of the law (v 18, v 22) but without being in contradiction to the Law; see v 23b: "against such things there is no Law". (47)

The conflicting views between Paul and his opponents are also seen in Gal 5:24, as already shown. Here, Paul stresses that the removal of the flesh together with its passions and desires is exclusively brought about by the believer's crucifixion with Christ, and not, as claimed by the opponents, tied to obedience to the commandment of bodily circumcision.

The conclusion is that Paul in Gal 5:19-24 continues the controversy between his opponents' view (built on the dualism between pagan desires and the life under the Law of Moses, and therefore requiring bodily circumcision) and Paul's own view (based upon a dualism between the (pagan) fleshly desires and the eschatological life of the Spirit, outside the jurisdiction of the Law of Moses, but not in contradiction with it). Consequently, Paul does not require bodily circumcision, but ties the removal of the fleshly desires exclusively to the believer's crucifixion with Christ.

In the next section, Gal 5:25-6:6 Paul elaborates upon and defines the thoughts of 5:13-15 about the community's life of love as fulfillment of the Law. The key term which expresses this theme is ἀλλήλους vv 13.14.15 and 5:26 and 6:2.

Paul's main point in 5:25-6:6 is to show that the Christian community's life of mutual love (vv 13-14) is a life in which they are to walk in the eschatological Spirit, 5:25, cf 6:1, and fulfill the Law of Christ, 6:2 (48) and thus not a life to be lived under the jurisdiction of the Law of Moses, as maintained by the opponents.

Against this background, it is evident that Paul's main concern here is not to criticize actual divisions and conflicts among the Galatian Christians themselves, but to show that problems and controversies among the believers are not to be solved by turning to the commandments of the Law of Moses, in spite of the central role played by the commandment of love, Lev 19:18, cited in Gal 5:14. The Galatian Christians are to solve community problems as those who have the Spirit, as οἱ πνευματικοί, 6:1. (49)

What then is the meaning of Gal 5:15: "If you bite and eat one another, take care that you do not consume one another"? When this verse is compared with the exhortations given by Paul in 5:26 and 6:1 ff no consistent picture of an inner conflict among the Galatian Christians becomes apparent. Thus Paul gives advice on how to solve such inner conflicts, rather than addressing himself in a direct way to one particular concrete situation.

Nevertheless, in Gal 5:15 the conditional clause of a real condition is used, and Paul therefore here probably refers to an actual example of such community conflicts. (50) He then probably refers back to some problem-solving exhortations he gave when he went to Galatia as a missionary and founded the congregations. If so, Paul here continues his warning against the influence in the Christian community of the wild behaviour that characterized them in their pagan contexts. Cf. the reference in Gal 5:20-1 to strife and divisions together with such pagan vices as idolatry, etc.

Again it should be stated, however, that Paul's main point here in Gal 5:13-15 and 5:25 ff 6:1 ff is to show that in spite of his use of the love command from the Law of Moses, Lev 19:18, such inner community problems are not to be solved by enforcing the Law of Moses, but by acting as those who walk according to the Spirit.

After Paul in Gal 5:13-6:6 has rebutted the claims of the opponents (i.e. his venerators) that he still preached circumcision, 5:11, and thereby the jurisdiction of the Law of Moses, he in 6:7-10 concludes with a sharp warning to the Galatians and with a final exhortation. In this way he also sums up main points from 5:13-6:6: He deals in 6:8 with ἡ σάρξ and τὸ πνεῦμα, the theme of 5:13-24, and he refers in 6:10 to the Christian community life, the theme of 5:25-6:6.

When Paul in 6:8 again formulates the contrast between flesh and Spirit, the question arises: Does Paul here, as in 5:13-24, understand ἡ σάρξ as expression of the pagan way of life according to the passions and desires, or as expression of the Jewish-Christian emphasis on the works of the Law of Moses? As already stated, Paul's eschatological understanding of the cross of Christ and the Spirit causes him to characterize the opponents' continued claim for works of the Law by the same term which he gives to the pagan life, σάρξ. Both attitudes express man's trust in himself and rejection of the cross of Christ and of the life of the Spirit. Both are expressions of ἡ σάρξ. (51) Thus, the main point of Paul's criticism against "the flesh" in 6:8 is his polemic against the circumcision campaign of his opponents, and his warning against the danger that the Galatians might follow them.

Gal 6:7-10 may then be paraphrased in this way: Be not deceived. God is not mocked: for whatsoever a man sows that shall he also reap; for he who sows in his own flesh, whether in fleshly passions, or in the boasting of the flesh of circumcision (6:13), shall, from his man-centered and rebellious attitude, reap corruption. But he who is crucified with Christ from the fleshly desires and the boasting of the flesh of circumcision, and thereby sows to the Spirit, shall from this eschatological Spirit reap eternal life.

Against this background, we, as believers, are to do good deeds to all, but primarily to our fellow believers within the Christian community.

Conclusion

The present observations show that features from the situation of Philo in Alexandria can throw light upon some aspects of Paul's situation, as reflected in his letters. On the basic of this discussion of controversies on circumcision in Philo's writings and in Paul's letter to the Galatians, other related matters might be discussed in a similar way, such as debates on the observance of feasts Gal 4:10 and related ideas.

As for Gal 5:11-6:10 the employment of material from Philo has made it possible to reach the following conclusion:

1. Paul's opponents in Galatia claimed that Paul agreed with them: he still preached circumcision.
2. When he came as missionary, Paul preached to the heathen Galatians that they should remove the desires of the flesh and enter the society of those who served and loved one another in accordance with the Law of Moses. According to Paul's opponents, this "ethical circumcision" was meant to be completed by bodily circumcision and a life under the Law of Moses.
3. In Gal 5:13-6:10 Paul repeats points from his missionary preaching in Galatia. At the same time he removes the misunderstanding made by his opponents, when they maintained that Paul here preached circumcision.

Although Paul and Philo reflect parallel conflicts about the observance of bodily circumcision, it would be wrong for that reason to characterize them as Hellenistic Jews in sharp contrast to Palestinian Judaism. As shown in the study, sayings attributed to Hillel and Eleazar from Modin indicate that similar problems and debates on circumcision, etc. existed also in Palestine.

NOTES

1) J. Munck, "Pauline Research since Schweitzer", in J.Ph. Hyatt (ed), The Bible in Modern Scholarship, (Nashville/New York, 1965) 166-7.

2) W.D. Davies, "Paul and Judaism" in J.Ph. Hyatt (ed), The Bible in Modern Scholarship, 178-95.

3) ibid, 186.

4) J. Drummond, Philo Judaeus, 1 (London, 1888; repr. Amsterdam, 1969) 20; E.R. Goodenough, By Light, 83-4 etc.

5) See Leg all I:6.18; Cher 87; Joh 5:17:, Exod Rab 30:6.

6) Cf. Hillel's view that the Sabbath joy applied to every day, b Beṣa 16 a. In the Old Testament joy and thanksgiving were already central features of the feasts: Neh 8:12; Jes 16:10; 9:2; 22:13; Sak 8:19; Neh 12:43; Ps 50:14.23 etc.

7) M. Friedländer, Die religiösen Bewegungen, 81, etc.

8) See f. ex. B.J. Bamberger, Proslytism, 38-52.

9) See D. Daube, ST, 1, (1947) 159.

10) The problem is formulated in a similar way by S. Bialoblocki, Die Beziehungen des Judentums zu Proselyten, 15 ff.

11) Cf. O. Linton, "The Third Aspect. A Neglected Point of View," ST, 3, (1950/51) 83.

12) See E. de Witt Burton, Galatians, ICC, 287.

13) G.S. Duncan, to the Galatians, MNTC, 159; A. Oepke/J. Rohde, an die Galater, 161; H. Schlier, an die Galater, 238; F. Mussner, Der Galaterbrief, 358; K. Müller, Anstoss und Gericht, 114: "Das δέ adversativum distanziert ἐγώ von dem in V 10 genannten part ὁ ταράσσων . Es belastet ἐγώ mit einem gewichtigen Akzent."

14) See G.S. Duncan, to the Galatians, 159; A. Oepke/J. Rohde, an die Galater, 161 f; H. Schlier, die Galater, 239.- F. Mussner, Der Galaterbrief, 359, just takes for granted that Paul has not preached circumcision and writes, - "Doch das Paulus jemals die Beschneidigung "gepredigt" habe, ist nicht anzunehmen." On the same page, n. 112, he attempts to explain away the fact that the conditional clause has the form of a real case: "Paulus stellt vielmehr aus zorniger Erregung heraus in dem εἰ-Satz einen schlechthin unwirklichen Fall als wirklich hin, um auf die Konsequenzen dieses "Falles" aufmerksam machen zu können.

15) R. Marcus, PLCL, Sup, 1, 253 and n.i.

16) See E. Lohse, Die Texte von Qumran, ad loc. Cf. R. Meyer, " περιτέμνω" TWNT, 6, 78-79. J.J. Günther, St. Paul's Opponents, 87-8; cf. H.A. Wolfson, Philo, 2, 225-37, who connects the concepts of desire and evil inclination.

17) A. Oepke/J. Rohde, an die Galater, 101; So also H. Schlier, die Galater, 123 f.

18) H. Schlier, die Galater, 239 f.: "περιτομή und σταυρός stehen sich für ihn als einander ausschliessende Mittel und Zeichen des Heiles entgegen..."

19) In Gal 6:13-14 there is another example where Paul makes the cross of Christ replace circumcision: The circumcision people place their boast in the flesh of circumcision, while Paul, accordingly, boasts in the cross of Christ.

20) Cf. E. Lohmeyer, Die Briefe an die Philipper, an die Kolosser und an Philemon, Meyer.K. (Göttingen, 1964 [6]) 113-4: "Nicht jedes menschliche, sondern alles heidnische Leben ist "tot". So wäre also das Dasein in der "Beschneidung" vor Gott "lebendig" und gerecht?". E. Lohse, Die Briefe an die Kolosser und an Philemon,[2] Meyer,K., (Göttingen, 1977) 161: "Die ἀκροβυστία an die die Heidenchristen errinnert werden, ist durch die περιτομὴ ἀχειροποίητος (2:11) beseitigt worden. In der Taufe ist die Wende vom Tod zum Leben vollzogen worden; Gott hat euch lebendig gemacht mit ihm (vgl 2:12)."

Cf. that according to Phil 3:2 ff the believers are the circumcision (ἡμεῖς γάρ ἐσμεν ἡ περιτομή) who serve by the Spirit of God, who place their boast in Christ Jesus, and put no trust in flesh, as do those who mutilate themselves by bodily circumcision. - Here also circumcision is transferred to the union with Christ and life in the Spirit.

21) See E.F. Scott, The Epistles of Paul to the Colossians, to Philemon and to the Ephesians, (London, 1958)[9] 74 ff.

22) Cf. M. Friedländer, Die religiösen Bewegungen, 356-62.

23) W.G. Kümmel, Einleitung in das Neue Testament, (Heidelberg, 1976 [18]) 261-3; see footnote, p 262 n 16, with survey of scholars who belong to this group. To the list is to be added E.E. Ellis, Prophecy and Hermeneutic, (Tübingen, 1977) 112 (with some waivering, see p. 94); F. Mussner, Der Galaterbrief, 366 f.

24) See survey of scholars in W.G. Kümmel, Einleitung, 261, notes 10 and 11, cf note 9.

25) W. Schmithals, Paulus und die Gnostiker, (Hamburg-Bergstadt, 1965) 9-46; W. Marxsen, Einleitung in das Neue Testament, Gütersloh 1963, 49-55, etc. Cf. W.G. Kümmel, Einleitung, 261 f. for criticism of this line of research.

26) See the similar analysis in A. Sand, Der Begriff "Fleisch" in den paulinischen Hauptbriefen, (Regensburg, 1967) 209, although Sand draws different conclusions from his analysis.

27) H. Schlier, Die Galater, 242: "Indem Gott (vgl 1:6.15; 5:8) rief, und zwar konkret durch das apostolische Evangelium von Jesus Christus"...

28) See E. de Witt Burton, Galatians, 291, with references to 1 Thess 4:7, Phil 4:10.

29) ibid., 292.

30) A. Oepke/J. Rohde, an die Galater, 169; H. Schlier, die Galater, 242.

31) See H. Schlier, die Galater, 244-5. Cf. Rom 13:8.

32) Cf. the Jewish view that to obey one commandment is the same as to obey the whole Law. See H. Schlier, die Galater, 245.

33) See P. Borgen, "Eine allgemein-etische Maxime", Temenos, 5, (1969) 37-53; Englisch version: id., "The Golden Rule, with Emphasis on Its usage in the Gospels," in P. Borgen, 'Paul Preaches Circumcision' and Pleases Men' and Other Essays on Christian Origins, (Trondheim, 1953) 99-114. Cf. the use of the Golden Rule in Mt 7:12. See also W. Grundmann, Das Evangelium nach Matthäus, (Berlin, 1968) 225-7. Cf. J. Jeremias, "Paulus als Hillelit", in E.E. Ellis and M. Wilcox (eds), Neotestamentica et Semitica, 89-90; M. Hengel, "Die Ursprünge der christlichen Mission", NTS, 18, (1971/2) 22-3.

34) Cf. Philo's use of the love commandment, Lev 19:34 about the right attitude of the Jews to the proselytes: Spec I:51-3; Virt 102-4.

35) See B. Gerhardsson, "The Hermeneutic Program in Matthew 22:27-40" in R. Hamerton-Kelly and K. Scroggs (eds), Jews, Greeks and Christians. Essays in honour of W.D. Davies, Leiden 1976, 129-150. See Str - B, I, 900-5; W. Bacher, Die exegetische Terminologie, 1, כלל

36) See Abot 6:2: The one who is occupied with the Torah, is free. b B Meṣ 85b: He who makes himself slave in this world because of the words of the Torah, he will be free in the world to come. See Str B, 2, 522 f; See also Josephus, Ant. IV: 187; Philo, Quod Omn 43-47; Joh 8:33.

37) See A. Oepke/J. Rohde, and die Galater, 169; H. Schlier, an die Galater, 241; F. Mussner, Der Galaterbrief, 366.

38) See f.i. F. Mussner, Der Galaterbrief, 366: "5:13. Der Vers ist durch das Pronomen ὑμεῖς und die Partikel γάρ eng mit dem Vorausgehenden verbunden. Wie ist aber eigentlich der Begründungszusammenhang? Wird nur V 12 begründet, wie manche Ausleger meinten? Kaum. Begründet wird vielmehr die ganze Ablehnung des "Judaismus" der Gegner durch den Apostel."
A. Bisping, Erklärung des zweiten Briefes and die Korinter und des Briefes an die Galater, 3, (Münster, 1883) ad loc, attempts to connect v. 13 directly with v. 12: "Die Verbindung durch γάρ ... ist so zu fassen: "Möchten diejenigen sich gar verschneiden lassen, die euch in Verwirrung bringen..., denn ihr (im Gegensatz zu jenen) seid zur Freiheit berufen, Brüder". F. Mussner, Der Galaterbrief, 366, n. 7, rightly objects that in this case v. 13 should have used δέ (as in some mss) instead of γάρ . It should be added that there is no support found in the Epistle for the suggestion that Paul in Gal 5:12 alludes to castration in the cult of Attis and Cybele. See H. Schlier, Die Galater, 240 f.

39) Cf. H. Schlier, die Galater, 241-278, who divides 5:13-6:10 into the following subheadings:" 1) 5:13-15: Der Grundsatz." " 2) 5:16-24: Die Erläuterung des Grundsatzes im allgemeinen". "3) 5:25-6:10: Die Erläuterung des Grundsatzes im besonderen." A. Oepke/J. Rohde, an die Galater, 167-197, has the following outline: 5:13-15: "Thema"; 5:16-6:6: "Durchführung"; 6:7-10: "Ausklang".

40) A. Oepke/J. Rohde, ... an die Galater, 173:" 16 Die Formel λέγω δέ führt einen bereits angedeuteten Gedanken weiter, so aber, dass er nach einer neuen Richtung hin entfaltet, dadurch erläutert und besonders unterstrichen wird (3:17; 4:1; anders 5:2)."

41) Cf. H. Schlier, die Galater, 250, who comes close to this interpretation of v. 18 (although not with the same polemic focus):" Solche Obmacht des Geistes bedeutet, aber, v. 18, die wirkliche Freiheit und das heisst das οὐκ εἶναι ὑπὸ νόμον, vlg. 5:1,3:23,4:4f.21. Denn - anders lässt sich diese Erinnerung an das Gesetz nicht verstehen - dann ist ja das Gesetz erfüllt, ohne das es dabei zur ἰδία δικαιοσύνη gekommen ist, dann ist der Christ endlich und voll und ganz dem Gesetz entronnen und entnommen."

42) See especially A. Vögtle, Die Tugend- und Lasterkataloge im Neuen Testament, (Münster i W., 1936) 223-6; S. Wibbing, Die Tugend- und Lasterkataloge im Neuen Testament, (Berlin, 1959) 106; cf. E. Kamlah, Die Form der katalogischen Paränese im Neuen Testament, (Tübingen, 1964) 178.

43) Cf. F. Mussner, Der Galaterbrief, 385: "Als erste "Tugend" im folgenden Katalog wird die ἀγάπη genannt ... Man braucht nicht zu zweifeln, dass dieser Stellenwert in Gal 5:22 mit der Aussage von 5:14 zusammenhängt, nach welcher im Gebot der Nächstenliebe "das ganze Gesetz" seine Zusammenfassung und Erfüllung findet."

44) The virtues listed by Paul in Gal 5:22-23 are akin to those with which Philo in Virt 18 characterizes the proselytes. Some of the virtues are even direct parallells: Paul, ἀγάπη and Philo, φιλάνθρωποι ,; Paul, χρηστότης and Philo, χρηστοί ; Paul, ἐγκράτεια and Philo, ἐγκρατεῖς .

45) Gal 5:19-21 has the form of a rule by which persons are excluded from the Kingdom of God. Such rules of exclusion - just as also rules of admission - were widespread in Judaism and in NT. See A. Vögtle, Die Tugend, 43; H. Windisch, "Die Sprüche vom Eingehen in das Reich Gottes", ZNW, 27, (1928) 163-192, etc. Here also Philo can produce a parallel connected with circumcision: In Quaest. in Gen II:52 he writes: "For the mind which is not circumcised and purified and sanctified of the body and the passions which come through the body, will be corrupted and cannot be saved." Cf. also Acts 15:1 (Gal 6:12).

46) F. Mussner, Der Galaterbrief, 389: "Der Satz klingt leicht ironisch und spricht eigentlich eine Selbstverständlichkeit aus." J.Chr.K.V. Hofman, Die heilige Schrift neuen Testamentes, II:1: Der Pauli Brief an die Galater, (1872 [2]) ad loc: "mehr als überflüssig".

47) Cf. For the interpretation of τῶν τοιούτων as neuter , see F. Mussner, Der Galaterbrief, 389.

48) Concerning the Law of Christ/Messiah, see W.D. Davies, Torah in the Messianic Age and/or the Age to Come, (Philadelphia, 1952); id., The Setting of the Sermon on the Mount, (Cambridge, 1966[2]) 447-9; 109-90.

49) See H. Schlier, die Galater, 270: the congregation as a whole are pneumatics, not only one group, the enthusiasts, as suggested by W. Lütgert, Gesetz und Geist, (Gütersloh, 1919) 12-14.

50) So H. Schlier, die Galater, 246f; F. Mussner, Der Galaterbrief, 273-4, has difficulties in making up his mind. He seems to favor the somewhat forced interpretation that Paul here uses the realis of preaching.

51) For the use of ἡ σάρξ to characterize man's trust in the works of the Law of Moses, in casu circumcision, see especially Gal 6:12-13.

CHAPTER FOURTEEN
THE CROSS-NATIONAL CHURCH FOR JEWS AND GREEKS

Paul's Letter to the Galatians takes us to the geographical region north-east and east of the Mediterranean Sea. From the north-east (Asia Minor) Galatia (1:2) and Cilicia (1:21) are mentioned, from the east, we hear of Syria (1:21), Damascus (1:17), Judea (1:22), Jerusalem (1:17-18; 2:1-10; 4:21-5:1) and Arabia (1:17). Many different ethnic groups lived in these geographical areas, but Paul looked upon them from a Jewish perspective and classified them in two categories: Jews and Gentiles (1:16; 2:2.9. 14-15) and Jews and Greeks (2:3; 3:28).

Paul's missionary work represented a geographical and ideological movement from the Jews to the Gentiles. He, Paul, the Jew, was called to preach about Christ to the Gentiles (1:16). He took traditions and events out of their Jewish context and put them into various ethnic contexts. In this way Early Christianity was transformed from being just part of a national religion into a religion with a cross-national structure.

The tension between national Judaism and cross-national Christianity was felt in many places in the Mediterranean world. Among them, Galatia in Asia Minor is of special interest, since Paul's Letter to the Galatians gives us a literary documentation of the struggle. Several issues played a central role in this struggle - circumcision, the cultic calendar and the role of the Jewish religious center, Jerusalem.

In this study the observations made in the previous chapters on Gal 5:11 ff. etc, will serve as point of departure. Then Gal 1:10 and on 2:1-10 (where Paul reports on the meeting in Jerusalem) will be analysed more fully. The question which will guide our investigation is: How is the conflict between the national and cross-national perspectives reflected in these passages?

Gal 5:11

In Gal 5:11 Paul says: "And I, brethren, if I am still preaching circumcision, why am I despite this fact persecuted? In that case the stumbling-block of the cross is done away with." (1) The conditional clause has the form of a real case. Thus, Paul's opponents had evidently been saying that he himself was still preaching circumcision.

H. Schlier and others refer to Acts 16:3, according to which Paul had circumcised Timothy. (2) Paul performed this observance from piety or out of convenience, without regarding circumcision as necessary for salvation. Paul's opponents misinterpreted such actions, and claimed that he still preached circumcision.

Many scholars find this interpretation to be unsatisfactory. F. Mussner states that even if Paul had circumcised Timothy, as said in Acts 16:3, such an isolated act did not give sufficient basis for the accusation that he preached circumcision. "Paul stellt vielmehr aus zorniger Erregung heraus in dem εἰ-Satz einen schlechthin unwirklichen Fall als wirklich hin, <u>um auf die Konsequenzen dieses "Falles" aufmerksam machen zu können</u>." (3)

Before resorting to such psychological speculations, however, one should make further attempts to take at face value the grammatical form of a real case. Thus, G. Howard tries to picture the situation presupposed. He suggests that the Judaizers, out of ignorance, actually thought that Paul practised circumcision. They considered Paul to be their ally, not an enemy. (4) This stress on the ignorance of the Judaizers does not harmonize well, however, with their accusation that Paul still <u>preaches</u> circumcision. Thus, they must have based their argumentation on the message presented by Paul in his missionary preaching to the Galatians.

There is good reason for raising anew the question whether the context of Gal 5:11 can yield more information about Paul's preaching of circumcision. The question may be formulated in this way: Does Paul in this context reiterate ideas from his missionary preaching in Galatia, ideas which the opponents have misunderstood and misused in support for their cimcumcision campaign?

In Gal 5:19-21 Paul states explicitly that he repeats points from his previous preaching to the Galatians: 'Now the works of the flesh are manifest, such as fornication, etc., respecting which I tell you beforehand, as I have already previously told you, that they who do such things will not inherit the Kingdom of God.' In his missionary preaching to the pagan Galatians, Paul spoke against the works of the flesh. With some variation in wording Paul repeatedly stresses this point in his missionary preaching:

Gal 5:13 εἰς ἀφορμὴν τῇ σαρκί
5:16 ἐπιθυμίαν σαρκός
5:17 ἡ...σὰρξ ἐπιθυμεῖ
κατὰ τῆς σαρκός
5:24 τὴν σάρκα...
σὺν τοῖς παθήμασιν καὶ ταῖς ἐπιθυμίαις

Against this background the following hypothesis can be

formulated: Paul refers pointedly to this topic from his previous preaching because his opponents have claimed that, in this way, he preached circumcision to be the removal of the passions and desires. On what basis could they make this claim? The reason was that, among the Jews of that time, circumcision was understood to portray the removal of passions, desires and the evil inclination, as can be seen in the works of Philo of Alexandria and the Dead Sea Serolls.

Of special interest is Quaes Gen III:52, since here the term "flesh" - central to Paul - symbolizes the passions: "The flesh of the foreskin, symbolizing those sensual pleasures and impulses (= ἡδονὰς καὶ ὁρμάς) which afterwards come to the body." (5)

In a similar way we read in the Qumran writings, in I Qp Hab II:13, that the foreskin of the heart is to be circumcised in addition to the circumcision of the body, which seems assumed. A parallel to the thoughts of Paul and Philo occurs also in I QS 5.5-6, where it says that the foreskin of the evil inclination is to be circumcised. (6)

In Migr 92 Philo shows that such ethical interpretations of circumcision might lead to different attitudes and practices. Philo criticizes some Jews who, although they have the right understanding of the ethical meaning of circumcision, nevertheless ignore the external observance. Philo himself stressed that the ethical ideas were of necessity tied to the external observance of bodily circumcision. Although Philo, according to Quaes Exod II:2, gave heathens the status of proselytes on the basis of ethical circumcision of the pagan pleasures, he meant that the observance of bodily circumcision was to follow. (7) In a similar way Paul's opponents have linked Paul's preaching against (pagan) fleshly desires closely to bodily circumcision: ethical circumcision was to be followed by obedience to the commandment for bodily circumcision.

The idea that the observance of circumcision should follow and complete ethical circumcision is supported by Gal 3:3, where Paul writes: "Having begun with the Spirit, will you now complete with the flesh?" A. Oepke suggests that Paul's opponents in Galatia argued that the Galatians needed a supplement, needed a completion by obeying the Law of Moses. (8) Circumcision played a basic role in this complete submission to the Law. In this way Paul's opponents - who appeared as his followers - said that he preached circumcision, Gal 5:11.

In Gal 5:11 there is another point which Paul comments upon, namely the stumbling-block of the cross. In 5:11 Paul formulates an 'either-or' between circumcision and the stumbling-block of the cross. (9) If in his preaching against the pagan vices of desire and the passions he has preached bodily circumcision, then the stumbling-block of the cross ceases to exist.

The idea of the cross is elaborated upon in 5:24. Against the background of 5:11, how is this elaboration to be understood? In 5:24 Paul writes: "And they who belong to Christ (Jesus) have crucified the flesh together with the passions and desires". Since Paul in 5:11 formulated an 'either-or' between circumcision and the cross, it is probable that Paul in 5:24 made the believer's crucifixion with Christ replace the function of bodily circumcision: crucifixion with Christ and not bodily circumcision has removed the passions and desires.

Philo gives support to this interpretation, since according to him, as we have seen, circumcision has the role of removing the passions and desires, a role which Paul in Gal 5:24 attributes to the crucifixion with Christ. As an example, Migr 92 can be quoted again:"... receiving circumcision portrays the excision of pleasure and all passions ..." The role of circumcision, removing pleasures and passions, has thus been transferred by Paul to the believer's crucifixion with Christ, to the exclusion of the observance of bodily circumcision itself. (10)

In a similar way the role of circumcision in Col 2:13 is transferred to the believer's resurrection with Christ, and reinterpreted on that basis: "For though you were dead in your trespasses, and in the uncircumcision of your flesh, he made you live with Christ". (11) Moreover, in Col 2:11 we read about the circumcision not made by hands, the circumcision of Christ, ἐν τῇ περιτομῇ τοῦ Χριστοῦ. The meaning is the circumcision which belongs to Christ, and is brought about by union with him. (12)

At this point there is a basic difference between the anti-circumcision-Jews criticized by Philo in Migr 86-93, and Paul. Those Jews accepted and practised the ethical meaning of circumcision, but ignored the observance of bodily circumcision. Paul, on the other hand, transferred the role of circumcision to another event, namely the believer's crucifixion (and resurrection) together with Christ. Paul also rejected the observance of bodily circumcision, but gave the ethical life a new and eschatological foundation in the death and resurrection of Jesus Christ.

We have reached the following conclusion: When Paul preached that the heathen Galatians should depart from the desires of the flesh and enter the society of those who serve and love each other, his opponents claimed that this was the ethical meaning of circumcision. Paul still preached circumcision, and their task was to persuade the Galatians to make bodily circumcision follow upon their ethical circumcision. By obedience to the commandment of circumcision they would make evident that they lived under the Law of Moses. Paul objected to this misunderstanding and misuse of his missionary preaching to the Galatians. For him their transition from the (pagan) desires of the flesh to a communal life in love was in an exclusive way tied to the believer's crucifixion with Christ, not to bodily circumcision and the jurisdiction of the Law of Moses. (13)

Gal 1:10b and 6:12-13

The Judaizers, who worked among the Galatians, claimed that Paul preached circumcision, as they did themselves. This claim implied that they meant that Paul, like themselves, wanted the Christian congregations to conform to the Jewish community.

In Gal 1:10 Paul seems to deal with this matter: εἰ ἔτι ἀνθρώποις ἤρεσκον, Χριστοῦ δοῦλος οὐκ ἂν ἤμην. "If I still tried to please men, I would not be the slave of Christ".

H. Schlier, F. Mussner and others rightly understand the sentence to be 'biographical': ἔτι "still", is then understood to refer to the time after Paul's call, 1:13 ff. (14) When Schlier and Mussner specify what Paul refers to when he talks about pleasing men, their interpretations become more problematic. They maintain that Paul's opponents criticized him for pleasing men when he proclaimed a gospel free from circumcision and the other requirements of the Law. (15) This interpretation of the opponents' criticism cannot be correct, however, since according to Gal 5:11 they maintained that Paul still preached circumcision.

It must be remembered that Paul and the Judaizers formulate the same point in different ways. Hence, what Paul in a derogatory sense would call pleasing men, they would evaluate in a positive way: Paul wished to be accepted by the Jewish community after he had heard the call to be an apostle.

When Gal 5:11 and 1:10 are seen together, they give clues to the way in which the Judaizers claimed that Paul represented their own cause. They claimed that Paul continued (cf. ἔτι) to preach and practise circumcision after he received his call.

In this respect there was continuity between his teaching before and after he became an apostle. As has been shown in our analysis of Gal 5:11 the conformists had reason for their claim: Paul continued to draw on traditions about circumcision and related Jewish tradition. Accordingly, they drew the conclusion that he wanted to be accepted by the Jewish community and please men by still advocating circumcision.

Paul's characterization of his opponents in Gal 6:12-13 supports this interpretation. So does Philo's treatment of an analogous situation in Migr 86-93. In Gal 6:12-13 Paul states the purpose of the Judaizers in the two ἵνα-clauses: v. 12: ἵνα τῷ σταυρῷ τοῦ Χριστοῦ (Ἰησοῦ) μὴ διώκωνται, and v. 13: ἵνα ἐν τῇ ὑμετέρᾳ σαρκὶ καυχήσωνται. According to Paul the Judaizers wanted to avoid persecution, and to boast over the circumcision of the Galatians.

The point about persecution has been estimated differently in recent research. Some scholars, who mention it, have difficulties in making it part of their hypotheses. They believe that Paul's opponents were Jewish Christian gnostics. If so, why should they seek to avoid persecution, presumably from the Jews? (16)

On the other hand, scholars such as R. Jewett and A. Suhl place much emphasis on the point about persecution, Gal 6:12. They maintain that Paul's opponents were Judaizers from Judea who sought to escape from persecution by persuading the Galatians to be circumcised. This threat of persecution was, in their view, due to pressures from zealot circles in Judea. (17) Jewett and Suhl are right when they take seriously Paul's own stress on this aspect of circumcision. Their theory about pressure from the Zealots in Judea must, however, be taken to be only one possible background, since Philo, for one, testifies in Migr 86-93 to the fact that in the Jewish communities in the Diaspora there was also a general threat of persecution against non-conformists who ignored or rejected the external observances.

In order to understand Gal 6:12-13 one has to realize that Paul here states his own polemical view. The Judaizers themselves would have formulated the same points in a positive way. Schmithals has ignored this distinction, and maintains therefore that Paul's opponents worked to avoid persecution for tactical reasons and to gain praise. Schmithals then draws the conclusion that the opponents cannot have been Judaizers, because _they_ fought for circumcision out of conviction, not from expediency. (18)

Philo, in Migr 86-93, shows that the aim of avoiding persecution and gaining acceptance/fame can be given positive evaluation as part of Jewish scriptural convictions. It is a gift from God when people receive "a great name" and fame because they conform to the Law of Moses and thereby accept and keep the customs, fixed by divinely inspired men in the past. Those who ignore the observances of the feasts and circumcision are taught by the sacred word to take thought of good repute. In this way they can avoid being subject to censure and hostile plotting against them from the Jewish community.

The Judaizers whom Paul criticizes have reasoned along similar lines. There is, however, one detail in Gal 6:13 which seems to speak against this view. Here Paul accuses the "circumcision people" of not keeping the Law themselves. Many commentators understand this to mean that the "circumcision people" were selective in their keeping of the Law of Moses, and therefore did not either represent a proper Jewish attitude, or have a regular Jewish community as background. (19)

A closer analysis of Gal 6:13 suggests that the explanation for Paul's accusation is that he and the Judaizers give a different appraisal of the fame they seek. With this question in mind, we see how the statement in Gal 6:13 places circumcision in sharp focus. In the first half, introduced by οὐδὲ γάρ , the term οἱ περιτεμνόμενοι (20) occurs, and in the second half, introduced by ἀλλά , we find περιτέμνεσθαι . There is then reason for interpreting the verse as an antithetic parallelism: the accusation that members of the circumcision party do not themselves keep the Law means that they have illegitimate reason for wanting the Galatians to be circumcised: they do it for the sake of their own fame. (21) As such Gal 6:13 is, then, about wrong intentions in connection with the conversion of proselytes. This question receives much attention in rabbinic sources, although there it is the wrong intentions of the prospective proselytes that are discussed, not, as here, the wrong intentions of those who seek to win proselytes. (22)

In Gal 6:14 Paul moves into a more basic evaluation of this boast. Fundamentally speaking it is not a question of the right or wrong intentions behind the circumcision of proselytes. The alternatives are rather whether one puts one's trust in the flesh, in this particular case in circumcision, or in the cross of Christ. Paul puts his trust in the cross of Christ (cf. 5:11, 24) to the exclusion of putting his trust in the flesh (namely in circumcision) and thereby in the works of the Law. (23)

It has been rightly pointed out that in Gal 6:12 Paul does not mention any danger of persecution for the Galatian Christians. This threat existed only for the group advocating circumcision.(24) The explanation is probably that the circumcision party (the conformists) came from a Jewish community, while the Galatian congregations were not Jewish communities. (25) The Judaizers went to the Galatian congregations to take care (in their own view) of proselytes already won by Paul. Thus, Paul does not picture them as missionaries, but as persons who in good Jewish manner sought to care for the proselytes. (26)

Our conclusion must then be that when Gal 5:11 and 1:10 are seen together, the following picture of the Galatian situation emerges: the Judaizers claim that Paul continued to preach (and practise) circumcision after he received his call to be an apostle. Thus, in their opinion, Paul wanted to be accepted by the Jewish community and to please men by continuing to advocate circumcision. In his letter Paul objects to this misunderstanding and misuse of his missionary preaching to the Galatians. His preaching did not imply that bodily circumcision ought to follow, and thus his service to Christ meant conflict with the Jewish communities: "If I still tried to please men, I would not be the slave of Christ" (Gal 1:10). Christianity was not a nationally bound religious movement, but crossnational in its nature.

Gal 2:1-10

In our observations we shall not raise the historical questions about the Jerusalem meeting itself, or the relationship between Gal 2:1-10 and the Jerusalem meeting reported on in Acts 15. Our concern is the role which Gal 2:1-10 plays in Paul's letter. This approach is akin to that of H.D. Betz in his commentary to the Letter. He interprets the Letter using the model of a legal defence plea in accordance with recommended practice of various standard authorities on rhetoric. (27) Our focus concentrates, however, on the actual issues in the controversy between Paul and his opponents and not on the formal norms of rhetoric.

In connection with Gal 2:1-10 two issues will be discussed; first, Paul's preaching and circumcision, and second, the different views on Jerusalem and the pillar apostles.

The issue of circumcision is explicitly mentioned in Gal 2:3 "... not even Titus who was with me and who was a Greek was compelled to be circumcised". Let us try to characterize in a precise way Paul's view and the view of the opponents as to this issue. Paul's reference to his preaching in Gal 2:2 will serve as a point of departure.

In Gal 2:2 Paul writes: "... and I laid before them the gospel which I preach among the gentiles..." A corresponding statement about Paul's preaching is found in Gal 5:11: "... if I still preach circumcision..." Several observations indicate that these two formulations refer to the same preaching by Paul:

1. The same technical term for preaching is used in both places: κηρύσσειν . H.D. Betz makes the following comment on Gal 5:11: (28) "The language suggests that κηρύσσειν περιτομὴν ("preach circumcision") is Paul's language, formulated in contrast to κηρύσσειν Χριστόν ("preach Christ"), his usual concept". This is probable, but a sharper distinction should be made between Paul's view and that of his opponents. The opponents represent the view that both phrases mean the same: to preach the gospel of Christ means to preach (physical) circumcision. Paul does not make this identification, however, but draws a contrast between the two formulations.

2. In both Gal 2:2 and 5:11 the gentiles are the addresses of the preaching. In Gal 2:2 there is an explicit reference to "the gentiles", and in 5:11 the preaching refers in particular to Paul's missionary activity among the Galatian gentiles, although the perspective here focuses on Paul's preaching since his call.

3. Paul does not make distinction between his preaching in Galatia and his preaching prior to the meeting in Jerusalem. His report from the Jerusalem meeting in Gal 2:1-10 is rather meant to give support to his preaching in Galatia, i.e. to counter the opponents' misunderstanding of it. Two observations in Gal 2:1-10 demonstrate this:

a. In 2:5 Paul states that his action in Jerusalem was taken for the benefit of the Galatians: "... in order that the truth of the gospel might remain with you".

b. The present tense used in Gal 2:2 presupposes that Paul preached the same gospel before the Jerusalem meeting and since that time up to the writing of the Letter: "Und schliesslich geht aus dem 'zeitlosen' Präsens κηρύσσω hervor, dass er dieses spezifische Heiden-Evangelium auch jetzt noch unter den Heiden verkündet und auch bei den Galatern verkündet hat (vgl. auch 1:11)". (29)

How can Gal 2:2 and 5:11 refer to the same preaching by Paul? In an earlier section of this essay, Gal 5:11 was discussed together with its context. In this analysis of Gal 5 we reached the following conclusion: When Paul, according to Gal 5:13-24, preached that the heathen Galatians should depart from the desires of the flesh and enter the society of those who serve and love each other, then his opponents claimed that such proselyte traditions gave the ethical meaning of circumcision. They therefore claimed that Paul still preached circumcision, and their task was to persuade the Galatian Christians to make bodily circumcision follow upon their ethical circumcision. By obedience to the commandment of physical circumcision they would make evident that they lived under the Law of Moses and were integrated into the Jewish nation as proselytes.

Both in Gal 5:11 ff. and in Gal 2:2 ff. Paul objected to this misunderstanding and misuse of his missionary preaching to the heathen Galatians. Although he preached Christ within the context of Jewish proselyte traditions, he did not imply that the gentile Christians should take physical circumcision and become citizens of the Jewish nation. In this polemic against the opponents and the Galatian Churches, Paul then tells them that he at the Jerusalem meeting presented the same gospel, exclusive of physical circumsion, and the pillar apostles agreed with him.

Our conclusion is then the following: The problem Paul faced in Galatia was that he, in his preaching of the gospel of Christ, drew on Jewish teaching about proselytes in which physical circumcision was an integral part. Correspondingly, when Paul reported on his preaching of the gospel in Jerusalem, the question became: When Paul preached Christ to the Gentiles within the context of Jewish proselyte traditions, did this mean that the Gentiles had to undertake physical circumcision and join the Jewish nation? Paul's opponents maintained that physical circumcision was basic. They claimed that Paul held this view as well. Paul, on the other hand, in utilizing the Jewish traditions about proselytes excluded from them physical circumcision and Jewish citizenship.

The conflict between the national and cross-national perspectives is also reflected in the different views on Jerusalem and the pillar apostles.

It is a much debated question as to what Gal 1-2 tells us about the relationship between Paul and the Jerusalem apostles. In recent years B. Holmberg has approached the question from a sociological perspective. He reaches the conclusion that "The dialectic between being independent of and being acknowledged by Jerusalem is the keynote of this important text ..." (30) J. Dunn agrees with Holmberg's understanding in general, but makes a distinction between the time of the Jerusalem meeting and the time when Paul wrote Galatians. At the time of the Jerusalem meeting Paul still acknowledged the authority of the Jerusalem leadership in the making of policy decisions which affected the whole Christian mission. By the time he wrote Galatians, however, he was no longer prepared to acknowledge the authority of Jerusalem to the same extent. (31)

Instead of discussing the historical questions connected with the Jerusalem meeting itself, we focus the analysis on its role within the conflict in the Galatian churches, and Paul's use of it in his letter. From this perspective it is important to characterize the views of Paul's opponents as background for Paul's presentation.

From Gal 4:21-5:1 we learn that different attitudes towards Jerusalem were part of the conflict between Paul and his opponents. In his study "The Allegory of Abraham, Sarah and Hagar in the argument of Galatians", C.K. Barrett attempts to characterize the view of the opponents and the view of Paul in this way:(32) At the heart of the theology of the opponents was the concept of the People of God (with its origin in Abraham), and the divine promise that constituted it. The opponents probably took the view (expressly controverted by Paul in 3:17) that the Abrahamic covenant had been redefined by the Sinaitic. The promise was made to Abraham and his seed; and the obligations, which follow thereof, were revealed in the law, fulfillment of which was made a necessary condition for receipt of the promised blessing.

The scriptural argument on which this position rested reached its climax in the story of Abraham, Sarah and Hagar. Only the Sarah-Isaac line was to count as seed; this was the line that included Moses and therefore the Law, and it had its seat in Jerusalem. It had found its fulfilment in Jesus and his disciples, notably James, Cephas and John, and was still administered in terms of the law of Jerusalem. The true descendants of Abraham are the Jews, who inhabit Jerusalem. They are the true people of God. It follows that Jerusalem is the authoritative centre of the renewed people of God, now called the church. Those who are not prepared to attach themselves to this community by means of circumcision must be cast out.

Paul challenged this view. He did not associate Sarah and Isaac with the Sinaitic law or with Jerusalem. Rather, Hagar, the slave-girl, and her child symbolize Sinai and the present Jerusalem. The free woman Sarah and her son Isaac, on the other hand, symbolize the Jerusalem above, the free city, in contrast to the present Jerusalem.

Barrett's interpretation accounts well for the passage on Abraham, Sarah, Isaac, Hagar and Ishmael in Gal 4:21-5:1. He does not draw the line, however, from Gal 4:21-5:1 to Gal 2:1-10. The question to be asked is: Can these different views on Jerusalem throw light on the section about the meeting in Jerusalem?

Several observations indicate that the answer must be affirmative:

1. Both sections deal with Jerusalem. If Barrett's interpretation of Gal 4:21-5:1 is correct, different attitudes to Jerusalem are reflected in the passage. These different views, held by Paul and his opponents respectively, serve as background to Paul's report on the Jerusalem meeting rendered in Gal 2:1-10.

2. In both places Paul has the non-Jewish Galatians in mind. In Gal 4:21, 31 and 5:1 Paul addresses himself directly to the Galatian readers and according to Gal 2:5 Paul did not give in to the argument of the false brethren at the Jerusalem meeting "that the truth of the gospel might be preserved for you (the Galatians)."

3. In both cases the conflict is described as a struggle between freedom and slavery. At Jerusalem false brethren infiltrated the meeting in order to bring the Christians into slavery (καταδουλώσουσιν) by demanding that non-Jews who confessed Jesus as the Christ were proselytes of the Jewish nation and therefore had to accept physical circumcision and keep the Law of Moses. On the other hand, Paul defended the view that non-Jewish Christians such as Titus, a Greek man who attended the meeting, should not have to submit themselves to physical circumcision and become Jews. Paul maintained that this was the meaning of freedom in contrast to slavery.

Similarily in Gal 4:21-5:1 Hagar, the Sinaitic covenant and the present Jerusalem are seen by Paul as representing slavery while the covenant associated with Sarah and the Jerusalem above, represents freedom.

Accordingly in Paul's view at the time when he wrote Galatians, both now in Galatia as also at the Jerusalem meeting in the past, the same struggle took place - that between freedom and slavery. The conflict between "the present Jerusalem" and "the Jerusalem above" was an issue at the Jerusalem meeting as well as in the debate about the role Jerusalem should play for the Galatian Christians. To be tied to "the present Jerusalem" meant to become an integral part of the Jewish nation and the Jewish Law. This was slavery. To be tied to "the Jerusalem above" meant that non-Jewish and Jewish Christians could confess Christ and worship God together without non-Jews having to become Jewish proselytes as a pre-condition. This was freedom.

Moreover, Paul and his opponents in Galatia interpreted the role of the Jerusalem apostles along different lines. The difficult verses in Gal 2:6 ff. must be discussed from this point of view:

v. 6 ἀπὸ δὲ τῶν δοκούντων εἶναί τι, ὁποῖοί ποτε ἦσαν οὐδέν μοι
διαφέρει,
πρόσωπον ὁ θεὸς ἀνθρώπου οὐ λαμβάνει.
ἐμοὶ γὰρ οἱ δοκοῦντες οὐδὲν προσανέθεντο,

v. 7 ἀλλὰ τοὐναντίον ἰδόντες ὅτι
πεπίστευμαι τὸ εὐαγγέλιον τῆς ἀκροβυστίας
καθὼς Πέτρος τῆς περιτομῆς.

The structure of vv 6-10 is complex. Verse 6 is an anacoluthon. The clause which begins the verse, is interrupted by a parenthesis, ὁποῖοί .... οὐ λαμβάνει , and is not completed, but is begun anew in v. 6c. (33)

In these verses Paul indicates his views concerning the chief apostles in Jerusalem, "those who were reputed to be something". The meaning of the parenthesis is much debated. One problem concerns the tenses of the verbs: (34) why did Paul put the verb in the imperfect tense ἦσαν ("they were") instead of the present tense, which would be consistent with the following present tense of οὐδέν..διαφέρει ("it makes no difference")? Some scholars take the ἦσαν ("they were") as a reference to positive qualities which the apostles once had, but which they no longer have. Schlier sums up the position of scholars who believe that Paul in this way refers to the life of the apostles before Pentecost: (35) "they may have had fellowship with the historical and, in particular, with the resurrected Jesus-Messiah; they themselves or others may base their reputation upon that fellowship... (yet) God did not pay attention to these historical qualification when he called Paul. Therefore, Paul does not pay attention to them either, when apostolic decisions must be made." Again, others believe that Paul refers to an advantageous situation that existed for the apostles <u>only</u> at the time of the conference, or prior to the proclamation of the Pauline gospel.

If this is what Paul means, he seems to undermine his own argumentation: if he disavows the authority of the apostles on doctrinal matters, why is it then important for him to gain their recognition of his work?

Kasting thinks that the phrase refers to a certain part of the apostle's past lives, when they circumcised converted Gentiles, a custom that Paul's opponents in Galatia knew about and had declared to be normative. (36) Holmberg objects to Kasting's interpretation that it leaves the second half of the parenthesis unexplained; the phrase πρόσωπον λαμβάνειν ("show partiality") seems to have something to do with a person's prestige rather than with a past demeanour. (37)

As indicated by Holmberg, this last phrase πρόσωπον ὁ θεὸς ἀνθρώπου οὐ λαμβάνει ("God shows no partiality") seems to give the key to the meaning of the parenthesis. It is important that the phrase also occurs in Rom 2:11 in a slightly different wording: οὐ γάρ ἐστιν προσωπολημψία παρὰ τῷ θεῷ. ("For God shows no partiality"). In the Letter to the Romans this principle is applied to the relationship between Jews and Greeks; both groups have basically the same status before God. In Gal 2:1-10 the issue at stake is the same: are Jews and non-Jews basically equal before God?

Paul's opponents defended the view that the Jews had an exclusive relation to God, so that non-Jews who confessed Jesus as the Christ had to become Jews. Paul, on the other hand, referred there to the Jewish principle of God's nonpartiality, (38) and argued on this basis for the equality of Jews and non-Jews.

This analysis throws light on the beginning words of the parenthesis ὁποῖοί ποτε ἦσαν οὐδέν μοι διαφέρει ("whatsoever they once were, makes no difference to me"). Paul here refers to a specific situation in the past which he acknowledges as a historical fact. The reason why this reference is included must be that this situation in the past in the view of the opponents supported their view and policy. Paul and his opponents agreed that the three "pillars", James, Cephas (Peter) and John, were once the center in Jerusalem for the Church within the borders of the Jewish nation, even before non-Jews were being reached by the Gospel. Paul's opponents maintained that that delimitation was basic, while Paul disagreed. To him the principle was that God shows no partiality between Jews and non-Jews, and therefore the role of the Jerusalem apostles as leaders of the Jewish Christian Church was not a matter of principle, although it was a historical fact. Thus, what the "pillars" were at the exclusively Jewish period of the Church, made no difference to him.

The "pillar"-apostles in Jerusalem agreed with Paul concerning this principle and not with his opponents: "those who were of repute added nothing to me; but on the contrary, when they saw that I had been entrusted with the gospel to the uncircumcised, just as Peter had been entrusted with the gospel to the circumcised (for he who worked through Peter for the mission to the circumcised worked through me also for the Gentiles) and when they perceived the grace that was given to me, James and Cephas and John, who were reputed to be pillars, gave me and Barnabas the right hand of fellowship, that we should go to the Gentiles and they to the circumcised..." (Gal 2:6-9).

<u>Summary</u>

The problem Paul faced in Galatia was that he, in his preaching of the Gospel of Christ, drew on Jewish teaching about proselytes, in which physical circumcision was an integral part. Paul's opponents, the Judaizers, then claimed that Paul continued to preach circumcision after he received his call to be an apostle. Thus, in their opinion, Paul wanted to be accepted by the Jewish community and to please men. Paul objected to this misunderstanding: Christianity was not a nationally bound religious movement. It was cross-national. His preaching did not imply that bodily circumcision was required, and thus his service to Christ meant conflict with the Jewish communities.

When Paul reported on his preaching at the meeting in Jerusalem, he presented the same Gospel, exclusive of physical circumcision, and the pillar apostles agreed with him. As a matter of historical fact, the pillar apostles once were the center in Jerusalem for the Church within the borders of the Jewish nation. The Judaizers in Galatia understood this national role of the apostles to be normative, but Paul stressed that this historical fact was not a matter of principle. Likewise, Paul did not reject Jerusalem as such, but he proclaimed the New Age which broke out of the national and geographical limitations of the Jewish religion. The "Jerusalem above" (Gal 4:26) was a cross-national entity, comprising both Jews and Greeks. (39)

NOTES

1) See E. de Witt Burton, Galatians, ICC, 287.

2) H. Schlier, an die Galater (1971), 238-9; R. Bring, Pauli brev til Galaterna (Stockholm 1969[2]), 259 f; E. Haenchen, Die Apostelgeschichte, 421.

3) F. Mussner, Der Galaterbrief, 358-9. J. Becker, Der Brief and die Galater, (Göttingen 1976), 63-4, thinks that Gal 5:11 does not refer to accusations made by the Judaizers: "Der Ausdruck" die Beschneidung predigen" ist kein Vorwurf an Paulus, sondern von Paulus selbst polemisch in Antithese zur Wendung "Christus verkündigen" ... gebildet. Sie soll den Inhalt der gegnerischen Verkündigung in Kontrast zu seiner eigenen kennzeichnen.' Becker does not take seriously, however, the fact that Paul in Gal 5:11 has given the conditional clause the form of a real case.

4) G. Howard, Paul: Crisis in Galatia, (Cambridge, 1979), 8-10, 39, 44, 91.

5) R. Marcus, PLCL Sup 1, 253 and n1.

6) See E. Lohse, Die Texte von Qumran, ad loc. cf. R. Meyer, "περιτέμνω ," TWNT, vi, 78-9; cf. H.A. Wolfson, Philo, 2, 225-37, who connects the concepts of desire and evil inclination.

7) See chapter thirteen.

8) A. Oepke/J. Rohde, an die Galater, 101; so also H. Schlier, an die Galater, 123 f.

9) H. Schlier, an die Galater, 239 f: "περιτομή und σταυρός stehen sich für ihn als einander ausschliessende Mittel und Zeichen des Heiles entgegen..."

10) In Gal 6:13-14 there is another example where Paul makes the cross of Christ replace circumcision: the circumcision people place their boast in the flesh of circumcision, while Paul, accordingly, boasts in the cross of Christ.

11) cf. E. Lohmeyer, Die Briefe and die Philipper, an die Kolosser und an Philemon, 113-14: "Nicht jedes menschliche, sondern alles heidnische Leben ist "tot". So wäre also das Dasein in der "Beschneidung" vor Gott "lebendig" und gerecht?" E. Lohse, Die Briefe an die Kolosser und an Philemon, Meyer, K., (Göttingen, 1977[2]), 161: "Die ἀκροβυστία an die Heidenchristen errinnert werden, ist durch die περιτομὴ ἀχειροποίητος (2:11) beseitigt worden. In der Taufe ist die Wende vom Tod

zum Leben vollzogen worden; Gott hat euch lebendig gemacht mit ihm (Vgl. 2:12)." cf. that according to Phil 3:1 ff the believers are the circumcision (ἡμεῖς γάρ ἐσμεν ἡ περιτομή) who serve by the Spirit of God, who place their boast in Christ Jesus, and put no trust in flesh, as do those who mutilate themselves by bodily circumcision. Here also circumcision is transferred to the union with Christ and life in the Spirit.

12) See E.F. Scott, The Epistles of Paul to the Colossians, to Philemon and to the Ephesians, 74 ff.

13) See chapter thirteen.

14) Contra the theological interpretation of ἔτι in A. Oepke/ J. Rohde, an die Galater, 54. The conditional clause has the form of a condition contrary to fact. Thus, Paul's own understanding and evaluation is expressed in the formulation, and not the understanding of the Judaizers. They regarded it as a fact that Paul wanted to please men.

15) H. Schlier, an die Galater, 42: "Und Ihr Vorwurf mag darauf gezielt haben, dass er die Freiheit vom Gezetz bzw. der Beschneidung und des Kalenders verkündigte." F. Mussner, Der Galaterbrief, 63: "Es geht Paulus bei seiner ganzen Verkündigung eines gesetzfreien Evangeliums nur um billigen Erfolg, und deshalb auch seine falsche Rücksichtnahme auf die Menschen."

16) W. Marxsen, Einleitung in das Neue Testament (Gütersloh, 1964), 52 ff; W. Schmithals, Paulus und die Gnostiker, (Hamburg, 1965), 28. The point on persecution is ignored to an even larger extent in W. Schmithals, Paulus und Jakobus (Göttingen, 1963), 90; K. Wegenast, Das Verständnis der Tradition bei Paulus und in den Deutero-Paulinen (Neukirchen, 1962), 34-49; D. Georgi, Die Geschichte der Kollekte des Paulus für Jerusalem (Hamburg/Bergstadt, 1965), 35-8; D. Lührmann, Das Offenbarungsverständnis bei Paulus und in den paulinischen Gemeinden (Neukirchen, 1965), 67-73; E. Güttmanns, Der leidende Apostel und sein Herr (Göttingen, 1966), 178-85; E.E. Ellis, Prophecy and Hermeneutic, 110, 230.

17) R. Jewett, "The Agitators and the Galatian Congregation", NTS, 17 (1970/1), 198-212; id., Paul's Anthropological Terms (Leiden, 1971), 19 f, 95 ff; A. Suhl, Paulus und seine Briefe, (Gütersloh, 1975), 15-25.

18) W. Schmithals, Paulus und die Gnostiker, 28.

19) H. Schlier, an die Galater, 281; J. Eckert, Die urchristliche Verkündigung im Streit zwischen Paulus und seinen Gegnern nach dem Galaterbrief (Regensburg, 1971), 34 f.

20) For the meaning of οἱ περιτεμνόμενοι and discussion of variant readings, see H. Schlier, an die Galater, 281; A. Oepke/J. Rohde, an die Galater, 201-2; F. Mussner, Der Galaterbrief, 412-13.

21) cf. the similar interpretation in A. Oepke/J. Rohde, an die Galater, 202.

22) See B.J. Bamberger, Proselytism, 32 f. See also Matt 23:15, where the Pharisees are criticized for having wrong aims in their work to win proselytes.

23) On the interpretation of boast as trust, see R. Bultmann, καυχάομαι , TWNT, 3, 649, n37.

24) See A. Suhl, Paulus und seine Briefe, 15 f; R. Jewett, NTS, 17 (1970-1), 203-6.

25) Against R. Jewett, NTS, 17 (1970-1), 209. This observation fits well the theory that Paul's letter was addressed to the North Galatian congregations.

26) See B.J. Bamberger, Proselytism, 24 etc; R. Jewett, NTS, 17 (1970-1), 200, has overlooked this point when he writes: "Why would Jewish Christians suddenly lose their traditional disinterest in the Gentile mission and embark on a circumcision campaign in Galatia?"

27) H.D. Betz, Galatians, (Philadelphia, 1979).

28) H. Betz, Galatians, 268-269.

29) F. Mussner, Der Galaterbrief, 102.

30) B. Holmberg, Paul and Power, (Lund, 1978), 15.

31) J. Dunn, "The Relationship between Paul and Jerusalem according to Galatians 1 and 2," NTS, 28, (1982) 461-478.

32) C.K. Barrett, "The Allegory of Abraham, Sarah and Hagar in the Argument of Galatians," in Rechtfertigung, Festschrift für Ernst Käsemann, (Göttingen, 1976), 1-16.

33) H. Schlier, an die Galater, 74; H.N. Ridderbos, The Epistle of Paul to the Churches of Galatia, (Grand Rapids, Michigan, 1953, repr. 1981) 86.

34) H.D. Betz, Galatians, 93.

35) H. Schlier, and die Galater, 75 f.

36) H. Kasting, Die Anfänge der urchristlichen Mission, (München, 1969), 120.

37) B. Holmberg, Paul and Power, 25.

38) See O. Michel, Der Brief and die Römer, (Göttingen 1966), 76.

39) The present study is a continuation of and brings further the analysis of Galatians in my essay "Paul Preaches Circumcision and Pleases Men", in M.D. Hooker and S.G. Wilson (eds), Paul and Paulinism. Essays in Honour of C.K. Barrett, (London, 1982), 37-46, included in my collection of essays: 'Paul Preaches Circumcision and Pleases Men' and Other Essays on Christian Origins, (Trondheim, 1983), 33-46.

CHAPTER FIFTEEN
PHILO, LUKE AND GEOGRAPHY

The geographical horizon of Philo

In his book Ptolemaic Alexandria P.M. Fraser states that an adequate understanding of the outlook of an individual in antiquity depends to a considerable extent on our ability to assess his geographical horizon. (1) Thus, in order to understand the situation of Philo and Alexandrian Judaism as a whole, it is of interest to examine the main points of their geographical world perspective. As reflected in Philo's writings, his world comprised the area from India in the east to Libya, Rome and the Atlantic ocean in the West, and from Scythia and Germany in the north to Ethiopia in the south. (2)

In this world three centers are emphasized by Philo:

1. Jerusalem;
2. Greece, with Athens as the main city;
3. Alexandria and Egypt, where Philo lived.

A fourth center is generally presupposed, and is explicitly mentioned in connection with the pogrom in Alexandria in 38 A.D: Italy and Rome.

With regard to Jerusalem Philo presents the common Jewish view: (3) Jerusalem and the Temple are the center of all Judaism, whether in the Diaspora or in Judea. Philo is an important source for knowledge of the Jewish Diaspora as well as for knowledge of the role of Jerusalem in this period. (4) In a letter attributed by Philo to King Agrippa, (5) the king writes:

> While she (the Holy City), as I have said, is my native city, she is also the mother city not of one country, Judaea, but of most of the others in virtue of the colonies sent out of divers times to the neighbouring lands Egypt, Phoenicia, the part of Syria called the Hollow and the rest as well, and the lands lying far apart, Pamphylia, Cilicia, most of Asia up to Bithynia and the corners of Pontus, similarly also into Europe, Thessaly, Boeotia, Macedonia, Aetolia, Attica, Argos, Corinth and most of the best parts of Peleponnese.
>
> And not only are the mainlands full of Jewish colonies, but also the most highly esteemed of the islands Euboea, Cyprus, Crete. I say nothing of the countries

> beyond the Euphrates, for except for a small part they all, Babylon and of the other satrapies those where the land within their confines is highly fertile, have Jewish inhabitants. So that if my own home-city is granted a share of your goodwill the benefit extends not to one city but to myriads of the others situated in every region of the inhabited world whether in Europe or in Asia or in Libya, whether in the mainlands or in the islands, whether it be seabord or inland (Gaium 281-3). (6)

In this list Philo shows special interest in the Jewish colonies in Greece, as various parts of Greece and the Greek islands are listed in particular detail. No mention is made, however, of the Jewish community of Rome nor of the Jews in Italy as a whole. In connection with his visit to Rome due to the Alexandrian pogrom, Philo speaks about the Jews in Rome (Gaium 155-7). (7)

The payment of the half-shekel and the fact of its being sent to Jerusalem gave a sense of participation in the Temple worship. Philo mentions several times the huge number of half-shekels from the Jewish Diaspora and says that there were collecting-places in every city for the money for the sacrifices. The money was then brought up to Jerusalem by groups of Jews (Spec I:77-8; Gaium 156). (8)

Moreover, Jews from the Diaspora went on pilgrimages to Jerusalem. Philo writes:

> Countless multitudes from countless cities come, some over land, others over sea, from east and west and north and south at every feast. They take the temple for their post as a general haven and refuge from the bustle and great turmoil of life ... Friendships are formed between those who hitherto knew not each other, and the sacrifices and libations are the occasion of reciprocity of feeling and constitute the surest pledge that all are of one mind (Spec I:69). (9)

Finally, Philo seems to give evidence for the expectation that God some day would gather together in the homeland the exiles from the end of the earth. (10)

This material in Philo shows that he regarded the Jews as one nation whether they lived in Jerusalem and Judea or were scattered around in the other parts of the world. His main aim is therefore not to assert the independence and greatness of Alexandrian Judaism over Palestinian Judaism. Consequently, when he refers to other Jewish scholars, he does not classify some as Alexandrian teachers in distinction from Palestinian rabbis. For example, when Philo in Mos I:4 refers to the elders who transmitted to him traditions about Moses, he calls them elders of the nation, although probably they were in fact largely Alexandrian teachers. The picture given above of pilgrimages (Spec I:69) indicates, however, that Jerusalem to some extent served as a pool of information and a place of exchange of traditions and news about Jews from Judea and from the various Diaspora communities.

it has already been noted that Philo shows special interest in Greece, since in Gaium 281-3 he listed various parts of Greece and the Greek islands in particular detail. In several places he expresses a high regard for Athens and Greece and their contribution to civilization. He frequently uses the Greek division of the world: Greeks and barbarians. (11) Although the importance of Athens had diminished in Hellenistic and Roman times, it still was one of the most celebrated and honoured cities. (12) In accordance with this view, Philo says that Athens ranks highest in Greece, "... the Athenians, the keenest in intelligence among the Greeks - for Athens is in Greece what the pupil is in the eye and reason in the soul ..." (Omn 140). The dry climate of Greece, though bad for the vegetation, is good for intellect (Provid II:66). Thus, Greece was a center for learning (Mos I:21-23).

Consequently, Philo draws extensively on Greek authors, many of whom he also names explicitly. Apart from Biblical names, most of the personal names mentioned by Philo belong to Greek culture. Also most of the pagan gods referred to by name are Greek ones: Koré, Demeter, Poseidon, Hera, Hephaestus, Apollo, Artemis, Aphrodite, Hermes, (13) Bacchus, (14) Heracles, (15) and Zeus. (16)

Besides Jerusalem and Athens, Rome is also of central significance to Philo, though in different way. In Philo's view Rome and the Romans have no culture or learning of their own, but serve as promoters of Greek culture. (17) Rome's importance is in the political sphere. Philo describes the Roman empire as a dominion not confined to the really vital parts of the world - the world between the Euphrates and the Rhine - but a dominion extending from the rising to the setting of the sun. (18) The Roman emperors are chief actors in Philo's treatises Flaccus and the Embassy to Gaius. (19)

A main problem was the worship of the emperor. Philo recognized that Augustus was venerated as god, and he refers explicitly to the worship of him in the temple Sebasteum in Alexandria. Philo stresses that Augustus did not directly claim to be God. (20) Although the Jews regarded emperor-worship with horror, Augustus still approved of them and permitted them to live in accordance with their Laws and worship only their one God. (21) Philo interpreted this to mean that Augustus was never elated or puffed up by the vast honours given to him. (22)

The emperor Gaius Caligula, on the other hand, made a direct claim to divinity, and enforced the worship of himself. The Jews were not to be exempted. Philo makes it clear that the Jews opposed him on principle, since they acknowledged only one God, the creator. In Philo's judgement, Gaius Caligula overstepped the bounds of human nature in his eagerness to be thought a god (Gaium 75). In this way Gaius Galigula acted against God's will and commandment, as stated by Philo in Virt 171-4: "Whosoever sets his hand to do anything with presumptuousness provokes God." (Num 15:30) (23) In this context Philo expressed his high evaluation of the Pax Romana created by Augustus, and charged Gaius Caligula with causing war and strife to flourish. (24)

As for Philo's picture of Alexandria and Egypt, he states that Egypt is delineated by the sea in the north, by Libya in the west, and by Ethiopia in the south. (25) Philo knows that Alexandria with its environs has status as a city in its own right distinct both politically and culturally from Egypt proper. He uses the double name, Alexandria and Egypt. (26) Moreover he knows that the Roman prefect of Alexandria and Egypt also rules over Libya. (27)

In passing Philo reports that Egypt is divided into provinces, the nomes. (28) It is surprising, however, that he names very few of the locations of Egypt. He tells that the Nile flows from Ethiopia through the whole of Egypt, and that the Egyptians have deified it. (29) Outside Alexandria the Mareotic lake was located. (30) A few Egyptian towns and cities, such as Memphis, are mentioned as places of history. (31)

At times Philo can express positive appraisals of the Egyptians. They are men of high learning, as teachers of arithmetic, geometri, the love of metre, rhythm and harmony, etc. (32) Mostly, however, his characterization of the Egyptians is of a negative nature. He offers sharp criticism of their worship of animals and of the Nile. He specifies the animal worship as worship of bulls, rams, goats, lions, crocodiles, asps, dogs, cats, wolves , and birds, as well as ibises and hawks, and also fishes. (33) The bull Apis is by Philo identified with the golden calf in Exod 32. (34) It is to be noted that other main Egyptian gods, such as Isis, Osiris, Hathor, etc. are not explicitly mentioned by Philo.

Philo is harsh in his criticism of the character of the Egyptians: they are arrogant whenever they have experienced good fortune. (35) Jealousy is part of the Egyptians' nature, and the Egyptians have an ancient and innate hostility to the Jews. (36) They are fools who prefer ease to toil and are at enmity with those who would advise them to their profit. (37) Thus, the Egyptians represent body and passion, evil and rebellion against God. (38) They are a seed bed of evil in whose souls both the venom and the temper of the native crocodiles and asps are reproduced. (39)

Among the cities of the Roman Empire, Philo describes only Alexandria, his home city, in any detail. The city has five quarters named after the first letters of the alphabet. (40) The locations most clearly identifiable from Philo's writings are the island Pharos and the temple Caesareum. Both places have an ideological importance. The island Pharos was the place where, according to tradition, the Laws of Moses were translated into Greek, and event which Jews and Greeks celebrated together on the island every year as a sign of the coming universal recognition of the Laws of Moses. (41)

The Caesareum, in turn, was a glorious temple for the worship of the emperor: "... there is no precinct elsewhere like that which is called Sebasteum, a temple to Caesar on shipboard, situated on an eminence facing the harbours famed for their excellent moorage, huge and conspicuous, fitted on a scale not found elsewhere with dedicated offerings, around it a girdle of pictures and statues in silver and gold, forming a precinct of vast breadth, embellished with porticoes, libraries, chambers, groves, gateways and wide open courts and every thing with lavish expenditure could produce to beautify it - the whole a hope of safety to the voyage either going into or out of the harbour." (42)

Among the other places in the city Philo mentions the gymnasium, with a statue said to be dedicated to Cleopatra. Other places are the market place, the palace, theatre, numerous synagogues in all parts of the city, especially one large and notable one. (43) Beaches, dunghills and tombs are also part of Philo's picture of the city as also are the harbours of the river Nile. (44)

Philo makes the prefect Flaccus praise Alexandria in the lament of his own downfall: "I am Flaccus, who but now was governor of Alexandria, that great city, or multitude of cities ..." In another place Philo tells that the city was close to the heart of Gaius. Gaius thought that this large city was admirably situated for commanding or serving the habitable world. He therefore wanted to make the city into a center for the worship of himself as god. Such praise of Alexandria's universal role was part of Ptolemaic ideology, but was also continued in Roman time. (45)

As for the Jews in Alexandria some details are to be added to the points already mentioned. The Jews were organized as a community with their own council of elders, the gerousia. (46) The names of three of these elders are given, Euodus, Trypho and Andro. Many professions were represented among the Alexandrian Jews, such as tradesmen, farmers, shipmen, merchants and artisans. (47) At other places, however, Philo's writings reflect that many of the Jews were poor. (48)

Philo was one of the most prominent Jews in Alexandria in the period culminating in the pogrom in 38 A.D. He was an old man by that time. (49) Philo was probably born between 20 and 10 B.C. and he died some time after 40 A.D. The one certain date in his life is bound up with the pogrom in 38. (50) He was then serving as head of a legation of five men. (51) They were to report to Emperor Gaius Caligula on the sufferings of the Jews and present their claims. (52) Philo's mission failed, and the Emperor sent the envoys away as foolish people who refused to believe that he had the nature of a god. (53)

There are points in Philo's writing which indicate that he had also been engaged in the political life of the Jewish community in Alexandria earlier in his life. It is impossible, however, to give a precise description of his function. In a rather general way he says that envy had plunged him into the ocean of civil cares. (54)

Although Philo may at times divide the population of Alexandria into two groups, the Jews and the others, he also makes it clear that there were three main groups in the city:

a) the Alexandrians proper,
b) the Egyptians, and
c) the Jews.

Thus, Philo tells at one point that there were differences between the scourges used in the city. The Egyptians were scourged with a lash, which was different from the one used when the Alexandrians were punished by scourging. The Jews used to be treated like the Alexandrians in this respect, but during the pogrom they were treated like Egyptians. (55)

From this survey of Philo's world, it becomes clear that religiously and culturally he identified himself with Jerusalem and Athens; politically he gave a positive evaluation of the pax romana, but in his relationship with the Roman government, he was nevertheless in a deep quandary since the very existence of Alexandrian Jewry was threatened by the tragic pogrom of 38 A.D. Alexandria played a universal role to Philo, both politically and religiously. Her central role for the Jews was especially made manifest in the Greek translation of the Laws of Moses.

The geographical horizon in Luke-Acts

Philo's geographical world perspective may serve as background for the discussion of the horizon of Luke-Acts, since Luke-Acts has the Jewish Diaspora as its setting. Already in the first volume of Luke-Acts, the Gospel of Luke, the world perspective is apparent. The birth of Christ is seen within the context of the whole Roman empire: "In those days a decree went out from Caesar Augustus that all the world (oikoumene) should be enrolled." (Luke 2:1). The universal perspective is emphasized in the second volume, the Acts of the Apostles, where the horizon is "the ends of the earth" (Acts 1:8), "every nation under heaven" (2:5), and "all Asia and the world" (19:27).

What are then the border areas of the world in Luke-Acts? In the East, the outermost areas mentioned are the biblical nations of the Medes and the Elamites. Philo goes even further East and refers to India. (55) In the north Pontus and Bithynia at the Black Sea are listed by Luke in Acts 2:9-11; 16:7, and by Philo in Gaium 281-283.

In Acts the regions north of Macedonia (56) are not specified, while Philo names the Scythians and Germans. (57) In the West Rome, Sicely and Libya are names common both to Acts and Philo. (58) Vaguely, Philo refers to areas further West beyond Rome, but Rome is the most western place identified by him, besides Carthage, which he mentions in passing. (59) In the South Luke and Philo have knowledge of Ethiopia. (60)

Luke joins Philo in regarding Jerusalem, Athens and Rome as the main centers of the world. Both in the Gospel and in Acts Luke is very occupied with Jerusalem. Both Luke and Philo tell about people coming to worship in the Temple of Jerusalem. Philo shows how Jews from all the world meet and enjoy fellowship in Jerusalem, and Luke informs us that Jews from all nations live in Jerusalem. (61) Travel to and from Jerusalem in Acts moreover serves the aims and needs of the emerging Christian movement. (62) The central and universal role played by Jerusalem in Luke and Philo is due, of course, to the fact that both represent the geographical outlook of Diaspora Judaism.

As for Athens, Luke depicts her in Acts 17:10-34 as the central representative of non-Jewish culture and religion. It was here that Paul presented the gospel to Epicurean and Stoic philosophers. (63) In spite of the respect for Athens expressed by both Luke and Philo, Philo's admiration of the city is even more marked, just as Greek philosophy and literature to a much greater extent have penetrated his writings.

In Luke-Acts the Greek division of the people of the world into "Greeks and barbarians" is not utilized, and the Jewish distinction between Jews and gentiles prevails, and occasionally the term used is "Jews and Greeks". (64) In this way Luke limits himself to the typically Jewish terminology more than do Philo and Paul. The growth of the gospel among Jews and gentiles, and its transfer from Jews to gentiles, are a main theme of Luke-Acts. This theme, however, cannot be pursued further in this context.

Acts 28:16-31 tells of Paul's coming to Rome, where he lived two years, teaching about the Lord Jesus Christ openly and unhindered. The precise role of Rome in this concluding section of Luke-Acts is much debated. Many scholars see here the fulfillment of Acts 1:8 in Rome the gospel has reached the ends of the earth. (65) Roloff follows this interpretation in a modified form. According to him, Rome replaces Jerusalem in Acts. The eschatological people of God do not any longer have Jerusalem as their center. God leads Paul to Rome, the center of the gentile world. (66) Some scholars will not interpret "the ends of the earth" in Acts 1:8 as a reference to Rome. Thornton, for one, states that there is no evidence that any Jew, Greek or Roman around the first century A.D. ever conceived of Rome as being at the end of the earth. All would have agreed that beyond Rome there lay other countries, Spain to the West and Gaul and barbarian Britannia to the North. Thornton suggests an alternative interpretation of "the ends of the earth" in Acts 1:8: the phrase points to the Ethiopian eunuch who, after having been baptized, returned to his country, Acts 8:26-39. (67)

Although knowledge of the regions West and North of Rome was widespread, as evidenced in Philo's writings, Thornton is mistaken when he says that no one around the first century conceived of Rome as being at the end of the earth. Thornton overlooks Psalms of Solomon 8:15: "He brought him (Pompey) that is from the end of the earth (i.e. Rome), that smiteth mightily." (68) Moreover, Philo, who lived in Alexandria, only identifies and describes one city in the West, Rome, and both in Philo's writings and in Luke-Acts Rome is the most westerly place where Jews reside. Actually, no certain evidence is found for the existence of a Jewish colony in the first century A.D. West of Rome, apart from one in Carthage. (69)

On the basis of these data the most probable conclusion is: Rome and her Jewish colony represent in Acts 28:16-31 "the ends of the earth" (Acts 1:8), because that city is the one place in the extreme West which stands out and is well known. (70)

Philo's home city, Alexandria, is also mentioned in Luke-Acts. The fact that she was a main center for shipping and commerce is reflected in Acts 28:11, which states that Paul sailed from Malta on board a ship of Alexandria. From Acts 6:9 we learn that Alexandrian Jews had settled in Jerusalem and shared a synagogue with other Diaspora jews. The impact of Alexandria is also seen in the Christian movement, through Apollos, who was an Alexandrian Jew, an eloquent man, well versed in the scriptures. Luke associates him with Corinth and Ephesus, Acts. 18:24-19:1. (71)

The major stage of the events recorded in Acts is not Alexandria, however, but Asia Minor, Macedonia and Achaia, besides Jerusalem and the surrounding area. In these regions it seems that Luke attributes a special role to Ephesus. Several observations point in this direction: 1. Luke reports the universal claim of the worship of Artemis, as stated by the silversmith Demetrius: Artemis "whom all Asia and the world worship". For comparison one might mention the way in which Philo makes non-Jews express the universal claim of Alexandria (Flacc 163; Gaium 338). 2. Ephesus is described as a place not only for magic activities but also for the pursuit of philosophy. From Acts 19:9f. we learn about Tyrannus' auditorium, where Paul lectured for two years "so that all the residents of Asia heard the word of the Lord, both Jews and Greeks". Paul is here envisioned as a philosopher who had a school for all of Asia. (72) As a result of his work in Ephesus "the word of the Lord grew and prevailed mightily" (Acts 19:20).

3. Most important, Paul's farewell discourse, Acts 20:17-38, was addressed to the elders of the Ephesian church. At the close of his churchfounding activity and missionary travel, Paul gives his "testament" and his legacy to the church at Ephesus.

This testament had paradigmatic character, and the Ephesian congregation thereby became the bearers of Paul's legacy. (73)

These points give a basis for the following hypothesis to be formulated. The horizon of Luke-Acts may be defined as the geographical perspective of the world as seen from the standpoint of pagans, Jews and Christians in Ephesus. If so, Ephesus has to Luke a function corresponding to that of Alexandria to Philo.

Paul's fare well speech offers the clue to the rest of Acts. His travel to Jerusalem, and then to Rome in the extreme West, is the completion of his ministry of preaching the gospel of the grace of God (Acts 20:24). His legacy to the church, however, he left with the church of Ephesus, and not with churches in Jerusalem and Rome.

NOTES

1) P.M. Fraser, Ptolemaic Alexandria, 1, (Oxford, 1971) 520.

2) Somn II:59.121f.; Spec III:15-23; Quod Deus 173-5; Ebr 133; Aet 141; Jos 134-6; Mos II:18-20; Gaium 10; 356.

3) See S. Safrai, "Relation between the Diaspora and the Land of Israel," CRINT, I:1, (Assen, 1974) 184-215.

4) See M. Stern, "The Jewish Diaspora", CRINT, I:1, 117-83.

5) See E.M. Smallwood, Philonis Alexandrini Legatio ad Gaium, (Leiden, 1961) 292.

6) See E.M. Smallwood, Legatio, 293-296.

7) M. Stern, Op.cit., 118.

8) E.M. Smallwood, Legatio, 237-238.

9) S. Safrai, op.cit., 191 ff.

10) Praem 117. Cf. S. Safrai, op.cit., 185.

11) Quod Deus 136; Mos II:18.20; Jos 134; Praem 165; Gaium 141, Omn 73.94.98.94.138; Provid II:15. This distinction is also applied to the classification of languages: Greek is the language of the Greek half of the world, while Hebrew serves as the main language of the barbarian world, Mos II:27 ff.; cf. Conf 68. - Cf. Paul's use of the distinction "Greek and barbarians" in Rom 1:14.

12) See H. Conzelmann, Die Apostelgeschichte, 96.

13) Dec 54.

14) Plant 148; Vita cont 85; Gaium 96.

15) Omn 99-104.

16) Opif 100; omn 102.127.130; Aet 81; Provid II:7.24; Gaium 188.265.346.

17) Gaium 147. See E.M. Smallwood, Legatio, 229; J. Palm, Rom, Römertum und Imperium in der Griechischen Literatur der Kaiserzeit, (Lund, 1959) 10-43; 130-136.

18) Gaium 10. See E.M. Smallwood, Legatio, 160-1; J. Palm, Rom, 14 f.; 56f.

19) Augustus, Gaius Julius Caesar Octavianus: Flacc 23.49.81. 103f.; Gaium 48.149.322; Augustus Gaius Caesar Caligula: Flacc 9-15, etc.; Gaium 32-9, etc.; Claudius Germanicus Caesar: Gaium 206; Julius Caesar is mentioned in Quod omn 118.

20) Concerning the emperor worship, see L.R. Taylor, The Divinity of the Roman Emperor, (Middletown, Conn., 1931); G.F. Moore, History of Religions, 1, (Edinburgh, 1950) 569-576.

21) For the religious liberty and rights of the Jews, see E.M. Smallwood, Legatio, 205-206; 231-233; and id., The Jews under Roman Rule, (Leiden, 1976) 120-143. See also P. Borgen, "Religiös pluralisme i nytestamentlig tid," i P. Borgen (ed.), Religiös Pluralisme i Bibelsk Tid og i Norge I Dag (Trondheim, 1979) 101-115.

22) Gaium 143-161.

23) Gaium 75-165. For details of Gaius' conflict with the Jews, see E.M. Smallwood, The Jews, 174-180; 236-245.

24) Gaium 143-149.

25) Flacc 43; Mos I:99.

26) Flacc 163. See P.M. Fraser, Ptolemaic Alexandria, 197f.

27) Flacc 152.

28) Mos I:21; Vita cont 21.

29) Mos I:6.98-101; 114-18; 202; II:195; Conf 29f; Heres 315f; Fug 179f; Somn II:255-9; 278; 300; Praem 90; Provid II.65. See T.O. Lambdin, "Nile", IDB, 3, 549-551.

30) Vita cont. 22.

31) Memphis, Mos I:118; other places are mentioned in Post 54-8; Somn I:77f.

32) Mos I:214.

33) Dec 76-80; Gaium 139.163. Cf. G.F. Moore, History of Religions, 1, 197-8, about the emphasis on animal worship in the Greek and Roman periods.

34) Sacr 130; Post 2.158-67; Ebr 95-124; Migr 85; Fug 90; Mos II:161-173; 270-4; Spec III:79.124-7.

35) Agr 62.

36) Flacc 29.

37) Mut 170.

38) Leg all III:38; Somn II:255; Post 156; Abr 103; Jos 151f; Conf 88; Congr 118.

39) Gaium 166: Philo here contemptously characterizes the Alexandrian "Greeks" as Egyptians. See E.M. Smallwood, Legatio, 225 and 246.

40) Flacc 55.

41) Mos II:35-44. See also Flacc 27.110.

42) Gaium 150-151. See E.M. Smallwood, Legatio, 231-232.

43) Flacc 34.37.45-48.64.74.84.92.95; Gaium 131-135.

44) Flacc 56; Gaium 127-129.

45) Flacc 163; Gaium 338; cf. 173. See P.M. Fraser, Ptolemaic Alexandria, 1, 513; 2, 702, n. 58, and 740, n. 160.

46) Flacc 38. 74. 76. See S. Applebaum, "The Organization of the Jewish Communities in the Diaspora", CRINT, I:1, 473-476.

47) Flacc 57.

48) Spec III:159ff.

49) Gaium 182. Concerning Philo's family and life, see especially J. Schwartz, "Note sur la famille de Philon d'Alexandrie", Annuaire de L'institut de philologie et d'histoire Orientales et Slaves, 13 (1953), 591-602 and 1 id., "L'Égypte de Philon", in Philon d'Alexandrie. Lyon 11-16 Septembre 1966: colloque, (Paris, 1967) 35-44.

50) Concerning the dating of the pogrom, etc. see E. Schürer, The History of the Jewish People in the Age of Jesus Christ, 1, 388-398.

51) Gaium 370. According to Josephus, Ant XVIII:257, the Jewish and the Greek embassies each consisted of three men.

52) Gaium 178-179.

53) Gaium 367.

54) Spec III:3.

55) Acts 2:9-11; concerning the biblical names of Medes and Elamites, see H. Conzelmann, Die Apostelgeschichte, 26. Philo, Somn II:59.

56) Macedonia: Acts 16:9-17:15.

57) Somn II:59.121.

58) Acts 2:9-11; 28:12-31; Gaium 283; Somn II:54; Leg all I:62.

59) Carthage: Quod Deus 174. Philo knows of the Atlantic Ocean, Ebr 133.

60) Acts 8:26-39; Quod Deus 174; Flacc 43, etc.

61) For example Luke 2:41-51; 9:51-22:38; Acts 8:27-39, 21:15-36; 2:9-11; 6:1-9; Philo, Spec I:69.

62) For example Acts 15:1-30.

63) See E. Haenchen, Die Apostelgeschichte, 454-455; H. Conzelmann, Die Apostelgeschichte, 95-96; G. Schneider, Die Apostelgeschichte, 2, (Freiburg, 1982) 231.

64) Acts 13:45-46; 14:2; 18:6; 28:28, etc.; Acts 14:1.

65) E. Haenchen, Die Apostelgeschichte, 112, n. 6; 654.

66) J. Roloff, Die Apostelgeschichte, (Göttingen, 1981) 289. 371.

67) T.C.G. Thornton, "To the end of the earth: Acts 1:8," The Exp Tim, 89, (1977-1978) 374-375.

68) See E. Hammershaimb et al. (trans), De gammeltestamentlige Pseudepigrafer, 5, (Copenhagen, 1970) 574, n. 15a. The English translation is taken from R.H. Charles, The Apocrypha and the Pseudepigrapha, 2, (Oxford, 1973, reprint of the first edition 1913) 641.

69) Cf. M. Stern, CRINT, I:1, 117-183.

70) Cf. B. Noack, Pinsedagen, (Copenhagen, 1968) 82.

71) See further I Cor 1:12; 3:4-6, 22; 4:6; 16:12; Tit 3:13. - The use of the Septuagint in Luke-Acts may also be listed as an influence from Alexandrian Judaism; cf. K. Stendahl, The School of St. Matthew. Uppsala 1954, 158.161-162.

72) H. Conzelmann, Die Apostelgeschichte, 110: "Paulus bietet hier das Bild eines Wanderphilosophen."

73) H. Conzelmann, Die Apostelgeschichte, 117; G. Schneider, Die Apostelgeschichte, 2, 293 ("Testament für die Kirche.")

ABBREVIATIONS
(PERIODICALS, SERIES ETC.)

ANRW	Aufstieg und Niedergang der Römischen Welt
BJRL	Bulletin of John Rylands Library
BZ	Biblische Zeitschrift
CBQ	The Catholic Biblical Quarterly
CRINT	Compendia Rerum Iudaicarum ad Novum Testamentum
FRLANT	Forschungen zur Religion und Literatur des Alten und Neuen Testaments
HNT	Handbuch zum Neuen Testament
HTKNT	Herders theologischer Kommentar zum Neuen Testament
HTR	Harvard Theological Review
HUCA	Hebrew Union College Annual, Cincinnati
JAOS	Journal of the American Oriental Society
JBL	Journal of Biblical Literature
JBR	Journal of Bible and Religion
JSJ	Journal for the Study of Judaism
LXX	Septuaginta
MGWJ	Monatschrift für Geschichte und Wissenschaft des Judentums
MT	The Masoretic Text
Nov T Sup	Novum Testamentum, Supplements
NTS	New Testament Studies
NTT	Norsk Teologisk Tidsskrift
PLCL	Philo, with an English Translation. Ed.F.H. Colson, Loeb Classical Library
SEÅ	Svensk eksegetisk årsbok
SJLA	Studies in Judaism in Late Antiquity
ST	Studia theologica
Str.-B/Str.-Bill	Kommentar zum Neuen Testament aus Talmud und Midrash von L. Strack und P. Billerbeck, München
TBL	Theologische Blätter
The Exp Tim	The Expository Times
ThR	Theologische Rundschau
TStJThS	Text and Studies of the Jewish Theological Seminary of America, New York
TWNT	Theologisches Wörterbuch zum Neuen Testament
VC	Vigiliae christianae
ZNW	Zeitschrift für die neutestamentliche Wissenschaft
ZTK	Zeitschrift für Theologie und Kirche

INDEX OF REFERENCES

I. OLD TESTAMENT

Genesis (Gen)

Exodus (Exod)

Leviticus (Lev)

Numbers (Num)

Deuteronomy (Deut)

Judges (Judg)

1. Samuel (1. Sam)

1. Kings (Kgs)

2. Kings (2. Kgs)

Isaiah (Isa)

Jeremia (Jer)

<u>Acts</u>

III. PHILO

De Somniis (Somn)

De Specialibus Legibus (Spec)

De Vita Contemplativa (Vita Cont)

De Virtutibus (Virt)

IV. JEWISH WRITINGS. MISCELLANIA

INDEX OF AUTHORS

The number of the page on which a work is cited with full title is underlined.

GENERAL INDEX

ACKNOWLEDGEMENTS

The studies are either reproductions, elaborations or modifications of essays which have been previously published. See my two books 'Logos was the True Light' and Other Essays on the Gospel of John, (Trondheim, 1983), and 'Paul Preaches Circumcision and Pleases Men' and Other Essays on Christian Origins, (Trondheim, 1983), and the following references:

PART I: PHILO

ARISTOBULUS AND PHILO
cf. "Philo of Alexandria", in M. Stone (ed), Jewish Writings of the Second Temple Period, CRINT II:2, (Assen, 1984) 274-279.

PHILOS WRITINGS
cf. "Philo of Alexandria", in M. Stone (ed), Jewish Writings of the Second Temple Period, CRINT II:2, (Assen, 1984) 233-252.

DEBATES ON CIRCUMCISION
cf. "Observations on the Theme 'Paul and Philo', in S. Pedersen (ed), Die Paulinische Literatur und Theologie, (Göttingen, 1980) 85-102.

PART II: JOHN

OBSERVATIONS ON THE TARGUMIC CHARACTER OF THE PROLOGUE OF JOHN, in New Testament Studies, 16 (1970) 288-295.

LOGOS WAS THE TRUE LIGHT,
in Novum Testamentum, 14 (1972) 115-130.

THE SON OF MAN SAYING IN JOHN 3.13-14,
See "Some Jewish Exegetical Traditions as Background for Son of Man Sayings in John's Gospel" (Jn 3,13-14 and context) in M. De Jonge (ed.). L'Evangile de Jean, (Leuven, 1977) 243-258.

OBSERVATIONS ON THE MIDRASHIC CHARACTER OF JOHN 6,
in Zeitschrift für die neutestamentliche Wissenschaft, 54, 1963, 232-240.

BREAD FROM HEAVEN. ASPECTS OF DEBATES ON EXPOSITORY METHOD AND FORM,
in 'Logos was the True Light' and Other Essays on the Gospel of John (Trondheim, 1983) 32-46.

BROWN JUDAIC STUDIES SERIES

140001	*Approaches to Ancient Judaism I*	William S. Green
140002	*The Traditions of Eleazar Ben Az'ariah*	Tzvee Zahavy
140003	*Persons and Institutions in Early Rabbinic Judaism*	William S. Green
140004	*Claude Goldsmid Montefiore on the Ancient Rabbis*	Joshua B. Stein
140005	*The Ecumenical Perspective and the Modernization of Jewish Religion*	S. Daniel Breslauer
140006	*The Sabbath-Law of Rabbi Meir*	Robert Goldenberg
140007	*Rabbi Tarfon*	Joel Gereboff
140008	*Rabban Gamaliel II*	Shamai Kanter
140009	*Approaches to Ancient Judaism II*	William S. Green
140010	*Method and Meaning in Ancient Judaism*	Jacob Neusner
140011	*Approaches to Ancient Judaism III*	William S. Green
140012	*Turning Point: Zionism and Reform Judaism*	Howard R. Greenstein
140013	*Buber on God and the Perfect Man*	Pamela Vermes
140014	*Scholastic Rabbinism*	Anthony J. Saldarini
140015	*Method and Meaning in Ancient Judaism II*	Jacob Neusner
140016	*Method and Meaning in Ancient Judaism III*	Jacob Neusner
140017	*Post Mishnaic Judaism in Transition*	Baruch M. Bokser
140018	*A History of the Mishnaic Law of Agriculture: Tractate Maaser Sheni*	Peter J. Haas
140019	*Mishnah's Theology of Tithing*	Martin S. Jaffee
140020	*The Priestly Gift in Mishnah: A Study of Tractate Terumot*	Alan J. Peck
140021	*History of Judaism: The Next Ten Years*	Baruch M. Bokser
140022	*Ancient Synagogues*	Joseph Gutmann
140023	*Warrant for Genocide*	Norman Cohn
140024	*The Creation of the World According to Gersonides*	Jacob J. Staub
140025	*Two Treatises of Philo of Alexandria: A Commentary on De Gigantibus and Quod Deus Sit Immutabilis*	David Winston/John Dillon
140026	*A History of the Mishnaic Law of Agriculture: Kilayim*	Irving Mandelbaum
140027	*Approaches to Ancient Judaism IV*	William S. Green
140028	*Judaism in the American Humanities*	Jacob Neusner
140029	*Handbook of Synagogue Architecture*	Marilyn Chiat
140030	*The Book of Mirrors*	Daniel C. Matt
140031	*Ideas in Fiction: The Works of Hayim Hazaz*	Warren Bargad
140032	*Approaches to Ancient Judaism V*	William S. Green
140033	*Sectarian Law in the Dead Sea Scrolls: Courts, Testimony and the Penal Code*	Lawrence H. Schiffman
140034	*A History of the United Jewish Appeal: 1939-1982*	Marc L. Raphael
140035	*The Academic Study of Judaism*	Jacob Neusner
140036	*Women Leaders in the Ancient Synagogue*	Bernadette Brooten
140037	*Formative Judaism: Religious, Historical, and Literary Studies*	Jacob Neusner
140038	*Ben Sira's View of Women: A Literary Analysis*	Warren C. Trenchard
140039	*Barukh Kurzweil and Modern Hebrew Literature*	James S. Diamond
140040	*Israeli Childhood Stories of the Sixties: Yizhar, Aloni, Shahar, Kahana-Carmon*	Gideon Telpaz
140041	*Formative Judaism II: Religious, Historical, and Literary Studies*	Jacob Neusner

BROWN JUDAIC STUDIES SERIES

140042	*Judaism in the American Humanities II: Jewish Learning and the New Humanities*	Jacob Neusner
140043	*Support for the Poor in the Mishnaic Law of Agriculture: Tractate Peah*	Roger Brooks
140044	*The Sanctity of the Seventh Year: A Study of Mishnah Tractate Shebiit*	Louis E. Newman
140045	*Character and Context: Studies in the Fiction of Abramovitsh, Brenner, and Agnon*	Jeffrey Fleck
140046	*Formative Judaism III: Religious, Historical, and Literary Studies*	Jacob Neusner
140047	*Pharaoh's Counsellors: Job, Jethro, and Balaam in Rabbinic and Patristic Tradition*	Judith Baskin
140048	*The Scrolls and Christian Origins: Studies in the Jewish Background of the New Testament*	Matthew Black
140049	*Approaches to Modern Judaism I*	Marc Lee Raphael
140050	*Mysterious Encounters at Mamre and Jabbok*	William T. Miller
140051	*The Mishnah Before 70*	Jacob Neusner
140052	*Sparda by the Bitter Sea: Imperial Interaction in Western Anatolia*	Jack Martin Balcer
140053	*Hermann Cohen: The Challenge of a Religion of Reason*	William Kluback
140054	*Approaches to Judaism in Medieval Times I*	David R. Blumenthal
140055	*In the Margins of the Yerushalmi: Glosses on the English Translation*	Jacob Neusner
140056	*Approaches to Modern Judaism II*	Marc Lee Raphael
140057	*Approaches to Judaism in Medieval Times II*	David R. Blumenthal
140058	*Midrash as Literature: The Primacy of Documentary Discourse*	Jacob Neusner
140059	*The Commerce of the Sacred: Mediation of the Divine Among Jews in the Graeco-Roman Diaspora*	Jack N. Lightstone
140060	*Major Trends in Formative Judaism I: Society and Symbol in Political Crisis*	Jacob Neusner
140061	*Major Trends in Formative Judaism II: Texts, Contents, and Contexts*	Jacob Neusner
140062	*A History of the Jews in Babylonia. I: The Parthian Period*	Jacob Neusner
140063	*The Talmud of Babylonia: An American Translation. XXXII: Tractate Arakhin*	Jacob Neusner
140064	*Ancient Judaism: Debates and Disputes*	Jacob Neusner
140065	*Prayers Alleged to Be Jewish: An Examination of the Constitutiones Apostolorum*	David Fiensy
140066	*The Legal Methodology of Hai Gaon*	Tsvi Groner
140067	*From Mishnah to Scripture: The Problem of the Unattributed Saying*	Jacob Neusner
140068	*Halakhah in a Theological Dimension*	David Novak
140069	*From Philo to Origen: Middle Platonism in Transition*	Robert M. Berchman
140070	*In Search of Talmudic Biography: The Problem of the Attributed Saying*	Jacob Neusner
140071	*The Death of the Old and the Birth of the New: The Framework of the Book of Numbers and the Pentateuch*	Dennis T. Olson

BROWN JUDAIC STUDIES SERIES

140072	*The Talmud of Babylonia: An American Translation. XVII: Tractate Sotah*	Jacob Neusner
140073	*Understanding Seeking Faith: Essays on the Case of Judaism. Volume Two: Literature, Religion and the Social Study of Judaism*	Jacob Neusner
140074	*The Talmud of Babylonia: An American Translation. VI: Tractate Sukkah*	Jacob Neusner
140075	*Fear Not Warrior: A Study of 'al tira' Pericopes in the Hebrew Scriptures*	Edgar W. Conrad
140076	*Formative Judaism IV: Religious, Historical, and Literary Studies*	Jacob Neusner
140077	*Biblical Patterns in Modern Literature*	David H. Hirsch/ Nehama Aschkenasy
140078	*The Talmud of Babylonia: An American Translation. I: Tractate Berakhot*	Jacob Neusner
140079	*Mishnah's Division of Agriculture: A History and Theology of Seder Zeraim*	Alan J. Avery-Peck
140080	*From Tradition to Imitation: The Plan and Program of Pesiqta Rabbati and Pesiqta deRab Kahana*	Jacob Neusner
140081	*The Talmud of Babylonia: An American Translation. XXIIIA: Tractate Sanhedrin, Chapters 1-3*	Jacob Neusner
140082	*Jewish Presence in T. S. Eliot and Franz Kafka*	Melvin Wilk
140083	*School, Court, Public Administration: Judaism and its Institutions in Talmudic Babylonia*	Jacob Neusner
140084	*The Talmud of Babylonia: An American Translation. XXIIIB: Tractate Sanhedrin, Chapters 4-8*	Jacob Neusner
140085	*The Bavli and Its Sources: The Question of Tradition in the Case of Tractate Sukkah*	Jacob Neusner
140087	*The Talmud of Babylonia: An American Translation. XXIIIC: Tractate Sanhedrin, Chapters 9-11*	Jacob Neusner
140088	*Mishnaic Law of Blessings and Prayers: Tractate Berakhot*	Tzvee Zahavy
140089	*The Peripatetic Saying: The Problem of the Thrice-Told Tale in Talmudic Literature*	Jacob Neusner
140090	*The Talmud of Babylonia: An American Translation. XXVI: Tractate Horayot*	Martin S. Jaffee
140091	*Formative Judaism V: Religious, Historical, and Literary Studies*	Jacob Neusner
140093	*The Integrity of Leviticus Rabbah*	Jacob Neusner
140094	*Behind the Essenes: History and Ideology of the Dead Sea Scrolls*	Philip R. Davies
140096	*The Memorized Torah: The Mnemonic System of the Mishnah*	Jacob Neusner
140098	*Sifre to Deuteronomy: An Analytical Translation. Volume One: Pisqaot One through One Hundred Forty-Three. Debarim, Waethanan, Eqeb*	Jacob Neusner
140099	*Major Trends in Formative Judaism III: The Three Stages in the Formation of Judaism*	Jacob Neusner

BROWN JUDAIC STUDIES SERIES

140102	*Sifra: The Rabbinic Commentary on Levit. us*	Jacob Neusner/ Roger Brooks
140103	*The Human Will in Judaism*	Howard Eilberg-Schwartz
140104	*Genesis Rabbah: Volume 1. Genesis 1:1 to 8:14*	Jacob Neusner
140105	*Genesis Rabbah: Volume 2. Genesis 8:15 to 28:9*	Jacob Neusner
140106	*Genesis Rabbah: Volume 3. Genesis 28:10 to 50:26*	Jacob Neusner
140108	*Genesis and Judaism*	Jacob Neusner
140109	*The Talmud of Babylonia. An American Translation. XXXV: Tractates Meilah and Tamid*	Peter J. Haas
140110	*Studies in Islamic and Judaic Traditions*	William Brinner/Stephen Ricks
140111	*Comparative Midrash: The Plan and Program of Genesis Rabbah and Leviticus Rabbah*	Jacob Neusner
140112	*The Tosefta: Its Structure and its Sources*	Jacob Neusner
140113	*Reading and Believing*	Jacob Neusner
140114	*The Fathers According to Rabbi Nathan*	Jacob Neusner
140115	*Etymology in Early Jewish Interpretation: The Hebrew Names in Philo*	Lester L. Grabbe
140116	*Understanding Seeking Faith: Essays on the Case of Judaism. Volume One: Debates on Method, Reports of Results*	Jacob Neusner
140117	*The Talmud of Babylonia: An American Translation. VII: Tractate Besah*	Alan J. Avery-Peck
140118	*Sifre to Numbers: An American Translation and Explanation, Volume One: Sifre to Numbers 1-58*	Jacob Neusner
140119	*Sifre to Numbers: An American Translation and Explanation, Volume Two: Sifre to Numbers 59-115*	Jacob Neusner
140120	*Cohen and Troeltsch: Ethical Monotheistic Religion and Theory of Culture*	Wendell S. Dietrich
140121	*Goodenough on the History of Religion and on Judaism*	Jacob Neusner/ Ernest Frerichs
140122	*Pesiqta DeRab Kahana I: Pisqaot One through Fourteen*	Jacob Neusner
140123	*Pesiqta DeRab Kahana II: Pisqaot Fifteen through Twenty-Eight and Introduction to Pesiqta DeRab Kahana*	Jacob Neusner
140125	*Comparative Midrash II*	Jacob Neusner
140126	*A Conceptual Commentary on Midrash Leviticus Rabbah: Value Concepts in Jewish Thought*	Max Kadushin